MARKETING RESEARCH

MARKETING RESEARCH

Planning, Process, Practice

Riccardo Benzo
Marwa G. Mohsen
Chahid Fourali

Los Angeles | London | New Delhi
Singapore | Washington DC | Melbourne

Los Angeles | London | New Delhi
Singapore | Washington DC | Melbourne

SAGE Publications Ltd
1 Oliver's Yard
55 City Road
London EC1Y 1SP

SAGE Publications Inc.
2455 Teller Road
Thousand Oaks, California 91320

SAGE Publications India Pvt Ltd
B 1/I 1 Mohan Cooperative Industrial Area
Mathura Road
New Delhi 110 044

SAGE Publications Asia-Pacific Pte Ltd
3 Church Street
#10-04 Samsung Hub
Singapore 049483

Editor: Matthew Waters
Editorial assistant: Jasleen Kaur
Production editor: Nicola Carrier
Copyeditor: Sharon Cawood
Proofreader: Kate Campbell
Indexer: Silvia Benvenuto
Marketing manager: Alison Borg
Cover design: Shaun Mercier
Typeset by: C&M Digitals (P) Ltd, Chennai, India
Printed in the UK by Bell and Bain Ltd, Glasgow

First published 2018

Library of Congress Control Number: 2017940908

British Library Cataloguing in Publication data

A catalogue record for this book is available from the British Library

ISBN 978-1-4462-9435-2
ISBN 978-1-4462-9436-9 (pbk)

At SAGE we take sustainability seriously. Most of our products are printed in the UK using FSC papers and boards. When we print overseas we ensure sustainable papers are used as measured by the PREPS grading system. We undertake an annual audit to monitor our sustainability.

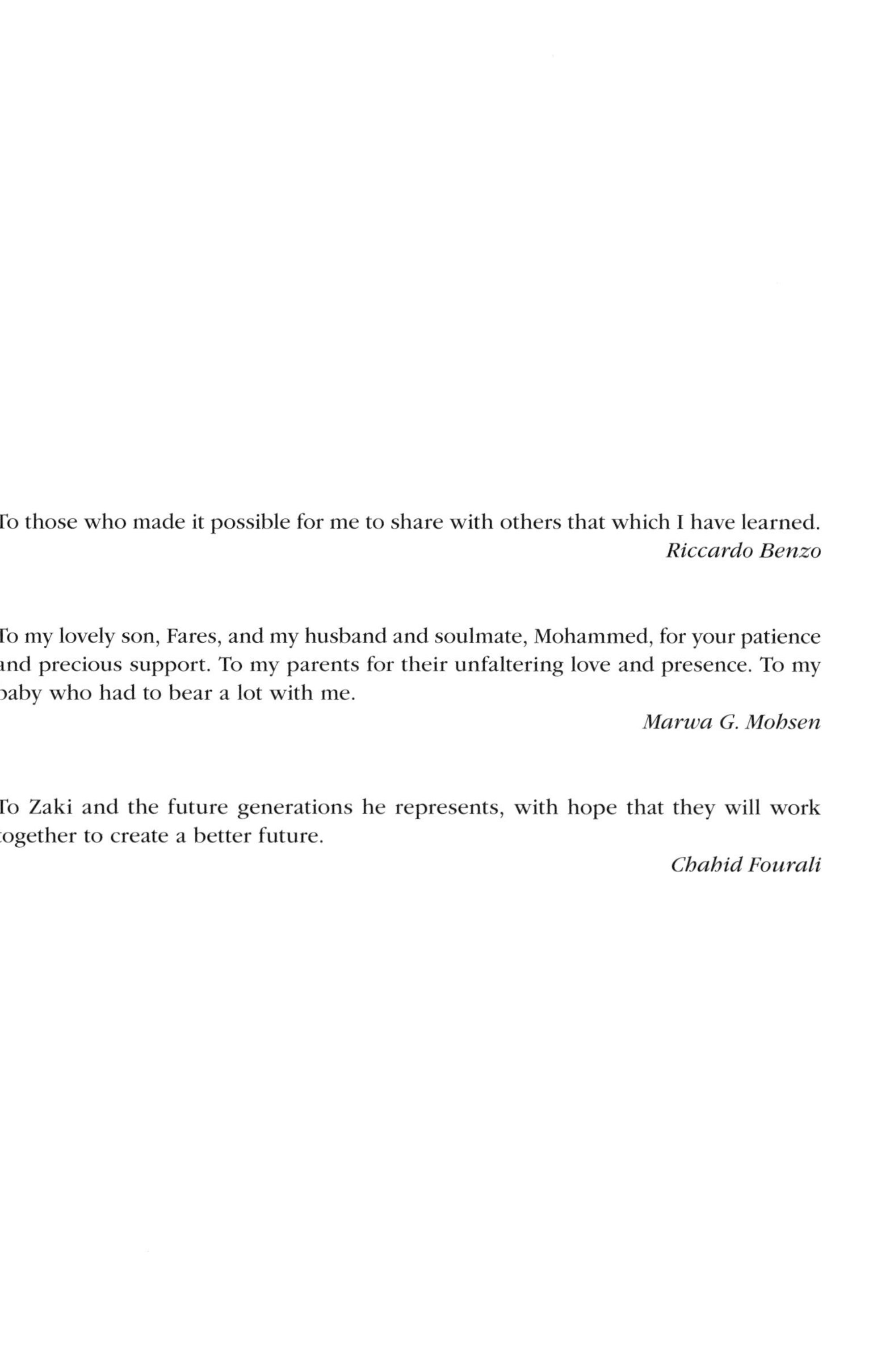

To those who made it possible for me to share with others that which I have learned.

Riccardo Benzo

To my lovely son, Fares, and my husband and soulmate, Mohammed, for your patience and precious support. To my parents for their unfaltering love and presence. To my baby who had to bear a lot with me.

Marwa G. Mohsen

To Zaki and the future generations he represents, with hope that they will work together to create a better future.

Chahid Fourali

Table of Contents

Extended Table of Contents

About the Authors

Riccardo Benzo is a Member of the Chartered Institute of Marketing (MCIM) and a Fellow of the Higher Education Academy (HEA). He has over twenty years of experience gained across multiple sectors and in marketing, sales and commercial roles for international organisations, leading and managing teams of professionals. In 2008, he founded Managing Expectations to provide a vehicle for market research, consulting and training. At the same time, he has been involved in teaching and supervising undergraduate and postgraduate students on a number of subjects including marketing and business research.

He conducted and commissioned several research projects in fields as far apart as beverages and professional services, including presenting findings on qualitative and quantitative investigations into the cruise industry in the UK and luxury retailing in China. Riccardo is passionate about ethical and sustainable marketing, and believes in helping organisations create value for the economy, society and the environment.

Marwa Gad Mohsen is an experienced scholar and researcher with a background in industry. At the start of her career, she worked as a practitioner for many years through contributing in various roles in Egyptian-EU funded programs, supporting and upgrading SMEs in various sectors. Marwa then embarked upon her academic career in the UK. Over years, she contributed to research and teaching at UK and international institutions. Marwa is an Associate Professor of Marketing and Founding Faculty at Prince Mohammad Bin Salman College of Business and Entrepreneurship (MBSC) in KSA.

Marwa is a Fellow of HEA (UK) and a Global Fellow of Babson College (USA). She holds a PhD in Marketing from Warwick Business School (UK) and MBA in Marketing & International Business from the American University in Cairo (Egypt). Marwa is published in many outstanding international journals including the Journal of Marketing Management, Journal of Services Marketing, and Advances in Consumer Research.

Dr Chahid Fourali (IoE, UCL) has backgrounds in psychology, education and marketing and has published in all three areas. He led the consultation with the UK Government to set up the Marketing and Sales Standards Setting Body, which he then led for eight years, as well as, the development of three sets of world-class national occupational standards (in Marketing, Sales and Social Marketing) that were supported by many internationally recognized marketing/business gurus. These standards are now the basis for all nationally recognized qualifications in the UK in the three professional areas. Dr Fourali is Senior Lecturer in Management at the London Metropolitan Business School and is examiner/subject expert for Cambridge University and University of Hertfordshire. He achieved Fellowship or professional membership status from several international organisations including FRSA, FCIM and BABCP. His recent book Social Marketing: A Powerful Tool for Changing the World for Good received very encouraging reviews including being selected for one of the Levitt Group 5 Great Minds events organized by the Chartered Institute of Marketing.

Online Resources

Marketing Research: Planning, Process, Practice is supported by a wealth of online resources for both students and lecturers to aid study and support teaching, which are available at https://study.sagepub.com/benzo

For students

- Further reading articles
- Multiple choice questions

For lecturers

- Instructor's manual
- PowerPoint slides

Students of marketing research should focus their attention on learning and applying practical skills to specific marketing issues or problems so that organisations can understand and serve their markets more effectively and efficiently. Part I of the book is concerned with defining the boundaries of marketing research as well as helping with recognising and developing solutions for relevant situations, for example international expansion.

Chapter 1 discusses the business environment in which marketing research takes place. It highlights how complexity affects our views of the world surrounding us and how learners can approach that. On this journey, the evolution of marketing research over time, the importance of technology and data in marketing research, and the impact of marketing research on generating value for organisations are presented to the reader alongside an overview of opportunities for a career in marketing research.

Chapter 2 presents and develops an approach to identifying topics for marketing-related inquiry. This refers to a system which helps with recognising issues, solving problems and understanding phenomena by making broad statements more specific, and by defining the fundamental contents of a marketing research idea. It provides students with a set of objective principles in order for them to arrive at a valid and reliable output for their work.

Finally, Chapter 3 addresses secondary data and research by drawing attention to the importance of knowledge in marketing research. It looks into a range of secondary data sources while describing the basic steps of secondary research, with a view to explaining what it means to be critical in this context. By mapping out key areas of knowledge and offering further suggestions on writing secondary research, it shows how to build appropriate literature reviews for academic purposes.

PART I

Setting Up Marketing Research

CHAPTER 1

Introduction: Adding Value with Marketing Research

LEARNING OBJECTIVES

The key learning objectives of this chapter are:

1. To define marketing research and its key dimensions
2. To appreciate different perspectives in marketing research and their significance
3. To discuss principles of and practices in marketing research
4. To highlight key skills and capabilities for marketing research practitioners

KEY CONCEPTS

By the end of this chapter, the reader should be familiar with the following concepts:

1. Complexity and its impact on organisations
2. What marketing research is
3. Basic and applied marketing research
4. Historical perspectives and the significance of marketing research
5. Technology in marketing research: scope and application
6. Creating value with marketing research
7. Attitude, confidence and skills for learners
8. Careers in marketing research

Riccardo Benzo

Introduction

Marketing is an essential function in any organisation: it relates to understanding and predicting current and future market trends, potential consumer demand, as well as responding to what stakeholders need and want. Moreover, it is the outward-facing department of a company. This is why learning how to do proper marketing research is critical to anyone studying and practising marketing around the world.

This opening chapter outlines the foundations of marketing research by introducing and clarifying a series of relevant topics in and around the field. More precisely, it deals with the idea of complexity in the modern business environment and how it informs the way companies compete. Key perspectives on the evolution of marketing and marketing research are also presented, together with a discussion of their influence on how research is, could and should be conducted. Continuing on this theme, we explore the impact of technology on the collection, handling, interpretation and use of data, especially considering the increasing ease with which information is now exchanged between different parties. Examples illustrating how to take full advantage of marketing research in relation to the application of its basic principles in a given context are provided.

Learners and non-specialist practitioners should not feel daunted when embarking on the study of marketing research. On the contrary, they should be excited as becoming familiar with a systematic process of discovery is going to enable them to understand their surroundings and how organisations operate within different environments and markets. The purpose is to acquaint you with the building blocks of marketing research and, in so doing, provide you with the practical skills and knowledge to facilitate overall critical reflection.

Marketing research is not a rigid sequence of steps that leads to a definitive conclusion. Rather, it is an iterative process, which requires an open mind and a drive for a holistic (i.e. the 'bigger picture') overview – sometimes a project may simply unearth the need for more research. With this in mind, let's start unpacking marketing research!

Snapshot: Nokia

In November 2011, Nokia executives were preparing to do battle in the highly competitive 'smartphone' market (Costa, 2011) while also planning to reinvent their brand to appeal to a youth segment, which had progressively shifted away from the Finnish handset manufacturer. This transformation appeared to be linked to a series of changes from brand principles to empowering local teams, from targeting to product development, and from recruiting marketing talent to innovation.

During Nokia World, Craig Hepburn – Global Director of Digital – reminded the audience that 'people don't want you to sell them products any more, they want you to add value to their lives' (Marketing Week, 2011). This statement was far-reaching in its implications as it meant that the company would effectively need to put more emphasis on social relationships and brand experiences (Joseph, 2011).

In other words, Nokia's new strategic perspective would aim to exploit commonalities between people around the world as further attention would be paid to understanding how to become more consumer-centric. Research took centre stage 'on every continent and really looking hard at what Nokia means to [consumers], who they are, what do they aspire to [be], what are their passions and what resonates with them' (Costa, 2011).

Doubts still remained about the suitability of the partnership with Microsoft, which had been announced just a year earlier, effectively as a result of the appointment to CEO of Steve Elop, previously head of Microsoft's Business Division (Peacock, 2010). Some analysts were critical of this move as they predicted it would not have the desired effect of allowing both businesses to compete against the might of Apple and Google (Troianowski, Grundberg, and Ante, 2012). It looked like Microsoft had chosen the wrong partner with whom to build a substantial presence in mobile technology.

It seemed as though Nokia had forgotten the words of former CEO Jorma Ollila, who between 1998 and 2001 had anticipated that 'the convergence of Internet to mobile phones will not lead to one single player becoming master of the universe'. He stated that the key challenge for technology companies at that point was how to remain novel in the face of shorter technological cycles. Highlighting that the full advantage of 3G mobile phone technology was dependent on the number of types of software built into the device, Ollila emphasised the key role played by software in shaping the industry going forward (Malik, 2011).

Nokia prided itself on conducting extensive marketing research to respond to market demands, yet many of its strategic choices from the mid-2000s have been debatable.

Complexity: Breaking Down Research into Manageable Bites

Complexity The quality of something that is made of many different parts and, as such, is difficult to understand

The relationship between management practices and complexity has never been a comfortable one, especially in an environment where control is a critical aspect of managerial activities. This is partly due to the fact that making decisions is far less demanding in a simpler context where fewer variables exist or are taken into account, and partly because of the lack of the necessary support, such as technology.

However, complexity is the norm in the world around us. The conditions in which we operate change, sometimes even suddenly and/or dramatically, bringing about fundamental disruptions as summarised in Schumpeter's idea of creative destruction (Elliot, 1980). More than ever, we need to come to terms with and understand the modern business environment, its evolution and its composition because 'its collective characteristics cannot easily be predicted from underlying components: the whole is greater than, and often significantly different from, the sum of its parts' (West, 2013: 14).

This is the reason why organisations need to acknowledge how much harder understanding our surroundings has become. What used to be relatively simple conditions where patterns could be recognised have transformed into complex, interconnected and interdependent systems. As organisations juggle their limited resources, it is reasonable to assume that the gap between what we can know and what we should know is growing ever wider, making us realise the fundamental role of marketing research further.

Companies must thrive despite operating in such complex environments. They need to be able to identify the key supporting aspects of decision making as efficiently and effectively as possible:

- identifying issues (before they become problems)
- solving problems (together with their causes)
- understanding phenomena (about the world around us)

- taking advantage of opportunities
- fending off threats.

This book explains how marketing research can help make sense of a reality that is increasingly hard to grasp and data that are more wide-ranging than ever, thus adding further layers of uncertainty as to what truly matters when designing and implementing strategy. It goes without saying that it is important to be selective in the way that research is conducted. Reflection is paramount because only good questions eventually lead to valuable findings and discoveries, which can aid the process of decision making.

Good marketing research is not just about turning data and information into knowledge. It is about making sure that findings are understood, appreciated and used in as productive a way as possible.

Understanding World Issues

Marketing as a business function provides analytic capability to organisations. Indeed, a business has to deal with issues, problems, phenomena, opportunities and threats relating to fields as disparate as innovation, new product development, pricing, marketing communications, brand management and consumer behaviour. This is the reason why, in order to arrive at useful insights, these factors have to be examined in the context of the environment in which a business operates.

The term marketing research can be ambiguous. Academics and practitioners often refer to two separate concepts: market research and market*ing* research, which are interconnected but not interchangeable. For the purposes of this textbook, market research is defined as research about specific markets; in short, it defines the macro-, meso- and micro-environments or country, industry and competition, respectively, which affect an organisation in its day-to-day routine (Hollensen, 2011).

Marketing research, on the other hand, is research into the whole marketing process of a company and can be defined as a systematic, critical and in-depth process of enquiry based on the collection and the interpretation of data and information to address specific requirements, which respond to the operational needs of organisations.

Looking at the definition above, the term systematic is crucial as it may be qualified as unbiased, objective in nature and following an explicit route. This means that any kind of unstructured research is not likely to generate valid and/or reliable knowledge. It is also important for the marketing research process to be critical, to consider and evaluate a variety of sources with a view to arriving at a conceptualisation of one's idea, which will act as its backbone, holding the work together. From there, further routes to theoretical and empirical evidence are possible, which can be crystallised through the construction of research paradigms, each and every one of them, as the assumptions made in relation to a particular piece of research and the logical plan that holds them in place (see Chapter 4 for more on conceptualising research).

Depth, too, is an underlying requirement of valid and reliable research in marketing. In general terms, it is useful for researchers to establish their competence through a thorough examination of the existing body of research in a particular field of interest and in order to defend one's view on a subject as well as evaluate the usefulness of ideas in a specific context (Hart, 1999). In undertaking this process, there is a fundamental difference between depth requirements at undergraduate level and at postgraduate level, or in the type of work you are planning – for instance, a pitch for new business as opposed to an investigation of new market opportunities.

Overall, a marketing researcher should be aiming to turn a variety of sources of data and information into a specific piece of new knowledge that will enable a decision to be made, while understanding the reasons for doing so – this will be referred to later as the 'trigger' of the research – and the meaning of the end result. Equally, it is important not to overlook the constraints that might limit the capacity for elaborating on and finding solutions to complex problems as well as the uses of research in an organisational context. There are different 'modes' that inform our actions, as depicted in Table 1.1.

Table 1.1 Dealing with information

Mode	Central Idea
Sense making	Environmental change → Interpret equivocal messages by enacting interpretations → Meaningful context for action Information is INTERPRETED
Knowledge creating	Knowledge gap → Convert and combine tacit and explicit knowledge → New capabilities, innovations Information is CONVERTED
Decision making	Decision situation → Search and select alternatives guided by premises, rules → Goal-directed action Information is EVALUATED

Source: Choo, 2006: 14

In the first instance, the data collected by the market and marketing research effort needs to be interpreted through a shared process of 'sense making', which is largely dependent on social interactions in the working environment. Therefore, the same process may lead some people towards radical change, while others may see the same set of circumstances as a minor glitch and do nothing about it. There is no right or wrong response in such situations and, above all, the individual competence of a person, student or professional has a bearing on the overall interpretation of facts.

'Knowledge creating' and 'decision making' are other possible ways of converting and evaluating information, respectively. In other words, the situation we need to understand – environmental change, knowledge gap or decision – is influencing the process we follow and the output we seek.

The learner perspective

Conducting marketing research can be a daunting prospect. People sometimes find it mysterious in nature, as its systematic character, in some respects, contrasts with the apparently disorganised patterns within which we live our daily lives. Therefore, it is only normal to feel apprehensive and to experience self-doubt as one embarks on something unfamiliar and not quite intuitive in nature. In particular, it has been noticed that in conducting research 'students can sometimes find themselves overwhelmed, with too many things to do and not enough time to do them' (Daft and Marcic, 2014: 124).

Professionals, too, might not have had much exposure to marketing research and may lack confidence in their ability to brief or manage projects of this kind. There is a way to simplify this challenge – by breaking it down into three components: attitude, confidence and skills. This book will address all three: improve attitudes towards learning marketing research by showing the positive side of this discipline, boost confidence by dispelling myths about marketing research, and build useful skills by focusing on the key requirements of marketing research.

Attitude

Employers tend to value knowledgeable employees who are willing to apply themselves and learn. In simple terms, this means that a person should remain open to new learning experiences and believe they can continue on the path of improvement. Remember that attitude formation is a function of personal background and experience as well as personality; for instance, motivating oneself differently helps overcome difficulties previously encountered in learning a specific subject. Likewise, branching out in different directions, such as reading about or taking part in online discussions on research, can provide further scope for improvement by adopting more suitable ways of learning. This is consistent with the fact that attitudes are not static, so more positive dispositions towards certain areas of knowledge can eventually allow students to become more successful with their marketing research studies. For instance, can you think of anything that you enjoyed in your previous experiences at university or at work which you can relate to the field of research by and large?

Confidence

Confidence can be gained in a variety of ways; it has to do with self-esteem and self-efficacy or, essentially, believing in one's ability to achieve personal goals. Marketing research is not to be seen as an obstacle to personal, academic or professional goals; it is an enabler and you should engage with it. For this reason, it is appropriate that you ask for clarification of learning outcomes, assessment criteria and grading (e.g. marking schemes) in order to ensure that there is no breakdown in communication between you and the teaching team at your university – or between you and your line manager at work.

Skills

In this respect, sharing is deemed a fundamental component of the learning process, which allows those involved to agree to and develop a set of desirable skills. Marketing research requires you to think critically: unfortunately, critical thinking is not defined uniformly across cultures and international students often discover this late on in their courses (Yoshino, 2004). It is necessary to try and think more deeply, to ask challenging questions, to assess evidence and to weigh arguments; these are necessary steps towards developing personal, academic and professional transferrable skills as a researcher. We will revisit all of these skills throughout the book to help develop a number of useful tools to add to your researcher's toolkit.

Skill, will and self-regulation

Skill development, greater confidence and a positive attitude can combine to help generate better study and learning habits, which can fuel a cycle of improvement for students and practitioners alike (Cano, 2006). This should result in an improved knowledge base, an ability to set and achieve goals, and a letting go of commonly held beliefs that might prevent you from approaching research with the right frame of mind.

Marketing Research Today

Those who have invested time in the development of research methods and methodologies over the years have done so because of one of two reasons: either a manifest interest in or across business disciplines such as marketing, or a specific concern for observed trends – for instance, the impact of technology on data collection online and offline in recent years.

Although the practice of market research can be seen in, amongst other things, the use of interviewing techniques and questionnaires, contemporary marketing research only dates back around 100 years. Therefore, it is not yet a well-established science in its own right; many long-standing debates are still unresolved. Its origin is the work of Daniel Starch, an American psychologist who, in the 1920s and 1930s, developed ways to measure advertising effectiveness after noticing that there was little understanding about how successful marketing efforts were made by companies.

From these beginnings, the development of methods has grown, together with the introduction of new tools and techniques leading to the birth of postmodern and post-positivist views of research, identified as 'pluralist' in Table 1.2 (see Chapters 4 and 5 for a more detailed discussion about the significance of these changes).

Table 1.2 Marketing research views over time

Market(ing) Research	When
No structured view	Before 1920
Quantitative view	1920–1960
Qualitative vs quantitative (debate) view	1960–1990
Pluralist view	After 1990

Source: Adapted from Bradley, 2007: 9

The early days of marketing research were characterised by a more specific emphasis on an overall quantitative outlook, as demonstrated by the pre-eminence of the survey method and the widespread use of statistical analysis. It was in this context that the first large consumer studies took place in the late 1920s and throughout the 1930s in the UK, such as the Gallup Poll, and the USA. This trend continued after the Second World War when companies like Procter & Gamble set up fully fledged research departments focusing on the application of scientific methodology to a variety of areas such as consumer behaviour, marketing management and, later, brand management.

Things gradually began to change in the 1950s with the birth of motivational research, introduced by authors like Martineau and Dichter, even though qualitative research continued to be met with scepticism and a lot of resistance. The hypothetico-deductive approach (in essence, the testing of hypotheses) still dominated the field and was largely regarded as the good science (for more on hypothesis testing, see Chapter 11).

With marketing's orientation shifting away from 'product' and 'sales' to 'market', 'customer' and 'relationships' (see Table 1.3), new perspectives emerged that took into account the importance of understanding consumer thinking, feelings, opinions, attitudes, and so on, for which qualitative research appeared to be at least equally well suited as its quantitative counterpart. In fact, the use of qualitative techniques, for instance focus groups and interviews, was already widespread amongst practitioners by the end of the 1970s because of the value of its interpretative models.

'Verstehen' *'Any approach that focuses on qualitative issues like social meanings'* (Brewer, 2003: 338)

In short, marketing research became interested in the meanings of social action, or 'Verstehen' in its original definition, in order to provide explanations for trends, patterns, phenomena and behaviours ultimately affecting organisations around the world. This (r)evolution first created a debate as to which tradition, quantitative or qualitative, was superior in generating valid and reliable knowledge. Academics and practitioners in opposing camps tried arguing in favour of one or other of these so-called competing views, constrained by a long perpetuated opinion that the scientific nature of quantitative research made it somehow the more worthy of the two. Part of the problem was identified in the 'blurred genres' (1970–86) and the 'crisis of representation' (1986–90), periods when qualitative researchers found themselves ill at ease with a radically changing research landscape (Denzin and Lincoln, 2005).

Eventually, a different outlook started to take hold: qualitative research became recognised as a valid and reliable route to obtain insight about, and even explain, complexity. It was no longer a matter of choosing between quantitative and qualitative positions; instead, these two ideas could finally be seen as complementary traditions, which provided differing systematic ways of investigating issues, problems and phenomena. Nowadays, the driver is achieving efficiency and effectiveness in understanding the global business environment. In this respect, it is advisable to spend time defining company challenges in research terms. The initial stages of marketing research are critical to the success of a project and its value to an organisation; asking the right questions in relation to marketing objectives is likely to represent the difference between staring at raw data and generating useful insight. Similarly, researchers must not underestimate resistance to change. Identifying key stakeholders within an organisation and obtaining their support (buy-in) before allocating resources need to receive more attention.

Marketing and Marketing Research

Earlier in this chapter, we pointed out that state-of-the-art business research (which, as a discipline for business, and marketing research within it) has effectively been influenced by changes in marketing orientation as a set of competing ideas. These are broadly depicted in Table 1.3.

In the late stages of the Industrial Revolution, the methods of Ford and Taylor essentially concerned themselves with 'production' as companies strived to make a variety of goods available to the masses by levering the division of labour and its main benefit: economies of scale.

Table 1.3 Marketing orientation and research focus

When	Orientation (marketing)	Focus (research)
1880s–1910s	Production	Generally unfocused
1920s–1940s	Product	Market composition (macro-)
1950s–1960s	Sales	Industry competition (micro-)
1970s–1980s	Market	Consumer studies (needs and wants)
1990s–2000s	Relationship(s)	Satisfaction and loyalty
2010s	Co-creation	Collaboration and content

'Inward-Looking' Orientations

Price-led approaches to marketing are still being used in fast-developing markets such as China; computer manufacturer Legend's focus on production efficiency is demonstrating a lack of consideration for consumer expectations, which could lead to a myopic view of their surroundings and possibly even their demise. There is in fact little or no emphasis on research in cases where organisations are not inclined to think about satisfying the current or future needs and wants of customers.

The consequences of being production-oriented are not often fully grasped by organisations. Despite being frequently referred to as a shining example of car manufacturing, the success of the Ford T-Model was short-lived. Launched in 1908, supply began outstripping demand once the assembly line got going in full swing in 1914. Besides the introduction of the electric starter in 1919, there was no major change to the car; Ford was obsessed with saving costs and never listened to customers. In today's world, sustaining competitive advantage without understanding consumer complexity is equivalent to accepting that products and services will eventually sell themselves as long as their quality is good enough. Even McDonald's had to move away from its tried-and-tested model to engage with a fast-changing customer base asking for different, healthier options and, ultimately, a much improved product proposition.

This trend continued in the years between the two world wars and immediately after, as firms paid more attention to the characteristics of the 'product' – i.e. the relationship between commodities and marketing functions – and 'sales' – i.e. the supporting activities of which marketing is made. There remained a general inward-looking approach to business, which essentially focused on transactions and eventually translated into what is now defined as a product-centric orientation. These views are generally regarded as the result of organisational competencies, or what companies can do as opposed to what consumers are asking them to do. They have developed over time and are still being used in some situations and for some industries, for example application software.

This kind of approach is typical when overall demand is thought to be unrestrained; for example in developing countries today, in these situations, it is relatively easy to come across new customers to fuel growth. As such, organisations might not actively look to develop long-term relationships, and show only a limited drive in the pursuit of knowledge through a more consistent and continuous use of marketing research.

Figure 1.1 Understanding the world using marketing research

The use of product orientation alone presents limitations. Typically, an organisation applies specific competencies (e.g. innovation) to create new, or improve existing, offerings, and then finds ways to market and sell them. Intel did this with the dual-core processor in 2005; this led to the development of new lines of personal computers by IBM, which were successfully introduced in the marketplace. Companies taking this position too literally end up developing products and services on a continuous basis, failing to appreciate market trends. If sales decline, a product-oriented company will head toward its own demise. This is why listening to customers and marketing research started taking centre stage: Intel adopted alternate cycles by being market-oriented as well. In this respect, needs and wants are explored and offerings designed to suit them, as in the case of its Centrino Mobile Technology in 2003. Integrating internal and external inputs through a systematic process involving marketing research indeed yielded good results.

Reflective Activity

- What kind of consumer research do you think global consumer electronics companies – for example, Apple, Samsung, Lenovo – conduct to help with new product development? Can you find any evidence of 'inward-looking' orientation amongst any of these businesses?

'Outward-Looking' Orientations

In the early 1960s, while there may not have been a conscious push to cause a revolution, McCarthy and Borden introduced and subsequently formalised the 4 Ps framework, hence effectively bringing about a massive change of direction in the way marketing worked. For the first time, executives were able to prepare full-blown marketing plans well beyond the scope of advertising, which had been the sole focus of attention for many years. This, coupled with the steep increases in costs facing businesses during the oil crises of the 1970s, led to a further transformation: customers were no longer to be considered a cheap commodity so a 'market' orientation began to take hold.

Understanding consumer patterns and trends turned out to be a winning formula for Ford, as it used research to develop one of the most important models in its history – the Taurus (Taub, 1991). Producing a car whose key features were customer-driven was also a strong departure from the prevailing corporate culture of that time, mostly content with perpetuating the status quo. Unfortunately, the importance of marketing research was then underestimated once more as the company lost its way again in the late 1990s.

Research in Practice: Consumer Studies – The Ford Taurus

In the late 1970s, there was a clear message being sent through Ford by its senior executives: the company had to become customer-driven and, for that to happen, marketing research had to add a qualitative dimension in order to understand rather than simply monitor consumer perceptions and feelings. The use of quantitative studies up to that point essentially limited insight; further, the organisation was not used to sharing information as divisions and functions were structured as separate entities and didn't communicate. A couple of years into the Taurus project, the marketing research team made the first of many important discoveries by going back to and re-testing some old findings relating to previous models to discover how the Edsel, a model launched more than 20 years earlier, had left a lasting negative impression on the American public. The promotional strategy, devised by J. Walter Thompson, was also put through its paces: consumers' interest in various concepts kept on changing and so would the execution as social trends influenced needs. The marketplace had evolved and marketing research was helping a more consistent market orientation to take hold.

The necessity of monitoring Return On Marketing Investment (ROMI), understanding market diversity and embracing technology became the drivers of development in marketing thinking and its application for years to come, particularly with respect to the birth of a 'relationship' orientation. The emphasis of research in the last 20–30 years has gradually shifted towards unearthing what motivates people and organisations to engage in relationships, while explaining how they effectively develop. It is also a reflection of the growing importance of designing sustainable marketing strategies in today's fast-paced business environment through the maximisation of Customer Lifetime Value. In this respect, a study by McKinsey & Company (2012) highlighted the need for relationships to be built by US car insurers through the use of marketing research; simply put, the industry didn't understand their customers and had a poor track record with regards to creating and maintaining meaningful relationships with them. In spite of record growth in marketing spend, these businesses were struggling to understand customer needs, their shopping habits and their decision-making behaviour. A better allocation of funds has since seen some players, such as EICO and State Farm, improve product propositions, the relevance of marketing messages and the level of customer retention through targeted studies about consumer preferences and shopping journeys.

The customer experience takes precedence as companies evolve and pursue closer relationships with customers and consumers; assessing drivers of value (competencies) for an organisation, knowing the competition and their offerings, and analysing customer expectations are key enablers to help create mutually rewarding value. It is therefore only fitting that the latest step in this journey from the 'production' orientation and the unfocused nature of marketing research over 100 years is represented by the coming together of companies and consumers in what has been characterised as value co-creation. The essence of this newest marketing orientation is the idea of value as generated by the customer in their preferred interaction with and/or experience of a company.

As such, marketing research has ultimately focused on collaboration and content by becoming all-encompassing (see Figure 1.2) and by taking advantage of platforms, which enable this co-creation of value to take place. Many companies have found Corporate Social Responsibility (CSR) a tough nut to crack. Setting up policies and programmes is a relatively easy endeavour; however, consumers often feel that CSR is a profit-driven attempt at increasing corporate domination dressed up as a genuine effort on the part of companies to listen to their audiences. However, marketing research has provided a revolutionary avenue for data collection and engagement that levers technology, specifically social media and communities. Crowdsourcing enables organisations to trace a direct route between opinions and ideas held by customers and the way these should be implemented to obtain support for a company's CSR (brand affinity).

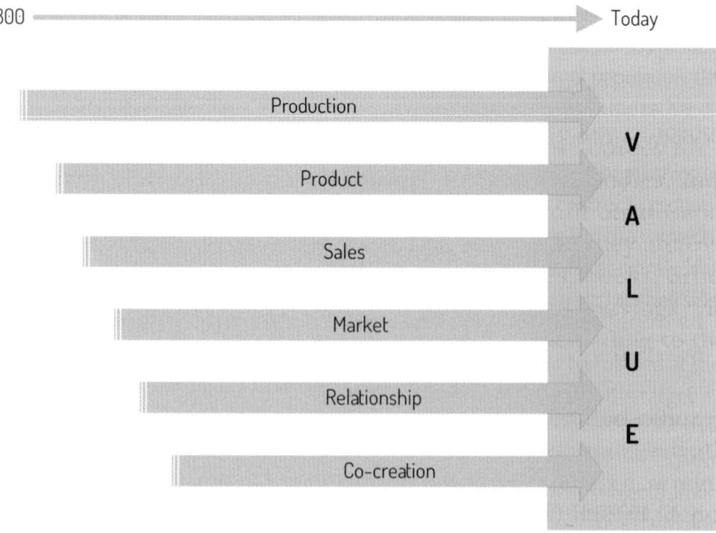

Figure 1.2 Marketing orientation and value creation

Reflective Activity

- What kind of impact can an 'outward-looking' orientation have for marketing research in a large-, medium- or small-sized business today?
- How can companies with rather different resources and budgets make the best of marketing research, for instance tracking online conversations?

As different viewpoints and theories have developed over time, they have come to co-exist with rather than replace each other. In this respect, the basic orientations of marketing and the fundamental directions of marketing research can now be seen as complementary as well as dependent on circumstances, for instance market, industry (or sector) or competitor set.

At the same time, technology has allowed marketing research to thrive as a variety of new tools have made their appearance, potentially enabling managers to make more informed decisions. What remains to be mediated is the complexity of the modern world, the increasing amount of data accessible to most and the widespread lack of familiarity with the research process.

Technology

The emergence of affordable computing power during the 1960s accelerated the evolution of empirical research in marketing, especially with the initial purpose of simplifying data (e.g. cleaning, summarising) and improving analysis (e.g. clustering, interpreting). This entailed going from relatively unsophisticated investigative techniques to advanced methods based on the use of statistics and computer power. The scenario was further enhanced by the arrival of the personal computer, extensive research software and communication devices, all of which were eventually made portable to open up a completely new era of observation and enquiry, spanning both quantitative and qualitative perspectives.

Marketing Information System (MIS)

Organisations have therefore benefited from the application of technology to marketing through the ever more precise treatment of information collected at all points of contact between them and their stakeholders. The Marketing Information System (MIS) gives structure and flexibility at the same time, essentially comprising a wide variety of resources, which are pulled together in the quest to aid reporting and decision making (see Table 1.4). Ideally, companies want to ensure that everything learned is internalised in the short to medium term and that the knowledge gained is shared in the long term.

The essence of an MIS is its ability to collect, store and interrogate information in a useful manner starting from a 'data warehouse'. A wide array of additional inputs from

'Data warehouse' A relational database containing historical data from many sources such as transactions, enquiries, requests, etc. at any possible point of contact/touch point between a firm and its stakeholders

Table 1.4 A schematic of the marketing information system (MIS)

Input	Processing	Output
Internal records (data warehouse) Market research Marketing intelligence Tracking Stakeholders (Partners)	Analysis systems Decision support systems Customer relationship management	Reporting Decision making

Source: Adapted from Bradley, 2007: 12; Zikmund et al., 2013: 22–6; Burns and Bush, 2014: 40

regular (e.g. scanner data, online panels) and ad hoc (e.g. consumer surveys, competitor benchmarking) research activities are then added to the mix and eventually evaluated on an 'as and when' basis, i.e. in the context of a particular situation or for a given purpose.

Building an efficient system requires a clear Single Customer View (SCV), a place where each record is consolidated, duplication eliminated, errors corrected and, ultimately, individual consumers identified as precisely as possible. This is a difficult endeavour, indeed, but one that can potentially provide a company with a chance to generate positive outcomes via analysis, decision support and customer relationships systems. Many companies, such as Zynga, the American videogame developer, have already showed the gains resulting from levering behavioural (tracking) and survey data, for instance.

Ultimately, four parameters have historically been paramount when designing a workable MIS: budget, 'macro specifications', level of sophistication and implementation strategy. Technology can help us make sense of the mounting amount of data available internally and externally: statistics show that 2.5 quintillion (as in 10 to the power of 18!) bytes of new data are being created every day.

'Big Data'

This rather large number is estimated to be doubling every three to four years and possibly faster. Besides the sheer volume of information now available, more widespread technology has brought about changes in velocity (instant access and availability) and variety; these three elements together have the potential to produce a move away from managerial practices that have too often relied on experience and intuition, generally as the prerogative of high-ranked executives within organisations. In order to take advantage of such potential advances, organisations have to get a fix on the type of internal and external data needed, they have to employ the right people and tools, and have to ensure that insights are eventually impacting the way decisions are made.

'Big data' Large amount(s) of data that are hard to capture, store, manage and analyse

It appears that there is a relationship between achieving better marginal results from marketing investments and better margins from pricing and marketing communications decisions, and asking the right questions in the first place. This is something that should never get overlooked, whether in the context of a first-year undergraduate student essay or a small piece of desk research commissioned by a marketing manager.

Indeed, the very solution we are staring at is undoubtedly adding to the complexity of the world we live in, thus raising some further issues rather than entirely fulfilling its promise. There is a powerful argument that it is going to be hard to come up with overarching answers because of a lack of a truly comprehensive theoretical framework, yet technology is going to allow for better data collection and data analysis, together with the integration of more perspectives to suit marketing decision making.

Reflective Activity: Nokia

Refer back to the opening chapter Snapshot and answer the following questions in relation to the organisation during the years 2005–16:

- What appeared to drive Nokia's decisions during that period, and why?
- How did Nokia deal with complexity to anticipate demand trends in the various regions and countries in which it operated?
- What fundamental questions could (or should) Nokia have asked in the marketplace to remain on the same wavelength as its target audiences?

Maximising Data Collection: The Internet and Other Sources

The origin of the use of the Internet for research purposes is linked to getting existing information as secondary data through searches in an era when users were mainly devoting their attention to compiling environmental, business and consumer intelligence from published sources. This is still an important part of the efforts made by researchers online, yet the development of data collections methods has been fast and furious since the mid-1990s, the heyday of Internet surveys. For instance, Google Consumer Surveys serve different purposes for those involved: data collection itself, revenue generation (for publishers), access to content (for users), and so on, thus going well beyond a mono-dimensional reality.

It is perhaps a little less known that, at around the same time, qualitative researchers also began to experiment with online methods, as bulletin boards allowed for some form of face-to-face interaction – this could be seen as an interview – to take place. The explosion of social media platforms has widened the range of possibilities, with the ability to entertain and observe conversations in real time; in fact, the amount of data from such activities has already made some people talk about 'little big data'. Nevertheless, organisations can benefit from getting to know their existing and potential customers intimately through the appropriate use of tracking software and the identification of opinion leaders within their 'community'. One of the most talked about tenets in marketing is that of listening to consumers; social media monitoring tools, such as Radian6, enable companies to gather real-time information about what people say about brands and where they go (virtually) to do so.

Firms can specify keywords in order to keep track of conversations people are having online in a sort of boundless focus group involving many participants around the world; they can then share this information with colleagues to add definition to strategic and tactical decision-making processes. Consumer insight can now be attained in a variety of ways; some observers have noticed that technology plays a big part in this process and, in fact, it always helps to obtain knowledge about target groups even when the primary objective is not necessarily to capture data. Because of the fundamental nature of technology, every interaction through a modern device can be recorded and documented in detail.

Ethics: Ethics in Cyberspace

The constant stream of information from consumers to organisations via electronic devices poses a variety of questions on how to deal with data. First of all, there needs to be clarity about who the data are provided to and, above all, for what purposes. This should then define if and how such information can be shared, which in turn brings about two further key issues: storage and security. The legal frameworks put in place by governments and the work of professional bodies do not guarantee ethical behaviour as they still require company employees to have moral fibre and make at least a minimal ethical effort.

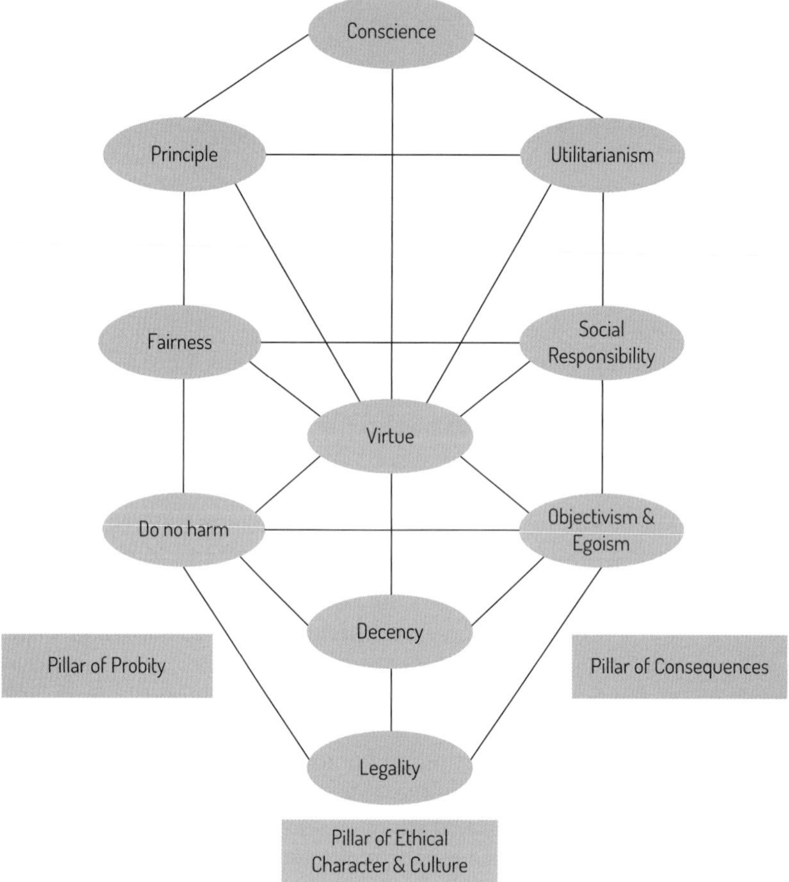

Figure 1.3 A framework for ethical theories

Business Ethics and Values, 4th ed, Fisher, C; Lovell, A; Valero-Silva, N, © 2013, 103, Pearson Education. Reprinted with permission by Pearson Canada Inc.

However, researchers, professional or otherwise, should not forget that the creation of new knowledge must be driven by reliability and validity; the ease with which we can now collect data as a result of technological advances does not make up for the need to continue applying the core principles of marketing research. Ideally, we are seeking consistent, replicable outcomes (reliable) that meet our objectives in the sense that they measure what we set out to measure (valid). In qualitative research, there is a further requirement for this to be true internally: researchers working on a project must also agree on what they are experiencing, while observations must, to a certain extent, match the theoretical concepts they refer to (more on validity and reliability in Chapter 15).

Maximising Analysis: Marketing Dashboard

In essence, making sense of data has become a rather demanding task because of the ever increasing options offered by technology in identifying suitable methods for collection. The mounting pressure on researchers and analysts in the marketing area has been eased by the evolution of marketing dashboards as tools that simplify:

- the integration of data – a synthesis of multiple sources in a common framework with the possibility of varying degrees of aggregation
- the integration of processes – the management of internal and external sources into an organisation-wide set of parameters
- the integration of viewpoints – an analysis of the market situation from common ground.

These instruments solve some of the typical organisational tensions, especially simplifying critical aspects such as socio-cultural trends affecting one's business, for non-marketing specialists; yet, the selection of specific information to be collected and its overall interpretation are factors that only well-prepared and naturally curious people are able to deal with. For example, social media management platforms like HootSuite help with handling multiple networks, tracking mentions of brands (or particular topics of interest), analysing online traffic, scheduling outgoing messages and monitoring activity in cyberspace. Teams can be allocated responsibilities for projects and given access to parts of the system, accordingly. The individual analytical tools attached to platforms like Twitter or Google+ can then be integrated further into HootSuite Reports in order to communicate selected facts about the outcomes of your social initiatives.

The quest for new product development illustrates how information can either be used instrumentally to arrive at decisions within a fairly structured framework or system, or conceptually by adding layers of new information to knowledge accumulated over time in order to establish meanings and implications. In this respect, technology allows for emphasis to be placed on a select number of variables, which might become crucial in determining a new direction or in supporting a particular strategic orientation (see Table 1.3 on research orientation and focus).

A dashboard can be fine-tuned to summarise and analyse data from disparate sources of marketing research with the aim of satisfying organisational objectives and the simultaneous achievement of relevant targets. Should something not be heading in the right direction, this would be immediately apparent as the main 'dials' in the dashboard provide an easy-to-read representation of the overall situation.

Advanced: Convergence and Democratisation

Technological advances have determined the destruction of those barriers that prevented human interaction such as distance, time lag and language. The science that has allowed connectivity – for instance, the Internet and social media platforms – is now helping deliver true convergence as a process bringing together several spaces, which generate virtual communities where self-expression can take place. Marketing research now has the potential to be truly pervasive rather than invasive as well as decentralised, while an increase in the democratisation of knowledge provides much-needed self-regulating mechanisms in order to ensure fair representations of these very interactions. By adding a layered approach, different users can access the right type of data both in terms of scope and depth; in other words, each user or stakeholder is able to obtain the answers they seek based on their needs and analytical skills. This means that even consumers, traditionally in a position of relative weakness, can benefit from the work of organisations that make data more open, searchable and actionable, i.e. consumable. Marketing research is a gateway to this change becoming widespread reality.

Academic (Basic) and Practitioner (Applied) Research

In spite of the progress made over the last 100 years, research remains an endeavour based on curiosity and necessity; in general, the former perspective is adopted more extensively in academic circles where furthering knowledge in discrete areas tends to be the preferred goal, whereas the latter approach is essentially for professionals in organisations as they attempt, among other things, to achieve defined marketing objectives.

When applied to marketing, basic research looks at understanding processes and their outcomes, whereas applied research investigates particular aspects of marketing (see Table 1.5) – this is perhaps how management consulting firms see the world. Yet, this can be regarded as a semantic distinction, which has mostly been perpetuated in the theory. There exists a fundamental connection between the two, which Pasteur defined as 'use-inspired'. Marketing research is informed both by basic and applied research, too, as a highly practical discipline wedged between art and science: the scientific rigour of basic research as an input for applied research. There is evidence of this, for instance, in how the General Electric Company highlights the necessity for a company to link its business objectives with benefits that might result in society, following a better understanding of the environment in which the operation and implementation of applied research responds to organisational and societal challenges.

It is with this in mind that this book attempts to place emphasis on both positions by embracing them and proposing to take a stance whereby basic research should inform

Table 1.5 Basic and applied marketing research

Basic Research	Applied Research
Knowledge driven	Problem driven
More formal	Less formal
Significant to society	Specific to organisations

Source: Adapted from Saunders et al., 2009: 8–9; Wilson, 2010: 22–3

applied research and vice versa. Indeed, skills gained as a result of studying for a university degree are transferrable to the business environment where more learning, perhaps of a different kind, can be sought.

Generating Organisational Value

The relay of information and knowledge relating to basic and applied marketing research highlights the direct connection existing between making sense of complexity and generating organisational value. For instance, Apple has been applying 'empathy' and 'focus': through its stores, it has created a platform to interact with its customers face to face in a constant drive to understand them; it has essentially put data collection at the core of the company philosophy.

The contribution of marketing research towards value is widely documented in the strategic process of organisations wherein external and internal analyses help inform and operationalise the overall direction of companies in their competitive environment. Similarly, the process of innovation is supported and influenced by the quality of the research that goes into it; value is added by understanding and framing issues (whether problems or challenges), coming up with ideas – typically through desk research or exploratory studies including expert opinions, proposing alternatives and solutions, pre-testing or testing with a variety of techniques of inquiry including toolkits and crowdsourcing – and fine-tuning offerings by looking at and interpreting outcomes.

Other perspectives relate value generation to an ability to achieve a differential advantage through answering two key questions: 'What do customers want?' and 'What are the competitors' strategies?' This demonstrates that the potential impact of marketing research as understanding the micro-environment allows for a more customer-centric orientation to emerge and, eventually, for stronger relationships between stakeholders to be formed.

It is not hard to grasp that knowing more, i.e. collecting and processing information for specific purposes, is a sensible way to produce incremental advantages for an organisation. The generation, interpretation and dissemination of market information is a powerful means of fostering organisational learning and memory, as much as it would be for individuals. The importance of information literacy should never be underestimated. This is manifested through questions asked about the frame of analysis ('know-what'), the dynamics of research ('know-why') and firm properties and market influences ('know-how'). In other words, learning should continue in the workplace and resources marshalled for maximum efficiency; collaboration is therefore paramount for success both internally across functions and externally in the way companies work with suppliers in this area.

A Career in Marketing Research

Besides forming an important and necessary part of any marketing degree, students should be aware that marketing research represents an exciting career option of its own. Learning and improving research-related skills will prove invaluable in the long term, whether you are required to write a research brief, manage a research project or run small-scale surveys, for example.

End users of marketing research are typically manufacturers, retailers, service providers or any organisation that needs a better understanding of their business environment to help them make appropriate decisions. Marketing research companies can also help with the co-creation of knowledge (and value), looking beyond traditional methods of data collection and analysis of information to include its interpretation and integration, the creation of insights and their ultimate dissemination. With a strong tradition for marketing research, it is no surprise that Sainsbury's has won coveted industry prizes like the Research Awards Best In-House Research Team 2011.

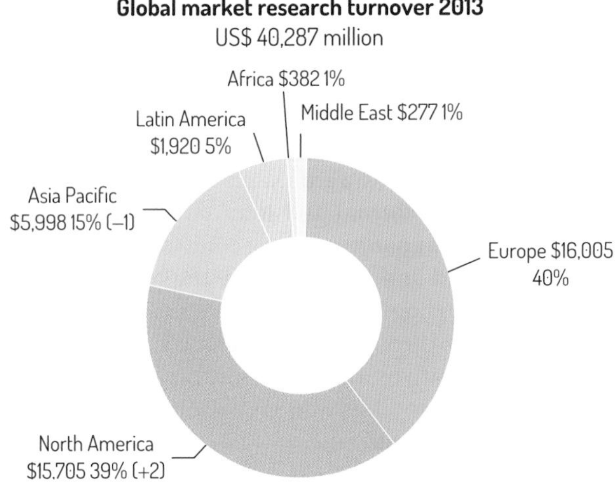

Figure 1.4 2013 Global market(ing) research spend

Source: ESOMAR, 2014

ESOMAR estimates. Rounded figures presented. Percentage point changes in market sharecompared to 2012 are provided between brackets.

Jobs in marketing research range from data collection to senior managerial positions. Graduates without specific experience might want to focus on marketing assistant vacancies to try and build general skills in proofreading, organising, administrative support and, less often, report writing. Another more specific route into marketing research is to become a marketing analyst and to build reports from multiple sources of information, including customer and consumer surveys, product testing and business intelligence. There are many roles at all levels, either agency or client side (see Table 1.6 for some examples); as might be expected, large organisations tend to look for more specialised skills, whereas SMEs take more of a holistic view and staff should be able to stretch across multiple tasks.

The evolution of marketing research over time from little more than an almost accidental or random occurrence to an extremely articulated set of qualitative and quantitative tools and techniques of enquiry (look back at Table 1.2 for further detail) has gone hand in hand with the development of industry best practices and standards. Bodies like the Marketing Research Association, formerly the Marketing Research Trade Association, incorporated in the State of New York in 1957, have provided an ever expanding platform for the promotion and advancement of the marketing research profession.

Table 1.6 Client and agency roles in marketing research

CLIENT:
Marketing Research Analyst: working on several tasks like data matching, manipulation and mining and data analysis from information available in an MIS
Marketing Research Manager: guiding and managing the research needs by defining and addressing appropriate company objectives while managing internal teams and external agencies
Head of Research (or Insight): bringing together information sources to develop business strategy and operations (implementation) in accordance with other departments
Marketing Research Director: directing and overseeing the entire research programme of a firm with responsibility for proposing and initiating new undertakings in line with the corporate mission
AGENCY:
Research Executive: assisting in designing and costing as well as implementing research together with analysing, interpreting and presenting results to clients (1 to 3 years of prior experience)
Senior Research Executive: seeing research projects through from start to finish with some specific people management and/or client liaison responsibility (3 to 5 years of prior experience)
Research (or Project) Manager: managing projects of reasonable size from proposal (brief) to presentation, including full client responsibility (around 5 years of experience)
Account Director: leading small research teams across a range of projects or for a large research programme with some additional responsibility for business development

Research in Practice: Market Research Society (MRS)

Marketing research specialists with interests in market, social and opinion research as well as business intelligence and customer insight can find support in the activities of the Market Research Society (n.d.). Founded in 1946, it now has members from more than 60 countries around the world. Work is being conducted in areas like quality assurance and standards, events and awards, and training and qualifications. Specific resources, including the *International Journal of Market Research*, provide students and professionals with a fertile ground for discussion and reflection on the role of research as a 'force for democracy, commerce and society'.

In the same vein, the European Society for Opinion and Marketing Research (ESOMAR, n.d.) has helped spread consistent guidelines and standards since 1947; today, around 5,000 members in over 130 countries maintain an ongoing dialogue through this network, with the mission of 'encouraging, advancing and elevating market research worldwide' while providing several opportunities for career development through events, awards, workshops, membership and scholarships.

Chapter Summary

The research professional of the future will have to come to terms with a profoundly different industry, as a result of the shift from traditional question-and-answer formats to technology-driven conversation tracking and consumer listening, as facilitated by software and electronic devices. As such, the marketing research sector as a whole is facing a number of challenges that arise from large amounts of relatively easily available data, and can be distilled down to:

- 'big data'
- a change of emphasis from asking to observing
- convergence
- democratisation
- the strategic imperative.

In particular, knowledge is expanding at an exponential rate because of (social) convergence: new combinations of factors and new relationships that create new opportunities for further development, thus requiring companies to boost relevant competencies in the field of marketing research in order to deal with the demands of ever richer data streams and their analysis in the context of the modern business environment.

As marketing research strives to make sense of the complex reality we referred to in the opening pages of this book (see Table 1.1), its value-adding properties very much reside in the contribution it can make to the strategic direction of organisations, so that it is ultimately possible for them to identify and exploit avenues for sustainable competitive advantage.

Table 1.7 Actionable marketing research

	Data	Information	Knowledge	Insight	Foresight	Strategy
Defining traits	Recorded observations	Dataset Datafile Topline Data cross-tabulations	Descriptive facts	Narrative understanding of relation and causation	Understanding projected into the future	Planned activity to achieve a goal within a competitive network
Generative activity	Collecting	Processing Structuring	Analysing	Synthesising Probing Causation	Anticipating	Planning
Temporal focus	Past Present	Past	Past	Present/ Future	Future	Future
Deliverable	Raw data	Datafile Topline data Cross-tabulation	Useful facts/'know how'	Actionable knowledge Implications	Probable and preferred futures	Sequenced actions Resource allocation

Source: Moran, 2012: 421

At the very least, people and companies must demonstrate a positive and inquisitive mindset, possess functional expertise and show an empathic character overall. In other words, there needs to be an in-built ability to marry logical and creative elements in order to generate useful competencies to achieve marketing research excellence (see Table 1.7) in the context of a democratised research space, one with few, or even no, boundaries, where data flows in many directions.

Case Study: Innovation at Singapore Airlines

Over the years, Singapore Airlines has consistently delivered on its promise for service excellence. In the first three months of 2014 alone, the airline received 14 different awards in Scandinavia, the USA, Spain, Indonesia, China, Australia and the UK (Singapore Airlines, 2014) across a range of categories including 'Best Inflight Service' from the AFAR Magazine. It has been its aim to be at the forefront of innovation in that elusive, yet fundamental requirement of a business: meeting and exceeding customer expectations. The company has concentrated both on 'hygiene' factors – those which are needed to avoid dissatisfaction – and 'motivation' factors – those which are needed to improve satisfaction. For instance, the on-board environment, whether you are flying in first, business or economy class, is designed to resemble the home, car or office. Items that we take for granted on the ground, for example vanity mirrors, cup holders, noise-cancelling headphones, are now found on Singapore Airlines flights.

Convenience is not the only organisational focal point as ergonomics, comfort and style are all given due consideration as part of the product development process, to allow the business to move forward without losing its hallmark features, which have made it so memorable and such a success over the years. Value-conscious customers are impressed by details such as atmospheric lighting and elegance, while the carefully arranged interiors also offer privacy within the space constraints of an aircraft.

Although Singapore Airlines is renowned for its service, such pre-eminence in the highly competitive world of business has been achieved through the application of sound practices. To begin with, there is a genuine complicity between the company and its customers as the airline observes and listens carefully in order to gain valuable insight into what interests its target segments, forever striving to build a picture of what people do and how they actually live. On the other hand, customers themselves are given the opportunity to share thoughts and ideas as well as to make suggestions through feedback platforms so that they are also directly involved in the future of the organisation, as Singapore Airlines actively seeks customer input with regards to specific activities and projects.

A picture of consistency emerges as the company makes every conceivable effort to establish, maintain and develop its relationship with existing and potential customers across all points of contact. This is reflected throughout the supply chain as stakeholders collaborate towards a common goal. In this respect, employees and managers have been found to be equally important in the assimilation and the interpretation of information. Ground and cabin crews are able to provide anecdotal experiences, which might contribute to clarifying certain customer behaviours, as well as their expectations. They can also be the source of precious recommendations as the eyes and ears of Singapore Airlines on a 24/7 basis. There is a culture of inclusion as everyone feels as though they can make a real difference to how the company will look like in the years to come.

Likewise, benchmarking competitors has become second nature in the organisation in spite of the fact that Singapore Airlines has been ahead of the pack since the 1950s. Indeed, the main preoccupation is to consolidate this leading position and, if possible, make the gap with the rest of the industry even wider. This is why improvements seen in hotels, banks, restaurants and retailers often find their way into the company's customer service culture in the form of innovative ways to improve amenities, convenience and comfort. It has

(Continued)

(Continued)

been noted that 'the culture of innovation is so pervasive in the company that most functional departments have the innovation objective as part of their mission' (Heracleous et al., 2005: 30).

In essence, Singapore Airlines is not happy with the status quo, i.e. what it has attained so far; it wants to leave other companies, whether in the industry or not, trailing in its wake through the application of a two-pronged approach to innovation. It is as much about planning and organising a comprehensive support system for innovation as it is about nurturing and developing an independent mentality to sustain and renew its business over time. This essentially fits within the definition of a learning organisation or an organisation whose members are working towards clear goals using expansive thinking patterns and 'where people are continually learning to see the whole together' (Senge, 1990: 3).

Case study questions:

1. What are the contexts in which Singapore Airlines might need to conduct market and marketing research?
2. How would you characterise the environment facing Singapore Airlines in light of the information presented in Chapter 1?
3. Who are the key stakeholders in the process of product development for Singapore Airlines, and why?
4. What is the approach of Singapore Airlines to marketing and marketing research?

End of Chapter Questions

These questions should help you reflect on your understanding of this chapter:

1. What is a possible definition of marketing research, and why?
2. What are the three key elements that can help with learning marketing research?
3. What are the key passages in the evolution of marketing research to date?
4. What is the main difference between market and marketing research?
5. What is the link between basic and applied research in marketing, and why?
6. What are the main themes concerning the application of technology to marketing research?
7. How does marketing research ultimately contribute to organisational value?
8. What are some of the applications of marketing research seen in Chapter 1?

Checklist

After studying Chapter 1, you should now be familiar with these key concepts:

1. The definition of systematic marketing research
2. How marketing orientations have influenced marketing research

3. What developments have occurred in marketing research
4. The importance of understanding complexity
5. Why the study of marketing research is important to businesses

Further Reading (in sequence from beginners to advanced)

McKinsey & Company (2013) Making data analytics work: three key challenges. *McKinsey & Company Interview* [online, March]. Available at: www.mckinsey.com/insights/business_technology/making_data_analytics_work

Straub, R. (2013) Why managers haven't embraced complexity. *HBR Blog Network* [online, 6 May]. Available at: http://blogs.hbr.org/cs/2013/05/why_managers_havent_embraced_c.html

Rallis, S. F. and Rossmann, G. B. (2012) *The Research Journey: Introduction to Inquiry*. New York: The Guildford Press.

Kaden, R. J., Linda, G. and Prince, M. (eds) (2012) *Leading Edge Marketing Research: 21st-Century Tools and Practices*. Thousand Oaks, CA: Sage Publications.

Merz, M. A., He, Y. and Vargo, S. L. (2009) The evolving brand logic: a service-dominant logic perspective. *Journal of the Academy of Marketing Science*, 37 (3), pp. 328–44.

Bibliography

Armstrong, G., Kotler, P., Harker, M. and Brennan, R. (2011) *Marketing: An Introduction* (2nd edition). Harlow: Pearson Education.

Bradley, N. (2007) *Marketing Research: Tools and Techniques*. Oxford: Oxford University Press.

Brewer, J. D. (2003) Verstehen. In R. L. Miller and J. D. Brewer (eds), *The A–Z of Social Research*. London: Sage Publications.

Burns, A. C. and Bush, R. F. (2014) *Marketing Research: International edition* (7th edition). Harlow: Pearson Education.

Cano, F. (2006) An in-depth analysis of the Learning Study and Strategies Inventory (LASSI). *Educational and Psychological Measurement*, 66 (6), pp. 1023–38.

Choo, C. W. (2006) *The Knowing Organization: How Organizations use Information to Construct Meaning, Create Knowledge, and Make Decisions* (2nd edition). New York: Oxford University Press.

Costa, M. (2011) New growth at Nokia. *Marketing Week* [online, 16 November]. Available at: www.marketingweek.co.uk/new-growth-at-nokia/3031928.article [Accessed 18 June 2013].

Cox, D. F. and Good, R. E. (1967) How to build a marketing information system. *Harvard Business Review*, 45 (3), pp. 145–54.

Daft, R. L. and Marcic, D. (2014) *Building Management Skills: An Action-First Approach*. Mason, OH: South-Western, Cengage Learning.

Denzin, N. K. and Lincoln, Y. S. (2005) *The SAGE Handbook of Qualitative Research* (3rd edition). Thousand Oaks, CA: Sage Publications.

Elliott, J. E. (1980) Marx and Schumpeter on Capitalism's Creative Destruction: A Comparative Restatement. *The Quarterly Journal of Economics*, 95 (1), pp. 45–68.

ESOMAR (n.d.) About ESOMAR: Mission & Statutes. *ESOMAR World Research* [online]. Available at: www.esomar.org/about-esomar/mission-and-statutes.php [Accessed 17 November 2013].

ESOMAR (2014) Global Marketing Research 2014: an ESOMAR industry report [online]. Available at: www.esomar.org/uploads/industry/reports/global-market-research-2014/ESOMAR-GMR2014-Preview.pdf [Accessed 23 August 2015].

Fisher, C., Lovell, A. and Valero-Silva, N. (2013) *Business Ethics and Values* (4th edition). Harlow: Pearson Education.

Hart, C. (1999) Doing a literature review: releasing the social science research imagination. London: SAGE [online]. Available at: www.sagepub.com/upm-data/28728_LitReview___hart_chapter_1.pdf [Accessed 7 September 2013].

Heracleous, L., Wirtz, J. and Johnston, R. (2005) Kung-fu service development at Singapore Airlines. *Business Strategy Review*, Winter, pp. 26–31.

Hollensen, S. (2011) *Global Marketing: A Decision-Oriented Approach* (5th edition). Harlow: Pearson Education.

Joseph, S. (2011) Nokia focuses brand strategy on retail stores. *Marketing Week* [online, 1 December]. Available at: www.marketingweek.co.uk/nokia-focuses-brand-strategy-on-retail-stores/3032389.article [Accessed 18 June 2013].

Kaufman, R. (n.d.) Singapore Airlines flies high thanks to its customer service culture. *Up Your Service* [online]. Available at: www.upyourservice.com/learning-library/customer-service-culture/how-does-singapore-airlines-fly-so-high [Accessed 17 June 2014].

Lewis, I. and Chadwick, S. (2012) New roles for marketing researchers. In R. J. Kaden, G. Linda and M. Prince (eds). *Leading Edge Marketing Research: 21st-Century Tools and Practices*. Thousand Oaks, CA: Sage Publications.

Lockley, L. C. (1950) Notes on the history of marketing research. *Journal of Marketing*, 14 (5), pp. 733–6.

Malik, O. (2011) How Nokia didn't listen to itself. GigaOm [online, 1 June]. Available at: http://gigaom.com/mobile/how-nokia-didnt-listen-to-itself [Accessed 27 October 2012].

Market Research Society (n.d.) About MRS: The world's leading research association. *MRS* [online]. Available at: www.mrs.org.uk/mrs/aboutmrs [Accessed 17 November 2013].

Marketing Week (2011) Matching insight with innovation at Nokia [online, 16 November]. Available at: www.marketingweek.co.uk/analysis/matching-insight-with-innovation-at-nokia/3031940.article [Accessed 18 June 2013].

Marketing Week (2013) Q&A: Alex Owens, head of insight, data, tools and segmentation, Sainsbury's [online, 29 August]. Available at: www.marketingweek.co.uk/trends/qa-alex-owens-head-of-insight-data-tools-and-segmentation-sainsburys/4007699.article [Accessed 16 November 2013].

McCartney, S. (2013) How Singapore Airlines upgraded three cabins. *Wall Street Journal* [online, 1 October]. Available at: http://online.wsj.com/news/articles/SB10001424052702304526204579097284121738684 [Accessed 17 June 2014].

McKinsey & Company (2012) Beyond price: the rise of customer-centric marketing in insurance. *Financial Services Practice* [online]. Available at: www.mckinsey.com/Search.aspx?q=beyond%20price [Accessed 1 November 2013].

Moran, R. (2012) The futures of marketing research. In R. J. Kaden, G. Linda and M. Prince (eds), *Leading Edge Marketing Research: 21st-Century Tools and Practices*. Thousand Oaks, CA: Sage Publications.

Peacock, L. (2010) Nokia appoints Elop as chief executive. *The Telegraph* [online, 11 September]. Available at: www.telegraph.co.uk/technology/nokia/7995243/Nokia-appoints-Elop-as-chief-executive.html [Accessed 27 October 2012].

Satell, G. (2013) 5 marketing problems we need to solve now. *Forbes* [online, 13 July]. Available at: www.forbes.com/sites/gregsatell/2013/07/13/5-marketing-problems-we-need-to-solve-now [Accessed 31 August 2013].

Saunders, M., Lewis, P. and Thornhill, A. (2009) *Research Methods for Business Students* (5th edition). Harlow: Pearson Education.

Senge, P. (1990) *The Fifth Discipline: The Art and Practice of the Learning Organization*. New York: Doubleday/Currency.

Shaw, E. H. and Jones, D. G. B. (2005) A history of schools of marketing thought. *Marketing Theory*, 5 (3), pp. 239–81.

Singapore Airlines (2014) Singapore Airlines: Our awards [online]. Available at: www.singaporeair.com/en_UK/about-us/sia-history/sia-awards [Accessed 16 June 2014].

Taub, E. (1991) *Taurus: The Making of the Car that Saved Ford*. New York: Dutton, Penguin Books.

Troianowski, A., Grundberg, S. and Ante, S. E. (2012) Nokia's problems haunt Microsoft. *Wall Street Journal*, European edition [online, 14 June]. Available at: online.wsj.com/article/SB10001424052702303822204577465771376539532.html [Accessed 27 October 2012].

West, G. (2013) Wisdom in numbers. *Scientific American*, 308 (5), p. 14.

Wilson, J. (2010) *Essentials of Business Research: A Guide to Doing Your Research Project*. London: Sage Publications.

Yoshino, A. (2004) Well-intentioned ignorance characterises British attitudes to foreign students. *The Times Higher Education Supplement* [online, 16 July]. Available at: www.timeshighereducation.co.uk/story.asp?storyCode=190126§ioncode=26 [Accessed 7 September 2013].

Zikmund, W. G., Babin, B. J., Carr, J. C. and Griffin, M. (2013) *Business Research Methods* (9th edition). Mason, OH: South-Western, Cengage Learning.

Find journal articles and multiple choice questions online at: **https://study.sagepub.com/benzo** to support what you've learnt so far.

CHAPTER 2

Identifying Marketing-Related (Business) Issues

LEARNING OBJECTIVES

The key learning objectives of this chapter are:

1. To select a suitable topic for marketing research
2. To explain the link between management formulation and actionable research
3. To prepare a rationale for a marketing research proposal
4. To outline the systematic process of marketing research

KEY CONCEPTS

By the end of this chapter, the reader should be familiar with the following concepts:

1. Choosing suitable research topics
2. Environmental analysis and marketing research
3. Generating viable research ideas
4. Key components of a research plan
5. A research proposal versus a marketing research brief
6. Linking data collection with data analysis
7. From proposals to full-scale projects

Riccardo Benzo

Introduction

The way in which we understand the business environment around us and how organisations operate within it is likely to influence the direction of marketing research. All the things that attract our attention are worth reflecting on and, possibly, investigating; however, we need to come up with suitable strategies to decide what to pursue and how to learn more about such matters. It would be presumptuous to think we know all that we need to, and it would be unwise to think that we can make sense of complexity without appropriate thinking and planning. The success of any research assignment is therefore dependent on the effort one puts into identifying researchable marketing-related business issues. These typically take the shape of research questions for which answers can be found within the constraints set by a company or by an academic institution.

This chapter aims to give a balanced view of how to define a marketing research issue, problem, phenomenon, trend, and so on, of interest and make it researchable. It is about keeping things in check as we strive to develop a suitable, systematic process for marketing research from its initial definition to secondary research and, if needed, from secondary research to primary research – the collection and analysis of fresh data for a specific purpose.

Based on our experience, the main reason why students fail in their marketing research endeavours is because of poor organisational and planning skills. The relative lack of knowledge of the methods and techniques required to gather, understand and interpret data can be overcome as these can easily be learned once they have been identified. With this in mind, the goal here is to break down the initial steps of the systematic process of enquiry that is marketing research. As such, we propose to start by looking into the business environment as a possible source of inspiration for investigation: marketing professionals and students should work to get to grips with identifying issues, solving problems, understanding phenomena, taking advantage of opportunities and fending off threats, which can be identified in the world out there.

As we proceed, we should aim to shed light on the type and extent of secondary research needed to frame a piece of marketing research or to address a particular assignment. This is because investing in the early stages of a research task tends to pay off handsome dividends by the end of it.

Snapshot: Yo! Sushi

With 91 restaurants worldwide, Yo! Sushi made the logical step of speeding up its international expansion by accepting an offer from Mayfair Equity Partners, giving the business a further boost on its way to bigger and better things. The chain was founded in the UK in 1997 where it still has the majority of its interests; however, it has moved into the USA, Ireland, Denmark, Norway, the United Arab Emirates and Saudi Arabia, where it either owns or franchises a small number of restaurants.

'Kaiten' (conveyor belt) sushi restaurants have proved rather successful outside of Japan where, from around 2012, they had in contrast begun experiencing tougher times. The evolution of the format has seen the introduction of more technology, with touchscreens to order a wide array of dishes and a single-track delivery system to get the food to customers quickly in a futuristic setting. The conveyor belt is disappearing as it requires larger physical spaces, which can be expensive in inner-city locations and lead to food wastage – dishes go around the conveyor belt and eventually have to be thrown away. As some parts of the world get introduced to 'kaiten' sushi, its homeland is seeing what might be the beginning of a (food) revolution.

As internationalisation goes, Yo! Sushi does not appear to have followed a classical path from a domestic market unable to sustain its growth to a close foreign market with further opportunity for expansion. It has perhaps taken advantage of the possibility to present itself within its network of contacts. Yet, it seems plausible to argue that the company wants 'to play active roles in local markets, but also globally, as new opportunities scattered around the world can be sensed and exploited' (Carrizo Moreira, 2009: 25). In so doing, Yo! Sushi faces a number of questions relating to making decisions with regards to marketing strategy and management.

The chain already has plans for more short-term openings in the USA, yet the recent injection of funds will no doubt trigger further business activity beyond this.

Choosing a Topic

It is only natural for students to struggle during their early attempts at dealing with the first step of a research project: choosing a topic. This is because we have a tendency to start writing without realising that a carefully argued topic of research will have a much better chance of standing up to the scrutiny of our lecturers and colleagues. It is all too often assumed that adjustments can be made later on in order to create compelling new knowledge that answers a particular research question. However, keeping a marketing research project moving forward is a function of the many decisions one has made along the way. Every rushed or unsupported choice takes us away from our main purpose, because there is a higher probability that the findings will eventually be invalid and/or unreliable.

In this respect, the relationship between us and our surroundings can be seen as a stepping stone in helping define a suitable topic for marketing research. The way we sense the world in which we live has a strong influence on how we learn about it; this eventually provides a wealth of knowledge and wisdom in order for us to define potential directions for the development of our research. Experiences, expertise, culture, personal and family life cycle are some of the factors that shape who we are and how we think about what is going on around us. Drawing inspiration from our backgrounds can lead to the discovery of general areas of interest from which to select topics for research. However, our values and passions can also introduce bias in the way we execute research, so we should always be careful that our views do not intercept the systematic process of marketing research. This is how we add valid and reliable knowledge to what is already known about marketing as a discipline by and large (see Chapter 4 for further details).

As a student, you must be able to discern between a topic that has potential and a topic that does not. The process of marketing research must be, to a great extent, about being able to support our ideas right from the start using empirical and theoretical evidence along the way. Everything we know comes from somewhere and enables us to put emphasis on an issue, problem, opportunity or phenomenon that is specific enough to be researchable.

What About Your Career Prospects?

If you are nearing the end of your undergraduate or postgraduate programme, you may soon have to choose a marketing-related research topic for your final project. This piece of work is extremely important in determining the final outcome of your studies and, possibly, your future career prospects. Several higher education institutions around the world miss the importance of putting enough emphasis on this last fact. This is why students take a rather mechanical approach to such larger-scale tasks, thus foregoing the opportunity to think deeper, focus their interests and specialise in a particular topic. They often seek to achieve a mere pass mark or to get this final hurdle out of the way, only to find themselves aimless in the pursuit of their next step, for example finding a job or getting a promotion.

There is merit in looking at alternative careers in marketing (see Chapter 1 for some examples), as the obvious choices, such as marketing communications, may be the road most travelled by tomorrow's graduates. Adding value to a degree through a more targeted dissertation is generally a sensible idea. This can be achieved by focusing on:

- particular areas of knowledge needed to pursue a specific path
- attractive (this could mean fast-growing) industries or sectors
- outstanding organisations with appealing marketing orientations.

Learning about something closely is an excellent way to improve your chances of being shortlisted for a job interview and to keep part of the selection process focused on something you are familiar with. The key advice is: avoid illogical and insignificant questions! Reflecting carefully on a dissertation topic can bring who we are and what we know to bear in a powerful way: it is the convergence of the past, the present and the future – something that should not be underplayed.

Ethics: Stage-Specific Ethical Issues

There is a general tendency to let considerations about ethics in research take a back seat; Hunt, Chonko and Wilcox (1984) state that 'Most of the ethics research pertains to the duties of researchers toward respondents and clients'. Indeed, in the past emphasis was mainly put on detailing the responsibilities of researchers. Little attention was paid to power relationships and the need to balance the interests of different groups. This is why more should be done to establish clear rules of engagement early on during a marketing research project.

For instance, students should not be forced into researching a topic in which they are not interested or that does not satisfy the assessment requirements of a particular module. It is important for researchers to take ownership of a project in full, i.e. to have the ability to 'call the shots' and define the boundaries of each and every relationship, so that they are guaranteed protection against stress, harm, discomfort, and so on, as much as any other stakeholder. In so doing, the researcher is free of coercion, the organisation or higher education institution gets meaningful research, and stakeholders obtain quality research based on the application of sound, systematic research principles.

The Business Environment

The choices we make as students or professionals should be dictated by a thorough understanding of the business environment in which we study or work. There is often a tendency to think loosely about a particular situation as being relevant and worthy of our consideration and time because of personal interest. We should try and reflect on why a particular topic has become relevant to us, to our organisation or society at large. What kind of evolution in the business environment have we been witnessing? This is a solid way to build a compelling basis for one's research. To this extent, it makes sense to review key tools for analysis first, as depicted in Figure 2.1.

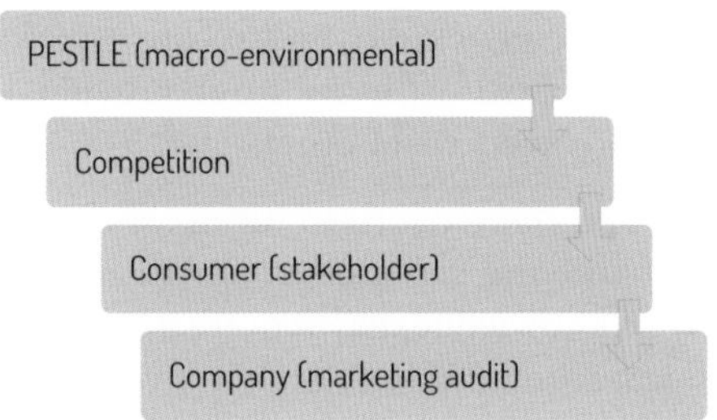

Figure 2.1 Environmental analysis in marketing research

Macro-environmental scanning originated in the second half of the 1960s. Although there are now several different acronyms to define it, the fundamental idea of a PESTLE is to offer a synthetic system to break down and list out uncontrollable factors that shape the way in which organisations do business. It starts by providing a list of important areas for observation – Political, Economic, Social, Technological, Legal and Environmental – and a structure to describe them in more detail according to the impact they may have on a firm. Using this kind of approach, a student can highlight the potential issues, problems and phenomena worth studying. This is the case for many laws coming into existence around the world, such as Australia's SPAM Act 2003, for how they eventually force changes to best practice in marketing and what this means for an industry, sector or company. In this respect, useful research could be conducted in a number of areas, including compliance, consumer perception and marketing communications.

The **business environment** includes internal and external factors that impact on how a company operates (does marketing)

As an example, Ugg, the world-renowned Australian sheepskin footwear manufacturer, had to contend with greater restrictions impacting their ability to do e-marketing within the afore-mentioned regulatory framework. These changes also shaped consumer perceptions – these can be thought of as the mental boundaries of acceptable practices – thus affecting the extent of eventual complaints, i.e. what was acceptable or otherwise. In other words, a researcher could dwell on how an organisation should adapt its marketing messages and techniques in order not to fall foul of the law and, equally importantly, not to alienate consumers. Such an investigation could eventually lead to the collection of qualitative data via expert interviews and ethnographic research (see Chapter 8 for further detail).

Further ideas for research assignments and projects typically originate from the intensity and the characteristics of the competitive environment that surrounds us (the micro environment); it is a given that companies have to contend with marketing strategies and tactics as put in place by their rivals. In this respect, marketing research can be driven by how decisions taken by businesses, with regards to innovation and product development, revenue generation and pricing, customer satisfaction and people (internal and external synergies), may influence their competitors.

Due to the seemingly unstoppable technological revolution and evolution of the last ten years, content marketing has grown massively in importance. The performance of organisations in this area is in fact in the public domain, so an analysis of practices in this field can prove useful in order to realise the effectiveness of particular programmes or activities within a small competitive set, for instance boutique hotels in the Bahamas. Such effectiveness can be measured in terms of the overall coverage in social media, the reach via influencers, the popularity of pages, the traffic generated, and so on. There is indeed a lot of scope in benchmarking others, studying industries, sectors and individual organisations, as much of what we do in marketing is 'borrowed' from others.

Irrespective of our starting point, there needs to be an awareness of what is going on near and around us in order for marketing research to gather momentum. As a matter of fact, enhancing the existing body of knowledge may require more than a one-dimensional effort. Both macro (PESTLE) and micro (competitive set) environmental analyses typically contribute to the successful identification, selection and development of a researchable topic.

Reflective Activity

- What recent macro-environmental changes have you noticed in your home country, which can affect marketing practices, e.g. product, price?
- For a sector of your choice, can you identify any strategic or tactical marketing action, which can stimulate research into existing practices, e.g. place, people?
- How might changes in macro- and micro-environmental conditions impact on one another?

This should also lead us to look beyond the widespread view that the key relationship in marketing is that between an organisation and its customers or consumers. For example, stakeholder theory has provided researchers with a much more comprehensive understanding of how companies can create and share value through a variety of properly managed relations with suppliers, distributors, governments, local authorities, communities, and so on. There is definitely an opportunity to recognise and study meaningful associations through the use of a simple power–interest matrix, a tool that examines and analyses the potential influence of certain stakeholders (power) and their willingness to act on it (interest) (Mendelow, 1991).

The increasing deregulation of the drinks industry in many countries around the world, from Chile to India via Nigeria, has given way to the rise of severe social disruption together with a growing impact on general health issues. The resulting heavier drinking habits displayed by large groups of people have kick-started a counter-process whereby states are considering how to control, and possibly regulate, this trend. This is why several alcohol producers have been working together to appease governments and law-makers, with campaigns aiming at educating the general public on enjoying responsible drinking, indirectly warning them about the risks of binge drinking. In spite of these efforts, the social cost of excessive alcohol intake – this would include short- and long-term medical issues, damage to private and public property – seems to continue escalating, hence understanding how to change opinions, attitudes and behaviours through the use of more appropriate marketing communications and other elements of the marketing mix (e.g. people, processes and physical evidence) is becoming key to achieving certain strategic marketing objectives.

The impact of marketing resources – be it their presence or absence – on an organisation can be another point of interest for research. Internal analysis in the form of marketing audits is a useful technique for spotting specific requirements as positive and negative associations in relation to important areas, for instance brand image, can be categorised and, among other things, the perceived quality of service delivery measured by assessing other parts of the marketing mix, for example processes. New product development and speed to market were tackled by Standard Bank Argentina as part of a capital investment whose broader aims included the management of project schedules, which gave the bank the ability to establish and meet completion dates for customer marketing campaigns more precisely and effectively. Budgets were also streamlined and savings achieved as a result of that.

Research in Practice: Sugar Consumption Trends

As the world finally caught up with the USA, more questions had to be asked as to what has been driving the increase in consumption of sugar-sweetened foods and drinks to an unprecedented level. Chile and Mexico now top the charts, with Argentina not far behind. A host of other countries, including Saudi Arabia and India, have seen similarly worrying trends, especially considering that high sugar consumption has been linked with weight gain, heart disease, diabetes and stroke. However, there may be some light at the end of the tunnel as research conducted in the UK showed a somewhat opposite trend, due to media coverage and a heightened perception of how sugar can affect one's health for the worse (Langley, 2015).

There appear to be some powerful forces at play, which are shaping the way audiences around the world are reacting to messages from different sources. On the one hand, there are the interests of food and drink manufacturers whose objectives may primarily be driven by financial considerations. On the other hand, not-for-profit and public sector organisations are providing a different voice to try and deliver facts about the effects of excessive sugar consumption. In this highly competitive market, there is definitely room for a variety of studies and investigations on the effectiveness of marketing activities, perhaps comparing how people in different countries understand and process inputs. In broad terms, the marketing objectives of social/societal campaigns are to instill, modify or stop a particular behaviour by changing beliefs, opinions, attitudes and behaviours. This is rather more difficult than enticing consumers to buy what in many cases is a low-involvement purchase.

Marketing-related investigation is about proactive and reactive research into solutions and innovations

The simple observation of a phenomenon can raise a host of potentially exciting ideas around a topic, in this case sugar consumption. Secondary data and research should be looked at first together with theories and theoretical frameworks in order to establish potential lines of inquiry. Further reflection is then needed to find some potentially interesting connections between some of these areas, thus establishing a 'blueprint' for eventual development.

In spite of its many upsides, environmental analysis should be treated with respect. First of all, it is static, whereas the world around us changes constantly, sometimes dramatically. Additional information might in certain circumstances be needed, thus sending researchers back to earlier stages of their projects for fine-tuning purposes. Conversely, over-analysing situations can often lead to the very opposite issue: paralysis. We should instead accept the fact that we live in a world where perfect information is not achievable and move forward in order to make the best possible decisions, having considered a sufficient range of valid and reliable sources to define the extent of a problem, issue or trend at least in the first instance, i.e. when we initially approach them.

Marketing-Related Investigation

The beginning of any research task is therefore a rather tentative, sometimes even messy, affair as we search for evidence to enable us to put together and support a solid rationale for what is to follow, for what we are going to try and study. This is the time when we win or lose support for our ideas; this is when students need to persuade their tutors or supervisors that they have spotted something worth investigating or that their arguments are logical in a given context. Furthermore, we should not get obsessed with just looking at problems and solutions as this encourages a mainly reactive mode. Marketing as the outward-facing function of an organisation has the task of reading and anticipating signs of change through the creation and interpretation of data and information, eventually leading to better decision making and long-term sustainability (see Chapter 1, Table 1.1). Here, we are going to look at how to effect a transition from a general topic to a research plan by providing a range of examples and illustrations, as depicted in Figure 2.2.

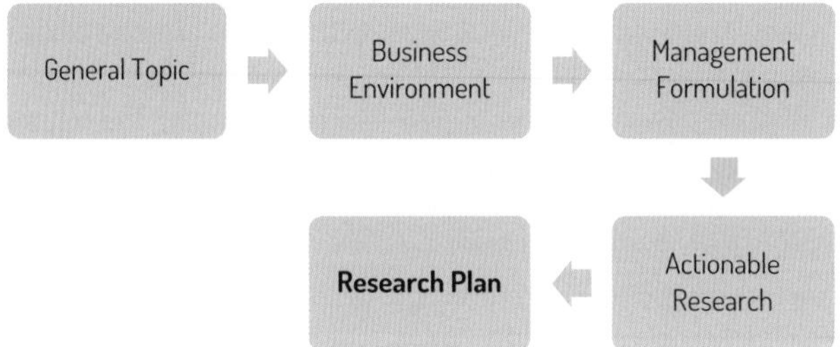

Figure 2.2 Narrowing down marketing research

In other words, we are trying to make connections between a particular area of interest – be that empirical, theoretical or both – and a business environment, so that it is possible to arrive at a suitable formulation of a managerial issue, problem or phenomenon. This will then help with the operationalisation of marketing research, eventually in the shape of a full-blown plan of action.

Identifying issues

General observations in the business environment more often than not lead to interesting findings and directions for research. This is applicable both to struggling as well as thriving companies. In fact, identifying issues becomes crucial during protracted periods of growth when there is little to worry about in terms of fundamental problem solving, and short-term views and executions for more immediate results tend to be preferred. There is indeed a tendency to accept the status quo and to let one's guard down.

For instance, since the revolutionary use of touchscreen technology gave Apple a head start on its competitors with the launch of the first iPhone in 2007, the American company has at times appeared seemingly unstoppable. This has been down to its willingness and ability to continue collecting and interpreting data, even though its success and resulting leadership position might naturally have pushed the firm to 'milk' its advantage or, in other words, to be content with its achievements. Indeed, Apple's success is the result of a widespread research effort in China where many, including arch-rival Samsung, have not been able to sustain business growth over time. For a start, the rather stringent control exerted by the Chinese government and competition from local electronics manufacturers created conditions rarely experienced elsewhere in the world. Looking at the distinguishing features of Chinese customers in relation to their preferences, together with the exploitation of mistakes previously made by others, provided a solid platform on which the company could build.

Along the way, Apple was also adamant that it would not compromise on product and on brand positioning by maintaining a consistent front, which eventually contributed to its strong performance in early 2015. Management executives have relied on the insights provided by research projects focusing on product development, product attributes and benefits (for instance, these led to the launch of the iPhone 6 Plus), brand image, brand equity and consumer relationships, in spite of Apple itself being acknowledged and celebrated as the leader in the specific mobile phone product category. These are all valid examples of angles that students can take in their quest for a suitable way to begin work on an end-of-term piece of assessment.

Research can stem from the desire to anticipate threats and spot opportunities, and it is more useful when it enables us to achieve this well before others can. In other words, there is a lot to be gained by identifying issues before they become problems: 'It's about getting better at sensing what the market wants or might do' (Rao, n.d.). Technology and social listening have indeed added to the armoury of each and every researcher, making data collection yet more flexible and powerful. It has also made it possible to produce quick and effective decision making, sometimes at a much reduced cost. Marketing research should indeed be proportionally more widespread nowadays than it has ever been because our ability to communicate two-way or many ways has greatly improved. The interpretation and presentation of data are still skills that need to be honed over time through study and practice (see Chapters 10, 13, 14 and 15 for more detail); acquiring these skills requires patience, application and reflection over time.

Solving problems

The use of tried-and-tested processes, for example marketing research, which helps in tracking and anticipating change, appears to be preferable to reacting to external and internal conditions. Ignoring potential shocks to the business environment is often the reason why organisations find themselves dealing with a host of undesirable situations. Based on our previous discussion, problems – for example, bad online customer reviews, slow-selling product lines, negative word-of-mouth – are likely to emerge when there is a tendency to take a short-term as opposed to a healthier, long-term view in business. Whatever their origin, these problems are in many circumstances the trigger of marketing research as we seek to come up with and implement solutions to them.

As an illustration, foreign banks in South Korea thought they could take advantage of an opening in the marketplace following changes in the structure of the financial system in the country after the 1998 Asian financial crisis. Their optimism was dictated by the prospect of renewed economic growth and a widespread habit in the local population of keeping large amounts of money in savings: these factors bore the promise of potentially quick returns. Yet, these facts proved insufficient in themselves as the country had, since the 1950s, been supported by and was dependent on a group of established conglomerates known as the 'chaebols', which include Hyundai and Samsung; failing to appreciate the historical evolution of the credit system in South Korea and the central role of these corporations in its society, foreign operators soon found themselves unable to compete.

One of the key problems in marketing terms was to establish their reputation. They lacked an understanding of the psychographic dimensions of consumer behaviour amongst South Koreans: values, beliefs, opinions and interests. As virtually new entrants, they lagged behind their local counterparts and could not enjoy the same kind of relationship with consumers. Standard Chartered is an example of a bank which has not quite captured the essence and nuances of this culture as its brand promise still reads: 'Here for good captures the essence of who we are. It's about sticking by our clients and always trying to do the right thing' (Standard Chartered, 2014). It is at best a shallow statement, especially if one does not know how to articulate what 'doing the right thing' means to a South Korean. The outcome of this absence of foresight is a series of problems linked to the lack of a meaningful and relevant positioning for the business, which would eventually make target audiences pay attention to the bank.

In this respect, a host of potential marketing research projects around brand preference, brand image and associations, consumer values, beliefs and opinions in relation to banking services and banks opens up in front of a student's eyes. The focus here is firmly on finding solutions to problems both at the strategic and the tactical levels in order to attain faster customer acquisition in a hard-fought market.

Reflective Activity

- What news items have you read during the past four weeks in relation to management problems relating to the wider marketing area?
- How did the companies you read about find themselves facing such situations?
- How could they address their problems using marketing research?

Since problems are somewhat part and parcel of our lives, it is sensible to have ways to deal with them, thus limiting their overall impact. As a well-supported systematic process of investigation, marketing research is therefore well placed to help provide solutions and steer decision making. It also makes the implementation of corrective actions more effective and efficient as we cannot expect the competition to stand still.

Understanding phenomena

Another way marketing research contributes to managerial activities – planning, organising, co-ordinating, commanding and controlling – is in the tracking of phenomena that may have an impact on the sustainability of a business over time. Students can discuss and look into changes in the fabric of society (e.g. morals and morality), the evolution of technology (e.g. crowdsourcing) and the development of markets (e.g. globalisation), as these act as powerful influencers. In many cases, such changes sweep across the world and their intimate understanding could make a huge difference to marketing strategy, its formulation through appropriate marketing objectives and its eventual implementation via detailed marketing programmes. Students should take an interest in exploring phenomena, trends and patterns, especially when they are new and little data, information and knowledge are available on them – this has been the case for the K-Pop wave as this phenomenon spread from South Korea to Vietnam where its understanding is still somewhat limited.

An incredibly dynamic area for marketing research is represented by the willingness of people to engage with others around them as multi-media platforms make broadcasting messages in real time extremely easy. Participation in these exchanges can lead to value co-creation, although this is not necessarily limited to the organisation–consumer relationship. A large amount of information regarding the opinions that people hold about the world around them is publicly available in online platforms and virtual communities alike. Companies have to come to terms with the fact that in these spaces they are not necessarily in control but still have an opportunity to learn from and somehow influence stakeholders.

Research in Practice: Making Sense of Selfies

The selfie as a phenomenon has become all pervasive in our digital-driven culture. People even take huge risks to get the perfect snap in rather dangerous situations, which have, in some circumstances, led to injury and death. There is no doubt that the selfie has influenced the way we live and socialise. One student recently thought about how this fascination might reflect itself in the relationship between brands and consumers. In spite of the popularity of selfies, research on the topic, especially in relation to marketing as a discipline, is still limited; hence, the first steps in the investigation proved rather challenging.

Reading around the topic brought back interesting findings from the field of psychology where the examination of selfies has been associated with narcissism, psychopathy and self-objectification. This contributed to raising some doubts about what branded selfies would eventually contribute to organisations, as consumers mainly appeared to be looking at self-promotion. In other words, the relationship between brands and consumers could turn out to be a shallow one, thus not adding much in terms of brand equity.

Therefore, the investigation moved on to consider different companies and, more broadly, product categories using the work of Interbrand to focus observations on specific brands and, eventually, the content of related branded selfies. At each step, a new field of knowledge would happen to provide another piece of the jigsaw puzzle that had appeared to be incredibly hard to solve. Some of the selfies might as well indicate meaning and value, so it eventually transpired that the relationship between brand and consumer could lead to desirable associations, indirectly identifying another relevant field of knowledge.

Ultimately, the process allowed the topic to be narrowed down at the intersection of narcissism, brand equity and brand associations, such as with celebrities, from what seemed a possibly sterile route for a marketing research project.

Let us now examine one of these new spaces. Although Pinterest may not be known as an environment primarily used to interact with other users, it is still a popular social media platform where people come together and share thoughts and opinions. There is a large amount of useful information for organisations and students to tap into as boards and group boards provide an ideal situation to showcase ideas in a visual format and encourage exchanges. Muji, the Japanese minimalist brand, benefited from the increasing popularity of Naoto Fukusawa, one if its designers, who went on to build a rather large following on Pinterest, where many of its creations are displayed and discussed. The company itself is officially present via a couple of boards (Products and Stores), yet the interest around the brand is much more widespread with hundreds of boards and pins associated with it.

The collection and analysis of data from this medium, therefore, can provide insight into trends and patterns, which can indicate the existence of particular phenomena and the implications these may have for a particular business. In other words, there may be indications as to what product features and benefits are becoming increasingly popular in order to understand how to engage with audiences on a long-term basis. Trawling through social media data can possibly indicate consumer motivations in general or in relation to a specific brand; these can be economic, hedonic or normative reasons for people to act in a particular way. Such activities enable a researcher to read between the lines and to interpret thoughts and feelings in order to take advantage of key trends as identified from screening peer-to-peer exchanges.

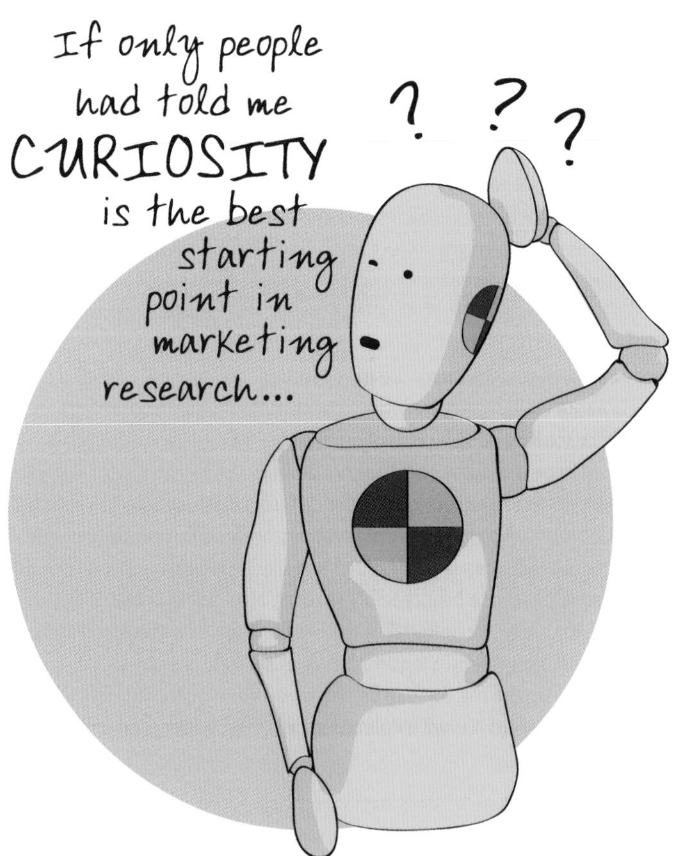

Figure 2.3 The world as a source of inspiration

As we reflect on a research topic in relation to its environment and with regards to its potential relevance in managerial terms, we get nearer to isolating a particular area of interest at the intersection of a number of components that have revealed themselves to us along this journey of reconnaissance. This takes us a step closer to fleshing out ideas in enough detail and, as such, to preparing a plan that can then be put into action.

Researchable Marketing Topics

The transition from marketing-related investigation to actionable marketing research is an important one as it is intended to help define the actual scope of a piece of work, thus ensuring that a desired output can be attained within the constraints, for example the time/deadline set by an institution. In other words, this phase is about operationalising a particular topic as the intersection of a set of fields of investigation that appear to be relevant for a given context.

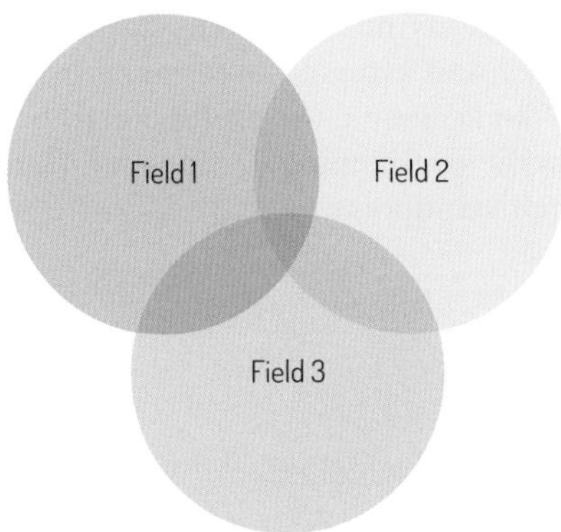

Figure 2.4 Operationalising marketing research

The small area in the middle of Figure 2.4 represents the focus of one's research project, or ideally how a student should think of their topic if they are to succeed with any endeavour. Broad marketing research tasks, such as talking about Starbuck's marketing strategy in China, do not lead to interesting research findings. They are too ambitious in their attempt to make sense of many things (e.g. variables, concepts, constructs) at once. Even worse, they tend to produce a descriptive, summative account of what a company might have been up to over an extended period of time in a particular country. Therefore, it is good practice to narrow down research to something actionable, bearing in mind that this improves its relevance to the researcher, student or otherwise, and ensures the creation of valid and reliable knowledge.

To illustrate, Ghana is one of the largest African economies with a lot of untapped potential, yet its gross domestic product growth has slowed down over the past few years. It seems that some external, uncontrollable forces are beginning to play a part in certain sectors and industries, which might affect the way pricing is approached at a strategic level. As time goes by, such conditions only make it harder to create and deliver consumer value; customers become more demanding, meeting their needs turns out to be increasingly difficult, and developing compelling propositions is a rather big ask. Competitors strive to remain relevant by trying to find ways to carve a 'monopolistic' position, which eventually allows them to charge a premium for their offerings. For instance, commoditisation has been rife within the telecommunications industry around the world and has led to a sizeable reduction in margins as customers do not perceive any fundamental differences between the services provided by operators. As an answer to a specific assessment brief, a student might be interested to discover the drivers of value for consumers in Ghana in order to understand what local brands can do to sustain meaningful relationships (and generate brand equity in the long term).

A few further concepts begin to emerge in relation to the initial topic, for instance pricing. Perception of value – in principle, this is seen as the benefits obtained less the costs sustained to acquire an offering – is important in order to define the boundaries of what a company can expect to charge its customers.

From the customer viewpoint, value can also be dependent on whether expectations are simply met or exceeded. However defined, customer satisfaction is thought to generate value and enhance relationships between customers and organisations. This may be one of the reasons why a company like Airtel Ghana has invested heavily in customer service 'beyond just the telecommunications needs of our customers' (ModernGhana, 2015). Yet another aspect can be identified and assessed in terms of its relevance to the topic initially chosen or assigned as part of an academic (or professional) brief. Different areas of knowledge are then selected so that the overlapping section (see Figure 2.5) is discreet enough to be manageable from a research standpoint.

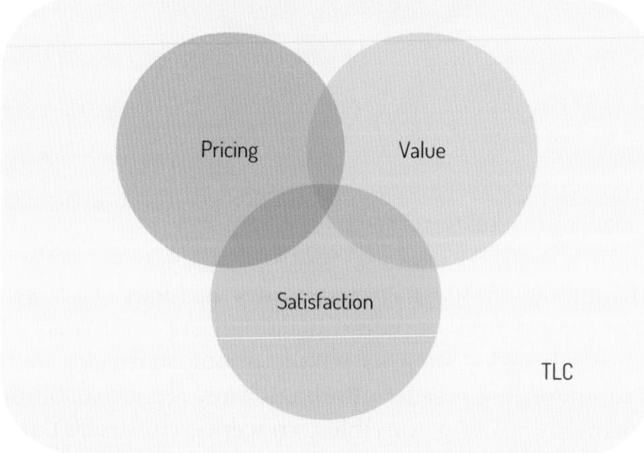

Figure 2.5 Intersecting pricing, value and satisfaction in the Telecommunications (TLC) industry in Ghana

In essence, students need to direct their efforts towards translating managerial issues, problems, phenomena and trends into reasonably self-contained pieces of marketing research. This is how a broad topic is shaped into a workable idea, which provides a sensible purpose in order for the remaining stages of a task to be lined up correctly. In many instances, this will also lead to the formulation of a first draft research question (see Chapter 4 for more detail), linking together all chosen components. During this process, we should try and visualise our thoughts using a large sheet of paper or suitable software in order to ensure that no idea or intuition is discarded a priori. Later on, a selection will eventually have to be made by arranging material according to its relevance so that less compelling pieces of information, concepts and theories are sidelined and a balance is found.

Reflective Activity

- Can you think of a general area of inquiry in marketing and restrict it by adding further layers of knowledge to it?
- What is the overall topic you are thinking of?
- What other concepts and theories are linked with it?

As a further case in point, we can observe the evolution of sport in the USA over the past few years where new and exciting sports have managed to enhance their profile; this has significantly closed the gap with the more traditional sports, such as American football. It has been the case for soccer and cage fighting, which have increased their popularity to a level where they are no longer isolated (e.g. regional phenomena). These sports are beginning to challenge American football, baseball, basketball and ice hockey matches as well as boxing bouts for popularity and attendance. Despite having been present and played in the country for well over a century, rugby union has so far been unable to achieve the same level of recognition. There is support at grassroots level, all the way from schools to colleges and universities around the country, yet rugby has struggled to impose itself. The sport possesses some characteristics that, at face value, should be attractive to many; these being discipline, control and mutual respect. However, it could also be viewed as old-fashioned, traditional and elitist, given that its origins trace back to England. There has certainly been little research into finding out the causes of this lack of progress; the values the game embodies could therefore be a good starting point for an exploration of the subject.

In order for its popularity to increase, rugby union would need to understand what key associations Americans make with it. Areas of knowledge like opinion and attitude formation appear to be important in defining desirable characteristics and set these against the backdrop of what people actually think and feel about the game. Ultimately, research could aim at building an appealing brand personality that resonates with specific target segments, with a view to bridging the gap that is currently holding back the development of the game. The overarching purpose could be to answer a why type of question in order to provide a reasonable set of recommendations as to what needs changing in the minds of American audiences for them to accept rugby as a viable entertainment alternative to other emerging sports in the country. After all, the performances of the national teams have provided some much needed limelight. It seems to be a case of using it in a more proactive fashion.

Reflective Activity: Yo! Sushi

Look back at the Yo! Sushi Snapshot and, given the company's more recent activity, try and answer the following questions:

- What kind of strategic plans in marketing terms could Yo! Sushi put in place in the next few years of operation?

(Continued)

(Continued)

- Based on these, what general topics for marketing research should Yo! Sushi focus on, i.e. try and understand further?
- How could you draw out a more specific research idea from any one of the general topics you have singled out?

Getting Started with Research

Narrowing down a particular marketing topic to a feasible piece of research is as much art as it is science. Likewise, scoping out an assignment can present a student with fundamental choices about what would have to be included, and why. These are hit-and-miss processes at best, during which a variety of thoughts, concepts, ideas and theories are examined, and accepted or rejected, according to their significance in our journey towards stating the purpose of a research project. The work we undertake in the initial stages of any type of inquiry is crucial to setting the direction of what is to come. For instance, the initial output required by academic institutions for an assignment or an end-of-term project could be a research proposal – a short document outlining the main phases of a full-scale piece of research. This can be a rather overwhelming task, as budding researchers can find detailing things out particularly confusing due to a lack of familiarity with their chosen topic as well as the methodological requirements of marketing research.

Preparing a Research Proposal

The basic components of a research proposal can be listed as follows:

- introduction
- research question
- (short) literature review
- methodology
- expected outcome.

In this respect, the definition of the issue, problem, phenomenon or trend of interest is still the most important aspect of this process as it looks to support the rationale for inquiry with credible sources of data and information.

Procter & Gamble failed to recognise important trends in emerging markets. As 2015 was drawing to a close, the company was hard at work, thinking over fundamental decisions about its future all the way from corporate structure to how to implement marketing strategy. Among other things, it appeared that the company had not quite grasped that its Pampers nappies brand in China could be targeted at high-end audiences, and also missed out on developing a wider range of products for segments with fundamentally different needs. Following these observations, it would appear sensible for a student to think of brand extensions as a sensible area for discussion. Both horizontal and vertical extensions could be considered together with the concept of stretching – the ability to remain relevant as a brand expands its lines and ranges.

Having depicted a sensible picture of the situation, students can then put together an initial research question with sufficient emphasis such that it is not too narrow or too broad. Starting with 'what', 'how' or 'why' indeed leads to much more compelling questions. A researcher would want to avoid restricting their inquiry to something that calls for a simple 'yes' or 'no' answer. It is important to treat this initial stage very much like work-in-progress: there is always time to go back and improve a research question (see Chapter 4 for more information on writing research questions). With regards to Procter & Gamble and Pampers, the following line of inquiry could be regarded as acceptable: *What are the attributes and benefits sought by high-end Chinese audiences with regards to nappies?* Such a question would then lend itself to further qualification, yet it is market-specific, product-specific and points at some marketing theory.

Research in Practice: The Marketing Research Brief

Decision makers and researchers come together to agree briefs with the intent of expressing the requirements of a marketing research project; they are normally meant either for external agencies or internal staff with responsibilities for this area. By and large, they should contain the following:

- Background – Why is the research needed? What kind of issue, problem, phenomenon, and so on, needs to be understood?
- Objectives – Who and what is the research for? What kind of decision is the research going to help with?
- Logistics – How is the research to be operationalised? What kind of constraints, such as time, budget, do we face?
- Sample – How are target audiences to be selected and accessed? What kind of people are we interested in?
- Methodology – How are we going to collect and analyse data? What kind of data do we need, and why?
- Deliverables – How is the research going to be presented? What kind of reporting format and dissemination strategy do we need?

Above all, the output of marketing research has to respond to the managerial requirements attached to it.

Whereas an introduction largely uses empirical data and news items and stems from an observation of the world around us, the literature review in a proposal attempts to establish a basic knowledge of relevant theories in a given context. Looking back at the Pampers example, brand extension, brand stretching, product attributes and benefits had all been touched on. Therefore, it would make sense to provide some coverage of these concepts and, above all, to offer a critical assessment of their individual importance as well as to make connections between them (see Chapter 3 for more details on how to write a literature review), in order to put forth some propositions about the direction of the primary research.

The next part is rather challenging as you may not have developed the necessary knowledge and skills to handle the transition from secondary research to primary research just yet. Drawing a conclusion from the literature review could help greatly. On the one hand, you might have found enough evidence to suggest that verifying an assumption would be the right way to proceed. On the other hand, you might instead be in a position to study something more in detail and suggest how to improve our understanding of it. This could be illustrated by looking at the difference between (a) theorising a causal relationship between the presence of certain features in the Pampers nappy and their overall attractiveness to certain target segments; and (b) exploring the credibility of the Pampers brand in order to evaluate its ability to stretch into a new product category. This would have a direct bearing on the methodology and data collection techniques, as well as on data analysis, with two rather different solutions: regression analysis (see Chapter 14 for an introduction to this topic) and grounded theory (see Chapter 8 for a practical discussion of this technique), respectively.

Reflective Activity

- What are the key components of a marketing research proposal, and why?
- What should the proposed research question be driven by?
- How can a reasonable methodological framework be put together at such an early stage in one's project?

Finally, it is good practice to outline the key expectations and possible limitations of the research project through building links with the introduction, the literature review and the methodology. In the case of the causal study regarding Pampers, a student could be expected to confirm some previously held assumptions based on the hypotheses under scrutiny. Limitations would most likely be found in areas such as access to and selection of respondents and the administering of questionnaires (and related time and monetary constraints). Of course, there is no certainty as to what would exactly happen, but, after all, a proposal is about providing a reasonable blueprint for a larger research project.

The Marketing Research System

The efforts that we make to clarify the direction of any assignment are going to generate a solid platform for discussion, especially in the case of large-scale research projects as they require more planning and attention. This is because a clear research purpose can more easily be developed into a strong sequence with two main goals in mind: (1) to improve the research question; and (2) to finalise the methodological framework. The next three chapters will provide more help in putting together a comprehensive literature review, linking secondary and primary research effectively, and designing a detailed research plan. Here, we will discuss some overarching basic principles in order to lay down the foundations of marketing research based on its initial definition (see Figure 2.6; see also page 6 in Chapter 1).

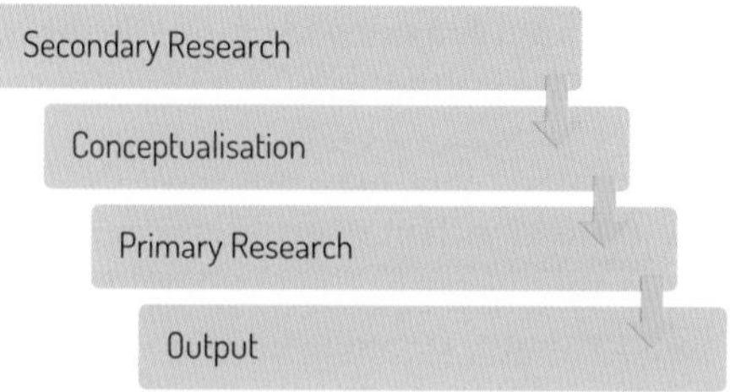

Figure 2.6 A simplified marketing research process

Secondary research

What we may claim to know about a certain subject is only limited by the amount of research that has gone into it. Notwithstanding the fact that there is always a time constraint to any marketing research task, the intensity with which we dig into available, secondary sources of information can generally make the difference between arguing reasonable points and making rhetorical statements which do not have to be answered! Secondary research helps define the fields of investigation we are interested in; it also allows us to find interesting empirical and theoretical evidence from a variety of sources (see Chapter 3 for a more detailed account). By using a critical approach, we can examine and ultimately select data and information in order to build a well-supported position with regards to a particular marketing research topic. In some instances, we can also find clarification on issues and solutions to problems through using existing data and information (Hague and Wilcock, n.d.) in new ways.

In short, secondary research is a route to gaining valuable insight into something, ultimately easing the process of generating a research question and, at times, answering it in full. Students typically use it for short pieces of work with limited scope or wherever the emphasis is restricted to a particular thought or idea. Whatever the need for it, secondary research has to be approached critically and not merely be confined to a footnote in your submission.

Conceptualisation

A conceptualisation summarises all secondary data into a simplified representation of the reality we plan to investigate (see Chapter 4 for further details). It helps generate categories for analysis as well as describe the fundamental character of an issue, problem or phenomenon of interest; it could also be seen as a 'model'. As such, it can serve as a platform for hypothesis generation or to establish connections between larger theoretical constructs for further investigation.

Students of all ages and skills looking to conduct research for a particular purpose should be aware of the importance of this step in order to understand in full how to build a watertight link between what is already known (secondary data) and what could be uncovered (primary data) about their topic of choice. This would play an important role in a marketing research project such as a practice-based paper or a dissertation. Ultimately, you want to figure out whether your research would aim at verifying assumptions or adding detail to existing knowledge.

Primary research

Once there is a clear sense of direction and purpose as a result of the work conducted around secondary data and towards the conceptualisation of a project, the task of a researcher is to take appropriate decisions as to how to collect and analyse the necessary primary data, or the data to be collected to answer a given research question or brief. In other words, the priority shifts to justifying a particular course of action; it is at this point that a full-blown research design should be firmed up in all of its components (see Chapter 5 for more information). At the very least, a researcher is to demonstrate a rationale for employing either an inductive or a deductive approach based

Primary research deals with the generation and analysis of new and unpublished data

on the arguments presented in the conceptualisation of their work, i.e. verifying suppositions from theory or plugging holes in theory (Blackstone, 2015).

Likewise, there needs to be a definite sense of how the data collected will eventually be analysed. For instance, quantitative research mostly looks at differences, associations and cause-and-effect relationships, so the identification of what type of method to choose should be relatively straightforward (and dependent on the research question and the research objectives). By keeping track of our progress and looking back at our objectives, we ensure that a realistic and consistent flow is maintained at all times. In this way, the implementation of a systematic process of marketing research is more often than not guaranteed.

Output

The closing stages of a research project are characterised by excitement as we set our sights on a tangible reward for our efforts: knowledge acquisition. The outcome of research is acceptable as long as the process followed is sound (see Chapter 5 for more detail). If a hypothesis is disproven, we may need to collect further data, such as increasing the sample size or understanding what went wrong by means of a new study with a different emphasis (i.e. inductive rather than deductive reasoning). Similarly, qualitative inquiry might unveil new categories or themes to be the subject of explanation or description, thus leading to more research being undertaken to complement the initial purpose. Whatever happens, a researcher must arrive at an answer for their original research question through presenting a logical final argument. They can then add their considerations about limitations and future endeavours. This is to ensure that the whole project has gone full circle, whereby a question or a brief was put out there for which an answer has been found.

Rarely will a student find an explicit reference to the fact that their research needs to flow from the top down and, most importantly, from the bottom up. This means that once a research question and some research objectives are settled on, the analysis of the findings should address them in full.

Advanced: Using Marketing Research

A large number of marketing research projects derive from strategic and tactical management issues and problems which organisations find themselves facing. As a result of this, the global revenue generated by companies operating in the field reached the US$40 billion mark in 2013; of course, this does not include internal budgets and the investments made to hire skilled staff in marketing research-related roles. It does sound like a lot of money and time are put into finding appropriate answers to research questions. Yet there are several obstacles to the use of marketing research, which can be linked back to the 'implementation gap' as well as 'individual marketing competencies' or, more precisely, the lack thereof (Meldrum, 1996). Even though organisations might have the potential to move forward by adding insight to their strategy and tactics, they fail to realise any of it because there is a poor fit with their capabilities, systems, policies and culture. This is why it is important to know how to use the output of marketing research and, above all, to have the necessary management buy-in for a project to succeed.

Chapter Summary

Looking at marketing-related issues, problems and phenomena raises a series of concerns as to the means of shaping a broad topic into a feasible piece of research. This chapter has drawn attention to some essential aspects of marketing research while touching on how to generate valid and reliable knowledge, irrespective of the methods used – in fact, these will be dealt with in Parts III and IV of this book.

To begin with, it was noticed that the business environment tends to influence the way in which we narrow down a general inquiry to a viable research question. This is not just about the uncontrollable, for example the political, legal variables that define a country or countries (frame of reference) where research is to be conducted. It also has to do with the sectors and industries a researcher might be interested in as well as specific organisations and the kind of strategic and tactical marketing dilemmas they might face at a specific moment in time. In this respect, the managerial formulation of issues and problems in marketing terms is an important element. It should lead us to consider a range of concepts and theories, especially when working as an insider – for instance, this could be the case for a student interning at an organisation and looking to provide insight into a specific area of marketing.

Then a researcher has to be able to translate data and information about a particular topic into an actionable piece of research by detailing out an appropriate research question (and eventually a research aim and some objectives). From here, a research plan should emerge; it would ideally look at how to collect and how to analyse data within the parameters set at the conceptual level. In other words, emphasis should be put on linking secondary research and primary research together in a meaningful and structured way that respects the systematic process of marketing research.

With an adequate plan in place, the researcher can then proceed to tie together all the various stages in order to obtain targeted data with which to attempt to answer the research question. As said, it is not necessarily about achieving a desired outcome, but about respecting the logical nature of the process. Any methodological imprecision would eventually detract from the conclusions of any piece of research and, at times, render them invalid, unreliable or both.

Case Study: The Perception of Sound

Streaming has changed the way we listen to and consume music as we no longer need to own LPs, CDs or any other physical medium. At the same time, this fundamental shift has opened the doors for new players to enter the market, developing new hardware, as traditional mass electronics and niche hi-fi manufacturers hadn't anticipated this revolution and the role mobile devices would eventually come to play in society. Sonos was founded in 2002 and has grown to offer a 'smart speaker system that streams all your favourite music to any room, or every room' (Sonos, 2015).

Despite a favourable location, South America has not quite warmed to the products the American company markets so successfully in other parts of the world. The newly appointed UK Chief Marketing Officer believes that the key to expanding further is in the speed at which innovation is adopted by consumers,

(Continued)

(Continued)

which might indicate how little Sonos is understood by consumers in countries as far afield as Argentina and Colombia (Ghosh, 2015).

There appears to be work needed to entice consumers, especially those not naturally inclined to try out new and exciting things, the so-called 'innovators'. However, achieving a certain critical mass could be an issue as, besides making people realise that they want wireless speakers, the products themselves come with a rather steep price tag and are beginning to be threatened by cheaper alternatives (e.g. those of Samsung).

Of course, the speakers, home cinema solutions and components come with a number of additional features such as music (content), telephone application (controller) and trueplay (optimisation, tuning software). Most importantly, several services have been made available on Sonos, including Spotify, tunein, GooglePlay Music, soundcloud, Deezer, Amazon Music Library, Napster and many others, depending on location. The company has indeed put quite a lot of effort into improving accessibility to these services around the world by signing deals with the likes of Deezer. It is a strategic choice to build long-term relationships and to reduce the time lag experienced by the brand while attempting to move consumers from awareness to consideration – this is a result of the work needed to overcome a lack of knowledge about the brand and to achieve a positive attitude towards the brand.

Like any company moving on to the international stage at pace, Sonos needs to consider its marketing distribution network in South America: what it has at present and what it needs going forward. It is not easy to strike the right balance, as the company doesn't want to enter into too many partnerships with distributors, before it has achieved a reasonable level of interest from consumers in the market. Partners like PreSonus, which cover several local markets, look well positioned to serve target segments for the time being, but where will the company be in five years as more pressure is applied by brands like Bose and Denon, which already have global presence and recognition (Fowler, 2015)? It seems that any competitive advantage Sonus enjoyed as a result of the disruption it introduced in the home audio market just over ten years ago has dissipated almost entirely.

The task is to see what can be done to crack South American markets within a relatively short space of time, in order to prevent others from catching up or, even worse, establishing themselves as category leaders in countries like Brazil or Colombia. The company itself recognises that 'The market 10 years from now will be huge with high penetration into homes around the globe [...] Ten years from now, the music that plays in a room will adapt even more to the room, who is in the room, what time of day it is, and even what type of day they've had' (Palenchar, 2015). There is a fundamental assumption that the demand for Sonus' offerings is going to be there, although the transition from selective to mass distribution does not appear to be as clear-cut.

These contrasting signs should be researched and interpreted more precisely. It is important for a business to maintain a can-do attitude, yet this shouldn't come in the way of understanding and pre-empting issues and phenomena that may turn into problems if left unchecked. There are several aspects of Sonus' marketing strategy in South America and marketing management in each of the countries where it operates to look into – these are and should be controlled.

Case study questions:

1. What kind of general topics for inquiry can you recognise (either relating to the empirical or the theoretical evidence provided)?
2. How would the observation of the business environment help you focus the discussion of any of these marketing-related issues?
3. What research question appears to be emerging from your work so far? Can you write anything down?
4. How could a research plan develop from the reflection you have conducted so far? Are there any elements that should be researched further?

End of Chapter Questions

These questions should help you reflect on your understanding of this chapter:

1. How can the (business) environment around us help with singling out suitable marketing research topics?
2. What can an internal marketing audit do for researchers?
3. How do managerial considerations potentially influence the direction of marketing research?
4. What are three common ways to think of marketing-related investigation?
5. How can marketing research be narrowed down to a viable research question?
6. What are the core components of a marketing research proposal?
7. What are the basic stages of a marketing research process?
8. Why should a piece of research work from the top down and, more importantly, from the bottom up?

Checklist

After studying Chapter 2, you should now be familiar with these key concepts:

1. The breakdown of the systematic marketing research process
2. How the business environment can influence marketing research
3. The boundaries of marketing-related investigation
4. The characteristics of researchable marketing topics
5. How to get started with research

Further Reading (in sequence from beginners to advanced)

Harris, J. (2007) The Web's secret stories. *TED* [online, March]. Available at: www.ted.com/talks/jonathan_harris_tells_the_web_s_secret_stories?language=en

McNally, S. (2015) How to write a market research brief that delivers actionable results. *Eris Strategy* [online]. Available at: http://erisstrategy.com.au/writing-a-market-research-brief-that-delivers-actionable-results [Accessed 3 December 2015].

Berman Brown, R. (2006) *Doing Your Dissertation in Business and Management: The Reality of Researching and Writing.* London: Sage Publications.

Slife, B. D. and Williams, R. N. (1995) *What's behind the Research? Discovering Hidden Assumptions in the Behavioural Sciences.* Thousand Oaks, CA: Sage Publications.

Cravens, D. W., Piercy, N. F. and Baldauf, A. (2009) Management framework guiding strategic thinking in rapidly changing markets. *Journal of Marketing Management*, 25 (1–2), pp. 31–49.

Lewis, S., Pea, R. and Rosen, J. (2010) Beyond participation to co-creation of meaning: mobile social media in generative learning communities. *Social Science Information*, 49 (3), pp. 1–19.

Bibliography

Allman, H. F. (2013) Vertical versus horizontal line extension strategies: when do brands prosper? PhD Thesis, University of South Carolina, Columbia [online]. Available at: http://scholarcommons.sc.edu/cgi/viewcontent.cgi?article=3438&context=etd [Accessed 29 November 2015].

Barbopoulos, I. and Johansson, L.-O. (2015) A multi-dimensional approach to consumer motivation: exploring economic, hedonic, and normative consumption goals. *Journal of Consumer Behaviour*, 33 (1).

Blackstone, A. (2015) Principles of sociological inquiry: qualitative and quantitative methods, v. 1.0. *Flat World Education* [online]. Available at: http://catalog.flatworldknowledge.com/bookhub/reader/3585?e=blackstone_1.0-ch02_s03 [Accessed 1 December 2015].

Boyles, S. (2015) World overtaking US in sugar consumption: diet gets sweeter in most countries, especially in developing world. *MedPageToday* [online, 1 December]. Available at: www.medpagetoday.com/PrimaryCare/DietNutrition/54946 [Accessed 3 December 2015].

Carrizo Moreira, A. (2009) The evolution of internationalisation: towards a new theory? Universidade de Aveiro, Working Papers in Management, G/n 1/2009. Available at: file:///C:/Users/ab5750/Downloads/WP1_2009.pdf [Accessed 29 November 2015].

Casey, D. (2015) Yo! Sushi sold in £81m deal. *Insider Media* [online, 25 November]. Available at: www.insidermedia.com/insider/national/yo-sushi-sold-for-81m [Accessed 29 November 2015].

CA Technologies (2013) Standard Bank Argentina reduces project delivery times with CA Project & Portfolio Management SaaS. *Customer Success Story* [online, February]. Available at www.ca.com/gb/~/media/Files/SuccessStories/ca-css-standard-bank-031212-eng-mw.PDF [Accessed 31 October 2015].

Communications Council (The) (n.d.) Emarketing: codes [online]. Available at: www.communicationscouncil.org.au/public/content/ViewCategory.aspx?id=313 [Accessed 25 October 2015].

De Pelsmacker, P., Geuens, M. and Van den Bergh, J. (2010) *Marketing Communications: A European Perspective* (4th edition). Harlow: Pearson Education.

Dvir, D., Raz, T. and Shenhar, A. J. (2003) An empirical analysis of the relationship between project planning and project success. *International Journal of Project Management*, 21 (2), pp. 89–95.

Fowler, G. A. (2015) Ditch your old hi-fi: wireless speakers make home audio easier. *Wall Street Journal* [online, 14 July]. Available at: www.wsj.com/articles/ditch-your-old-hi-fi-wireless-speakers-make-home-audio-easier-1436900550 [Accessed 1 December 2015].

Ghosh, S. (2015) How Sonos is using diffusion of innovation to foster brand love. *Marketing Magazine* [online, 1 December]. Available at: www.marketingmagazine.co.uk/article/1375269/sonos-using-diffusion-innovation-foster-brand-love [Accessed 1 December 2015].

Hague, P. and Wilcock, C. (n.d.) How to get information for next to nothing. *B2B International* [online]. Available at: www.b2binternational.com/publications/desk-research [Accessed 1 December 2015].

Helmrich, B. (2015) Pinterest for business: everything you need to know. *Business News Daily* [online, 23 February]. Available at: www.businessnewsdaily.com/7552-pinterest-business-guide.html [Accessed 22 November 2015].

Hunt, S. D., Chonko, L. B. and Wilcox, J. B. (1984) Ethical problems of marketing researchers. *Journal of Marketing Research*, 21 (3), pp. 309–24.

Lambin, J.-J. and Schuiling, I. (2012) *Market-Driven Management: Strategic and Operational Marketing* (3rd edition). London: Palgrave.

Langley, S. (2015) Lessons for food marketers as sugar consumption in UK tumbles. *AFN* [online, 18 March]. Available at: http://ausfoodnews.com.au/2015/03/18/lessons-for-food-marketers-as-sugar-consumption-in-uk-tumbles.html [Accessed 3 December 2015].

Leshem, S. and Trafford, V. (2007) Overlooking the conceptual framework. *Innovations in Education and Teaching International*, 44 (1), pp. 93–105.

Meldrum, M. (1996) Critical issues in implementing marketing. *Journal of Marketing Practice*, 2 (3), pp. 29–43.

Mendelow, A. (1991) Proposed model on stakeholder ranking. Paper presented at the Second International Conference on Information Systems, Cambridge, MA.

ModernGhana (2015) Airtel Ghana celebrates customers. *Business Desk* [online, 5 October]. Available at: www.modernghana.com/news/647230/1/airtel-ghana-celebrates-customers.html [Accessed 28 November 2015].

Morrison, M. (2012) History of PEST analysis. *RapidBI* [online, 11 June]. Available at: https://rapidbi.com/history-of-pest-analysis/#.ViysaLfhDIU [Accessed 25 October 2015].

Mundy, S. (2013) Foreign lenders struggle to gain a foothold in South Korea. *Financial Times Banks* [online, 19 September]. Available at: www.ft.com/cms/s/0/6f1d4f04-14f9-11e3-b3db-00144feabdc0.html#axzz3qKQwsSE9 [Accessed 3 November 2015].

Nasr, R. (2015) Apple's success in China can teach US firms a lot. *CNBC* [online, 29 January]. Available at: www.cnbc.com/2015/01/29/apples-blowout-success-in-china-what-it-did-right-and-what-us-companies-can-learn-from-it.html [Accessed 2 November 2015].

Noboa y Rivera, R. (2015) Can American rugby move beyond the college campus? *The Guardian* [online, 25 September]. Available at: www.theguardian.com/sport/2015/sep/25/rugby-america-college-university-world-cup [Accessed 28 November 2015].

Owens, J. (2014) 7 big ideas about researching images in social media. *Pulsar* [online, 26 November]. Available at: www.pulsarplatform.com/blog/2014/7-things-we-learnt-at-picturing-the-social [Accessed 8 December 2015].

Palenchar, J. (2015) Sonos at 10: streaming into the future. *Twice* [online, 20 July]. Available at: www.twice.com/sonos-10-streaming-future/57924 [Accessed 1 December 2015].

Rao, A. (n.d.) Social listening: how market sensing trumps market research. *PwC* [online]. Available at: www.pwc.com/gx/en/services/advisory/consulting/risk/resilience/publications/social-listening-how-market-sensing-trumps-market-research.html [Accessed 3 November 2015].

San Cornelio, G. and Goméz Cruz, E. (2014) Co-creation and participation as a means of innovation in new media: an analysis of creativity in the photographic field. *International Journal of Communication*, 8, pp. 1–20.

Seidman, G. (2015) Are selfies a sign of narcissism and psychopathy? *Psychology Today* [online, 8 January]. Available at: www.psychologytoday.com/blog/close-encounters/201501/are-selfies-sign-narcissism-and-psychopathy [Accessed 8 December 2015].

Shuttleworth, M. (n.d.) Writing a conclusion. *Explorable* [online]. Available at: https://explorable.com/writing-a-conclusion [Accessed 1 December 2015].

Siegel, M. (2015) Selfie madness: too many dying to get the picture. *Reuters* [online, 3 September]. Available at: www.reuters.com/article/us-life-selfies-idUKKCN0R305L20150903#HfwfkRya0qG3GQRk.99 [Accessed 8 December 2015].

Sonos (2015) What is Sonos? [online]. Available at: www.sonos.com/en-gb/system?r=1 [Accessed 1 December 2015].

Standard Chartered (2014) Our brand and values [online]. Available at: www.sc.com/en/about-us/our-brand-and-values [Accessed 7 November 2015].

Statista (n.d.) Statistics and facts on the market research industry. *Business Services* [online]. Available at: www.statista.com/topics/1293/market-research [Accessed 3 December 2015].

Steele, B. (2015) Deezer Elite streams on Sonos systems outside of the US. *engadget* [online, 10 February]. Available at: www.engadget.com/2015/02/10/deezer-elite-sonos-europe-asia-latin-america [Accessed 1 December 2015].

St. Michel, P. (2015) The future of conveyor-belt sushi. *The Japan Times* [online, 27 November]. Available at: www.japantimes.co.jp/life/2015/11/27/food/future-conveyor-belt-sushi/#.Vlq0mHbhDIV [Accessed 27 November 2015].

Sutter, B. (2015) How to outsmart your competition with content marketing. *Forbes* [online, 29 September]. Available at: www.forbes.com/sites/briansutter/2015/09/29/how-to-outsmart-your-competition-with-content-marketing [Accessed 30 October 2015].

Uniyal, P. (2015) How excessive sugar is poisoning our diet; India no different. *indiatoday* [online, 3 December]. Available at: http://indiatoday.intoday.in/story/how-excessive-sugar-is-poisoning-our-diet-india-no-different/1/537539.html [Accessed 3 December 2015].

Whipp, L. (2015) Plot twist in the soap opera. *Financial Times*, 21 October, p. 9.

World Bank, The (2015) GDP growth (annual %). *Data* [online]. Available at: http://data.worldbank.org/indicator/NY.GDP.MKTP.KD.ZG/countries/GH?display=graph [Accessed 27 November 2015].

Find journal articles and multiple choice questions online at: **https://study.sagepub.com/benzo** to support what you've learnt so far.

CHAPTER 3

Secondary Research: Facts and Theory

LEARNING OBJECTIVES

The key learning objectives of this chapter are:

1. To categorise sources of secondary data
2. To outline the secondary research process
3. To understand the nature of a critical literature review
4. To build critical arguments and frameworks

KEY CONCEPTS

By the end of this chapter, the reader should be familiar with the following concepts:

1. The secondary research process
2. Internal and external sources of secondary data
3. Relevance trees and 'funnels'
4. Organising knowledge for research
5. How to read and write critically
6. Basic referencing requirements
7. What a critical literature review is and does
8. Theoretical frameworks

Riccardo Benzo

Introduction

The development of an appropriate direction in marketing research is directly related to the amount of knowledge one possesses about a subject of interest. In other words, no badly researched piece of research has ever produced compelling results in the field of business studies, or any other discipline for that matter. This suggests that commencing a new research project is a rather demanding endeavour. Any student or professional researcher would do well to keep that in mind; indeed, an effective plan of action starts from the collection and analysis of secondary data.

This chapter aims to provide a sound description and discussion of concepts and practices with regards to finding and handling secondary data. It does so with a view to defining what a theoretical framework and a conceptualisation (see Chapters 2 and 4 for more on conceptual frameworks) are in the transition from secondary to primary research. It intends to offer a series of tools and techniques for students and researchers in order for them to deal with the intricacies of choosing valid and reliable sources of information, examining them in a critical manner and elaborating them into useful results – these can turn out to be either answers to research questions, or new and challenging research questions.

In other words, a great deal of data, information and knowledge are available to us as students in any subject. It is important to distinguish the 'good' stuff from the 'bad' stuff, the useful from the useless or, put more simply, the relevant from the irrelevant material in the context of our research. This means that at the beginning of a task or a project we would have to come to terms with two facts:

(1) A literature review is going to be time-consuming; and

(2) Extensive reading is going to be required before suitable sources are identified.

Also remember that this is an exciting process, one that will open doors to a variety of new ideas, concepts and theories which can add to your personal, academic and professional development.

Snapshot: How Original is Your Research?

Students looking for a topic for their dissertation projects may ultimately find this process frustrating. As they come into contact with concepts and theories, there is a chance that specific areas of interest have already been researched extensively, thus making the selection of an original topic for their research seemingly unmanageable. However, this is not a problem per se as improving on previous studies and combining ideas in different ways are valid approaches to undertaking research at undergraduate and postgraduate levels. In other words, students are encouraged to provide a fresh outlook on a subject matter rather than coming up with a wholly original piece of research.

The field of brand management is particularly dynamic; several perspectives have been developed over time as to how brands should approach their strategies based on several years of academic research and professional practice in the field. There are also further variations depending on what type of brand is being looked at: products, services, goods, people, places, ideas, and so on. In spite of this extensive body of knowledge, students continue to be drawn to this topic and, indeed, should not stop studying it in detail.

The seminal works of Aaker (1992), Kapferer (1997) and Keller (1999) can be considered the backbone of brand management, yet over the years more articles, books, web pages and blogs have been added to this body of knowledge as researchers branched out in all sorts of directions, for example into brand tribalism (Taute and Sierra, 2014). This raises some critical questions regarding how a student can define the breadth and depth of their investigation of a topic as they approach brand management for the first time. What should they eventually include or discard? Above all, where should they draw a line and stop digging into a particular idea?

Striking a balance between the number of areas to investigate and the level of detail to include is essential as students become familiar with their chosen topics and carry out their literature review.

Secondary Research

Secondary research uses previously published data, information and knowledge to help understand a new research problem, issue or phenomenon

Also known as desk research, secondary research is a system that generates actionable knowledge based on the access, collection, synthesis and analysis of the widest possible array of existing sources of data, information and knowledge. It is defined as 'secondary' because it has to come up with valid and reliable outcomes by relying on data and information that were not necessarily designed and executed for the specific research at hand. Indeed, it uses what we can simply describe as 'old' or already existing knowledge to generate something new, where the latter is specifically applicable to our current research endeavours. In turn, this new output will become secondary in nature as soon as it is finalised and ready for dissemination – whether it is accessible internally within an organisation, externally for public knowledge, or both.

Secondary research is hence undertaken as the first step in any research project and it can, at times, be sufficient in achieving the objectives of a particular task (see Chapter 5); in other words, in certain research projects, secondary data can on its own be used to find answers to the research question.

Before considering how to make good use of secondary research tools and techniques, it is important to outline the main sources of secondary data as well as their advantages and disadvantages.

Ethics: Secondary Data Confidentiality

Academic institutions around the world are rightly concerned with ensuring that students understand the importance of ethics when collecting primary data. They provide precise frameworks that regulate undergraduate and postgraduate research – do look up the specific requirements of your university!

However, the application of sound ethical principles needs to be more clearly extended to earlier stages of the systematic process of marketing research. In particular, we ought to start considering the origin of our secondary data and, more specifically, whether it is acceptable to use certain data and information, or not.

(Continued)

(Continued)

Several websites, such as SlideShare (www.slideshare.net), allow for the sharing of presentations; these files are uploaded by their rightful owners and made available to others online. This means that, considerations about their validity and reliability aside, we should feel entitled to use them in our work given that we explicitly cite them. On the other hand, sometimes it is not so easy to understand the provenance of certain documents.

For instance, a presentation from YouTube for Havas Media and its client El Corte Ingles, marked as 'YouTube Confidential and Proprietary', can be found on the iab Europe website (www.iabeurope.eu). As students engage in a research project, they should question the moral legitimacy of using this information; from an Internet search, it is not at all clear whether this YouTube video is openly accessible to everyone.

In this respect, the conscientious researcher must first approach the owner of the data or information in order to ensure that there has been no breach of any confidentiality agreement between two, or more, parties. This would be even more crucial when we bump into extremely recent publications, which might not yet have been ready for release in the public domain.

Privileged information should remain as such even though it might be disclosed through the negligence of others – for example, two executives having a conversation about sensitive material on a train or plane. Listening in (eavesdropping) would provide us with an unfair advantage and our moral and ethical standards must prevent us from taking advantage of such a situation.

Secondary Data Sources

Secondary data can be classified by its source as internal or external. Internal records are easily accessible on a continuing basis and tend to be relevant to an organisation's circumstances. They cover a variety of functional areas including customer feedback, customer preferences and customer satisfaction. External data exists outside of the company and can be further classified into 'published', 'syndicated services' and 'databases' (Burns and Bush, 2014). Understandably, students find internal records more difficult to access, if not entirely inaccessible, and may have to rely on external sources to carry out their work.

Internal data sources

Any organisation possesses a wealth of data, information and knowledge about its business performance over time (see Table 3.1). A Marketing Information System (MIS) is a repository of all such things (see Chapter 1 for more on this) and is normally organised as a database giving a company the ability to glean important sales trends and patterns, assess opportunities for new offerings, formulate customer acquisition and retention strategies, and so on. For instance, it can provide an invaluable resource for a range of below-the-line marketing activities aimed at establishing, developing and consolidating stakeholder relationships.

Amtrak is a good example as it started this process of familiarisation with its customers very early on. By 1992 it already had access to basic information for millions of its customers and used it 'to deliver specific travel opportunities to Amtrak's most potentially lucrative niche markets' (Jones, 1998). Following in its own footsteps, more internal data sources were made available as technology enabled effective online tracking through mechanisms such as @Amtrack and indirect mentions on Twitter. The company discovered that a lot of positive comments were left by its passengers on this and other media channels, thus affecting the way its marketing communications took place. As a result, it developed a highly evocative Instagram account whose content is often shared by users.

From a student's standpoint, though, the availability of internal data such as this is limited by the degree of access to and the eventual extent of the agreement reached with a target organisation. In many cases, the researcher can only observe from a distance and rely on external data sources; if it is possible to get hold of some internal data sources, their use may still be bound by confidentiality issues.

Table 3.1 Examples of internal data sources

Source	Information
Sales (data, reports, etc.)	Individual and aggregate transactions by volume and value, composition, etc.
Sales team	Customer/client product requirements, usage, feedback, etc.
Financials	Contribution, profitability, credit, returns, etc.
Feedback	Comments, regular surveys, statistics, complaints, etc.
Experts	Heads of department, non-executive directors, etc.
Audits	Supply chain, value chain, product/service delivery, processes, etc.

It is also essential to remember that using internal data effectively can be affected by the format in which the data are available to us as marketing researchers and by the quality of such data. For instance, accounting information is often compiled with different objectives and goals than answering questions with regards to decision making in marketing strategy and management. This may lead to marketers needing to go back to and deal with raw data in order to arrive at more useful insights regarding particular product lines or ranges, geographical locations or time frames. Similarly, the information collated by a sales team can be biased by personal opinions and assumptions. Once it is input into an MIS, any pre-existing partiality will be lost, thus making it almost impossible to assess the overall quality of the source(s) in an objective manner. The separation between sales and marketing departments has on several occasions magnified this kind of issue; marketing staff accompanying sales people during visits helps reduce uncertainty as to the reliability and validity of the data collected.

The integration of internal data across multiple platforms in multiple countries also throws up many challenges. One of the most fundamental is how to handle the volume of data from traditional to digital to neuropsychological, such as eye-tracking sources through the use of homogeneous metrics – these may range from customer engagement value to share of wallet and service recovery. Making sense of internal data sources ultimately has an impact on decision making, so there has to be a 'focus on getting new data right': simple, fast and target-driven (Redman, 2013).

External data sources

There is an extensive range of external sources, especially when we take into account how technology has influenced the way we search and access data, information and knowledge nowadays. If anything, one of the key issues for any student who embarks on researching and writing a critical literature review is to be able to assess the material available to them in terms of genuineness. In order to help increase the likelihood of good search results for external data sources, students should get organised by:

1. Defining what is to be known about a topic
2. Putting together a list of keywords for inquiry
3. Seeking help from experts, such as a subject librarian
4. Re-working the list of keywords based on their initial findings

It is an iterative process that aims at honing in on useful material, which is then going to be synthesised and analysed critically.

Research in Practice: In Other Students We Trust, Or Should We?

Human beings tend to lose their objectivity when they are directly involved in a decision-making process; when it comes to their own coursework, students appear less able to be critical and often resort to using short cuts as a result of time pressure (i.e. lack of planning). The choice of sources one makes, especially in the early stages of an assignment, can have disastrous effects on its outcome. Take the work posted by a student for their marketing research module at Boston University in their personal blog (Meister, 2012). Although he is clearly attempting to share his assignment to help others, the actual research design is not supported by a proper rationale. Both the data findings and the data analysis are confusing and there is no direct referencing for anything that is being reported. Would you trust this? The fact that a large amount of material is available via many websites does not make using it right at all. Each piece of work should be planned carefully and thought over in order for an appropriate justification to be provided. We should always be on the safe side and avoid dubious sources of data, information and knowledge.

'Published'

Published sources of secondary data encompass a variety of sources for unrestricted distribution via many channels such as libraries, professional bodies, industry/sector associations, companies, governments, universities, not-for-profit organisations, publishers, and so forth. Everyone can in principle access them whether they are freely available or not. In turn, these can take the form of guides, directories, books, articles, reports, white papers, case studies, newsletters, bulletins, pamphlets, blogs/vlogs, videos, and so on. Some more specific information follows and is arranged according to the ownership of the material itself.

Governments, central and local branches of the administration and other public sector organisations such as health authorities produce a wide-ranging output, including statistical collections (raw data), reports and white papers on a continuous basis, i.e. at regular intervals. They are indeed highly reliable and, in many instances, offer additional, dependable commentaries from experts. Non-governmental organisations with international standing, such as the World Health Organisation, provide a similar type of data, information and knowledge with a much wider scope, potentially helping to identify sweeping worldwide trends and how these may then be associated with or even be responsible for macro-environmental conditions in a particular country (see Chapter 2 for more on the business environment).

Libraries are often a friendly environment for students and researchers as both physical and virtual sources are easily accessible, together with help from knowledgeable staff. An incredible range of directories, guides, handbooks, books, journals, magazines, databases, and so on, are available on location as well as remotely. Libraries serve different audiences and you may find it useful to access different types: academic, public, school and special libraries. Besides, they work together to preserve and further knowledge over time by sharing resources across regional and international borders using a document exchange catalogue such as WorldCat for the WorldShare Interlibrary Loan. As repositories of large amounts of data, libraries interact with publishers such as Sage, who in turn are responsible for the printing or electronic publication and distribution of books, journals, magazines, databases, case studies, and so on. Some of these businesses are highly specialised, whereas others have broad remits.

Reflective Activity

Books and blogs are possibly at the two opposite extremes of a hypothetical range of written resources:

- What would you use either for?
- Why are books important in the context of a literature review?
- What do blogs contribute to secondary data?

Professional bodies around the world provide access to a lot of data, information, knowledge and advice to members, including students of relevant undergraduate and postgraduate programmes, and non-members. In the field of marketing, organisations like the Chartered Institute of Marketing (CIM) and the American Marketing Association (AMA) have, over the years, helped disseminate information and consolidate practices, while developing a range of publications from books to white papers, and from surveys to conference proceedings. They also offer extensive learning resources including tools and templates. Similarly, business and trade associations can be a useful port of call for industry and sector data as well as other information on trends and patterns with regards to particular micro-environmental characteristics. For instance, the Mobile Marketing Association comprises more than 800 companies from around the world offering a whole host of research and insight resources in the form of reports and case studies. It is also common for these bodies and associations to disseminate interesting and up-to-date content via webinars.

Companies can also be handy sources of published information; it is quite common for marketing agencies to promote their work through the dissemination of white papers based on their experiences. These contain valuable insights from respected organisations and in the best cases provide clear applications of theory to practice. They also make other kinds of secondary data available, such as case studies, videos and podcasts. At the very opposite end of the spectrum, independent consultants and freelancers tend to be particularly active with blogging and contributing articles, especially given the plethora of online publications out there nowadays. Some of these individuals are considered to be gurus in their professional capacity and attract sizeable followings, but do be careful when using some of the thoughts, analysis and critique provided by them (Nagi, 2015).

Universities offer a comprehensive collection of secondary data; indeed, this is not limited to having a library service through which many sources are accessible. It has to do with their mission to further knowledge by sharing working papers, departmental resources, study programmes, student support, official publications, theses and dissertations, and so forth. Some higher education institutions have become well-known publishers in their own right (e.g. Harvard Business Publishing) on the back of their work as consultants to other organisations, thus enhancing their profile and attractiveness to students and executives around the world.

See Table 3.2 for some examples of secondary data.

Table 3.2 Sources of secondary data

What	Type of information	Available from (examples)
Books	Established knowledge in the field of marketing	Library; Dawsonera; Project Gutenberg (free)
Newspapers	Current information about contemporary issues (in business)	Library; LexisNexis; direct, e.g. *Financial Times*, *Wall Street Journal*
Magazines	Specialist marketing news and information	Library; LexisNexis; direct, e.g. *Marketing Week*, *AdAge*
Professional bodies	Contemporary knowledge about marketing as a profession	American Marketing Association; Chartered Institute of Marketing; Warc; ESOMAR
Trade associations	Data and information about particular markets, sectors and industries	OICA (automotive); IFPMA (pharmaceutical); TIA (telecommunications)
Reports	Market, competition and consumer analysis	MINTEL; KeyNote; Datamonitor; GEM
Journals	Peer-reviewed sources of marketing-related academic research	Library; EBSCO Business Source Premier; Emerald; ProQuest; JSTOR; ABI/Inform
Conferences	Proceedings of academic and non-academic marketing-themed symposia	Academy of Marketing Science; ANZMAC-GAMMA Joint Symposium Digital Marketing World Forum; Marketing Sherpa World Summit
Theses (PhD)	In-depth knowledge on specific marketing subjects	Library; British Library; Inter-library loan system
Agencies	Selected practitioner information and knowledge about marketing	WPP; Ogilvy & Mather; JWT; Leo Burnett; BBDO; McCann Erickson; Edelman
Companies	Competencies and offerings in the field of marketing	IBM Digital Marketing; P&G Core Strengths; Unilever Advertising & Marketing
Publishers	Data, information and knowledge across all marketing subject areas	SAGE Publications; Pearson Education; Kogan Page; Routledge

'Syndicated services'

Syndicated services are much more specialised sources of secondary data, which are not freely accessible or made available to the public via libraries. This type of research is typically undertaken by a market research company because it may be something an organisation in a particular industry could find useful or appealing. There is a pooling of resources between companies as well as individual studies aiming at generating actionable knowledge (insight). In some instances, it is possible for firms to collect specific information about their performance as a part of ongoing research – this is the case for the Harris Poll, a 'proprietary survey of public opinion' that has been running for over 40 years.

'Databases'

Databases include all external data and information organised for a series of different purposes and are generally searchable using dedicated software. They can be statistical collections or financial data such as Reuters; academic articles such as Ebsco; business information such as Factiva; industry reports such as IBISWorld; directories such as EDSA; or case studies such as The Case Centre. Nowadays, databases tend to be accessible online via the Internet, from vendors or producers, or through networks in their entirety or partially, depending on the needs of a specific user. Students can find that some of them allow for some data and information to be downloadable without restriction, but they generally have to rely on a university library, professional body or trade association subscription to find what they may need for a particular piece of assessment. In recent years, more precise search functions have made databases easier to navigate and hence search results are more relevant as a consequence.

Research in Practice: Censuses and Panels

Detailed information about the overall population of a country is typically produced every 10 years as generating large statistical collections for publication is a resource-intensive endeavour. Governments invest sizeable sums of money to collect, analyse and disseminate data about all residents. In India, the Office of the Registrar General & Census Commissioner has been working with the Jawaharlal Nehru University, Delhi, to produce 'specialized tables', which are available on request (Census of India, 2012). The census is organised around various categories and integrated with other pieces of research, such as the Annual Health Survey. It is a valid and reliable source whose power relies on the extent and precision of its coverage.

Of course, decision making in marketing can be supported by different types of secondary data, which are not necessarily as exhaustive as those obtained with a census. In recent years, technology has provided the opportunity for online panels to be developed and accessed at relatively short notice. Companies may tap into the results of these panels to find specific information on a topic. In so doing, they wouldn't necessarily have to brief a marketing research agency, which could be a more expensive and much slower process overall. Nielsen provides several solutions in this sense and makes some of the data collected via their Opinion Quest facility available to organisations: it would be worth your while to subscribe to its regular newsletter (www.nielsen.com/uk/en/newsletter.html).

An even more extensive discussion of secondary data sources would eventually draw our attention to two key facts: (1) there is an almost limitless range of material for a researcher to work from; and (2) secondary research could begin from any data source and evolve from there in an iterative process towards developing more meaningful and useful pieces of information in the context of a research project (see 'The Process of Secondary Research' later in this chapter for further detail).

Advantages and Disadvantages of Secondary Data

Before moving on to the secondary research process, it is worth pointing out the main pros and cons of using secondary data to help with the definition of topics of interest and, in the long run, with decision making in marketing.

It is highly likely that there is an availability of enough secondary data for any subject matter a student may be looking to study. Compared to primary data, secondary data can be gathered quickly and is less expensive to get hold of, so it is often used in the first instance. Secondary data can help build a solid rationale for a research project, before more time and effort are committed. They can also enhance primary data and/or indicate methodological solutions in terms of data collection, such as questionnaire design and data analysis techniques.

For example, with the outlook for the Moroccan economy strengthening and inflation remaining low (IMF Survey, 2015), the retail food industry is gearing up for further expansion and substantial changes to the food distribution system as more outlet and supermarket openings are planned by the four major players operating in the country: SNI, Label Vie, BIM and Aswak Essalem. However, a quick review of the information available in order to help with deciding where to locate these new shops, would quickly highlight the fact that in smaller cities and towns competition also comes from traditional local importers. This could trigger further research into how modern food retailers are to appeal to consumers in terms of product lines and ranges, as well as merchandising and service delivery, as they try to become relevant to more traditional audiences in Morocco. It might even be possible to address a specific requirement for strategy formulation and implementation using secondary research only.

In addition to clarifying or providing a solution for some issue or problem, it is possible to use secondary data to redefine a piece of research during its exploratory phase and to

Table 3.3 General pros and cons of secondary data

Advantages	Disadvantages
• Quick to obtain • Clarify an issue • Relatively inexpensive • Answer a research question • Widely available • Provide methodological alternatives • Alert to problems • Build credibility • Define a sample frame • Scope of information	• Lack of availability • Relevance to research • Purpose of publication • Accuracy of data • Fit with research question • Comparability between sources • Outdated information • Insufficiency • Inconsistent categorisation • Dubious quality

provide alternative methodological frameworks (research paradigms). It can be used to uncover potential stumbling blocks, such as sample selection difficulties, ineffective data collection methods and low survey conversion rates from previous studies conducted in similar fields or circumstances. Furthermore, one should be aware of how secondary data, mostly in the form of databases, can function effectively as the source of a sample frame (see Chapter 6 for more details).

However, there are both pros and cons to secondary data (see Table 3.3). It can present some notable downsides, starting with the fact that it is not always up to date (see Table 3.4). This becomes a problem, especially where a researcher is aiming at building a reliable snapshot of a market, sector or industry; in terms of working on a theoretical framework, a mix of established and contemporary theories is often the preferred solution instead. Other typical issues arise from a lack of availability and/or a lack or relevance of secondary data, the latter manifesting itself through fundamental differences: (a) in the definitions of categories within a particular area of knowledge, (b) between measurement units, and (c) in the context of comparisons over time or, more often, amongst several countries.

An example of this is in the way statistical information is put together and reported in relation to alcohol consumption habits. It is common for experts in the sector to refer to millions of hectolitres, gallons or cases, depending on the scope of the source and the origin of the data. Some of the statistics are also given in aggregate form as opposed to per capita, thus making comparisons somewhat hard or requiring some form of data manipulation first. On top of this,

Table 3.4 Inaccuracy – sources of error in secondary data

	Potential Issue
Who asked for the data?	Bias towards the 'position' of the organisation that commissioned the research, e.g. an advertising agency measuring their own ad effectiveness for a client
Who gathered the data?	Difference in capabilities (as resources plus competencies) between organisations, e.g. a start-up trying to understand potential customers
What questions were asked?	Lack of clarity in the formulation of the questions; illogical sequence; unclear explanation of the purpose of a study (introduction)
How were the questions asked?	Varying response rates depending on administration of research, e.g. face to face, telephone, email, online; bias in answers due to self-selection
When were the data collected?	Impact of the timing of the research, e.g. opinion about wearable technology at time of CES Las Vegas; unreliability of data when respondents are thinking about the past or hypothesising about the future
Who answered the questions?	Accuracy of the sample (based on the availability of a sample frame representative of the population to be studied)
How were the data analysed?	Reliability and validity of the results as a result of the analytical techniques employed, e.g. confidence level and confidence interval in inferential statistics
How were the data reported?	Misrepresentation of the outcome of research, e.g. using quantitative language in qualitative research

Source: Twyman, 2016

the individual consumption categories used in reports are in many instances not compatible, as local traditions tend to determine what societies consider it important to observe in each and every country. In any case, the existence of secondary data, its relevance and accuracy are not always enough to know what is needed, which invariably determines the need for primary data to be collected and analysed with a specific research question in mind.

Reflective Activity

Now go back to the 'Snapchat' at the beginning of the chapter and consider an area of marketing communications, such as public relations or viral marketing:

- What kinds of ideas appear to have already been researched extensively?
- Who are the main authors in the context of your chosen topic?
- What can be considered as the earliest piece of relevant theory with regards to the aforementioned topic?
- What is the latest, most up-to-date source of relevant information you can find on the topic?

The Process of Secondary Research

Like many other aspects of marketing research, secondary research is a rather complex process, which requires the rigorous application of sound principles to a systematic process of investigation (see 'Criticality in Secondary Research' below). At a fundamental level, things can be organised as per the four steps in Figure 3.1.

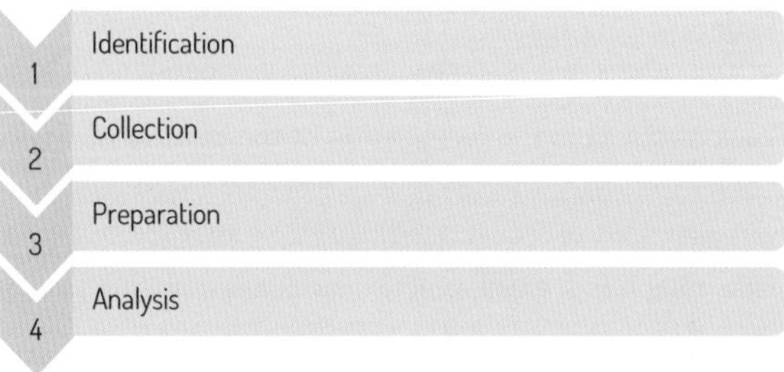

Figure 3.1 Basic steps of secondary research

Each step requires further specification. To begin with, 'identification' refers to understanding the subject of interest itself; there are questions to be asked in order to determine the components of a literature review, to select compelling keywords and phrases for searches, and to list out synonyms for each area of knowledge eventually 'to enable the researcher to map and to assess the existing intellectual territory, and to specify a research question' (Tranfield et al., 2003). In a similar way, the 'collection' of secondary data should be looking to make considerations as to the starting point, the extent or scope and the end point of a literature review.

What are the boundaries of secondary research? Ideally, students should proceed from the more general to the more specific field of investigation (see an example of a 'relevance tree' in Figure 3.2), while thinking about related subjects. In other words, it is important not to be drawn away from the central idea of an assignment to pursue seemingly useful, yet not crucial, themes. We should establish a cut-off point at which the data collected appears to be sufficient for the purposes of the study undertaken.

Designing Marketing Distribution Channel Structures										
Intensity Decisions					Type Decisions					
Downstream Channels		Upstream Channels			Ownership	Location		Technology		Intermediary
Intra-brand	Inter-brand	Contract	'Pull'	RPM		In-store	At-home	Catalogue	Web	(many options)

Figure 3.2 Relevance tree for marketing distribution channels

Source: Adapted from Palmatier et al., 2015: 155–92

'Preparation' is instead concerned with making sense of data. This phase looks at how data from different sources are captured and eventually combined. In the case of market, sector and industry information, students should aim to ensure that there is a common ground in order to make comparisons possible. When dealing with theoretical and empirical evidence, a literature review should aim to produce robust arguments using a critical approach.

Finally, 'analysis' refers to moments of constructive reflection on all the steps in the secondary research process in order to review and merge the steps taken, thus recognising that the process itself is iterative in nature rather than linear. This means that a solid enough literature review should eventually be built by going through this cycle at least twice, restricting the field of observation, while improving depth through the creation of subsequent drafts, thus culminating in a final version.

Criticality in Secondary Research

The basis for criticality is the use of argumentative practices and good reasoning: this is the opposite of rhetoric and fallacies. We should always strive to understand and explain secondary data by making clear points that are logically organised towards a conclusion, thus writing proper arguments rather than exposing personal opinions. This simple premise is particularly powerful and researchers should make an effort to ensure that both their reading and writing are guided by this premise in order for a literature review to be deemed truly critical.

Critical thinking refers to the application of an active, structured and skilful process to evaluate and use information as a guide to belief and action

Multiple sources

In this respect, critical arguments within a literature review are a function of the extent of the background research that goes into retrieving valid and reliable sources of data, information and knowledge. If we take customer acquisition, for instance, it will not be hard to argue that companies should have a clear proposition and ensure there is a strong link between marketing activity and desired outcomes using appropriate metrics. In fact, this very last paragraph just started presenting two valid and reliable sources to support such a statement. Using multiple sources for support makes it easier to transform an opinion into a logical argument.

Building arguments

From there, further ideas, thoughts, concepts and theories can be embedded in order to enhance the assertiveness of what is being said, thus avoiding empty, rhetorical statements. A student may want to continue reflecting on specific practices that lead to efficient customer acquisition, making reference to specific sources as well as pointing out factors that may play against 'maximising acquisition efforts' (eMarketer, 2015). The intensity with which information is provided to build an argument and the way in which it is soundly organised contribute to creating a defensible position based on findings that demonstrate critical knowledge of a subject (see Figure 3.3).

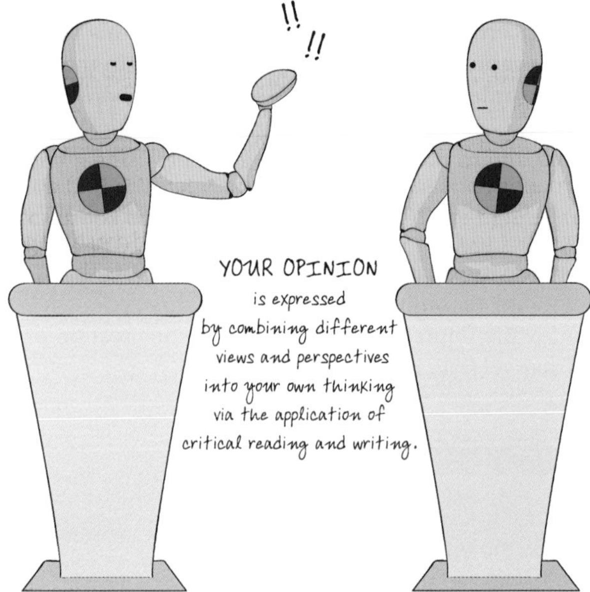

Figure 3.3 Argue your points comprehensively

Referencing work

The construction of critical arguments based on multiple sources of data, information and knowledge is typically done by paraphrasing a wide range of material, which has to be correctly referenced along the way. By doing so, a student is making sure that they: (a) provide as neutral an argument as possible; (b) reduce, or altogether eliminate, their personal bias; and (c) display a critical understanding of a particular topic.

At times, it may also be tempting to go back to previous work in order to capitalise on topics one is familiar with. If needed, this should not be done by self-referencing – even though this is a fair practice in academic terms – because citations from work previously submitted for assessment cannot be awarded any more marks. Thus, it is always preferable to integrate already known sources with up-to-date ones in order to boost the depth of a literature review (and, by extension, that of a piece of research).

These are just some initial thoughts on our way to becoming more well versed in how to deal with secondary data. Please ensure that you read on and later come back to this and the previous sections in order to make the best of all tips and suggestions.

Reflective Activity

The words, sentence, phrase, statement, point and argument have arguably the same meaning:

- How would you characterise the difference between a sentence and an argument?
- How would you structure an argument?
- Choose a marketing topic and write a short, 2–3 line argument about it.

Mapping Out Knowledge

In Chapter 2 (see 'Researchable Marketing Topics', p. 43 for more detail), the book proposed a simple method to narrow down topics into more discrete fields of study based on the intersection of some relevant areas of knowledge. Within this framework, it is now possible to take further steps forward by proceeding from the general to the specific using a 'funnel' (inverted pyramid) technique (see Figure 3.4). This can help students eliminate less important facts and information in order to map out knowledge more precisely, starting from a relevance 'tree' and by choosing the most promising path or creating a completely suitable one. In other words, when writing about a subject a student should be able to identify the beginning, the middle and the end of a reasonable literature review on a given subject: a set of relevant ideas, thoughts, concepts and theories that define the topic of interest and contribute to critical argumentation.

For instance, let's assume that you are planning to study marketing in relation to the hospitality industry. The broadest area of knowledge for you to look into could be the marketing of services. From there, you could then choose to focus on customer expectations by narrowing down your searches to those factors which are thought to have an impact on what customers might expect from a service, such as hospitality (see Figure 3.4).

Eventually, you could isolate two possible options amongst five service gaps (Parasuraman et al., 1985): the difference between actual customer expectations and what managers believe these expectations to be ('Gap 1'); and the distance between customer perceptions regarding their experience of a service and their original expectation of it ('Gap 5'). If this were your theoretical basis for discussion, it would then make sense to put more emphasis on the aforementioned service 'gaps', looking for relevant knowledge around these concepts and, wherever possible, adding industry-specific information and knowledge.

Figure 3.4 Services marketing 'funnel'

This would potentially draw our attention to the role beliefs and perceptions might play in this context. Indeed, the Greek philosopher Epictetus highlighted long ago the fact that beliefs and perceptions could be affecting our thoughts, feelings and behaviour. By making this kind of observation, you could then spark a new search into a related field of knowledge, which also appears to be a promising area.

Joining 'Funnels'

Following the example above, research should raise two main questions with regards to how this area of knowledge would ultimately help with the project, and how these two now relevant subjects could be presented as part of the same piece of work. In the first instance, there should be a judgement call based on whether or not it is felt that the link between beliefs and perceptions and the two service gaps is meaningful, i.e. how it adds value to the theoretical framework of the study. In the case of a positive answer, you should focus on finding a way to blend the existing critique of services marketing with the ensuing reflection on beliefs and perceptions. It is very much an exercise in splitting these theories into two separate, yet complementary, 'funnels'.

The first step would therefore have to consider how the last part of the services marketing inverted pyramid in Figure 3.4 can be linked to the opening of the beliefs and perceptions 'funnel'. This could be achieved by ensuring that the critical discussion about the service gaps is gradually moving on to beliefs and perceptions, so that the writing would naturally and smoothly flow towards the following section of the literature review.

The second step would be to identify a new path from general principles regarding this new subject, and eventually choose a middle and an end for it. By sticking to these simple rules, a literature review tends to gain momentum and eventually arrive at a conclusion in the form of a solid and coherent conceptualisation (see Chapters 2 and 4 for more detail), as in a description of the kind of reality a student is wishing to study.

The Content of Literature Reviews

Framing a literature review is a rather challenging process; the previous section pointed out some techniques to deal with structural issues when doing secondary research. You should also think of a literature review as a four-part scheme of work that enables you to organise the secondary data for a given project or piece of assessment. The four parts are:

- introduction
- sector overview
- marketing theory
- conclusion (conceptualisation).

They are not necessarily to be used at all costs and their content can vary depending on the type of research you are undertaking, which in turn determines the scope and depth of each stage.

Advanced: Where Companies Look for Secondary Data

Companies have benefited from the increasing array of data the Internet has made available over the course of the past 10–15 years. There are plenty of free data sources like Socrata or Open Data Network, Amazon Web Services Public Data Sets or Facebook Graph API, some of which come with basic analytic tools. Other data are accessible from the likes of Internet Service Provider (ISP) networks directly or via software such as Hitwise by Connexity. This allows companies with a limited, or no, research budget to access useful data in order to come up with (marketing) questions and possibly get answers to them.

Benchmarking has also been helped by the presence of data aggregators such as Coremetrics (now part of IBM), Google Analytics, Fireclick and benchmarkindex, as well as public services such as the Local Government Benchmarking Framework (this is part of the improvement service in Scotland). Comparisons for industries and sectors – for example, software, retail – can be provided in terms of customer conversion rates, time spent on a site, visits, page views, and so on. Websites report accurate data so companies can have a reliable picture of what is going on around them; however, data may only include some competitors, which might not be totally representative of the industry or sector in which an organisation operates.

Moreover, intelligence data like voice of the customer (VOC) has been made more readily available through internally designed programs, which aim at enhancing customer experience. Companies like iPerceptions and Qualtrics provide services in this area; in both cases, companies look to obtain insight by interpreting customer satisfaction statistics as well as task completion rates. This can eventually be taken to a higher level of 'predictive' analysis by measuring sentiment and behaviour with regard to the post-purchase evaluation of experiences, or by embedding 'early warning systems' through the use of statistical analysis to monitor data on a daily basis and to identify sizeable changes (HGS, 2015).

The Value of an Introduction

It is often the case that students spend time and effort drafting superficial introductions mostly based on personal opinion. The overriding question at this very early stage of a report, proposal, essay or dissertation should really be about what value an 'introduction' adds to the whole. Typically, there should be an indication of what prompted the researcher to look at an issue, explain it and provide enough references to get the process started. This background research shows that a student knows about the issue and its implications. It could also include the research question and research aim before summarising the overall structure of the document – this in the case of a dissertation project. All content should be relevant and concise, looking at a maximum of 10% of the word count, for instance 250 words for a 2,500-word report.

Looking back at our earlier example about the hospitality industry, the introduction would be the best place to start, steering the secondary research in a given direction using data and information about a notable, recent pattern, trend or phenomenon. For instance, the events sector is highly specialised, resilient to economic downturns and service driven. Air charter users are a particularly demanding audience in a fiercely competitive part of the hospitality sector. Minimising the aforementioned gaps would be important for any operator so as to improve reputation and secure further business expansion, as in the case of Australia's AVMIN. Thus, an initial description of events and the presentation of key facts about this segment of hospitality would fit well in an introduction to a research project about this topic. An eventual research question could then be framed in terms of service gaps, beliefs and perceptions, with a view to understanding what customers regard as, for instance, 'exceeding expectations'.

Industries and Competition

Secondary research in marketing often focuses on industries, sectors and markets. As a stand-alone exercise, you may be required to describe a particular micro-environment, such as the pharmaceutical chemist retail sector. In a more comprehensive report, this may have to follow an introduction and become a so-called 'sector overview' in order to frame a particular issue or problem, which would then be investigated accordingly. In both cases, it would be advisable to work from broad to narrow, adopting the logic of the inverted pyramid. If we take the context of the ongoing example, this could be framed as follows: hospitality (beginning); air charters (middle); and AVMIN (end).

Research in Practice: Fast Turnaround Secondary Research

Over the last ten years, marketing research agencies, like TNS, have introduced fast turnaround services to help organisations with issues such as understanding audiences and pitching for new business. One of the quickest and most cost-effective ways to do so is through compiling several data sets and information about a particular market, sector or industry into a report, which may also include some form of expert commentary or analysis.

Given the relative political instability of some markets, a manager going into a meeting to discuss market entry strategies could at times use a fresh overview. For instance, Egypt is a promising market of 93 million people where several car manufacturers already operate.

What would be the likelihood of a successful launch for a company not yet present in the country? Putting together a picture of the industry, its size and attractiveness, key competitors would need to source and combine statistics (raw or aggregate data) to generate useful marketing intelligence. The availability of such information for Egypt is not extensive, yet the Egyptian Auto Feeders Association (EAFA), the International Organization of Motor Vehicle Manufacturers (OICA), the Royal Automobile Club of Egypt and the Egyptian Automobile Manufacturers Association provide a solid basis for secondary research. Other regional, international and global trade associations, together with specialist news outfits, should allow a researcher to integrate these data, thus ensuring that a reasonable picture of present events and future developments (forecasts) can be drawn and made available by an agency to a client, ideally overnight.

Some people may be of the opinion that dedicating a part of their literature review to talking about market data is inappropriate as an introduction can contain similar information. However, the definition of general business parameters for marketing research purposes is advisable, especially if there is a sensible approach to it; charts, graphs, tables and other visuals are preferred to text descriptions – this with a view to saving precious words for a critical commentary of the data and bringing the point home explicitly through a visual display. It could lead to restricting the field of observation, sometimes providing a clear-cut exemplification or an opportunity to work on a case study by singling out a particular organisation (see Chapter 9 for more detail).

Theoretical Frameworks

Students do not always think of a literature review as a full-blown critique of secondary data. They tend to present summaries of some ideas, theories or journal articles rather than establish appropriate and coherent theoretical frameworks (for marketing). Furthermore, it is important to understand where theory sits in the context of an assignment. When writing an essay, we look to apply ideas, thoughts and concepts where they matter and according to a particular plan or outline. In other situations, we might have to implement a smooth transition between sections.

This would be the case when proceeding from 'sector overview' to 'marketing theory'. In order to do so, we would first have to point at a relevant area of marketing knowledge in the closing stages of the overview. Using the 'funnel' technique in our example of the hospitality industry, it would seem acceptable to end the sector overview by talking about the potential damaging effect of AVMIN, not understanding whether its service delivery may, or may not, meet expectations (however these are initially set). The inverted pyramid in Figure 3.5 could ideally 'follow' our previous one, which covered services marketing, customer expectations and service gaps.

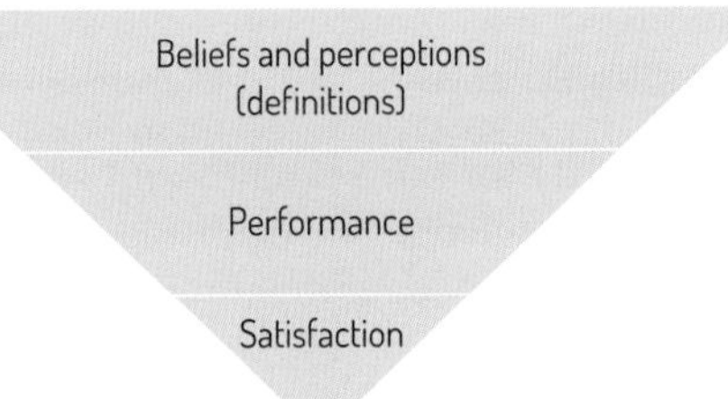

Figure 3.5 Perceptions and beliefs 'funnel'

Reflective Activity

A literature review needs to display a balance between its scope (breadth) and its detail (depth):

- How would you go about including or excluding theory and theoretical frameworks?
- What would be a sensible way to evaluate the relevance of old(er) and new(er) sources of knowledge?
- How would you deal with an apparent limited availability of knowledge in one or more of your field(s) of interest?

Beliefs and perceptions should be defined first and then more theory added to this theoretical framework. For instance, expectations and satisfaction can be connected with perceived performance and a disconfirmation of beliefs using the Expectation Confirmation Theory. In this respect, there may be a need to dig into other areas of knowledge to ensure that relevant factors such as promises, intensifiers and their respective impact on expectations, perceptions and experiences are identified along the way (Wilson et al., 2008). Once more, there is a tension towards narrowing down the literature review in such a way that the main marketing constructs should emerge with regards to key areas of knowledge and in relation to the business context.

The same principles could be applied to the relevance tree for marketing distribution channels shown in Figure 3.2 (and within any market, sector or industry where a subject matter of this kind appears to be relevant). Designing marketing distribution channel structures involves decisions about intensity and type. If we take the former first, it is important to consider whether we are looking at an 'intensity' or a 'type' decision before we can make a choice between downstream and upstream channel member options, as opposed to ownership, and so forth. Relationships are eventually a critical aspect of these perspectives.

The result of the initial investigation is that the first inverted pyramid is now pointing at the type of relationships that typically exist within brands and their distributors within a particular network. This can then be linked to the amount of pressure that a particular organisation eventually chooses to apply to their intermediaries in order for them to obtain certain desired outcomes, such as the discontinuation of a competing brand (see Figure 3.6). Studies are available to cover a variety of competition versus co-operation ideas in relation to fields like commercialisation, distribution and business strategy. From there, a student can ultimately focus on different results of how a given organisation works within its distribution network; further solutions such as "coopetition" are available, and more complex ideas such as game theory are applicable, too.

By selecting appropriate keywords for our searches and amending them as we delve more deeply into a particular area of knowledge, we can isolate the most relevant ideas, concepts and theories and reflect on how they come together to define and describe a reality that we intend to study.

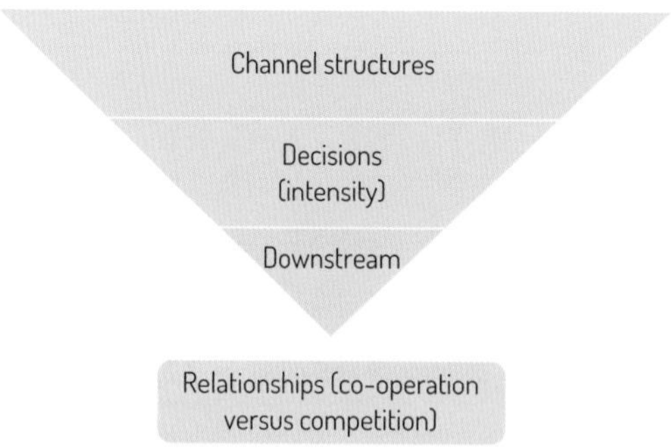

Figure 3.6 Marketing distribution channels 'funnel' and link

The Conclusion

A **conclusion** is the necessary consequence of a series of arguments, propositions or theses

Ending a literature review can be a rather difficult task to accomplish. Students should go back and think about their research question and how this is affected, if at all, by what they have found out, so that they can link the beginning to the end and close the research circle. Above all, they should strive to arrive at a critical conclusion, which attempts to make sense of the key ideas, thoughts, concepts and theories presented and discussed along the way.

Every piece of secondary research should eventually lead to a theory, model or conceptualisation that deals with a key ontological question (see Chapter 4 for more detail), i.e. what is the nature of the reality we are investigating? This would help us come up with a rationale for primary research (see also Chapter 2).

Instead, there is often a lack of understanding of this notion, which means that, more often than not, we are unable to make the best of a literature review, for instance, in response to an assignment brief. This is particularly noticeable in large research-driven projects where it would manifest itself as a jump, or gap in the flow, from secondary research to primary research. Students would then find it much harder to answer their research question (see Chapter 5 for further reflection on this topic). In the example about the hospitality industry, we could end up with our own developed model about the gap between customer experience of an air charter service and their expectation of it, using some of the elements learned while researching beliefs, perceptions, performance and satisfaction. This would finally enable us to work out a suitable methodology for data collection and data analysis based on the reliability of such a model, i.e. its ability to predict an outcome, or otherwise.

More Tips for Secondary Research

Secondary research is a fundamental part of any piece of work or assessment. Whether we are fully aware of it or not, every time we search for data, information and knowledge in relation to a topic, we are in fact conducting secondary research. It should tell a story.

Avoid summarising

Reporting the work of others, even though properly paraphrased and referenced, can often lead to simple summaries of books, articles, web pages, reports, and so on. As such, students will not be able to make any sizeable progress because this is effectively the same as listing out different ideas without understanding the possible implications of their work. We should instead make an effort to analyse data, information and knowledge about a subject, to offer a deeper understanding of how different views go together or otherwise diverge. For instance, looking at an apparently simple task like defining 'marketing', we can draw from plenty of definitions, but what are the key elements emerging from an analysis of this discipline? We should attempt to identify commonly shared components in order for us to arrive at a synthesis of something new, which can eventually underpin a critical argument (see the previous 'Criticality in Secondary Research'), i.e. our view of an idea supported by valid and reliable sources.

Sensible tales

Students tend to be too loose in the way secondary research is structured and executed. As discussed, the 'introduction' should be a writer's main driver, while a research question should constitute the focus of the literature review.

Let's assume that you are looking to find an answer to the following question: How does the co-operation between fashion brands and bloggers in the UK influence consumer perceptions in the short term?

You should build a free-flowing account of the fashion industry, specifically about the UK and possibly about a brand. From there, blogging, PR (persuasion and collaboration) and consumer perceptions would all be areas of interest to weave into this document. You should bear in mind the kind of conclusion it is reasonable to make in relation to how these different ideas, concepts and theories link together, thus demonstrating either the existence of a theory or the need for one to be created (see Table 3.5).

Table 3.5 Use of language

Introducing ideas	studies showed that; there is evidence that; some authors say; the literature reveals; this approach is; contributions from <name(s)> highlight; <name(s)> contend(s)
Reinforcing links	further; furthermore; moreover; besides; additionally; in addition; what is more; also; as well; likewise; equally; similarly; in a similar way; by the same token; in fact
Expressing difference	however; though; conversely; on the other hand; despite; in spite of; notwithstanding; even though; although; nevertheless; nonetheless; still; but; yet; otherwise
Making connections	so; then; thus; hence; as a result; consequently; therefore; because of this; for that reason; accordingly; in view of that; for example; for instance; finally; lastly

Source: Adapted from Thomas, 2013: 65

Iteration

Secondary research is not static. It adds value to a piece of assessment only if a student is able to refine their work while they establish a direction for their writing and use information to constructively debate their topic, research question, literature review and/or conceptualisation. In this respect, secondary research must be seen as an iterative, circular process and not as a discrete sequence of steps. For instance, a new article on service-dominant logic may steer a research question in a slightly different direction as theory on the subject is updated and may impact the understanding of a problem, issue or phenomenon, for instance 'The customer is always a co-creator of value' (Vargo and Lusch, 2016: 8). Going back to previously written sections and integrating other material is part and parcel of studying and learning about a given topic.

Critical reading

Another aspect that should not be underestimated while dealing with secondary data and research is the content of what we are reading. There is a widespread assumption that writing is more important than reading; the fact is that it is hard to produce compelling critical writing without in-depth knowledge of a subject, as gained through extensive critical reading. An approach to this often time-consuming task is to try and get a sense of what you are about to read by looking at any abstract, introduction or list of contents first. From there, you can decide whether or not to carry on with your reading and eventually select relevant parts, sections or chapters to study. It is then advisable to skim read these pieces before committing to spending the necessary time on understanding and reflecting on them in full.

Taking notes

Once the process of critical reading has started, it is crucial to keep track of those words and sentences that are related to your research question by highlighting them, if possible – try to avoid doing so when borrowing material from libraries, unless you make your own copies! You must also create a document to which you add chunks of text, notes and full details of how to retrieve the original material – it is wise not to do this in the main body of your secondary research write-up as it may later lead to confusion and involuntary plagiarism. Constructive note-taking is personal, selective and critical; this means that you need to be able to identify what for your work are important passages in the text and to critique sources using your own words. Direct quotes should be included only when the way in which something is being said is paramount to its meaning, i.e. paraphrasing may change its meaning, significance and impact. As mentioned in many other instances throughout this chapter, taking notes is also about establishing links with the topic of interest: what might something be useful for?

Style and content

Eventually, it is possible to arrive at a set of practices for students to consider when dealing with secondary data and writing up secondary research:

- Be organised and structured, i.e. follow a suitable process.
- Be focused and coherent: remember to define the topic clearly.
- Be straightforward and concise, thus avoiding lengthy sentences and repetitions.
- Be mindful of seminal work and influential research in the fields of knowledge you are interested in.
- Stay alert to recent developments in knowledge related to your subject matter(s).
- Be critical both when reading and writing.
- Use the appropriate terminology for your field of marketing.
- Be open-minded: do not settle for the first idea you come across.
- Be careful with online sources as their origin can be hard to ascertain.

Chapter Summary

Starting off secondary research is often a tough proposition as students need to have at least identified a topic through some preliminary information gathering. Without an idea, as rough as that might be (see Chapter 2 on marketing-related investigation), it is nearly impossible to define the parameters of a search or to put emphasis on specific areas of knowledge.

Thus, the first part of the secondary research process must focus on the choice of relevant keywords to develop an understanding of a particular topic based on valid and reliable sources of relevant secondary data, information and knowledge. This is not a practice that uses brute force – as in the more references, the better – but a systematic exercise whereby a range of books, articles (academic and non-academic), websites, reports, white papers, and so on, are selected for adding depth to what is needed to be known. This also helps towards defining, and perhaps answering, a research question, as well as articulating some specific, measurable, achievable, relevant and time-bound (SMART) research objectives.

This chapter, therefore, has covered issues relating both to process and content, with a view to providing a set of ideas and suggestions regarding how to handle key aspects of 'desk' research. This is shaped by the fact that the purpose of secondary research is, at the very least, six-fold:

1. Collect more background information on a topic of interest.
2. Define the various areas of knowledge within the general topic.
3. Identify useful sources of data, information and knowledge.
4. Discuss critically how other authors addressed similar issues, problems, phenomena, patterns and trends.
5. Improve your understanding of the research question.
6. Generate a suitable conceptual framework as a link with primary research.

Secondary research is indeed an effective system, which allows us to make sense of different views and perspectives in a critical fashion. Both reading and writing have to be informed by a strong sense of direction; conversely, widening a search aimlessly is not a substitute for adding detail to the main elements of a review. In this respect, students should ensure that they build sensible, well-supported arguments by analysing and synthesising material into compelling 'stories'.

Ultimately, secondary research points at some form of conceptual framework, a way to rationalise data, information and knowledge into a 'model'. This is an important aspect of secondary research because it offers the opportunity to crystallise our understanding of a subject, and also to showcase it to our research audience afterwards, whether in order to answer a research question or to establish the overarching principles of a research paradigm for primary data collection and analysis.

Case Study: Technology and Marketing

The growing interest in social media has had an impact on the kinds of fields of research students are looking into for their dissertation projects or other large assignments. Indeed, this is re-shaping knowledge; the way stakeholders interact is changing all the time and there is non-stop access to everyone, everywhere in the world (or near enough). In this respect, it is reasonable to assume that studies about social media could yield some interesting results. However, this does not mean that anything with the words social and media in it will in fact turn out to be of value. So, let's try and reflect on some ideas and understand how secondary research could and should be conducted in relation to these.

For a start, it is important to restrict the field of observation as social media is a huge collection of different tools. In the first instance, what kind of communication would one want to focus on: visual or text? The former appears to have taken over for Generation Z: 'Emojis, pictures, videos and GIFs replace words to make text conversations and social networking fast and visual' (Andrus, 2015). By the same token, being active on social media is gradually becoming more important than being passive (a spectator). This may suggest some further relevant areas of knowledge, perhaps around variety (forms of data), velocity (speed) and/or veracity (trust). Relationships between organisations and consumers, or customers, must indeed be framed following new rules of social interaction.

This has led to the development of social network analysis as people are eager to know where opinions about a brand are shared, what is being said and how this could eventually be managed in a public space such as the Internet. Notwithstanding some technical issues that may arise from not being familiar with this approach to gaining knowledge, the nature of the connection and how word-of-mouth spreads across nodes from a subject to the next, or comes to an end as interest wanes, is potentially crucial in terms of explaining how social media users interact, where online opinion leaders are (and who they talk to), and so forth. For instance, it may be a matter of singling out content marketing practices that foster certain types of relationship and arriving at setting up more captivating research questions about the links between individuals at different levels of the 'food chain': Social Broadcasters; Mass Influencers (Mass Connectors; Mass Mavens); and Potential Influencers (Ray, 2010).

In a similar vein, the widespread use of #hashtags has raised questions about how best to stand out, about what works and what does not work in a world in constant flux. There is a problem of identification, especially as brands want to be able to monitor reaction to particular marketing activities such as product launches. In other words, students could look at the rules determining the acceptance and subsequent popularity of a #hashtag, or otherwise. Some success is still down to the basic rules of sales promotion within the bigger area of marketing communications; hence, the application of principles that have been codified over a century of research in the field to a new platform such as Twitter could possibly make for exciting reading. Theory building appears to be a natural direction for the development of research with regards to how existing practices apply to the fast-moving world of technology in marketing.

The key to a sensible research project for undergraduate as well as postgraduate students is in the way the old and the new are combined to generate knowledge. There is plenty of material we can draw on and a virtually endless virtual world (pun intended!) to apply it to. Likewise, any study can also be restricted to look at a particular occurrence, i.e. within a sector or for a company. The fundamental process of secondary research should always unfold from a topic down to a 'model', making appropriate selections along the way.

Let's take a further example regarding Apple iBeacon – fundamentally, this is a device that communicates with iOS via Bluetooth so that marketers can send promotions and content to Apple users based on their location – in Singapore by EpiCentre, which shows how it is possible to build relationships by being first with technology that makes life easier, i.e. solves a problem. This strikes as an opportunity to investigate functional/utilitarian motivation in relation to adopting such technology in the first place and, above all, what the boundaries of what an organisation can do with it are. This is a fundamental question as consumers may in the future be pushed to live with a constant stream of communication 'Minority Report style'.

One of the issues for students planning to tackle projects in such novel areas is that they tend to privilege technology and technical aspects over and beyond theory, as it is easy to assume that much of the existing body of knowledge in marketing – for example, consumer behaviour, brand performance – would not be applicable to how consumers conduct themselves on social media platforms or react to things like

(Continued)

(Continued)

location-based marketing. Therefore, planning secondary research becomes even more important as new territory is possibly being explored; you should feel entitled to think creatively about possible linkages between knowledge that has been codified over a relatively long period of time and emerging technologies in marketing.

Case study questions

1. What technological developments in marketing can you identify from the text (and from recent Internet news)?
2. How do you think these developments could impact marketing practices (management) and/or consumer behaviour?
3. If you choose a particular 'technology' and some specific marketing theory, how can you link the two together in a short literature review outline?
4. What other kinds of connections, e.g. market, sector or industry, can you possibly make, which define the extent of secondary research further?

End of Chapter Questions

These questions should help you reflect on your understanding of this chapter:

1. How does secondary research help with answering a research question?
2. What kind of secondary data are there?
3. Why are some secondary data thought to be invalid, unreliable or both?
4. How can students deal with the issue of confidentiality in secondary research?
5. What are the main steps of the secondary research process?
6. How is criticality evidenced in secondary research and, in particular, in a literature review?
7. What is the difference between a 'sector overview' and 'marketing theory' in a literature review?
8. What is a conceptual framework there to achieve?

Checklist

After studying Chapter 3, you should now be familiar with these key concepts:

1. The range of internal and external sources of secondary data
2. How to organise secondary data, information and knowledge for marketing research
3. The role of relevance trees and 'funnels'
4. How to understand and produce critical arguments
5. The importance and practice of referencing work

Further Reading (in sequence from beginners to advanced)

Mao, A. (n.d.) Literature reviews. *TED-Ed* [online]. Available at: http://ed.ted.com/on/ymKKdaGz [Accessed 5 February 2016].

Bairfelt, S. and Wilkinson, T. (2015) Secondary (desk) research from Purple Market Research. *Purple Market Research* [online]. Available at: http://purplemr.co.uk/wp-content/uploads/Purple-Desk-Research-Services-Overview-2015.pdf [Accessed 18 February 2016].

Cleverism (2015) How to perform an insightful secondary market research. *Marketing 101* [online, 13 May]. Available at: www.cleverism.com/how-to-perform-insightful-secondary-market-research [Accessed 16 February 2016].

University of Derby (2012) A guide to Harvard referencing [online, 7 September]. Available at: www.youtube.com/watch?v=NDgqqPvMn0U&feature=youtu.be [Accessed 11 February 2016].

Ridley, D. (2012) *The Literature Review: A Step-by-Step Guide for Students* (2nd edition). London: Sage Publications.

Wallace, M. and Wray, A. (2011) *Critical Reading and Writing for Postgraduates* (2nd edition). London: Sage Publications.

Bibliography

Aaker, D. A. (1992) Managing the most important assets: brand equity. *Planning Review*, 20 (5), pp. 56–8.

American Library Association (2016) Types of libraries. Explore a Career in Libraries [online]. Available at: www.ala.org/educationcareers/careers/librarycareerssite/typesoflibraries [Accessed 17 January 2016].

Andrus, A. (2015) Gen Z vs. Gen Y: does the hype add up? *sproutsocial* [online, 1 September]. Available at: http://sproutsocial.com/insights/gen-z-vs-gen-y [Accessed 14 February 2016].

Bowell, T. and Kemp, G. (2010) *Critical Thinking: A Concise Guide* (3rd edition). Abingdon: Routledge.

Burns. A. C. and Bush, R. F. (2014) *Marketing Research: International edition* (7th edition). Harlow: Pearson Education.

Census of India (2012) Workstation for research on census data [online, 10 May]. Available at: www.censusindia.gov.in/2011-common/Workstation-Research.html [Accessed 7 February 2016].

Chaykowski, K. (2016) How esurance engineered its way to winning the Hashtag Bowl. *Forbes* [online, 8 February]. Available at: www.forbes.com/sites/kathleenchaykowski/2016/02/08/how-esurance-engineered-its-way-to-winning-the-hashtag-bowl/#4bc822b6266e [Accessed 16 February 2016].

Coghlan, A. T. (1985) Competition and cooperation in marketing channel choice: theory and application. *Marketing Science*, 4 (2), pp. 110–29.

Cronin, P., Ryan F. and Coughlan, M. (2008) Undertaking a literature review: a step-by-step approach. *British Journal of Nursing*, 17 (1), pp. 38–43.

Denz, A. (2014) What is syndicated research and what are the benefits? *Fresh MR* [online, 2 April]. Available at: www.marketstrategies.com/blog/2014/04/what-is-syndicated-research-and-what-are-the-benefits [Accessed 30 January 2016].

eMarketer (2015) What's your customer acquisition strategy? Lack of data prevents retailers from maximizing customer acquisition efforts. *Retail & Commerce* [online, 16 January]. Available at: www.emarketer.com/Article/Whats-Your-Customer-Acquisition-Strategy/1011821 [Accessed 5 February 2016].

FAO (n.d.) Secondary sources of information. *Corporate Document Repository* [online]. Available at: www.fao.org/docrep/w3241e/w3241e03.htm [Accesses 12 January 2016].

fabcom (n.d.) Marketing agency white papers [online]. Available at: www.fabcomlive.com/strategic-marketing-agency/marketing-agency-white-papers [Accessed 29 January 2016].

Fardaoussi, M. (2015) Morocco 2014 Retail Foods Report. *USDA Foreign Agricultural Service* [online]. Available at: http://gain.fas.usda.gov/Recent%20GAIN%20Publications/Retail%20Foods_Rabat_Morocco_10-5-2015.pdf [Accessed 5 February 2016].

Harris Interactive (n.d.) The Harris Poll [online]. Available at: www.theharrispoll.com [Accessed 30 January 2016].

Harvard Business Publishing (n.d.) Insights & publications [online]. Available at: www.harvardbusiness.org/insights-publications [Accessed 29 January 2016].

Heding, T., Knudtzen, C. F. and Bjerre, M. (2009) *Brand Management: Research, Theory and Practice*. Abingdon: Routledge.

HGS (2015) Innovating analytics in customer care beyond the voice of the consumer. *Hiduja Global Solutions* [online]. Available at: www.teamhgs.com/sites/default/files/case-studies/innovating-analytics-in-customer-care-beyond-the-voice-of-the-consumer.pdf [Accessed 17 June 2016].

IMF Survey (2015) Moroccan economy on the right track. *Economic Health Check* [online, 23 February]. Available at: www.imf.org/external/pubs/ft/survey/so/2015/CAR022315A.htm [Accessed 2 February 2016].

inspireblog (2015) cievents and AVMIN link up to expand horizons. *cievents* [online, 10 December]. Available at: www.cievents.com/cievents-and-avmin-link-up-to-expand-horizons [Accessed 11 February 2016].

Istat (n.d.) Data and products [online]. Available at: http://en.istat.it/dati [Accessed 17 January 2016].

Jones, C. B. (1998) Applications of database marketing in the tourism industry. *Economic Research Associates* [online]. Available at: www.hotel-online.com/Trends/ERA/ERADataBaseTourism.html [Accessed 12 January 2016].

Kapferer, J.-N. (1997) Managing luxury brands. *Journal of Brand Management*, 4 (4), pp. 251–9.

Keller, K. L. (1999) Managing brands for the long run: brand reinforcement and revitalization strategies. *California Management Review*, 41 (3), pp. 102–24.

Kumar, V., Chattaraman, V., Neghina, C., Skiera, B., Aksoy, L., Buoye, A. and Henseler, J. (2013) Data-driven services marketing in a connected world. *Journal of Services Marketing*, 24 (3), pp. 330–52.

Lazenby, A. (2016) 10 effective ways of working in customer acquisition. *warc* [online]. Available at: www.warc.com/Pages/Taxonomy/Results.aspx?DVals=4294951423&Sort=ContentDate%7c1&Filter=All [Accessed 5 February 2016].

Lyons, W. (2015) Who's driving world wine consumption? *Wall Street Journal* [online, 28 January]. Available at: www.wsj.com/articles/whos-driving-world-wine-consumption-1422461583 [Accessed 5 February 2016].

Market Research Bulletin (2014) TNS launches quick turnaround tool to identify winning concepts for business growth. *Research Industry News* [online, 2 July]. Available at: http://marketresearchbulletin.com/tns-launches-quick-turnaround-tool-identify-winning-concepts-business-growth [Accessed 11 February 2016].

Marr, B. (2016) Big data: 33 brilliant and free data sources for 2016. *Forbes* [online, 16 February]. Available at: www.forbes.com/sites/bernardmarr/2016/02/12/big-data-35-brilliant-and-free-data-sources-for-2016/#bba239b67961 [Accessed 17 June 2016].

Meister, M. (2012) The Wendy's Case: a demonstration how marketing research and analysis can help resolving a management decision problem. Undergraduate, Boston University. Available at: https://martinmeisterg.files.wordpress.com/2012/03/marketing-research-paper.pdf [Accessed 17 February 2016].

Mobile Marketing Association (2016) Who we are: about us [online]. Available at: www.mmaglobal.com/about [Accessed 19 January 2016].

Nagi, K. (2015) Top 15 internet marketing gurus changing people's lives. *bloggingcage* [online, 6 October]. Available at: www.bloggingcage.com/top-15-internet-marketing-gurus-who-are-ruling-blogosphere [Accessed 29 January 2016].

Nielsen (2016) Comprehensive end-to-end consumer insights for faster, smarter, better decisions to help your business grow. *Solutions* [online]. Available at: www.nielsen.com/us/en/solutions.html [Accessed 7 February 2016].

OCLC (2016) Overview. *WorldShare Interlibrary Loan* [online]. Available at: www.oclc.org/en-UK/worldshare-ill.html [Accessed 17 January 2016].

O'Meara, R. (2013) How our perceptions and beliefs influence our thoughts, feelings and behavior. *Baltimore Health Examiner* [online, 12 November]. Available at: www.examiner.com/article/how-our-perceptions-and-beliefs-influence-our-thoughts-feelings-and-behavior [Accessed 11 February 2016].

Palmatier, R. W., Stern, L. W. and El-Ansary, A. I. (2015) *Marketing Channel Strategy* (8th edition). Harlow: Pearson Education.

Parasuraman, A., Zeithaml, V. A. and Berry, L. L. (1985) A conceptual model of service quality and its implications for future research. *Journal of Marketing*, 49 (4), pp. 41–50.

Patzer, G. L. (1995*) Using Secondary Data in Marketing Research: United States and Worldwide*. Westport, CT: Quorum Books.

Rampton, J. (2014) Content marketing funnel: 5 steps to customer acquisition. *Forbes Tech* [online, 12 August]. Available at: www.forbes.com/sites/johnrampton/2014/08/12/content-marketing-funnel-5-steps-to-customer-acquisition/#7b84dc543c25 [Accessed 5 February 2016].

Ratcliff, C. (2014) A look inside Amtrak's excellent content marketing strategy. *Econsultancy* [online, 19 August]. Available at: https://econsultancy.com/blog/65338-a-look-inside-amtrak-s-excellent-content-marketing-strategy [Accessed 12 January 2016].

Ray, A. (2010) Tapping the entire online peer influence pyramid: a social computing report. *Forrester* [online, 26 February]. Available at: www.forrester.com/Tapping+The+Entire+Online+Peer+Influence+Pyramid/fulltext/-/E-res56537 [Accessed 16 February 2016].

Redman, T. C. (2013) Data's credibility problem. *Harvard Business Review* [online, December]. Available at: https://hbr.org/2013/12/datas-credibility-problem [Accessed 14 June 2016].

SAGE Publishing (n.d.) eBooks. Products [online]. Available at: https://uk.sagepub.com/en-gb/eur/EBOOKS [Accessed 16 January 2016].

Sandison, N. (2008) TNS launches 24-hour turnaround service. *Brand Republic* [online, 4 February]. Available at: www.brandrepublic.com/article/780881/tns-launches-24-hour-turnaround-service [Accessed 11 February 2016].

Statista (2016) Wine consumption worldwide in 2014, by country (in million hectoliters). *Alcoholic Beverages* [online]. Available at: www.statista.com/statistics/266165/wine-consumption-worldwide-by-selected-countries [Accessed 5 February 2016].

Taute, H. A. and Sierra, J. (2014) Brand tribalism: an anthropological perspective. *Journal of Product & Brand Management*, 23 (1), pp. 2–15.

Thomas, G. (2013) *How To Do Your Research Project: A Guide for Students in Education and Applied Social Sciences* (2nd edition). London: Sage Publications.

Tranfield, D., Denyer, D. and Smart, P. (2003) Towards a methodology for developing evidence-informed management knowledge by means of systematic review. *British Journal of Management*, 14 (3), pp. 207–22.

Trinity College (n.d.) The literature review process. Library [online]. Available at: www.tcd.ie/Library/assets/pdf/Library%20HITS%202014/HITS%20Literature%20Review%20Process.pdf [Accessed 5 February 2016].

Twyman, J. (2016) Public opinion polling. PR Masterclass. London College of Communication, 4 February.

Vargo, S. L. and Lusch, R. F. (2016) Institutions and axioms: an extension and update of service-dominant logic. *Journal of the Academy of Marketing Science*, 44 (1), pp. 5–23.

vindicia (2012) Best practices for customer acquisition [online]. Available at: www-304.ibm.com/partnerworld/gsd/showimage.do?id=34071 [Accessed 5 February 2016].

The Wallace Foundation (2009) Workbook B: Conducting secondary research, collecting and using data resources [online]. Available at: www.wallacefoundation.org/knowledge-center/after-school/collecting-and-using-data/Documents/Workbook-B-Secondary-Research.pdf [Accessed 6 January 2016].

Wilson, A., Zeithaml, V. A., Bitner, M. J. and Gremler, D. D. (2008) *Services Marketing: Integrating Customer Focus across the Firm*. New York: McGraw-Hill.

Wine Institute (2015) Wine consumption in the US. Statistics [online, 26 August]. Available at: www.wineinstitute.org/resources/statistics/article86 [Accessed 5 February 2016].

World Health Organisation (WHO) (2016a) Global Health Observatory (GHO) data. Data [online]. Available at: www.who.int/gho/en [Accessed 16 January 2016].

World Health Organisation (WHO) (2016b) Publications [online]. Available at: www.who.int/publications/en [Accessed 16 January 2016].

YouTube (n.d.) El Corte Ingles: Multimedia campaign effectiveness. *iab Europe* [online]. Available at: www.iabeurope.eu/files/4213/6852/4542/el20corte20ingles20case20study20final204.pdf [Accessed 7 February 2016].

Find journal articles and multiple choice questions online at: **https://study.sagepub.com/benzo** to support what you've learnt so far.

After considering how marketing research can help generate value for organisations, Part II deals with planning marketing research using a sound systematic process of inquiry. The following chapters define and examine useful theoretical and practical tools, techniques and frameworks to support the collection and analysis of secondary and primary data, while helping you make sense of research designs and population sampling.

Chapter 4 covers the initial steps of the marketing research process. Starting with a description of the reality under investigation, and its importance as a guiding principle of a research paradigm, it ends with a discussion of research objectives and the way a student should organise research into manageable chunks. It centres on the fact that planning should be at the forefront of the research process in order to boost one's chances of creating valid and reliable knowledge.

Chapter 5 concludes our critical discussion of the systematic process of marketing research, by connecting secondary and primary research through the conceptualisation of theoretical and empirical concepts. In addition, it presents and develops different research designs and examines their suitability for studying a problem, an issue, a phenomenon or a trend. The aim is to attain useful research outcomes irrespective of the researcher's beliefs, attitudes or opinions relating to a particular topic.

Chapter 6 offers an overview of different sampling techniques and the way in which students can choose suitable participants for their study in light of its research question and objectives. It looks at defining a target population and the steps needed to draw a sample for the purposes of primary data collection (either qualitative or quantitative in nature), while respecting the fundamental premise of the underlying research paradigm.

PART II

Planning Marketing Research

CHAPTER 4

Conceptualising Research: From Secondary to Primary Research

LEARNING OBJECTIVES

The key learning objectives of this chapter are:

1. To illustrate the sequential steps in conceptualising research
2. To describe the key concepts of the research philosophy in marketing
3. To analyse the potential benefits of planning marketing research systematically
4. To reflect on the overall structures of proposals and projects

KEY CONCEPTS

By the end of this chapter, the reader should be familiar with the following concepts:

1. Characterising reality for marketing research purposes
2. Basic perspectives in knowledge generation
3. Approaches and traditions in marketing research
4. Theory contribution in marketing research
5. Secondary and primary research and data: the relationship
6. Drafting research questions and objectives
7. The iterative nature of marketing research

Riccardo Benzo

Introduction

Deciding on the components and characteristics of any marketing research task can have a significant impact on its successful completion. Experienced professional and academic researchers and students alike should be aware of the implications of badly argued proposals. These range from insufficiently clear arguments in favour of marketing research to ineffective operational plans about how data will be collected and analysed. This can result in no meaningful knowledge being generated, whether in relation to basic or applied research, as discussed in Chapter 1.

This chapter is a stepping stone to understanding how marketing research can contribute to organisational value, by concentrating on the development of a systematic process to help isolate and deal with essential dilemmas – starting from the definition of reality and its relationship with the decisions researchers make along the way. It also reviews some of the most widely accepted principles of the philosophy of research and their application to marketing, including the way valid and reliable knowledge can be created, a description of suitable approaches to reasoning, the scope and the depth of marketing research and the achievement of solid conceptualisations for marketing research proposals as well as fully fledged projects.

At times, readers might question these ideas, thoughts, concepts and theories, and their place in marketing research. They have formed the basis of development in marketing as a discipline for a long time and continue to provide invaluable support in a variety of situations, so it is important to familiarise yourself with them. Try reading and answering the 'Reflective Activity' boxes provided, and try to reflect critically on real-life issues, problems and phenomena.

It is also essential to remember that marketing research is an iterative process; the concepts explored in this chapter link to those in other parts of the book, in particular Chapter 3 (Secondary Research: Facts and Theory) and Chapter 5 (Marketing Research Design). The links are signposted throughout the chapter to allow you to refer back or read ahead, to help you gain a broad understanding of the topics under discussion.

Snapshot: Chasing Customer Satisfaction

Customer satisfaction is one of marketing's most talked about concepts. Companies around the world make considerable efforts and spend large sums of money in order to figure out whether or not their customers are satisfied with the products or services they purchase from them. For instance, IKEA (2012) claimed that they continued building on long-standing relationships by becoming more relevant to and ultimately satisfying their customers by acting on the feedback they had collected. How, though, can we measure satisfaction?

The American Customer Satisfaction Index and its companions, affiliates and licensees around the world provide a methodology to obtain insight into this important business driver and to improve customer experience overall. An index, as a numerical measure of a phenomenon, is able to provide a summary for such an occurrence, the level of one's satisfaction, yet it does not in itself aim to give an account of the thoughts, feelings and opinions that lead to the score recorded by a company.

A detailed assessment of these dimensions can provide a better way of understanding the reasons behind satisfaction. This is because meaning is multi-faceted and cannot be reduced to a single index. Indeed, it was found that elements such as capability, continuity, creativity, consistency, commitment and credibility help define customer satisfaction, and are what organisations should aim for on their way to forming, developing and maintaining relationships over time.

There seem to be two ways of looking at customer satisfaction. On the one hand, there is an objective representation of the concept itself, which could be useful in different situations because it is deemed to be independent of them. Conversely, customer satisfaction can be seen in a subjective way, which is dependent on the situation/circumstances one is facing and the people involved.

The Ritz-Carlton hotels ensure that employees know a little bit about their guests to personalise the experience and improve satisfaction; being close to their customers allows them to apply a personal touch, thus standing out in a sea of undistinguished service.

Looking at the World

This book makes several references to complexity as a catalyst of curiosity and a driver of investigation. However, human beings do not spend time reflecting on it, mainly because it is a normal manifestation of reality; in other words, it does not appear to us as an anomaly. While this might not make a difference in our personal interactions, appreciating how complexity unfolds in front of our eyes could instead help focus our business efforts (see Chapter 2 for more information). We should thus start asking ourselves more questions relating to the nature of the reality surrounding us.

It may seem a purely academic debate, worlds away from the more managerial-style thinking encouraged in business schools. However, asking more compelling questions and digging deeper to understand what we are presented with on a daily basis, could provide a more solid foundation for personal, academic and professional development. For example, it is hard not to notice that, with ever growing global competition, companies in all sorts of consumer and industrial sectors tend to sacrifice margins by pricing themselves against the competition.

Through relying on benchmarking, companies stay 'relevant' for their target segments. In so doing, they typically forego opportunities to understand what motivates their audiences and provide value to them. This in turn affects their ability to come up with a compelling positioning strategy and to create and maintain a competitive advantage over time. Value is indeed defined by the trade-off between the benefits one obtains and the sacrifices one makes on their way to acquiring an offering. Above all, it is a dynamic concept that depends on circumstances, moods, ease of access, and so on, and, as such, should be researched in more detail. Let's try and make informed decisions by establishing how much our target audiences are prepared to pay for what they value.

Reflective Activity

- What recent issue or phenomena have you seen in the news that might be an interesting candidate for marketing research?
- How can you describe its potential impact on a business and its marketing strategy, in particular?
- What kind of data are there to help you define what is going on?

Brookes and Palmer referred to 'pressures from the outside' as the reasons for organisations to engage with the world more fully, using a process that is a combination of practical and theoretical practices, which could hopefully open up different avenues for development (2003: 20). In other words, they suggested that it would be sensible to keep on looking around, to explore the environment in which businesses operate, to update and improve marketing thinking and to bring about change as a result of all this. On their way there, companies could also find solutions to those paradoxes that, at times, stop evolution and might ultimately prevent success.

The Nature of Being (Ontology)

Marketing research can be thought of as a useful aid to help reach sound judgement based on a systematic study of the reality surrounding us, which can manifest itself as issues, problems, phenomena, trends or patterns (see Chapter 1 for a more detailed account of this area). The first step in this process is to come to terms with the essence of these things, or to lay out the assumptions we make with regards to how the world works. In this respect, it is important to accept the fact that people have different views and that the same aspect of life can be framed and perceived in different ways.

At the root of this discussion, there is an essential split, or separation, between objective and subjective interpretations of reality. Let's take a marketing department, for instance; it is possible to think of it as an entity made up of several parts and with an existence of its own, independent of the staff employed to run it. This is because a marketing department comprises relationships and behaviours to which staff conform, or should be expected to conform, according to the processes and the procedures set by an organisation. People comply with standardised practices, impart and follow orders and apply company values to their activities.

However, it can also be held true that reality stems from the perceptions of the individuals involved in it. In the case of a marketing department, this would essentially recognise that employees are active within the processes and the procedures that might exist at any one point in time. They influence what is happening, perhaps by not following a particular instruction to the letter, in which case an explicit, formal description of the department itself would not be entirely suitable anymore. Everything becomes the product of experiences, be those individual or social.

Ontology is a central part of metaphysics that deals with the nature of reality

This short illustration aims to highlight the fact that one might look at reality from fundamentally different angles (see Figure 4.1). A marketing department can be something that an organisation has or possesses and which operates according to and within certain parameters as held true by objectivism. Subjectivism, on the other hand, would view the same marketing department as something that shapes an organisation through constantly evolving interactions. Indeed, when carrying out research, we need to come to terms with the situation we are presented with and, later on, figure out how to deal with it. Students and practitioners should not see these passages as inward-looking philosophical enquiry, but as a stimulus for a more accurate observation of what is around us, especially when it comes to areas like consumer psychology, consumer behaviour and relationship marketing.

Objectivism is an ontological position claiming that the nature of reality is not influenced by the people who are part of it

SUBJECTIVISM	OBJECTIVISM
Multiple	Single
Symbolic	Tangible
Constructed	Structured
Situational	Independent
Holistic	Measurable

Figure 4.1 Reality through the ontological lens

The apparently opposing views presented in Figure 4.1 are simply telling us that we need to sort out what is significant from what is insignificant in our observations should we want to arrive at an acceptable model for the nature of the reality that interests us as researchers in any given context. It is about having a reliable thinking system to characterise situations based on perceptions, opinions, attitudes, and so on, that we hold, instead of having to make absolute choices at every single juncture. More questions can be asked to define reality, which need not necessarily bring about 'Yes' or 'No' answers, but consider intermediate solutions; in other words, it may all depend once more on the level of complexity in front of our eyes.

Subjectivism is an ontological position claiming that the nature of reality is affected by human perception (thus questioning an objective understanding of the world)

The majority of marketing research begins with an investigation of existing material in the form of independent reports, company reports and accounts, government publications and white papers, journals, books, newspapers, websites, abstracts and encyclopaedias. Some of these sources of information, such as conference proceedings, manuscripts and company archives, are often central to research and become primary evidence; besides their usefulness as data, what do they tell us about the reality we are observing?

Much documentary evidence is written for a specific audience and might be skewed or misrepresented. For instance, the international success of the online music streaming service Spotify, launched in 2008, might be explained in rather different ways depending on what types of source a researcher is able to access or simply look at. E-mail exchanges between executives might highlight a fairly informal process of internationalisation as the organisation took advantage of circumstances, for instance spontaneous demand from certain markets. Structured reports commissioned to external consultants might instead indicate a more strategic approach, including specific market screening and market entry strategies. Thus, the reality emerging from such investigations would not necessarily be the same, which potentially affects the way we understand things in the end.

Research in Practice: Managing B2B Relationships

Business networks are particularly important in industrial settings, especially with regards to the necessity for an organisation to maintain continuity over time. The overall duration of a relationship between a vendor firm

(Continued)

(Continued)

and its customers may be hampered by the loss of key personnel; if a key staff member leaves or is moved or promoted, the vendor may be left exposed. Research was conducted to understand the dynamics of such exchanges and, eventually, what organisations can possibly do to mitigate the impact of losing an employee with specific skills, competencies and, above all, knowledge.

The premise of this piece of research was influenced by the lack of previous secondary data. In other words, in spite of the fact that business-to-business (B2B) customer relationships had been studied before, there was little or no material addressing the issue outlined above, in any detail. As such, it seemed logical to proceed 'from the ground up' by trying to provide a clearer definition of the mechanisms at play without holding any particular view true. In this way, the ontological position was that the reality under investigation was dependent on perception.

Perhaps this is something that many would not consider as the starting point for marketing research, especially in an industrial, business-to-business setting and in relation to internal marketing areas within a firm. On the contrary, reflecting on the theoretical background enables researchers to frame the issue clearly and then proceed with the rest of their task assuredly. This means that the input from the chosen population sample was analysed to find patterns in the data, thus providing a solid platform for a research paradigm to develop from that point and as a consequence of the initial critical discussion.

Any 'reality' can contain objective and subjective dimensions. Phenomena can be made up of concrete and abstract elements. As a result, we can arrive at generally applicable systems as well as socially accepted ones. Being aware of this is all the more important when we consider that ontological issues have not been particularly important to marketing as a discipline and as a science. There is a long overdue debate to be had about reality as a continuum between a 'concrete structure' and a 'projection of human imagination' (Cunliffe, 2011: 650).

Generating Knowledge (Epistemology)

After defining the world through the lens of the ontological assumptions we make, the next step is to attempt to establish how best to gather knowledge about it. In its broadest sense, researchers have to clarify to themselves first and then to others what constitutes 'acceptable' knowledge in justifying the systematic research process they intend to follow towards answering a specific question (see Chapters 7 and 15 for information about validity and reliability in marketing research).

There is no right or wrong answer and it is important that learners do not feel their perspective on this matter is irrelevant. The sum of our experiences affects our epistemology. The characterisations eventually available to us are helpful in informing marketing research and in recognising tried-and-tested pathways to knowledge generation; yet, they are not the only possibilities. With this in mind, we can highlight some of the more widely discussed and applied epistemological philosophies, while establishing links between these and the nature of the reality under scrutiny as defined in the previous section (see Table 4.1).

In Chapter 1, we examined the evolution of marketing research over the years and focused briefly on the debate around the application of scientific methods of discovery used in the natural sciences. Positivist epistemology has been influenced by a fundamental principle that knowledge is created from what can be sensed, recorded and measured with a

Table 4.1 Establishing the boundaries of a research paradigm

Ontology	Objectivism		Subjectivism
Epistemology	Positivism	Realism	Interpretivism
Approach	Deductive	Abductive	Inductive

certain degree of statistical precision (refer to Chapter 14 for a discussion of 'confidence level'); in order to do this, large amounts of quantitative data need to be collected and a deductive approach adopted (see Chapter 11 for more on 'hypothesis testing'). In this way, the researcher is detached from the reality they are interested in studying, and able to make predictions about particular problems, issues or phenomena. This would be the case for a brand manager evaluating brand resonance through the use of an appropriate theoretical framework linking awareness, associations, attitudes, attachment and activity, which are each expected to influence the former in a specific fashion. It would, therefore, be possible to come up with a response to the initial assumptions, for instance whether they hold true, or not.

The structural forms offered by this epistemology are less than ideal though. It is extremely hard to accept the implied argument made by positivists that marketing can be treated like physics for all intents and purposes. After all, marketing is, in many respects, a lot less absolute in its manifestations than physics where, instead, there is a constant tension towards a working theory of everything. In this respect, realism provides an alternative stance which acknowledges the possibility that the typologies we employ to understand reality are variable. This is equivalent to accepting that there are some forces at play, which are shaping reality on an ongoing basis; the aim of the researcher is to discover the hidden mechanisms responsible for what we are seeing (Matthews and Ross, 2010). In other words, the job of the researcher is to add a critical perspective to the development of a picture of the reality that surrounds us, knowing that not everything is knowable and accepting that certain claims may not represent reality correctly.

There is an initial perception of reality. Then the stimuli are processed and further explanations may be proposed by adding theoretical elements whose existence can only be presumed. Looking at brand resonance now, it seems plausible to assume that how a brand resonates with target segments could realistically be down to more, or at least different, concepts such as image and reputation, than those that might initially have been envisaged. Researchers subscribing to this particular epistemological position would accept the possibility of using qualitative or quantitative types of data, or both, to uncover ideas that might challenge the status quo.

Taking this further, it is possible to adopt an even more uncertain view of the process of knowledge generation. It is possible to argue that there is a virtual absence of proper laws in the realm of marketing, which in turn provides a chance for reflection about the role of the researcher in making sense of reality (also see p. 99 later in this chapter on substantive theory). This is how interpretivism came to be a powerful force: knowledge can be seen as stemming from socially constructed meanings and as interpreted by other human beings. The key emphasis shifts from explanation to exploration, as the ultimate goal of this epistemological position is to equip researchers with the means to generate theory through the collection and analysis of qualitative data. Inductive reasoning, or the bottom-up approach, takes precedence here because the lack of an 'a priori' rationale allows for new paths and patterns to emerge. In the context of brand resonance, this could refer to the emergence of emotional responses and reactions beyond those which might have been theorised in past research.

Whatever route to knowledge generation we take, the following three statements should be satisfied by any one piece of research:

1. There is a belief something is true (ontology).
2. There is evidence that something is true (epistemology).
3. Something is true.

The problem with the last statement is that it seems to presuppose that there is a single 'truth' rather than several possible truths, all of which are plausible and acceptable as long as we uncover them by using a systematic process of inquiry. In other words, marketing research has value as long as it creates the conditions for different solutions to emerge. Such findings may not be in line with our expectations, yet they will contribute by adding insights and value to the body of knowledge for any chosen topic of inquiry.

Advanced: Research Paradigms

As the discussion about marketing research proceeds from considerations about the nature of reality to writing up findings, conclusions and/or recommendations, a number of thoughts will surface, which can be considered as the constituent parts of a research paradigm. Much has been written about this subject, yet a research paradigm can simply be defined as a container box in which all assumptions about this systematic process are stored. Thus, a researcher should always be able to boil their thinking down to a set of ideas that allows them to plan and execute a certain project.

The path that we follow from secondary data and research to primary data and research, via a conceptualisation of our work, is influenced by the ways in which we see reality, understand knowledge, approach theory and design data collection. There is no fixed research paradigm; in fact, it is easier to think of all the possible permutations one could arrive at. However, some research paradigms have been classified in terms of cultural differences stemming from the background and experiences that researchers might have had. This evolution over time might also have defined a preferred course of action, an overall paradigm a researcher would essentially be most comfortable with – both practitioners and students could conduct some self-reflection on those research-related aspects they believe in and identify their (paradigmatic) stance.

At this point, a systematic process of research can be thought of as something that synthesises data into information, which is in turn interpreted and converted into knowledge. It finally appears that any philosophical orientation needs to inform the methodology of discovery through the use of a suitable 'glue', which holds every component together nicely.

Theory and Marketing Research

A large proportion of marketing professionals jump straight into tackling problems, yet their actions are driven by educated guesses based on experience and assumptions. This section discusses the following basic premise: everything we know must come from somewhere.

Theory essentially represents a source of predictive power whether we are fully aware of it or not. The fundamental issue in marketing research, as well as in other management disciplines, is that theory is not something absolute with a capital T, as illustrated in Table 4.2.

Table 4.2 Different types of theory

Grand theory	Middle-range theory	Substantive theory
General applicability in a variety of different contexts and over time	Significant reliability in a more specific context and over time	Restricted validity to a particular context, time and group (population)

Source: Creswell, 2002

In many instances, marketing makes use of substantive or middle-range theories; studying the effects of some internal marketing initiatives in a Chinese organisation by relying on a few similar studies conducted in the USA during the 1990s exemplifies the application of substantive theory to generate further substantive theory; indeed, this makes the scope of such a piece of work ultimately rather restricted. At the same time, we should also start raising questions about the nature of the reality we intend to observe and how knowledge could be generated in such a setting.

However, what any theory does is to order concepts and principles for us to be able to advance predictions about what may happen in a chosen context, at a particular moment in time (or over time) and for a more or less specific, observable audience.

Ethics: More Than a Chore...

The act of planning a piece of marketing research is a systematic endeavour steeped in critical reflection. It does not consist of a series of random steps that might seem to fulfill a poorly thought-out research purpose. Ethics is part and parcel of such a process, yet it is far too often seen as an add-on; in a final rush before handing in their work, many students write a few paragraphs about ethics in order to 'get it out of the way'. However, there is a fundamental truth to contend with: each decision involves choices, and these choices, even the less significant ones, influence the ethical acceptability of choice outcomes.

On the one hand, there is a familiarity with ethical frameworks and guidelines that help assess whether an action is ethical or not, according to a specified system. In fact, several research ethics committees exist at all levels to regulate academic and professional marketing research. They establish fundamental norms and provide tools for people to refer to – your university will have something like a research ethics approval form or checklist to help evaluate the risk to participants, researchers and other contributors for any given project.

Normative ethics does not ask difficult questions of us; it is relatively easy to answer a few questions on a form or tick a few boxes on a checklist. Our moral compass, however, is not put to the test until we face some 'ethically important moments' (Guillemin and Gillam, 2004: 262). Let's assume that during the course of a face-to-face interview with a marketing director of a renowned multinational company you discover that bribes have been paid to secure exclusive distribution contracts around the world: what would you do?

(Continued)

(Continued)

Applied ethics is essentially dealing with unforeseeable situations in the practice of research. It is advisable to have a network to rely on such as supervisors, mentors and advisors, to establish appropriate responses.

A researcher also has to deal with their own morals: how high have you set your ethics bar? The Internet is widely regarded as an extremely useful source of data, information and knowledge. Unfortunately, many of us have lost some of the ability to assess the reliability and validity of such sources. Even more so, we tend not to pass ethical judgement about whether or not we should use some of these sources. During secondary research, it is not uncommon to come across documents online which might have been published by accident or fraudulently. You should contact their rightful owner, first, and ask for permission to use them – or should we?

Conceptualisation: From Secondary to Primary Research

Once we have defined our main field of interest and narrowed it down to a series of existing theories of interest to us (see Chapter 3 for more information on handling secondary data), we can use these to come up with a conceptualisation of our own. Blaikie referred to this as a model, 'a hypothetical explanatory structure or mechanism', warning that a model is built systematically and not thought up as a desirable (or, in other words, manufactured) representation of reality, as this would demote it to a set of beliefs without an appropriate grounding in theoretical and/or empirical evidence (2000: 165–6).

The way we proceed from here is then determined by how comprehensive, or otherwise, a model is. Essentially, are we trying to verify theory or are we trying to build theory? Clarifying this should help us determine a starting point in a standard cycle of research, as illustrated in Figure 4.2.

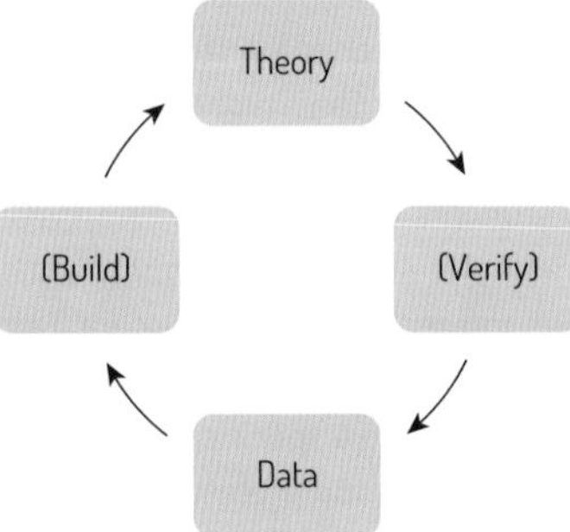

Figure 4.2 The cycle of research

If we are taking a relatively under-researched area like brand equity appropriation, there may eventually be a fairly strong case for attempting to build new theory; this could be likened to plugging a gap in knowledge. Conversely, if we are able to access a sizeable chunk of material about a particular topic in marketing like advertising effectiveness, there may be a reasonable rationale for the verification (or testing) of any model stemming from our critical literature review. Both cases do not represent a definitive approach to theory development: they should not be seen in isolation, but more as a continuous, iterative cycle.

Typically, a student should try and be realistic when planning a project such as an undergraduate dissertation, and focus on only half of the cycle, whereas a professional could consider a wider remit when evaluating strategic options, such as research for product innovation, and attempt to build and verify theory or, alternatively, verify and (re)-build existing theory in full.

If we take the example of P&O Cruises, the market leader in the UK, it seems reasonable to assume that it should want to keep its offering relevant and appealing over time. Returning (loyal) passengers need to be offered new, exciting things to do; they might choose a different ship on which to spend a holiday. Other consumers might be persuaded to join, either as first-timers to P&O or newbies to cruising in general.

When the cruise liner Azura was added to the fleet in 2010, it featured Sindhu, a high-end Indian restaurant whose concept and menu were created by Atul Kochhar of London's one-star Michelin restaurant Tamarind. The process of putting together a compelling proposition for such an idea was based on verifying some commonly held assumptions. For a start, Indian food is a mainstay of the British 'diet'; also, P&O Cruises has a long-standing connection with India. In this respect, it is possible to test a series of hypotheses and then figure out how to make the offering distinctive by adding detail to the initial (substantive) theory. This is why Sindhu has two areas (an all-day bar offering street food and a dining room), provides an affordable treat to everyone, features all-time favourites and contemporary dishes, and so forth. The overall experience can then be adjusted, such as the menu composition, on a continuous basis, knowing that the basics have been thoroughly checked and that they respond to what consumers want.

Reflective Activity

- What kinds of substantive or middle-range theory can you identify in the general area of consumer behaviour?
- How can any one of these theories help you choose a starting point in the cycle of research (Figure 4.2)?
- How can more theories (and concepts) be used to define a 'model' for a particular purpose?

To summarise, you can apply existing substantive theory on a subject to a different situation in order to find out how it works in that particular context and perhaps come up with new theories as a result. Conversely, you could try and characterise a particular trend, pattern, and so on, by arriving at a theory of it through the systematic application of research. Finally, researchers could be interested in defining a theory further in order to test its predictive power and gauge their progress on that specific subject matter or otherwise. There are different ways of operating, largely depending on the motivation for the research.

Approaches to Research in Marketing

The 'ways' we have been referring to can be categorised further in order to identify suitable research designs to choose from (see Chapters 5, 10 and 12 for further detail on

Model A possible representation of the reality a researcher intends to study

this topic). In practice, they are defined by the extent to which a model is able to describe the reality under observation and what interests us at a particular moment for a particular reason, for example the lack of response from a key marketing distribution channel. We have already introduced some of these approaches in relation to research in marketing. Due to historical developments in the field, deduction or deductive reasoning is usually the first approach to be addressed. We will carry on the tradition here with the proviso that this does not express a judgement of value on the importance of one approach over and beyond that of the others, which we will come on to discuss later.

Deductive reasoning relies on the existence of extensive theoretical evidence as a starting point (see Figure 4.3 for more detail). As such, a researcher is able to come up with a solid representation of reality (model) and, most importantly, to hypothesise specific outcomes from it (see Part IV for more on this subject).

1. THEORY (MODEL)
2. HYPOTHESIS
3. OPERATIONALISATION
4. DATA COLLECTION AND ANALYSIS
5. HYPOTHESIS TESTING (ACCEPT OR REJECT)
6. REVISION

Figure 4.3 Deductive reasoning explained

Construct A specific way to think of a concept based on some of its components/parts

Deductive reasoning works from a general assumption or premise to a specific occurrence or illustration. In this respect, it is the method that arrives at conclusions by using solid proof. This approach employs a known theory – perhaps in the shape of a conceptual framework – and tests whether or not it holds true in a particular situation. Snieder and Larner (2009, p. 16) noted that 'the deductive approach follows the path of logic most closely. The reasoning starts with a theory and leads to a new hypothesis. This hypothesis is put to the test'. Therefore, it is important to ensure that the concepts are translated into variables that can be measured correctly so as to enable the overall process of deduction to be completed in full. Hypotheses may then be accepted or rejected, and theory revised if needed – indeed, this is more likely to be the case when a model is found not to be working the way it was anticipated.

Let's examine how deduction might be used to investigate an improvement in the extent to which UK consumers trusted The Co-operative Bank after it was hit by a number of scandals between 2013 and 2014. A study by YouGov found that its 'Buzz' score – this represents 'the net balance of the positive or negative people hear about a brand' – shot up from –11.3 to –4.2 over a period of six months, during which the Bank had made a conscious effort to highlight its values and ethics through a marketing communication campaign (Parsons, 2014). Progress such as this can be explained by using hierarchy-of-effects theory, which argues that a sequence of events exists in which brand knowledge is paramount to brand trust as the former precedes the latter. In other words, the more one knows about a brand, the more one is likely to trust the brand – this would be our overarching proposition here. The research project would then need to look into ways to measure both constructs, collect data and analyse them, perhaps using a simple regression equation (see Chapter 14 for information on inferential statistics).

We may ultimately find that there is a statistically significant probability that our hypothesis is true, thus accepting it, in which case we can argue that providing more knowledge about a brand is a good way to increase trust in a brand. If it is not possible to accept our hypothesis, this would open up a debate about what happened instead; this would lead to a revision of theory and, above all, to considering a complementary approach to research.

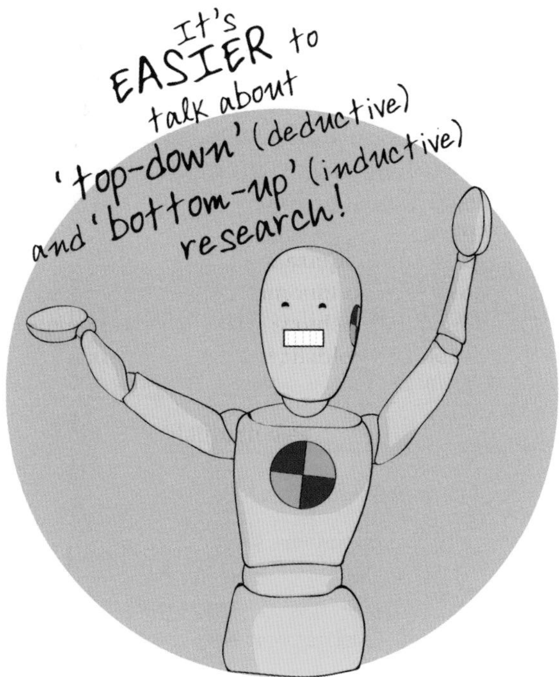

Figure 4.4 Top-down and bottom-up research

This is when induction comes into play as a logical way of proceeding. Inductive reasoning is not constrained by the existence of theory, or otherwise, and by our ability to arrive at a robust model of the reality we want to come to terms with. Its appeal resides in a more open-minded disposition as to what the causes of something might be; referring back to Figure 4.2, this is represented by the arrows going from 'data' to 'theory'. In simpler terms, this route would be advisable, or preferable, when our literature review or desk research (secondary data) is not enabling us to come up with any firm proposition. If this is the case, the only reasonable process to follow is the general idea of attempting to draw out themes, patterns, ideas and suggestions, which eventually provide the chance to find connections most likely in the form of a substantive piece of theory.

With this in mind, let's see how induction could be used to try and explain why several large companies considered turning away from Facebook after they had invested considerable time and money over the years in building a presence there. There are at least two key reasons why it would be almost impossible to crystallise a trend like this into a model: first, there is not yet enough dedicated research into a field as novel as social media; and second, and perhaps more importantly, decisions such as these are strategic in nature, hence internal to these organisations, which does not make it easy for an external observer to gauge them.

However, there are opinions available as to what might have been the root cause behind this behaviour: 'it's tough to beat free' is one of them (Burns, 2014). It would be interesting to assess how founded these are through the use of different instruments of inquiry, which leave space for interpretation and, ultimately, theory-building.

The study could aim to talk to key decision makers within a sample of suitable firms (see Chapter 6 for information on sampling techniques) in order to produce a large amount of data and to index them according to the originally selected themes as well as emerging ones (see Chapter 10 for details on qualitative data analysis). The goal here would be to provide an initial rationalisation for the choices made by the organisations sampled in the research. If this is considered to be weak or incomplete, you could continue by using inductive reasoning and perhaps expand the research by enlarging the sample further. If the research yielded a possibly consistent theory for such behaviour, you could move through the standard cycle of research to consider testing it via deductive reasoning.

Reflective Activity: The Ritz-Carlton

Considering the opening Snapshot for this chapter, discuss the following questions:

- How has The Ritz-Carlton approached customer satisfaction?
- Which solution does The Ritz-Carlton seem to have adopted in order to exceed industry standards?
- What is the influence of expectations on customer satisfaction, and how can this be taken into account in marketing research?

Although they can be used individually to achieve good results, deductive and inductive strategies are two halves of a whole. There has indeed been a conscious effort to portray them as complementary approaches because marketing research can benefit from their systematic application over time.

An additional perspective on finding answers to research questions is abductive reasoning.

Abductive Reasoning

Abductive reasoning is based on the idea of imperfect information – again, this ties in with complexity in as much as in the multi-faceted, ever-changing business environment of today it is virtually impossible to have a full picture at any moment in time. Put in very simple terms, this approach can be viewed as a process in which some sort of explanatory hypothesis is put together and examined. As such, it might be incomplete in its formulation, yet worth pursuing.

This seems to be the case when taking into consideration private labels – products manufactured by one company for another company's brand – for example, Kellogg's manufacture Tesco's private label cornflakes. In the USA, during the last recession, the company managed to shake off the lower-quality perception that American consumers had always associated with them. This change of heart was inconsistent with previously observed post-recessionary behaviour; nevertheless, 'the premise ... was that this recession was going to leave a scar, not a bruise, on American consumers' (Birkner, 2014). Researchers had in fact used the depth of the impact of what was happening, its more than vague resemblance to the 1929 Wall Street crash, to predict what the long-lasting effects of the recession would be. This actually represented an application of abductive reasoning – that is, filling in the blanks with a somewhat educated guess. The prolonged trial period forced on US consumers by economic conditions of uncertainty supported an implied prediction whereby brand switching, in this case from 'premium' to 'private', did eventually stick. People continued going back to private labels until it became second nature and, as such, perfectly acceptable: A further piece of theory emerged along the way.

Research in Practice: Silent Needs

The development of curved TV sets appears to have been led by a holistic approach to marketing, focusing on innovation, competition, customers and revenue (MaRS, 2009). A series of assumptions was made about the existence of a market, or a demand, for this type of offering, its appeal both in rational and emotional terms, and customer perceptions about the eventual viewing experience. Ultimately, there had to be a justifiable belief that an innovation such as this would come to satisfy customers, thus providing a solution to a specific problem.

Manufacturers like Samsung and LG concluded that curved TVs would provide a 'better viewing experience', although this might simply turn out to be down to perceptions rather than the actual ability of the human eye (and brain) to see a real difference between more traditional TVs and these new ones (Robarts, 2014). Similarly, these companies borrowed ideas from other fields, such as neuroaesthetics, explaining the attractiveness of curved shapes over and above linear ones as a driver of product development and design.

Several theories on shopping motivation could also be applied to this context. This is the case for some ideas like 'gratification shopping' or 'role shopping', which are linked with personal and social aspects of consumer behaviour (Arnold and Reynolds, 2003). Sales of curved TV sets could be expected based on the understanding of general characteristics found in shoppers, even though these do not necessarily relate to the product category under investigation here.

This is how organisations more or less explicitly make use of the various approaches to marketing research in the way they collect and interpret data, information and knowledge to help with their decision making. In this instance, we can think of the work undertaken by electronics manufacturers as influenced by abductive reasoning – an overall understanding of a situation based on a number of propositions from different fields.

Whichever approach is deemed to suit a specific situation the most, it essentially has to provide a link between existing knowledge in the chosen field of enquiry and the generation of new (valid and reliable) knowledge.

Generating Compelling Research Questions

A research approach is inextricably linked with the purpose (or aim) of the research – this aspect is crucial as it essentially establishes a direction to head in to answer a chosen research question. The key point here is to make every conceivable effort to stick to the purpose of the research as closely as possible throughout, without getting distracted by perhaps appealing, yet unimportant or, even worse, unrelated, strands of enquiry. To aid this process, it is useful to know that the following research purposes by and large cover a researcher's requirements (more information on them is also available in Parts III and IV):

- *Exploratory*: an initial attempt to investigate an issue, a problem, a phenomenon, and so on, about which there is limited prior understanding and research, for example the consumption patterns of Pakistani workers in the Middle East.
- *Descriptive*: an effort aiming at mapping out or summarising a particular issue, problem, phenomenon, and so on, about which some historical and current information is available, for example the strategic internationalisation of European SMEs via networks.
- *Explanatory*: an endeavour primarily focused on shedding light on the causes behind an issue, a problem, a phenomenon, and so on, about which theory exists, for example the key motives of American consumers visiting shopping malls in large metropolitan areas.

Any research question would therefore tend to fit within one of these categories or container boxes, as we have referred to them before, but how do you generate a research question? Figure 4.5 offers a sensible sequence to help with this task.

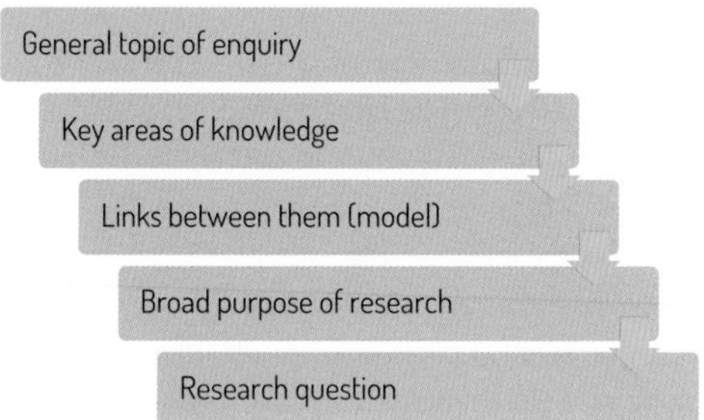

Figure 4.5 The road to a research question

Newcomers to research generally find it hard to narrow down their field of enquiry from a topic of interest to a workable research question. Abercrombie & Fitch, a renowned clothing brand in the USA during the mid- to late 1990s, was recently challenged by the likes of H&M and Zara and made a decision 'to take the North American logo business to practically nothing' (Linshi, 2014). There is little doubt that this would affect the overall recognition of the brand over time, yet it is hard to say what the ultimate impact of such a move would be on, for instance, brand equity. From this 'general topic of enquiry', there is an immediate need to isolate 'key areas of knowledge'; in marketing terms, these might be things like brand awareness, brand knowledge, brand image and brand reputation. It is at this stage that a researcher needs to look into 'links between them' and understand what the 'broad purpose of research' could be: exploratory, descriptive or explanatory? Representations of brand equity exist (Keller, 2013) so it should be possible to arrive at a model (conceptualisation) of the issue and then frame the 'research question' either in a descriptive or an explanatory format. For instance, imagery is thought to be related to feelings and judgements about a brand, so a reasonable descriptive question to ask could be: What is the impact of a key imagery change on feelings and judgements for a 1990s iconic brand: Abercrombie & Fitch in a radical US re-think?

The ability to get to this point relatively quickly is somewhat determined by the familiarity of a person with a topic of interest. In other words, it is not possible to guess research questions; there needs to be a sufficient level of understanding to start with, which is directly related to the amount of background research conducted as part of the literature review (or the desk research, if in the professional field). As students are always advised at this stage, the keyword is Read, Read, Read. Likewise, it is not possible to answer a research question without having it operationalised, i.e. reduced to some manageable steps that make the journey possible.

Articulating Research Objectives

There is a certain amount of confusion as to what a research objective is because the word objective itself has different meanings within marketing. In this context, a research objective is an operational statement stemming from a research question as part of a systematic process of enquiry. It is something that allows for a breakdown of the main purpose, or aim, of a given research project to be sequenced: how does a researcher organise their work?

If the research question is establishing the boundaries of a research project by defining what should be accomplished and by reflecting on what is to be expected, the research objectives are the steps you need to take in order to answer the research question. The objectives are phrased as individual statements, normally three or four of them, which more specifically identify a way to complete the research project (see Figure 4.6 on how to operationalise research at a glance). In the earlier case, what is the impact of a key imagery change on feelings and judgements for the 1990s iconic brand Abercrombie & Fitch (A&F) in a radical US re-think? There seems to be a basic necessity to understand feelings and judgements before an answer to the research question can be provided. A sensible research objective would be to investigate how feelings and judgements about brands are formed (Research Objective 1).

The use of precise and unambiguous verbs is extremely important as the research objectives must fit the overall purpose of the research, which in this example had been found to be descriptive in nature. In other words, there is little sense in setting explanatory research objectives to answer a research question whose general purpose is exploratory. Indeed, it is paramount not to lose track of the final goal and to build towards it. A further research objective in relation to the aforementioned study about Abercrombie & Fitch could be to characterise the relationship between US consumers and A&F (Research Objective 2).

Eventually, the researcher would edge progressively closer to the finishing line, and figure out that a third step could be to assess the potential influence of A&F ditching the use of

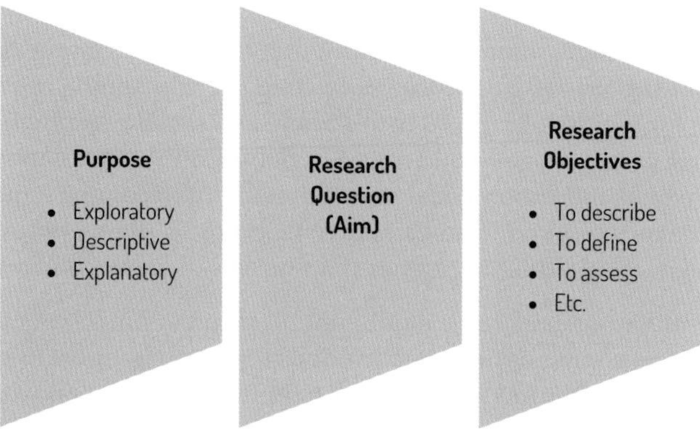

Figure 4.6 Operationalising research

its North American logo business (Research Objective 3). This is a realistic objective only because it is based on empirical evidence from recent marketing activity by the brand and what is known about branding theory. Furthermore, it ensures that the research question is articulated effectively and efficiently, thus making it possible to cover the journey back from interpreting the data to answering the research question.

Indeed, one of the most common mistakes made by young professionals, trainees and students, both at undergraduate and postgraduate level, is to set up a series of research objectives, each with a different research aim of its own, or, in other words, objectives that effectively refer to different research questions from the one they originally set out to deal with. There must be a thread ideally going from ontological considerations to research objectives; as pointed out in the previous paragraph, a researcher should be able to make the return trip when looking back at their data and their significance (see Part V for information on analysing findings as well as drawing conclusions and recommendations).

Chapter Summary

Conceptualising research throws up a number of challenges as it raises several key points for reflection and discussion. However, these very elements contribute to the richness of a piece of research by adding depth and detail to the way an issue, a problem, a phenomenon, a trend, and so on, is looked at and eventually understood. There is a voyage of discovery to be made, which starts from the necessary efforts one should make to get to grips with the nature of the reality around them. Summing up the various stages of the systematic process of marketing research covered so far, the following aspects should be uppermost in the minds of everyone involved in the discipline:

- ontology
- epistemology
- theory
- conceptual framework
- approach
- research purpose
- research question
- research objectives.

Although some readers might already feel as though things are getting rather complicated too fast, the truth of the matter is that the more time spent planning at the beginning of a research project or for a particular piece of academic assessment, the higher the probability of success – there is in fact a positive correlation between these two constructs. This is an opportunity for personal and professional development, for becoming a more accomplished individual and manager who understands and contributes to the world in an assertive way borne out of strategic critical thinking rather than hearsay, legends and anecdotes.

Therefore, a keen student of marketing should not be afraid to branch out into philosophical considerations when assessing options and avenues for an assignment, a proposal or a project. Critical reflection of this kind is only going to enhance the way in which we can create valid and reliable knowledge under a set of widely recognised and accepted systematic rules.

Case Study: Studying Visual Social Platforms Online

Sarah is a part-time student in her final year of an undergraduate marketing degree, which she has studied for while working for a Bentley car dealer. Robert is her dissertation project supervisor, a senior lecturer with prior experience in the sector and an interest in social media platforms. Together, they have already identified the rise in popularity of visual platforms like Pinterest and Instagram as an exciting topic for research, yet they do not seem to agree as to what to focus on. While Robert is keen to make connections with existing theoretical frameworks, Sarah wants to keep an open mind as to what is happening in this fast-growing area – the outcomes of information exchanges between organisations and Internet users are still not quite understood.

Reputation and brand image have been linked with sales; for instance, there is a wide body of evidence pointing at sales drops at times when companies struggle with their reputation and overall image. There is indeed a connection between reputation and image, too, and it is also fair to say that a corporate entity and its brands affect one another: in this particular instance, Robert is thinking about the influence of Volkswagen AG (a proven German automotive group) on Bentley (a traditional British stalwart). A picture is beginning to emerge, which can be described in a reasonable amount of detail, thus pointing to the existence of certain causal relationships, including the way visual social media platforms might contribute to eventual sales via reputation or image, as the latter essentially are yet another marketing communication channel at a company's disposal.

After some careful consideration, a model is crystallised that assumes that the popularity of Bentley on Pinterest, together with the reputation of its German owner, can have a positive effect on the brand's image and ultimately its sales (Harrysson et al., 2014). Constructs are by now being researched so that firmer representations of the possible dynamics between them can be prepared in the form of a set of hypotheses for testing. Further elements are still to be defined, but the overall feeling is that this is a viable piece of research to undertake.

However, Sarah does not share Robert's enthusiasm for this 'restrictive' approach as she is curious about the way Internet users interact with visual social media platforms in a more inclusive way, and what that may mean for a business like Bentley, which has an aura of exclusivity and still manages to attract the attention of such a wide-ranging set of audiences. She wonders what a platform like Instagram, Pinterest or Tumblr could add to the ongoing relationship between people and Bentley at a more emotional level.

The initial background research conducted to shed light on the topic from this viewpoint did not return a great deal of useful information or knowledge, although statistical data are available with regards to usage patterns, and it is clear that many companies are taking action to become proficient at making the best of these platforms. This should not mean that every organisation is bound to be involved with visual social media, yet an organisation like Bentley had better explore the overall idea of getting close(r) to people out there, in order to gauge the opportunities for more meaningful experiences to be had in the future.

In this respect, there is heightened awareness of the subjective nature of the research and that its interpretation may reveal unexpected themes and patterns. As such, the systematic process of research appears to call for an altogether different paradigm, making connections between the way individuals form opinions and attitudes, and what this may mean for Bentley as a brand.

Back at the office, Sarah is reviewing her notes before meeting with Robert; there is no single way to go about the research and, ultimately, the decision should be made considering what Bentley's requirements are – the business is seeing a lot of competition as more car manufacturers try to encroach their traditional space at the top end of the market (Kim and Trudell, 2014). The company does not have a problem per se, but there is definitely the potential to establish a more compelling direction for the future, starting from deciding what the role of visual social media platforms could be. Both researchers know and agree that the quality of the process is paramount: any badly written proposal or badly executed study is guaranteed to yield no contribution to existing knowledge about any topic.

(Continued)

(Continued)

Case study questions:

1. What are the key components of the two studies in relation to the material presented in this chapter?
2. How would you depict the conceptualisations of each project, considering the role of theory and Sarah and Robert's ability to specify a model?
3. What would be the pros and cons of each piece of research for an organisation like Bentley, and more in general?
4. Why could one say that a positivist and an interpretive stance are equally useful to the modern marketing professional?

End of Chapter Questions

These questions should help you reflect on your understanding of this chapter:

1. What are the key reasons for marketing research to challenge complexity?
2. How can the nature of being (ontology) be described?
3. What are some valid ways to generate new knowledge through marketing research?
4. What is the simplest way to define a marketing research paradigm?
5. Why is a conceptual framework important for a marketing research project?
6. What difference is there between normative and applied ethics?
7. What kind of approaches can be adopted in marketing research, and why?
8. What are the relationships between a research question and research objectives?

Checklist

After studying Chapter 4, you should now be familiar with these key concepts:

1. The nature of reality
2. How knowledge can be generated using marketing research
3. The relationship between theory and marketing research
4. What a research design is made of
5. How to identify the purpose/aim of marketing research

Further Reading (in sequence from beginners to advanced)

Grover, R. and Vriens, M. (2006) *The Handbook of Marketing Research: Uses, Misuses and Future Advances*. Thousand Oaks, CA: Sage Publications.

Pascale, R. T. (1984) Perspectives on strategy: the real story behind Honda's success. *California Management Review*, 26 (3), pp. 47–72.

Research Methodology (2016) Inductive approach [online]. Available at: http://research-methodology.net/research-methodology/research-approach/inductive-approach-2 [Accessed 1 May 2016].

Hunt, S. D. and Hansen, J. M. (2008) The philosophical foundations of marketing research: for scientific realism and truth. *Belk College of Business* [online]. Available at: http://belkcollegeofbusiness.uncc.edu/jaredhansen/Research/Scientific%20Realism%20and%20Truth.pdf

Cunliffe, A. L. (2011) Crafting qualitative research: Morgan and Smircich 30 years on. *Organizational Research Methods*, 14 (4), pp. 647–73.

Guillemin, M. and Gillam, L. (2004) Ethics, reflexivity, and 'ethically important moments' in research. *Qualitative Inquiry*, 10 (2), pp. 261–80.

Bibliography

Arnold, M. J. and Reynolds, K. E. (2003) Hedonic shopping motivation. *Journal of Retailing*, 79 (2), pp. 77–95.

Atkinson, P. and Coffey, A. (2004) Analysing documentary realities. In D. Silverman (ed.) *Qualitative Research: Theory, Methods and Practice* (2nd edition). London: Sage Publications.

Bargar, R. R. and Duncan, J. K. (1981) Cultivating creative endeavor in doctoral research. *The Journal of Higher Education*, 53 (1), pp. 1–31.

Bendapudi, N. and Leone, R.P. (2002) Managing business-to-business customer relationships following key contact employee turnover in a vendor firm. *Journal of Marketing*, 66 (2), pp. 83–101.

Birkner, C. (2014) Losing the label. American Marketing Association, *Marketing News* [online, August]. Available at: www.ama.org/publications/MarketingNews/Pages/losing-the-label.aspx [Accessed 25 August 2014].

Blaikie, N. (2000) *Designing Social Research*. Cambridge: Polity Press.

Brookes, R. and Palmer, R. (2003) *The New Global Marketing Reality*. Basingstoke: Palgrave Macmillan.

Bryman, A. and Bell, E. (2011) *Business Research Methods* (3rd edition). Oxford: Oxford University Press.

Burns, M. (2014) Why brands are un-friending Facebook to follow Twitter. *Marketing* [online, 14 August]. Available at: www.marketingmagazine.co.uk/article/1307727/why-brands-un-friending-facebook-follow-twitter [Accessed 25 August 2014].

Chia, R. (2002) The production of management knowledge: philosophical underpinnings of research design. In D. Partington (ed.) *Essential Skills for Management Research* (pp. 1–19). London: Sage Publications.

Creswell, J. (2002) *Qualitative, Quantitative and Mixed Methods Approaches* (2nd edition). Thousand Oaks, CA: Sage Publications.

Cunliffe, A. L. (2011) Crafting qualitative research: Morgan and Smircich 30 years on. *Organizational Research Methods*, 14 (4), pp. 647–73.

Dvir, D., Raz, T. and Shenhar, A. J. (2003) An empirical analysis of the relationship between project planning and project success. *International Journal of Project Management*, 21 (2), pp. 89–95.

Gallo, C. (2011) Wow your customers the Ritz-Carlton way. *Forbes* [online, 23 February]. Available at: www.forbes.com/sites/carminegallo/2011/02/23/wow-your-customers-the-ritz-carlton-way [Accessed 23 July 2014].

Guillemin, M. and Gillam, L. (2004) Ethics, reflexivity, and 'ethically important moments' in research. *Qualitative Inquiry*, 10 (2), pp. 261–80.

Harrysson, M., Métayer, E. and Sarrazin, H. (2014) The strength of the 'weak signals'. *McKinsey Quarterly* [online, February]. Available at: www.mckinsey.com/Insights/High_Tech_Telecoms_Internet/The_strength_of_weak_signals?cid=other-eml-alt-mkq-mck-oth-1402 [Accessed 20 September 2014].

Hines, K. (2014) How brands successfully leverage visual social media platforms. *iacquire social media* [online, 8 May]. Available at: www.iacquire.com/blog/how-brands-successfully-leverage-visual-social-media-platforms [Accessed 20 September 2014].

IKEA (2012) IKEA's focus on its customers brings outstanding results for 2012. *IKEA News Room* [online]. Available at: www.ikea.com/gb/en/about_ikea/newsitem/buisness_results_fy12 [Accessed 23 July 2014].

Keller, K. L. (2010) Brand equity management in a multichannel, multimedia retail environment. *Journal of Interactive Marketing*, 24 (2), pp. 58–70.

Keller, K. L. (2013) *Strategic Brand Management: Building, Measuring and Managing Brand Equity* (Global Edition). Hoboken, NJ: Pearson.

Kim, R. and Trudell, C. (2014) Bentley sees $272,000 cars facing mounting competition in Korea. *Bloomberg* [online, 18 September]. Available at: www.bloomberg.com/news/2014-09-18/bentley-sees-272-000-cars-facing-mounting-competition-in-korea.html [Accessed 20 September 2014].

Kochhar, A. (2010) P&O cruise ship Azura has high tastes on the high seas with celebrity chef Atul Kochhar. *Mail Online* [Online, 23 February]. Available at: www.dailymail.co.uk/travel/article-1252046/P-O-cruise-ship-Azura-high-tastes-high-seas-celebrity-chef-Atul-Kochhar.html [Accessed 20 September 2014].

Leszinski, R. and Marn, M. V. (1997) Setting value, not price. *McKinsey Quarterly* [online, February]. Available at: www.mckinsey.com/insights/marketing_sales/setting_value_not_price [Accessed 29 July 2014].

Linshi, J. (2014) Here's why Abercrombie & Fitch is ditching its logos. *Time* [online, 28 August]. Available at: http://time.com/3210312/abercrombie-fitch-logos-clothing-business [Accessed 30 August 2014].

MaRS (2009) Identifying market problems: building products to meet customers' needs. *MaRS Library* [online, 6 December]. Available at: www.marsdd.com/mars-library/identifying-market-problems [Accessed 1 May 2016].

Matthews, B. and Ross, L. (2010) *Research Methods: A Practical Guide for the Social Sciences*. Harlow: Pearson Education.

Parsons, R. (2014) Co-op Bank readies major brand push to highlight values. *Marketing Week* [online, 22 August]. Available at: www.marketingweek.co.uk/sectors/financial/news/co-op-bank-readies-major-brand-push-to-highlight-values/4011458.article [Accessed 25 August 2014].

Paternoster, L. (2011) Model of world class service. *Institute of Customer Service* [online, 9 March]. Available at: www.instituteofcustomerservice.com/1848-6942/Model-for-World-Class-Service.html [Accessed 23 July 2014].

Queen's University Belfast (n.d.) Research proposal: aims and objectives. School of Education [online]. Available at: www.qub.ac.uk/schools/SchoolofEducation/Research/DoctoralResearchCentre/PhD/TheResearchProposal/ResearchProposal-AimsandObjectives [Accessed 1 September 2014].

Robarts, S. (2014) What's the point of a curved TV? *New Atlas* [online, 11 December]. Available at: http://newatlas.com/curved-tv-benefits/34689/ [Accessed 3 January 2015]

Snieder, R. and Larner, K. (2009) *The Art of Being a Scientist: A Guide for Graduate Students and their Mentors*. Cambridge: Cambridge University Press.

Teddlie, C. and Tashakkori, A. (2009) *Foundations of Mixed Methods Research: Integrating Quantitative and Qualitative Approaches in the Social and Behavioral Sciences*. Thousand Oaks, CA: Sage Publications.

Walter, E. (2014) Why marketers love Instagram and Pinterest. *Fast Company* [online, 19 May]. Available at: www.fastcompany.com/3030677/why-seasoned-marketers-are-looking-to-newer-tools-like-instagram-and-pinterest [Accessed 20 September 2014].

Find journal articles and multiple choice questions online at: **https://study.sagepub.com/benzo** to support what you've learnt so far.

CHAPTER 5

Marketing Research Designs

LEARNING OBJECTIVES

The key learning objectives of this chapter are:

1. To define key features of feasible marketing research
2. To understand the systematic implementation of conceptual frameworks
3. To justify suitable research designs in a variety of contexts
4. To reflect on symmetry in research and its significance

KEY CONCEPTS

By the end of this chapter, the reader should be familiar with the following concepts:

1. The route from research question to research design
2. Recognising limitations in research
3. Qualitative and quantitative research
4. Single-, multiple- and mixed-method research
5. The relationship between research objectives and findings
6. Comparing and contrasting secondary and primary research
7. Answering a research question
8. The role of recommendations and implementation in marketing research

Riccardo Benzo

Introduction

Planning marketing research is a challenging activity that rests on a researcher's ability to organise their work in as much detail, and with as much clarity, as possible. In other words, students and practitioners should in the first instance attempt to think carefully about the nature of the reality they are observing in order to distil down a viable research question and articulate the necessary research steps. Ultimately, we should generate a valid and reliable answer for the research question itself. Having begun setting out a systematic process of research for marketing purposes in Chapter 4, the following pages deal with the remaining parts of this journey.

Therefore, this chapter looks to define several practical aspects of marketing research, such as resources and limitations, while tackling methodological issues regarding the selection of appropriate research designs in relation to a particular aim or purpose. The use of either qualitative research or quantitative research is going to be discussed first, touching on single- and multiple-method designs, and then debating the potential for using these two together in a mixed-method research design.

The systematic process of marketing research is then unpacked further by taking additional steps to close the ideal loop that links findings with research objectives and, ultimately, research objectives with the research question. This is consistent with previous indications that research objectives should be seen as a way to operationalise a research question, thus being directly related to it. The ensuing discussion also offers opportunities for further integration between primary data and secondary data as newly created knowledge is compared and contrasted with existing knowledge, especially with regards to any theoretical and/or conceptual frameworks (premise) a researcher might have been working from.

Once more, it is important to bear in mind that marketing research is an iterative process and more detailed information about how to come up with a feasible research design should always be sought by moving forwards and backwards between the different phases of an assignment or brief. This book helps you in this quest by providing further material in Chapter 7 (Qualitative Research Methods) and Chapter 12 (Quantitative Research Methodology) as well as Part V (Reporting Marketing Research). Ensure you consult these sections as well as the book's online resources to support your learning.

Snapshot: Meaningful Selections in Marketing Research

The premise of integrated marketing communications is that the coherent, consistent, continuous and complementary use of a range of methods, tools, channels, techniques and media tends to deliver better results than the same methods, tools, and so on, would achieve separately. This 'is about connecting a brand truth with a real human emotion' (Benady, n.d.). One of the issues of integrated marketing communications is that being focused on such a holistic view might make it hard to distinguish what method, tool, channel, technique and medium does what in terms of helping deliver specific marketing objectives.

Within this context, researchers are likely to be able to come up with several compelling research questions; however, there are a number of considerations to be made as restrictions will invariably affect what can realistically be achieved. For a start, there must be a concern as to whether or not a research question is logically connected with existing knowledge and fits a chosen conceptual framework. Nike has invested large sums of money in integrated marketing communications around the Olympics using ambush/guerrilla tactics. For instance, although the brand chose not to be a sponsor during London 2012, its 'Find Your Greatness' campaign included substantial TV advertising and online exposure, such as on Twitter, throughout the duration of the event.

Indeed, there may be reasons to want to study such behaviour both from a practical and an academic standpoint – the general purpose being to try and understand what the outcomes of guerrilla tactics might have been for Nike and, perhaps, how these compare with what the official global sponsor, Adidas, achieved through its marketing investment in the event. There is some evidence that consumers were confused as to which brand was actually involved with the event, raising the question as to how this might affect perceptions of a number of marketing-related concepts such as opinions, attitudes and trust.

Now imagine that, following a thorough critical literature review, a student has come up with the following research question for their undergraduate dissertation: What is the long-term impact of Nike's online guerrilla tactics as implemented during the London 2012 Olympics?

Although it appears to be connected with the aforementioned purpose, it would be wise to reflect on how a specific activity, or set of activities, can be isolated and examined in detail. Further, researching the past is generally a hard thing to achieve as people might no longer have clear recollections of facts, feelings and perceptions.

Resources, Commitment and Contribution

The use of secondary sources of information (data) and their critical analysis (see Chapter 3 for more detail on this topic) is a defining step on the way to drafting research questions (see Figure 4.6). However, the fact that one can arrive at a research question and even articulate that into a few research objectives does not mean that a piece of research would ultimately be viable.

Before we get to operationalise research projects, it is advisable to undergo some important reflection on the following aspects of research: resources, commitment and contribution.

Resources

Both practitioners and students frequently assume that once they have identified a problem, an issue, a phenomenon, a pattern, and so on, it is possible to generate relevant knowledge about it. At this point, the resources have to be listed out and checked:

- budget
- time
- access
- expertise
- equipment
- support (e.g. management, supervision).

Some of the main mistakes made by marketing research agencies are related to pricing, revenue generation and profitability. Scoping out a piece of research needs to be realistic;

under-pricing the services one provides is never a good idea as funds will eventually run out and research outcomes may even cease to be viable/attainable. The issue of time, instead, is proving to be tricky both in absolute and relative terms. While a student might worry about the number of weeks they have to complete and submit an assignment, the importance of the various phases in such an endeavour is, in many instances, overlooked. In other words, planning is generally where researchers should spend relatively more time than they think is needed before they set off collecting data and, even more so, writing. Furthermore, they should not see the systematic process of marketing research as a linear sequence of steps; it is likely that two or more stages will run simultaneously (see Figure 5.1).

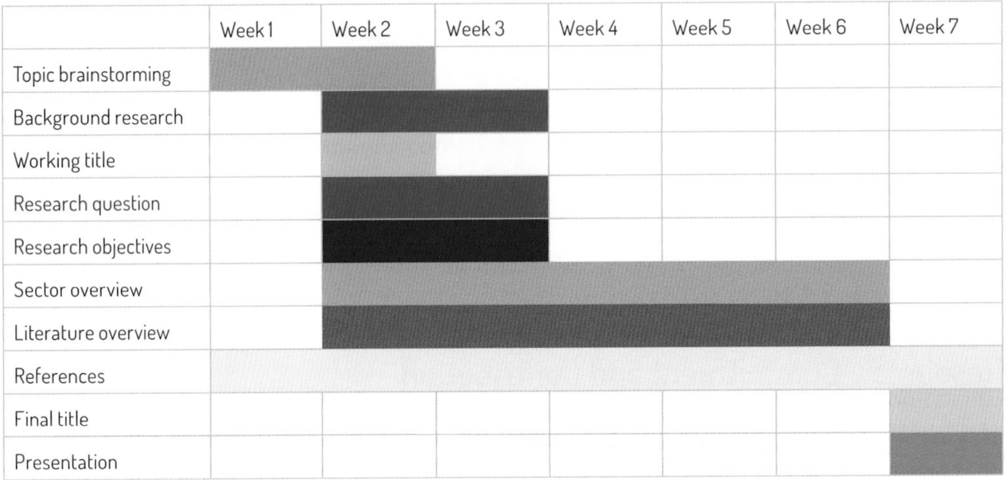

	Week 1	Week 2	Week 3	Week 4	Week 5	Week 6	Week 7
Topic brainstorming							
Background research							
Working title							
Research question							
Research objectives							
Sector overview							
Literature overview							
References							
Final title							
Presentation							

Figure 5.1 Marketing research timeline example

Anticipating certain needs and bringing forward particular aspects of a project can be the difference between success and failure – for instance, gaining access to a specific population sample should be a consideration in the early days of a project (see Chapter 6 for more information on sampling techniques). Let's assume that a piece of research has been commissioned to understand the views of Chief Marketing Officers (CMOs) on how Toyota, Volkswagen and other car manufacturers could recover from the impact of scandals concerning their reputations. Targeting such a group of high-powered, busy individuals would definitely be challenging, so appointments should be scheduled early on to give everyone enough advance notice. If the research was to be undertaken under the auspices of a well-known professional association, such as the Chartered Institute of Marketing, chances are that getting hold of such individuals would be easier and quicker than if an agency were to run the same research independently, for instance to publish a white paper.

Even though marketing research professionals would tend to disagree, the issue of expertise is just as important in the practical field as it is in the academic world. It would be presumptuous to believe that an individual is able to master all there is to know about methodological concerns. As such, people could find themselves needing help with research design, data collection, data analysis and reporting. This could take the form of suggestions from more experienced colleagues, expert advice from an industry or an academic authority in a particular area and/or access to modern equipment, such as software, online and mobile applications. Finally, it is important to have a support structure in place for all types of research and at all levels – as an instructor, a tutor or lecturer for undergraduate and postgraduate students, a mentor for an intern or a manager for a research executive. Developing a two-way or many-way communication network is the ultimate goal as this would provide a platform for sharing practice and information as well as ensuring dialogue and debate.

Ethics: Further Support in Marketing Research

No matter the size of a marketing research assignment, a project requiring the collection and the handling of data is to conform to ethical principles and guidelines. Universities set their own specific standards and procedures, typically aiming at ensuring that there is a full justification for the suggested process and that access to the information considers confidentiality and privacy, including sharing and storage. In the case of human respondents, their rights, such as anonymity, and, eventually, their informed consent should be carefully considered and handled – respondents should not be at any risk when sharing their views with researchers.

Marketing research in the academic field is also regulated by the institutions that provide funding and guidance such as the Economic and Social Research Council (ESRC) in the UK and the Indian Council of Social Science Research (ICSSR): principles, procedures and minimum requirements are detailed out and organised in governance systems generally tied with useful tools such as an initial 'checklist' to help researchers identify whether a complete application for ethics approval is to be submitted. Professional bodies also exist to regulate the activities of market and marketing research agencies and practitioners all over the world. ESOMAR, the World Association for Social, Opinion and Market Research, comprises individual, corporate, honorary, academic, association and affiliate members including, amongst others, the Associação Brasileira das Empresas de Pesquisa (ABEP) in Brazil, the Marketing Research and Intelligence Association (MRIA) in Canada and the Market Research Society (MRS) in the UK. Further, the industry as a whole has now been able to increase transparency and consistency with the adoption of the international standard ISO 20252, which refers to the way 'market research studies are planned, carried out, supervised and reported to clients commissioning such projects' (International Standards Organisation, 2006).

It appears to be wise to start by allocating funds to ideas that are likely to improve competitive advantage and sustain growth rather than to continue pouring money into the same areas without reflecting on the outcomes. There is indeed a potent argument in favour of the practical rather than the flashy, i.e. covering the areas that are doing well and those where clear potential for development can be identified.

Commitment

Symmetry in research holds that the outcome of research is valuable because the process is systematic

Besides the aforementioned research-enabling aspects resulting from the availability of sufficient resources, the amount of passion one has for a subject and, more to the point, a specific piece of work is an important, if not necessary, driver to overcome any difficulty in answering a research question. In other words, the fact that something can be researched does not mean that it will be researched. Typically, researchers feel more strongly about certain areas of knowledge for which they have an affinity and some form of personal interest. This is generally the case for a marketing manager trying to develop some dynamic capability within an organisation by aiming to understand the psychology of buying for their customers; projects with organisational 'buy-in' also tend to be approved and carried out in full more often than those without backing.

Contribution

There is a further element that should be considered in relation to the feasibility of marketing research: its overall contribution to knowledge. No matter the type of research endeavour, i.e. basic or applied (see Chapter 1 for more detail), identifying issues before they become problems, solving problems together with their causes, understanding phenomena about the world around us, taking advantage of opportunities and fending off threats can all be regarded as ways to generate new knowledge. In other words, any piece of marketing research should be measured against its ability to provide additional knowledge using a recognised approach, something valid and reliable.

Symmetry in Marketing Research

A reliable research process forms the basis of symmetry in marketing research. This is equivalent to stating that one's research outcomes will be of value whatever they happen to be as long as the process adopted is sound. Let's take an organisation interested in gauging the impact of mediated marketing communications in the fast-moving consumer goods public relations arena. On the basis of previous applications of blogging in this context – for instance, this was the case for L'Oréal and their 'Journal de ma Peau' campaign in 2005 – one would expect a negative reaction to a company trying to influence consumer perceptions by using this specific PR medium. This assumption could be likened to a hypothesis and, as such, tested (see Chapter 11 for more information) by collecting and analysing the appropriate quantitative data. The result could indicate that consumers do not necessarily have an aversion to this type of communication, provided that it is not being passed for something that it is not; for instance, this would be the case for an organisation pretending that one of its blogs has been written by independent sources. From a purely technical standpoint, such findings would not be a problem as long as the researcher has followed a systematic path for hypothesis testing (see 'Deduction' in Figure 5.2). It is simply that the observed sample does not behave as expected.

The same would be true when using inductive reasoning (see Chapter 4 for details), i.e. when looking to make sense of a subjective reality through an interpretive stance. Social media have been re-shaping the nature of marketing relationships for almost ten years now; in spite of this, research in the field is still comparatively limited, especially in light of the 'foundational' nature of communications systems in society (Breakenridge, 2008: 132). This describes a trend whereby many areas have been subject to radical change, but we can only guess at the actual breadth and depth of this shift. In this respect, it should be possible to list out some initial themes for inquiry, yet there could be new themes, and categories within these themes, emerging from the research (see Chapter 10 for more information about qualitative data analysis). In other words, one could find out that more elements than expected happen to be relevant in the chosen context. In technical terms, this means that one's ability to imagine a conceptualisation of the reality under observation has simply been proved insufficient. The research participants have raised more question marks as to what has been going on, which would then need to be taken into account.

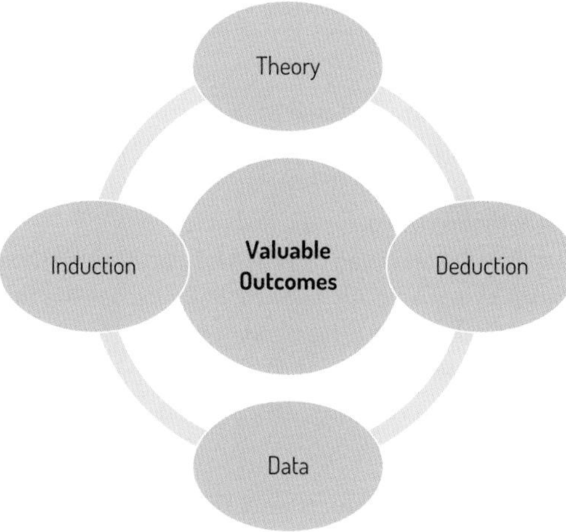

Figure 5.2 Symmetric outcomes in marketing research

Recognising Limitations

This brings us closer to realising and admitting (first to ourselves) that research projects have intrinsic limitations that practitioners and students must be aware of. The systematic process of marketing research is what we ought to be respecting at all times. As long as there is a sound, iterative plan in place, valid and reliable knowledge will be produced – it may only apply in a limited context, that is.

Research in Practice: 'Self-Selection' Limitation

During the last recession, many organisations noticed rather different consumption patterns, which have been shaping the way in which they market their offerings today. Insurance providers found out that 'selective perception' was having an impact on their target audiences' habits (Baker, 2007: 229). Existing and prospective customers needed to be profiled again in order to ensure that meaningful propositions were still being made to them. Extensive secondary research would have to be conducted to define those which appeared to be key variables in the decision-making process relating to purchasing insurance services. The sample population would then have to be made up of consumers who were either primary or co-decision makers. Given the rather large scope of such projects and their projected duration, data collection would be organised online to allow respondents to complete surveys at their own leisure. This segmentation process would provide robust insight through the use of statistical analysis (see Chapters 13 and 14 for further information), yet there would be cause for some concern.

If online surveys have been proved to be a rather efficient and cost-effective method at reaching target audiences and bringing back data speedily, the lack of face-to-face contact with the respondents does present researchers with the issue of self-selection bias, or problems resulting from the fact that respondents are entirely able to decide whether or not to participate in a survey by themselves. This may lead to outgoing and vocal individuals being over-represented, with the result that the overall findings would not necessarily

(Continued)

(Continued)

be representative of the target population. The same could be true because a respondent's propensity for taking part in a study has been shown to be positively correlated with the interest (and perhaps the knowledge) they have in a specific topic. Once again, this may bring about skewed results as less opinionated and less experienced subjects would rule themselves out in the first place.

There is a need to assess the situation in an objective fashion. Online surveys definitely have a place amongst data collection techniques in marketing research; however, one has to be aware of their potential limitations and ensure that these are dealt with either by adjusting them (at data collection level) or by making adjustments later on (at data analysis level).

In short, in presenting findings, conclusions and recommendations (see Part V for a more extensive treatment of these topics), it is sensible practice to point out as many limitations as possible – these might indeed cover resources, commitment and contribution. Also, it makes sense to highlight any effort that has been made to minimise the impact of such shortcomings and/or to overcome them, if at all possible. No one piece of marketing research can be perfect and proposing solutions to gaps that might be present contributes to improving the solidity of the process itself and the credibility of the researchers as well as that of the data.

What cannot be done today, whatever the reason, may be done in the future. In this respect, any lack in scope or detail of a given piece of work can be remedied with further research. It is possible to deal with two research questions, one at a time; we will shortly see that it is also possible to deal with complexity by employing multiple or mixed methods. What is not possible is arriving at valid, reliable and even generalisable research outcomes without a systematic process of marketing research in place.

Organising Research Projects

As the road to answering a research question becomes clearer, researchers are confronted with the need to identify a workable design to fit with the general purpose of the project itself: exploratory, descriptive or explanatory (see Chapter 4 and Parts III and IV for additional information). It is important to answer questions about the underlying approach to research, its relationship to theory and its potential limitations, in order for the systematic process of marketing research to continue building on itself in a virtuous cycle (see Figure 5.3).

A specific topic like the impact of customer misbehaviour on how an organisation might develop offerings appears to be influenced by its subjective nature: each customer is different and they might misbehave in radically different ways. This might lead a researcher to adopt an interpretive stance and, as a result of that, an inductive approach to exploring this area. The development of the 'Events' feature in Facebook is an example of this kind of situation as the company noticed users 'friending' classes, fraternities and other types of group entities that had regular social events, such as reunions and parties. This unusual and clearly unexpected behaviour pushed Facebook to respond to a sort of subconscious need: this was made possible through pattern observation.

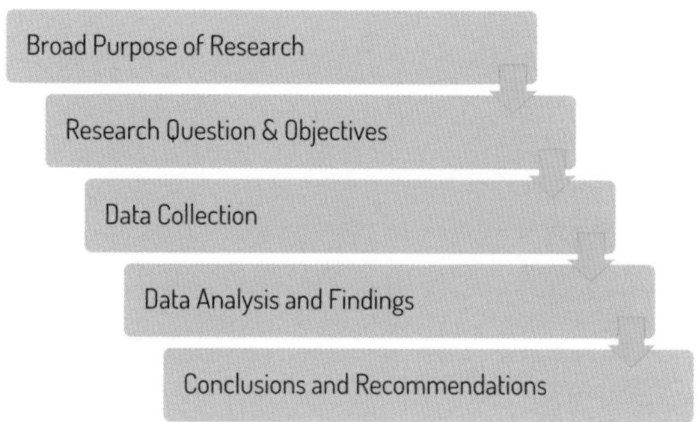

Figure 5.3 From purpose to conclusions in marketing research

Qualitative research

Developing such a project requires qualitative data to define, delineate and depict a particular experience and, as a result of specific analytic work, to arrive at some sort of substantive theory that can help characterise a phenomenon, an issue, and so on (see 'Theory and Marketing Research' in Chapter 4). Non-numerical data, as qualitative data are often referred to, generally provide a platform to unearth previously ignored meaning within interactions between different actors and variables in a chosen environment. Qualitative research is understood to be a rather wide-ranging collection of methods (see Part III for more detail), for example participant observation and focus groups, which are primarily, but not exclusively, used to conduct exploratory research.

Within this tradition, due consideration and reflection must be paid to the researcher, to research perspectives, research strategies, methods for collection and analysis and interpretation, as there is undoubtedly a blurring of lines between different methodological concepts and ideas, especially in the field of practice; companies are driven by being better at marketing and they tend to be rather matter-of-fact in their pursuit of sustainability over time.

This is why experience, in the form of assumptions, is often used in business, with a view to providing ready-made justifications for decision making. Marketing research should be considered as an empowering instrument that can verify these long-held beliefs by using a systematic process of inquiry. Numerical data can therefore be collected and analysed to determine whether or not certain ideas have foundation, given the external (business environment) and internal (marketing assets) conditions experienced by a company. Quantitative research (see Part IV for more detail) adopts a scientific position to conduct studies.

Quantitative research

The typical fields of scrutiny for quantitative research are either descriptive or explanatory (Mazzocchi, 2008). With the former, research essentially attempts to provide valid and reliable descriptions of issues, phenomena, and so forth, through basic statistical analysis, while the latter seeks to arrive at relevant explanations for particular problems, trends, and so on, by making comparisons, establishing relationships or assessing causality using quantitative variables (i.e. categories or numbers that can be counted).

Reflective Activity

- What do you perceive as your 'strengths' and 'weaknesses' in terms of research skills?
- What kind of marketing topic would lend itself more naturally to be studied using qualitative research?
- What is the main difference between qualitative and quantitative data?
- What assumptions about marketing-related topics that you hold could be tested through the collection and analysis of quantitative data?

Research Designs

Quantitative research is a systematic process of investigation that seeks to test theory through the use of statistics

Qualitative research and quantitative research are not mutually exclusive; they can be used individually or together as parts of large projects. In fact, primary research as a whole is only a part of what is available to researchers in their quest to answer questions about marketing, by and large. The presence of and ease-of-access to large amounts of data have made decision making for marketing purposes more nimble, whereby a good analyst might be able to use secondary data to complete a task, thus combining existing information into new knowledge. This would be the case for a PR agency pitching its business to a prospective client, having only a limited amount of time to determine the right balance between their and the target company's values, for instance. A straightforward piece of desk research using the Internet, industry databases such as FAME and other published sources of information would most likely generate an answer to a research question borne out of this kind of need.

In other instances, many marketing problems will require ad hoc research activity to be carried out. In this respect, we can categorise research designs involving the collection of primary data according to three typologies:

- single method
- multiple method
- mixed method.

Single-method research

Single-method research is based on the use of either a qualitative or a quantitative data collection method. This is a straightforward option, which is applicable when it is possible to conceptualise a marketing issue in clear yet contained terms. Let's assume that Ecover, the manufacturer of environmentally friendly household products, is interested in understanding the drivers of attitudes and personal and cultural factors that influence consumers in their purchases of environmentally friendly products. Ajzen's Theory of Planned Behaviour (Kalafatis et al., 1999) provides a solid premise to do so; a deductive approach to research can thus be chosen and appropriate quantitative data collected using a survey. Specific hypotheses can be set up and tested to establish what kind of associations might exist between some of the variables observed in the process. Findings are then presented and linked back to the research objectives; eventually, a conclusion is arrived at which should address the key research question.

Research in Practice: The Issue of Time – Cross-Sectional and Longitudinal Studies

In spite of the vast majority of research, especially that undertaken by undergraduate and postgraduate students, occurring within a rather limited time horizon, choosing a suitable research design might indeed entail decisions about collecting data in one go or at certain intervals. This is the difference between cross-sectional and longitudinal designs. The former are characterised by what can be considered research at a single point in time, with quantitative or qualitative data gathered until a sufficient number of cases has been attained; an example is the case of a customer satisfaction survey at US mobile provider Verizon Wireless.

Conversely, a longitudinal design puts emphasis on collecting data at intervals over time, such as in a panel survey whereby questionnaires are administered to a specific sample – a panel – at regular intervals, such as a GESIS panel. Although it is more resource-intensive, a longitudinal study can shed more light on causal relationships as changes of opinions, attitudes and behaviour can be examined more thoroughly at different points in time using the same sample.

A large majority of undergraduate projects, such as final-year dissertations, can be dealt with by following the single-method route. It is relatively simple to frame an issue, problem or phenomenon in such a way that a single-method research design allows researchers to make sense of what they are observing. This could be the case for someone interested in understanding the process of internationalisation of Moroccan Argan oil producers due to a witnessing of the growth in the use of this ingredient in personal-care products in the USA between 2007 and 2011 (Johannes, 2012). Realistically, it would be hard to come up with a single prediction based on one of the existing theories of internationalisation, for instance the Uppsala model; however, the existence of several options could lead to setting up an exploratory study based on qualitative data collected via an in-depth interview method using a sample of the aforementioned producers (see Chapter 6 for more detail on sampling). In other words, the researcher would aim to identify some patterns in the way these companies approach international expansion to figure out whether this could fit any of the existing theories, or point them in a new direction altogether.

Any type of single-method design is, therefore, useful as it gives practitioners the ability to generate knowledge for better decision making in marketing, especially at a tactical level, i.e. when there is a need to improve the implementation of a long-term plan (marketing strategy) in a relatively timely manner. Nonetheless, there may be situations calling for more comprehensive structures to be put in place.

Multiple-method research

Multiple-method research essentially advocates the use of more than one data collection method in order to answer a research question; this design has become more popular in recent years, yet it needs to be treated carefully as it may push the boundaries discussed earlier in this chapter with regards to resources (Curran and Blackburn, 2001). In essence, it is about combining different, but still either quantitative or qualitative only, data collection techniques.

If a retailer, like Primark, wanted to gauge the responses to particular in-store stimuli, it could employ the work of Mehrabian and Russel (1974) to build a prediction of the emotional impact of these inputs and their effect on consumer behaviour by using the Stimulus-Organism-Response (SOR) and Pleasure-Arousal-Dominance (PAD) models as proposed by the authors. These concepts would help formulate hypotheses in order to anticipate possible results with regards to the influence of atmospherics on people visiting the company outlets. However, obtaining meaningful data from shoppers might prove rather complicated given the general inability of human beings to remember facts clearly some time after experiences occur. In other words, it might be wise to combine a survey with quantitative observation to compare and contrast recollections and behaviours – what people say they do and what people actually do.

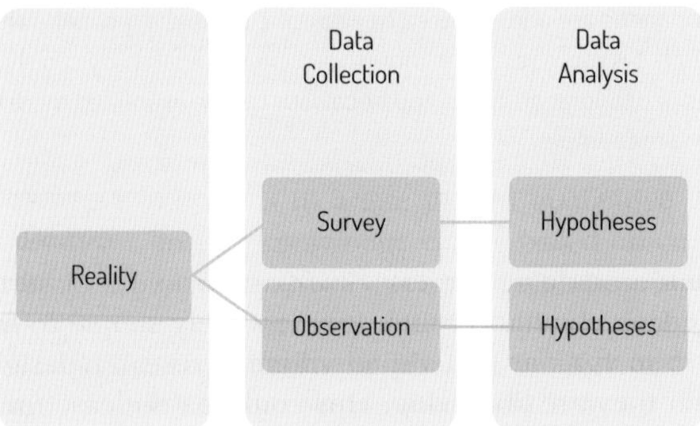

Figure 5.4 Testing hypotheses with multiple quantitative methods

In other words, hypotheses might be tested more thoroughly through the use of two (or even more in some cases) data collection methods and their independent evaluation (see Figure 5.4): is there any fundamental similarity or difference that should be taken into account when discussing the potential generalisability of findings further? By using multiple methods, it may be possible to advocate a point more strongly, or highlight some weakness in a theory's ability to explain the behaviour of a certain group of people.

Qualitative methods could equally be brought together to provide a more robust characterisation of the reality under scrutiny as a researcher tries to improve the validity and reliability in their work. Managing word-of-mouth in marketing communications has indeed proved extremely hard as organisations strive to understand what opinion leaders are made of and what makes them attractive to others in the first place. For instance, Rolex is a well-known brand with a specific brand identity built around 'excellence, performance, prestige and innovation'. As such, it could make sense for it to come up with a profile for opinion leaders in the sector who might be influencing its target audiences; this could be done by conducting semi-structured interviews and focus groups (see Chapter 8 for more detail) with Rolex owners and watch enthusiasts alike to ascertain what a credible source of information – one that consumers would trust – looks like and how this eventually impacts on consumer decision making from information search to post-purchase evaluation. This type of multiple-method design, or any type of design for that matter, can be made more comprehensive through the adoption of different planes of analysis, for example thematic or narrative (refer to 'Data Analysis' in Table 5.1 later on in this chapter).

Research in Practice: Not Just Triangulation

It is quite common to hear researchers talking about triangulation when they employ multiple or mixed methods. However, this term often indicates a general concern with internal, external and/or construct validity. Greene, Caracelli and Graham offer a more comprehensive view of those factors which researchers should consider in order to justify and support their choice of research design involving the use of more than one method with linkages between them – in other words, expansion and complementarity may be seen as purposes/objectives of triangulation as well as goals in their own right (1989: 259):

- triangulation
- complementarity
- development
- initiation
- expansion.

The rationale for undergoing a project involving more than one method could be linked to a need for extra scope in the investigation (expansion), whereby each and every method brings back data with regards to a particular element of the study.

Let's imagine that Holiday Inn would like to develop its hotel offerings; in doing so, it could use interviews, observations, suggestion cards, and so on, to look into the core benefits, basic products and expected products. It would essentially try and re-define the various 'product levels' based on the assumption that customers change over time, i.e. display selective perception. This process clearly offers the highest level of flexibility as many methods can be applied to try and satisfy the requirement of such a task.

Similarly, different methods can help define or re-define the direction (initiation) for research as well as discover new ideas, concepts, thoughts and perspectives. A report by Beehive Research (Barnett, 2014), based on the use of quantitative and qualitative methods, showed that new approaches to retention-based marketing would have to be put in place to overcome a general sense of mistrust when it comes to enticing existing customers to stay in relationship with a brand. Testing hypotheses about messages revealed that many companies do not provide enough benefits to engender loyalty.

Different methods can also be used in a sequence (development) in order to build on their individual strengths, or, in other words, to try and initiate a virtuous cycle of research whereby the outcomes from what is implemented first are applied to inform the main aspects of the next method to be employed. Another possibility is to apply qualitative and quantitative methods to attain an in-depth understanding of a phenomenon (complementary) or even of some components only; interactivity in such circumstances tends to produce more compelling findings and analysis.

This effectively means that triangulation in itself is not as commonly used as one might assume from all the talk about it because it entails a 'logic of convergence', so that the selected quantitative and qualitative methods have inherently different strengths and weaknesses in relation to the contribution they can make to the specific study at hand.

It is also possible to frame the use of multiple methods within the general purposes of research: exploratory, descriptive and explanatory. For instance, different sections in a topic guide could be used to straddle between exploring (semi-structured or unstructured interview) and describing (structured interview) a particular issue or pattern as long as the research objectives are respected. Indeed, coming up with an appropriate research design may require a number of iterative cycles to ensure many perspectives are considered, and even broader viewpoints included.

Mixed-method research

Mixed-method research allows researchers to combine the use of both qualitative and quantitative data to attain a particular aim (see Chapter 9 for more detail). First of all, researchers must consider the problem at hand: does mixed-method research really fit best? The next step is to pick a manageable design, while dealing with the issues of priority and sequence. Priority refers to the decision about whether qualitative or quantitative research is to take precedence, i.e. to be regarded as more important in terms of how conclusions would eventually be drawn out of the data obtained by the researcher. A standoff might present itself in case equal weight is given to these different routes, as one would ultimately have to find a way to discriminate between the qualitative and the quantitative findings, and devise a way to deal with the disproportionate or contradictory knowledge emerging from a study. Instead, sequence is a technical issue about which type of data would be collected and analysed first, why, and so forth. The simultaneous application of qualitative and quantitative data collection methods within a mixed-method design increases its logistical complexity and generally requires a broader set of skills than it might be realistic to expect; such projects are likely to involve several researchers with different backgrounds and experiences. (See Figure 5.5.)

Figure 5.5 Beware of mixed-method research

Simultaneous design

A study employing qualitative and quantitative research methods in parallel would essentially seek to remedy the implicit weaknesses of each area using the strengths of the other one to achieve a fuller picture for a problem or trend of interest. In rather basic terms, this is exemplified by a coming together of the detail provided by the in-depth nature of qualitative research and the ability to generalise through the use of large samples typical of quantitative research. The application of models like Kapferer's brand prism (2008) is seldom supported by extensive marketing research; yet, companies feel comfortable that they understand their brand identity and how this is perceived in the public domain. A simultaneous design in this context could test assumptions about physique, personality, and so on, with the collection and analysis of quantitative data from a sizeable sample of consumers, while separate qualitative data could be obtained internally from staff and examined in the context of these widely held assumptions. The outcomes of these two strands of research would then have to be merged to assess how they relate to each other, if at all, and what that might mean with regards to a particular research question. In the example, this could highlight a radical weakness in one of the elements of the brand prism such as reflection (from quantitative research) and a potential explanation for that (from qualitative research), as the business environment in which organisations operate evolves rapidly over time.

Advanced: Paradigm Issues in Mixed-Method Research (MMR)

In many circles, mixed-method research is seen as the coming together of qualitative research and quantitative research. This might have led some people to believe that, because of its lack of a fixed perspective across everything and for everyone, MMR does not conform to any particular paradigm. On the contrary, there is a need for order and structure in the pursuit of truth, which seems to fall well within pragmatism as 'a fallibilist anti-Cartesian approach to the norms that govern inquiry' (Hookway, 2013). It is not about abandoning all considerations regarding ontology and epistemology, but about accepting that subjectivity and objectivity are part of the nature of the reality we attempt to make sense of and that can therefore be known through abductive reasoning (see Table 5.1). In other words, researchers have the opportunity to dispel assumptions that might arise from our background beliefs using acceptable and coherent methodologies without prejudice. There is no clear indication as to which methodological tradition should come first or be regarded as dominant, although there is evidence that some researchers have given precedence to qualitative research, and vice versa (refer to Chapter 9 for further discussion in this area). This is also the case for studies in the general area of marketing where a wide variety of MMR designs have been used with a view to attaining more compelling answers to research questions. Ultimately, MMR must refer to a process of 'systematic inference' that moves from the particular to the general with the aim of crystallising meaning.

Unfortunately, there is often a tendency to see one of the two sets of data as more important than the other, which creates an imbalance and essentially reduces the effectiveness and potential benefits of a simultaneous design. Researchers appear to pay more attention to facilitation than to complementarity. When this is the case, a range of other mixed-method designs can be considered, depending on the purpose of the research and the overall starting point for it (see also Figure 4.6).

Serial designs

These are a set of designs which use qualitative and quantitative data in a pre-specified, ordered sequence. In general, they can be linked with exploratory or explanatory types of research, depending on the stated purpose of an assignment or a project.

Exploratory serial design

In case there is a void in the way a particular area of knowledge or organisational issue is understood, researchers tend to proceed from qualitative to quantitative research methods; the general principle here is to build some sort of substantive theory using an inductive approach and to verify its accuracy with the application of statistical analysis to quantitative data – is it eventually possible to discover some sort of generalisable pattern? (See Figure 5.6.)

Figure 5.6 Exploratory serial design

For instance, Starbucks has entered several markets around the world since the beginning of its global expansion in the 1980s. While the company has undoubtedly made sizeable steps forwards into South-East Asia, it has been hard to pin down what this success is due to. One could refer to the process of 'Americanisation' (or 'Westernisation'), the country of origin effect, such as the USA, or existing local predispositions, as in the case of Vietnam where the population has traditionally drunk coffee. Therefore, the use of grounded theory (further explored in Chapter 8) – this refers to a 'research design in which the inquirer generates a general explanation [from] the views of … participants' (Creswell, 2013: 83) – in the analysis of qualitative data would help categorise events, occurrences, episodes and experiences in relation to particular themes as identified in the literature (see Chapter 10 for further detail on the 'analytical framework'). As a picture emerges for a specific country, it is possible to generate some hypotheses and test them; it could be relevant in this scenario to attempt to ascertain the existence of meaningful relationships between variables as isolated in the initial, exploratory step by calculating correlation coefficients and interpreting them in the light of what seemed to be plausible assumptions to go with (see Chapter 14 for further detail).

It is likely that some of the proposed associations will not be confirmed by the outcomes (e.g. weak correlation coefficients), yet an organisation like Starbucks would be in a better place to steer its marketing activities in a more specific direction.

Explanatory serial design

Conversely, an explanatory serial design aims to address a research question through the collection of quantitative data first. This reflects the existence of a reliable theoretical framework in the general topic area one intends to look into, which indeed allows for predictions to be made and verified. Such a deductive approach is then developed with the addition of a targeted piece of qualitative research to build detail around particularly promising or extremely poor results (see Figure 5.7) as emerging from the initial step. Pepsi Cola has been at loggerheads with Coca-Cola for more than 100 years in possibly the longest-standing rivalry between two brands today. Their marketing staff ought to be wondering what makes their branded soft drink generally less appealing than its main competitor's. Awareness, image, knowledge, meaning, trust, and so forth, are all components of what make people like these popular brands and in fact underlie existing brand equity theory, thus providing a solid rationalisation of how relationships develop between a consumer and a brand: what does Pepsi Cola score well with?

Figure 5.7 Explanatory serial design

It might turn out that while it is clear what Pepsi Cola is about (meaning), there is a problem with trust; in this kind of occurrence, the qualitative step would have to put emphasis on clarifying why this is happening and how to select and develop more impressive points of difference to support the brand going forward.

No-nonsense serial design

A third serial design is the one normally favoured by practitioners as a way to generate insight into strategic options as well as tactical alternatives for decision making in marketing. No-nonsense serial design works from publicly available sources of information, levering qualitative research in order to define a descriptive quantitative phase (or even explanatory at times), to confirm commonly held beliefs, or otherwise, as shown in Figure 5.8.

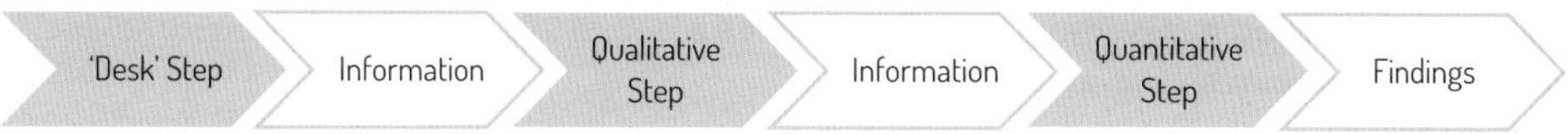

Figure 5.8 No-nonsense serial design

Carnival-owned Costa Cruises entered China in 2006 to try and build a first-mover advantage in one of the fastest growing economies in the world, as plans for a steep increase in capacity called for further expansion away from its home market: Italy. As a radically alien business environment was being approached, the cruise line would have asked itself several questions in relation to key socio-cultural factors, the actual and potential competition and consumer segments. In this respect, secondary ('desk') research was a logical starting point to define such elements and begin shaping a more suitable product proposition for the emerging Chinese middle class. Given the limited access to the country prior to that point in time, the collection of qualitative data from potential cruisers was deemed crucial to identify the prevailing behavioural patterns. Interviews were used instead of focus groups as Chinese consumers were perceived as more reserved than their European counterparts. 'Information' from the first step was fed into the 'Qualitative Step' to generate more 'Information' to be fed into the 'Quantitative Step' (see Figure 5.8). The onboard experience and expectations of it were detailed out and tested with a large sample of suitable participants from affluent metropolitan areas such as Shanghai (the homeport eventually chosen by Costa Cruises) and cities with easy air connections. Numerous differences were highlighted as statistically relevant driving changes in service delivery, yet a certain fascination with Western cultural icons, such as food, wine and music, was also confirmed which meant parts of the offering did not need adaptation.

Serial designs enable researchers in marketing to tackle any given conceptualisation of the reality around us in a more thorough fashion. They also require more extensive resources, thus should be treated with caution; in other words, these designs are appealing yet they might not necessarily be the best solution (see the 'Single-method' and 'Multiple-method' sections earlier in this chapter).

Joined design

Large programmes with a long-term goal such as the development and evaluation of economically, socially or environmentally driven marketing strategies often require the extensive application of qualitative and quantitative methods both simultaneously and serially (see Table 5.1 for a quick description of this type of research design). In other words, mixed-method designs can also be a combination of 'simpler' designs, as seen thus far in this chapter. This was the case for a US Agency for International Development (USAID)-funded effort called NetMark, which aimed at increasing the affordability, availability, demand and usage of mosquito nets in Africa between 1999 and 2009. A project like this required wide-ranging marketing research over time to fulfill three main purposes: (1) the identification and segmentation of audiences; (2) the planning and execution of appropriate marketing activities; and (3) the monitoring and control of progress made. Amongst other things, the successful implementation of the NetMark strategy was shown to be highly dependent on understanding the motivational triggers of manufacturers and distributors of nets to adopt the desired behaviours, which highlighted the need for 'using a joint risk/joint investment process'; dealing with different types of organisations and decision makers within them meant that combining mixed-method designs was a necessity rather than a fanciful exercise in marketing research (Lee and Kotler, 2012).

Table 5.1 Summary of mixed-method designs

	Simultaneous	**Serial**	**Joined**
Data collection	Parallel implementation of qualitative and quantitative data collection	Sequential implementation of qualitative and quantitative data collection	Combined implementation of simultaneous and serial mixed methods in phases (each with multiple steps)
Data analysis	Independent data analysis and reconciliation of data sets between methods	Interdependent data analysis: Step 1 informing data collection for Step 2, and so forth	Interdependent data analysis: devising analytic models that allow for the assessment of interdependence
In short:	Merging qualitative and quantitative research designs	Connecting qualitative and quantitative research designs	Joining mixed-method designs

A joined design allows for any number of research questions to be dealt with, especially those which arise as a result of the evolution of a broad marketing plan. With this in mind, the principles of simultaneous and serial mixed-method research designs continue to apply, so robust procedures to hold together key phases and individual steps should be devised before data are collected (see Chapter 9 on action research for a further perspective on mixed-method design).

Reflective Activity

- What are the main types of marketing research designs?
- How does 'desk' research help in the context of marketing research?
- What is the difference between simultaneous and serial research designs?
- How does the 'no-nonsense' research design work, and why?

Answering Research Questions

Any marketing research brief, whether it is for a short assignment or a longitudinal study, is driven by a main research question. No matter what design one adopts, there always has to be a clear focus on producing a valid and reliable answer for a research question within the parameters originally set. This essentially completes the systematic process of research (see Figure 5.3) by looking back at what was known in the beginning and by assessing the contribution made.

In so doing, it is important to consider the following final aspects:

Findings (primary data) → Research Objectives ← Literature Review (secondary data)

Data analysis and findings from primary data collection are to be directly linked with the research objectives. This bottom-up part of research practice is critical in determining what kind of new knowledge has been created with regards to the objectives articulated in the early stages of the process itself. It does also offer the opportunity to compare and contrast the primary data obtained through any of the designs and methods available to a researcher (in whatever permutation) with the secondary data as put together via a critical Literature Review (see Chapter 3 for further detail on this topic) or 'desk' research.

Looking back at the 'Snapshot' at the beginning of this chapter, a researcher might have wanted to verify what kind of inspiration everyday athletes draw from the key message of the Nike campaign (research objective). Changes in attitudes and, more to the point, behaviours such as hours of exercise per week before and after the campaign, can be measured using quantitative methods and eventually discussed in light of the secondary evidence collected in the initial stages of the project: Do the new data reinforce or contradict existing knowledge?

Research Objectives → Research Question

Finally, conclusions and, if part of the original brief, recommendations are to reflect the overarching aim of a study. The research objectives themselves should contribute to answering the research question in as comprehensive a way as possible (see Chapter 15 for a detailed account of how to write up marketing research). This is why research objectives that are not related to a project's research question are extremely dangerous and actually stray researchers away from their intended field of study.

Reflective Activity: Nike

Following up on this chapter's opening vignette regarding Nike, reflect on the research question by answering the following questions:

- What kind of operational issues (in research terms) would have to be tackled, and why?
- What ethical challenges might be encountered in addressing this question?
- How could one articulate research objectives to fit within the boundaries set by the research question itself?

Implementing Marketing Research

In a business context, companies are on many occasions willing to commission marketing research to explore or to explain specific aspects of their competitive environment, internal practices and external activities. Maintaining a team of analysts and researchers as well as working with agencies to find solutions to problems, understand market trends and patterns, deal with pressing issues, and so forth, isn't quite the same as embracing marketing research outcomes:

Conclusions → Recommendations ← Implementation

It is quite common for the results of marketing research to fall on deaf ears. In other words, once a research question has been answered, people may not be inclined to do anything about what they have discovered. Reports may end up in a bottom drawer – indeed, many nicely bound pieces of marketing research are found hidden away at the bottom of a desk drawer, or chucked randomly in a cupboard in some archive room.

There are several reasons why marketing research projects are not followed through. To begin with, it would be advisable to have a 'powerful' sponsor or advocate internally, someone whose opinions are respected. When a research brief is written, it would also be wise for that to be the natural evolution of discussions with colleagues; management theory has it that 'buy-in' from senior figures within a firm increases the chances of a successful implementation of recommendations. Further, guidance and leadership on how to maximise the operationalisation, the management and the rolling out of a marketing research study are to be considered. The ability of an organisation to use new information and knowledge in a constructive manner is a function of the resources available at any point in time, of what can eventually be acquired and/or developed (if not present), and of the time horizon within which the implementation must occur.

Chapter Summary

Designing marketing research is a delicate endeavour that depends on the conceptualisation of a project itself as much as on the technical choices a researcher is being faced with at every juncture. Every step is to be framed as a logical consequence of what comes before and a pillar that introduces and supports what comes after:

- conceptual framework
- research question
- research objectives
- viability
- data collection
- data analysis
- findings
- conclusions
- recommendations
- implementation.

A researcher should indeed be able to specify a whole research paradigm (see 'Research Paradigms' in Chapter 4, page 98) based on the identification of a particular need, i.e. in response to a problem, an issue, a phenomenon, a trend, and so on. This underlines the importance of planning in advance as opposed to sorting things out as a study takes shape. In this respect, another point should be considered with regards to data analysis as an often underestimated part of the marketing research process. Once the research objectives have clearly been established and a suitable design has been selected, a researcher is in a strong position to link data collection and data analysis together. The type of direction, such as exploratory, should inform the analytic framework to be used once data have been gathered. Developing meaning might require the application of discourse analysis to qualitative data (see Chapter 10 for more information on qualitative data analysis), which should be justified in full before data collection even takes place.

Outlining a research brief in response to a relevant topic of interest would almost invariably yield results that respect the principle of symmetry in research. The use of a codified system helps avoid surprises by highlighting possible pitfalls and anticipating eventual problems; it is worth devoting some extra thinking to how to organise ideas before one commits resources to a project.

Case Study: Marketing Wine in China

In spite of steep growth in overall sales, marketing and selling non-French wines to Chinese consumers remain a challenge; this is the experience of companies like Rathbone Wine Group, in spite of their having established some of the most successful wine brands in the country. There are a number of macro-economic trends that are contributing to making life hard, as the traditional preference for high price labels – these are

(Continued)

(Continued)

often associated with high quality as is the case for fashion brands – is beginning to wane as new consumer segments start looking at less expensive options. Furthermore, socio-cultural factors like the preference for the colour red is pushing sales of red wine up, making China the biggest market for this type of wine; many records are also being broken as the 1.5-billion-strong population provides wine exporters with almost boundless opportunities for development.

The speed of change within the country has essentially taken many organisations and commentators by surprise. There appears to be some basic rules with regards to how to differentiate one's brand in the eyes of Chinese consumers. Good imagery and storytelling are important, especially for companies that can lever heritage, history and tradition, as part of their positioning. On the other hand, it seems particularly hard to beat commonly held beliefs, which is why many promotional bodies have set up educational programmes to improve general wine knowledge as well as to build consumer understanding. This has also seen an increase in training directed at local market educators, influencers and opinion leaders. Above all, how can a foreign wine producer market its brand and product range effectively in a relatively unknown territory such as China?

There is little doubt as to the necessity of getting a more detailed picture of what has been happening in the country as a result of the recent influx of wealth. For a start, an interested party might want to distinguish between trends in metropolitan and rural areas as competition for traditional wine drinkers has definitely intensified (Zito, 2014). This brings about two key questions for marketing research: what to do and how to do it. First of all, the definition of the type of study needed in a particular circumstance for a foreign company is crucial. It may depend on the stage of internationalisation and the mode of entry as well as the marketing objectives.

A Chilean trailblazer like Montes (2013), with an established reputation and a solid distribution network, should be able to tap into existing relationships to plan a 'descriptive' piece of research as a way to clarify the next step(s) in their targeting strategy. Decisions about the research design would then have to be made, starting with the kind of data to collect: qualitative, quantitative or both – this might also be linked to the population sample, consumer or trade (see Chapter 6 for further suggestions). Describing the characteristics that have contributed to Montes' success through the collection and analysis of qualitative data could be a reasonable way to tackle such a project, given the lack of specific published/secondary research in this respect.

The company would indeed want to understand what aspects of the brand underpin its current reputation. It is then possible to frame this as a multiple research design aiming at generating explanations from two different groups of people – consumers and trade experts – in order to glean particularly interesting thoughts about Montes itself. The data collection could take place using the same method, such as unstructured interview, or different ones; the data analysis would have to be consistent, e.g. grounded theory. Ultimately, the research should look back at the research objectives and the overall research question – this would have been drafted respecting the above-mentioned marketing objective – in order to generate some conclusions and recommendations.

Two sets of factors should be considered with regards to marketing Montes wines in China:

- alternative marketing research designs
- follow-up research.

Case study questions:

1. What kind of alternative research designs are available to Montes?
2. Specifically, what would be the different design in case they adopted either an 'exploratory' or an 'explanatory' orientation?
3. How could a marketing manager justify further research into the Chinese market?
4. What would be the rationale for any investment based on the findings of the above-mentioned qualitative study?

End of Chapter Questions

These questions should help you reflect on your understanding of this chapter:

1. What is the relationship between a conceptual framework (secondary research) and a research design (primary research)?
2. What is the nature and relevance of resources, commitment and contribution in marketing research?
3. How would you define the concept of symmetry in marketing research?
4. What is the main difference between qualitative and quantitative research?
5. What are the key research designs, and why are they important to researchers?
6. What should a researcher take into consideration about data analysis while planning a research design?
7. Why is the link between findings and research objectives fundamental in marketing research?
8. What is the overall aim of conclusions and recommendations in marketing research?

Checklist

After studying Chapter 5, you should now be familiar with these key concepts:

1. The relationship between secondary and primary research
2. How to structure and develop research designs
3. The role of qualitative and quantitative research methods in marketing research
4. The characteristics of viable marketing research
5. How to provide 'symmetric' answers to research questions

Further Reading (in sequence from beginners to advanced)

Market Research Bulletin (n.d.) TNS launches quick turnaround tool to identify winning concepts for business growth [online]. Available at: http://marketresearchbulletin.com/tns-launches-quick-turnaround-tool-identify-winning-concepts-business-growth [Accessed 21 November 2014].

Creswell, J. (2013) What is mixed methods research? University of Nebraska-Lincoln [online]. Available at: www.youtube.com/watch?v=1OaNiTlpyX8 [Accessed 25 July 2016].

Teddlie, C. and Tashakkori, A. (2009) *Foundations of Mixed Methods Research: Integrating Quantitative and Qualitative Approaches in the Social and Behavioral Sciences*. Thousand Oaks, CA: Sage Publications.

Economic and Social Research Council (ESRC) (2012) Framework for Research Ethics (2010), Updated September 2012 [online]. Available at: www.esrc.ac.uk/_images/framework-for-research-ethics-09-12_tcm8-4586.pdf [Accessed 1 November 2014].

Hall A. L. and Rist, R. C. (1999) Integrating multiple qualitative research methods (or avoiding the precariousness of a one legged stool). *Psychology & Marketing*, 16 (4), pp. 291–304.

Whetten, D. (1989) What constitutes a theoretical contribution? *Academy of Management Review*, 14 (4), pp. 490–5.

Bibliography

Ang, S. H. (2014) *Research Design for Business and Management*. London: Sage Publications.

Baker, M. J. (2007) *Marketing Strategy and Management* (4th edition). Basingstoke: Palgrave Macmillan.

Barnett, M. (2014) Retention marketing falls flat for untrusting customers. *Marketing Week* [online, 4 December]. Available at: https://www.marketingweek.com/2014/12/04/retention-marketing-falls-flat-for-untrusting-consumers/ [Accessed 30 June 2014].

Bauer, T., Gordon, J. and Spillecke, D. (n.d.) The dawn of marketing's next golden age: $200 billion and counting. *McKinsey & Company* [online]. Available at: www.mckinsey.com/business-functions/marketing-and-sales/our-insights/the-dawn-of-marketings-new-golden-age [Accessed 24 July 2016].

Bethlehem, J. (2008) How accurate are self-selection web surveys? *Statistics Netherlands* [online]. (Discussion paper 08014). Available at: www.cbs.nl/NR/rdonlyres/EEC0E15B-76B0-4698-9B26-8FA04D2B3270/0/200814x10pub.pdf [Accessed 29 October 2014].

Benady, D. (n.d.) Nike, Snickers and Fosters have created powerful integrated campaigns – so what's their secret? *The Guardian* [online]. Available at: www.theguardian.com/best-awards/powerful-integrated-campaigns-secret [Accessed 2 January 2015].

Breakenridge, D. (2008) *PR 2.0: New Media, New Tools, New Audiences*. Upper Saddle River, NJ: Pearson Education.

Brown, R. (2009) *Public Relations and the Social Web: How to Use Social Media and Web 2.0 in Communications*. London: Kogan Page.

Burrell, A. (2014) Aussie wine is hard to sell in China. *The Australian Business Review* [online, 12 August]. Available at: www.theaustralian.com.au/business/aussie-wine-is-a-hard-sell-in-china/story-e6frg8zx-1227021029607?nk=6d9e07a88259b49f6b5167406b159abc [Accessed 3 January 2015].

Bryman, A. and Bell, E. (2011) *Business Research Methods* (3rd edition). Oxford: Oxford University Press.

Chow, J., and Gu, W. (2014) China's wine market shifts toward entry level: crackdown on lavish gift-giving sours high-end segment, but lower priced wine is in bloom. *Wall Street Journal* [online, 13 July]. Available at: www.wsj.com/articles/chinas-wine-market-shifts-toward-entry-level-1405305923 [Accessed 3 January 2015].

Creswell, J. (2013) *Qualitative Inquiry and Research Design: Choosing Among Five Approaches*. Thousand Oaks, CA: Sage Publications.

Curran, J. and Blackburn, R. (2001) *Researching the Small Enterprise*. London: Sage Publications.

De Keulenaer, F. (2008) Panel survey. In P. J. Lavrakas (ed.) *Encyclopaedia of Survey Methods* (pp. 563–648). Thousand Oaks, CA: Sage Publications.

Denzin, N. K. and Lincoln, Y. S. (2011) Introduction: the discipline and practice of qualitative research. In N. K. Denzin and Y. S. Lincoln (eds) *The SAGE Handbook of Qualitative Research* (pp. 1–19). Thousand Oaks, CA: Sage Publications.

Fisher, M. (2014) Misbehaving customers are most valuable. *wired* [online, 6 March]. Available at: www.wired.co.uk/magazine/archive/2014/04/ideas-bank/misbehaving-customers-valuable [Accessed 22 September 2014].

Fortune (2013) The 50 greatest business rivalries of all time. *Fortune Leadership*, Brand Marketing [online, 21 March]. Available at: http://fortune.com/2013/03/21/the-50-greatest-business-rivalries-of-all-time [Accessed 27 December 2014].

Gill, J. and Johnson, P. (2010) *Research Methods for Managers* (4th edition). London: Sage Publications.

Greene, J. C., Caracelli, V. J. and Graham, W. F. (1989) Toward a conceptual framework for mixed-method evaluation designs. *Educational Evaluation and Policy Analysis*, 11 (3), pp. 255–74.

Healey, M. J. and Rawlinson, M. B. (1994) Interviewing techniques in business and management research. In V. J. Wass, V. J. Wells and P. E. Wells (eds) *Principles and Practice in Business and Management Research* (pp. 123–46). Aldershot: Dartmouth Publishing.

Hookway, C. (2013). Pragmatism. *The Stanford Encyclopedia of Philosophy*, Stanford University [online, 7 October]. Available at: http://plato.stanford.edu/archives/win2013/entries/pragmatism [Accessed 30 June 2014].

International Standards Organisation (ISO) (2006) New ISO international standard for the market research industry. *ISO* [online, 9 May]. Available at: www.iso.org/iso/home/news_index/news_archive/news.htm?refid=Ref1005 [Accessed 1 November 2014].

Johannes, L. (2012) Hard nut to crack: beauty and antioxidant oil. *Wall Street Journal* [online, 11 June]. Available at: http://online.wsj.com/news/articles/SB10001424052702303768104577460504019108684?mg=reno64-wsj&url=http%3A%2F%2Fonline.wsj.com%2Farticle%2FSB10001424052702303768104577460504019108684.html [Accessed 22 November 2014].

Kalafatis, S., Pollard, M., East, R. and Tsogas, M. H. (1999) Green marketing and Ajzen's theory of planned behaviour: a cross-market examination. *Journal of Consumer Marketing*, 16 (5), pp. 441–60.

Kapferer, J.-N. (2008) *The New Strategic Brand Management: Creating and Sustaining Brand Equity Long Term* (4th edition). London: Kogan Page.

Kaushal, P. (2012) 5 tips: executing fast-turnaround research. *CEB Blogs* [online, 20 July]. Available at: www.executiveboard.com/blogs/5-tips-executing-fast-turnaround-research [Accessed 21 November 2014].

Lee, N. and Kotler, P. (2012) *Social Marketing: Influencing Behaviors for Good* (4th edition). Thousand Oaks, CA: Sage Publications.

Mazzocchi, M. (2008) *Statistics for Marketing and Consumer Research*. London: Sage Publications.

Mehrabian, A. and Russell, J. A. (1974) *An Approach to Environmental Psychology*. Cambridge: MIT Press.

Merrington, C. (2014) The seven most expensive research agency mistakes. *research*. [online, 23 October]. Available at: www.research-live.com/features/the-seven-most-expensive-research-agency-mistakes/4012424.article [Accessed 28 October 2014].

Montes Wines (2013) *Montes News 13*. [online]. Available at: www.google.co.uk/search?site=&source=hp&q=Montes+wine+China&oq=Montes+wine+China&gs_l=hp.3...1031.6587.0.6903.18.17.0.0.0.0.861.3573.3-2j2j2j1.7.0.eprnk%2Cekomodo%3Dtrue%2Ckpnr%3D100...0...1.1.60.hp..12.6.3123.0.FcB92r6LUVo [Accessed 3 January 2015].

Morgan, D. L. (1998) Practical strategies for combining qualitative and quantitative methods: applications to health research. *Qualitative Health Research*, 8 (3), pp. 362–76.

Sharon, T. (2012) *It's Our Research: Getting Stakeholder Buy-in for User Experience Research Projects*. New York: Morgan Kaufmann.

Willsher, K. (2014) China becomes biggest market for red wine, with 1.86bn bottles sold in 2013. *The Guardian* [online, 31 January]. Available at: www.theguardian.com/world/2014/jan/29/china-appetite-red-wine-market-boom [Accessed 3 January 2015].

Zito, M. (2014) The maturing tastes of China's wine industry. *China Briefing* [online, 9 May]. Available at: www.china-briefing.com/news/2014/05/09/maturing-tastes-chinas-wine-industry.html [Accessed 3 January 2015].

Find journal articles and multiple choice questions online at: **https://study.sagepub.com/benzo** to support what you've learnt so far.

CHAPTER 6

Sampling

LEARNING OBJECTIVES

The key learning objectives of this chapter are:

1. To describe probability and non-probability sampling
2. To understand how to select cases from a given target population
3. To critique key sampling techniques
4. To highlight advantages and disadvantages of the different approaches to sampling

KEY CONCEPTS

By the end of this chapter, the reader should be familiar with the following concepts:

1. Definitions of target population and sample
2. Fundamental steps in sampling
3. Differences between researching consumers and organisations
4. Screening participants, respondents and subjects
5. Samples for use in qualitative and quantitative research
6. Non-probability and probability sampling techniques
7. Sampling and non-sampling errors
8. Drawing samples from target populations

Riccardo Benzo

Introduction

Finding compelling answers to marketing research dilemmas largely depends on the application of a systematic process of investigation. As said thus far in this book, the fundamental steps of a given piece of research have to be identified early and supported by a solid rationale. This tends to guarantee that the output of an assignment is valid and reliable, and ultimately respects the principle of symmetry in research (see 'Symmetry in Marketing Research' in Chapter 5, page 120).

However, researchers in the field of marketing can rarely make absolute statements about the business environment they are interested in because they can only work with a limited number of people, or sample, as opposed to all the people or a population. The fact that resources are limited and, above all, time is a precious commodity means that researchers have had to come up with ways of selecting suitable participants for a study while respecting its general aim and its specific objectives.

It might seem reasonable to assume that this selection process is fairly straightforward, if a piece of research is focusing on a problem, issue or phenomenon with clearly defined boundaries. This is not always the case and is the reason why this chapter focuses on the many facets of sampling, as the technique that makes it possible for researchers to choose an appropriate group of people (sample) from a target population; ultimately, the aim is to uncover the truth about how they think, feel and behave.

Sampling should be regarded as an integral component of a research design (see Chapter 5, 'Marketing Research Designs'). In other words, students and professionals should reflect on sampling as they develop the overall structure of a project, starting from the moment they begin to consider who would best be suited to provide relevant information. Once a specific path for primary research data collection emerges, a sample should be selected using one of the techniques illustrated in this chapter.

Snapshot: Respondents, Participants and Subjects

However we term people who agree to take part in marketing research, there is little doubt that they are a fundamental component of a project, possibly determining the eventual reliability of findings and outcomes alike. The way in which we single them out is highly likely to influence the resulting data, information and knowledge. Sampling is in fact an area often neglected by researchers, academic or professional, and it does not normally register on the student radar until it is perhaps late in an assignment, or even too late.

One of the world-defining studies on national culture is a typical example of the importance of striking a balance between who is being observed and the conclusions being drawn from the observation. In this specific instance, a large database was used as a platform to make comparisons 'across individuals, across occupations, across countries, between the sexes, among age groups, and over time (1968 to 1972)' (Hofstede, 1983a: 49). Due to its global presence, IBM (International Business Machines Corporation) was thought to be ideally placed to provide the necessary pool of data. Of the original 67 countries included in the study, only 40 made the cut, although a further 10 were added later on together with three regions.

A staggering 116,000 people were surveyed along the way: 'It soon appeared that those items in the questionnaires that dealt with employee values rather than attitudes showed remarkable and very stable differences between countries' (Hofstede, 1983b: 77). These and other findings have regularly been applied to marketing decision making as they allow for certain assumptions to be made in relation to how people might react to specific promotional messages, for example. Combinations of the four dimensions (Power Distance, Uncertainty Avoidance, Individualism versus Collectivism, Masculinity versus Femininity) proposed in the research also provide interesting explanations of human behaviour.

In spite of their apparent reliability, data from Hofstede's initial project have been the subject of extensive debate among academics and practitioners because of the potential over-simplification, for instance, in accepting that IBM employees around the world could be truly representative of overall nations (or countries). For a start, organisations exhibit certain specific traits (or values) that might suppress or altogether negate those which are instead cultural characteristics of nations.

Choosing the right respondents, participants or subjects for a particular piece of research is something that should be reflected on in the early stages of a study and with reference to its other components, within a specified research paradigm.

Who Are We Researching?

Before any step is taken along the data collection trail, the question 'Who are we researching?', or put more simply, 'Who are we interested in knowing more about?' has to be carefully considered. Secondary research is particularly helpful with getting a sense of where to dig for fresh data and information. In this respect, it can lead to a conceptualisation of data and information from published empirical and theoretical sources (see 'Conceptualisation: From Secondary to Primary Research' in Chapter 4, page 100) and can eventually provide a valuable indication of how to arrive at a precise description of the entities, people or organisations which appear to represent a good place to start in the investigation.

For example, Coca-Cola has been operating in Mexico for almost 90 years; its investments in the country have increased and stand at between $1 and $2 billion a year, with firm commitment for similar budgets until 2020. Let's assume that the company is planning a rationalisation of its distribution via vending machines to benefit its relationships with both consumers and wholesale supplier and distributor partners. They would need to understand the shopping patterns of those who appear to be the heaviest users of these automated devices, in order to provide them with a more appealing range of products at the location they expect to find Coca-Cola drinks. It is unlikely that everyone in Mexico would be part of the so-called target population.

Identifying the Population of Interest

The first stage of the sampling process is to characterise in detail those people whose opinions, judgements, attitudes, behaviours, and so on, matter the most. In the aforementioned case of Coca-Cola, the target population might be determined by isolating key groups of interest based, for instance, on an off-the-shelf consumer segmentation such as Cameo Mexico Analysis, thus taking advantage of CMA's 48 descriptive categories as part of one of 10 'discriminative marketing groups'.

What this would entail is an examination of currently known facts about sales patterns in order to arrive at a more compelling and useful profile of who is more likely to use vending machines in Mexico from existing, standardised segments. A researcher should

A target population defines the entire extent of the group of people under examination in relation to the stated research objectives

eventually be able to describe their target population using a series of parameters normally available from the chosen classification – these are typically bunched up under the standard geo-demographic, psychographic, behavioural (or behaviouristic) and lifestyle (usage, habit, etc.) categories – and establish a starting point for sampling purposes.

Therefore, the concept of target population must not be confused with the usual definition of the word population, that is, the inhabitants of a country, city, town or village. If you require a specific piece of information or type of knowledge, you might only look at a few hundred people – this would be the case if expert views from a narrow technical field were sought, for instance.

Research in Practice: Researching Small Enterprises

Small enterprises form the backbone of several economies, yet there is often confusion as to what exactly is meant by this term. The European Commission defines them as organisations employing between 11 and 50 people or turning over between €2 million and €10 million per year. However one looks at them, it is fundamental to recognise what a population of interest might be for small enterprises or, even more crucially, a single small enterprise.

It is a common endeavour of research to try to shed some light on small enterprises within a specific area of business – these would typically be identified using a classification system like the Global Industry Classification Standard (GICS®). The organisations included in this pool would then be treated as the target population, thus determining the maximum size of the 'observable universe' for the research. From this point, a suitable approach to sampling would help select suitable candidate organisations while respecting the chosen research paradigm. Within each organisation, researchers would also have to get in touch with those employees who possess the appropriate knowledge to take part in the research.

For instance, if you wanted to study the influence of cost, competition or value on price setting for small organic food retailers in Japan, you might find a rather narrow target population, as the development of this specific sector has been slow, especially in comparison with the USA and Europe. The selection of a group of organisations, or even of a single organisation, to become the object(s) of a piece of research such as this would then be done according to the paradigmatic stance in order to fit the general aim of a study: exploratory, descriptive or explanatory.

Put more simply, target populations are defined considering a particular temporal span to ensure they are of an acceptable standard for the purposes of a project (see 'The sampling technique' later in the chapter for more information on cross-sectional versus longitudinal studies). The researcher is in charge of this process and must put in reasonable effort in order to come up with a concise description of what is included in a target population, and why (see Table 6.1 for an example). They should also be wary of possible changes in circumstances that might affect the composition of the target population, together with the availability of and access to certain individuals or organisations within the target population.

Taking the case of India's top 10 universities, and for a study on the impact of the overall customer experience on the likelihood of students recommending their institution to others, it makes sense to think about variations in university rankings as one of the factors affecting

Table 6.1 The 'observable universe' of the 'population of interest'

Population of Interest ('Persians' living in rural areas of the Republic of Georgia)		
Georgia	**Rural**	**Persian Heritage**
People with citizenship (passport) of the independent state situated at the crossroads between Europe and Asia (BBC News, 2016)	'an open swath of land that has few homes or other buildings, and not very many people' (National Geographic, n.d.)	Those who see themselves as a part of a pan-national group referred to as 'Persians', which can include non-Modern Persian speakers (Amanolahi, 2005)

the composition of the target population. Beyond this, it is also crucial to bear in mind that undergraduate students in their last year would be likely to have radically different opinions than those who just started their programmes. These reflections are expected both of professionals and students in order for credibility to be established early on in the life of a research assignment.

Drawing a Sample from a Target Population

With one's eyes now firmly set on a group of people or organisations, the next step for a researcher is to clarify the rationale behind sampling. Having spent time defining the target population does not in any way, shape or form guarantee that we will eventually be able to get in contact with any one of the individuals or businesses in which we are interested. In other words, we need to establish a viable course of action from target population to sample (refer to Figure 6.1), yet this might prove rather complicated as different obstacles exist along the decision-making path.

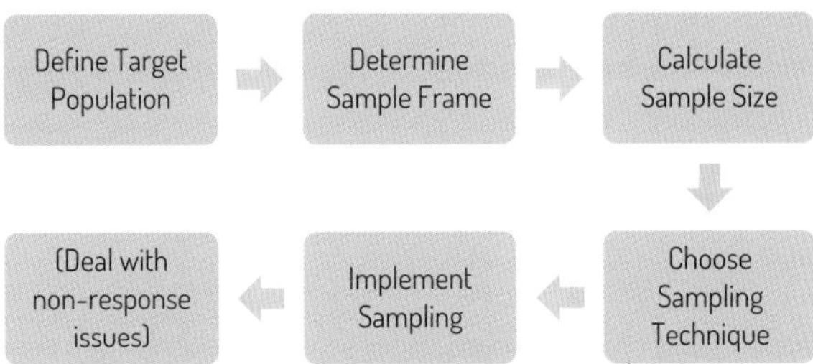

Figure 6.1 Step-by-step sampling

First, there is a tendency to think of sampling as more important for quantitative research than qualitative research, due to the fact that statistics is the language in use, samples are larger in size and generalisations from research outcomes may eventually be possible. However, the quality of a piece of research expressed through its reliability, replicability and validity is important, irrespective of the type of data collected. This means that the selection of a sufficient number of representative participants, respondents or subjects for research should be thought of as the overriding factor here and, as such, an appropriate screening procedure should eventually be put in place to get there.

The sample frame

A **sample frame** is a set of cases (or units) that approximate the target population as precisely as possible

We need to remember that knowing our target population is not the same as knowing exactly who (or what in the case of companies) it comprises. There is always a practical issue in terms of whether or not a comprehensive list of all people or businesses in a target population is available. The closest you will get to this is when a searchable census exists from which each and every case in the target population is determinable. In the not-so-distant past, telephone books and other types of directories served the purpose of approximating a target population well enough for the purposes of most research. Because of the fact that people nowadays communicate differently, this is not the case anymore. It is easier to build a sample frame for companies as industry associations – for example, the Canadian Pharmacists Association and databases such as FAME can still provide this level of detail.

In emerging economies like Vietnam, it is not uncommon to encounter difficulties when looking for adequate sample frames. Although official statistical collections such as the Statistical Handbook of Vietnam (General Statistics Office of Viet Nam, 2014) exist, information within it is provided in aggregate format and access to a detailed list of residents is not easy. This can affect a researcher's ability to identify suitable subjects – indeed, we will see that this restricts the possible choices to non-probability sampling techniques alone.

Eventually, it becomes important to acknowledge the existence of discrepancies between the overall size of a target population and that of the sample frame we can draw. In some instances, the gap will be small, but more often than not it will be large enough to raise some fundamental methodological questions. This highlights the existence of a sample frame error, or the fact that the sample frame does not reflect the target population in full or correctly. This might lead to situations in which not every case is accounted for, some cases not of interest are included, or both (see Figure 6.2). For instance, if a researcher planned to talk to Pakistani consumers about using Thalgo face treatments, but could only find a sample frame for people who purchased this product category (i.e. any face treatment product) in the past, this would lead to the sample frame being (probably much) bigger than the actual target population.

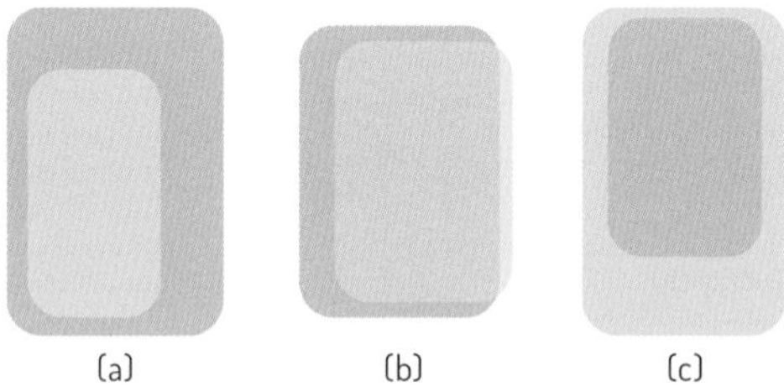

Figure 6.2 Types of sample frame errors

Screening

A practical way of dealing with the issues brought about by the imperfect nature of sample frames is to ensure that every case we are selecting belongs to the relevant target population. In other words, we have to put in place yet another system to single out subjects, respondents or participants who actually fall within the target population: this is achieved using a so-called screening process.

Take, for example, an organisation like Innocent Drinks wanting to attract a new audience, such as drinkers of carbonated sodas in Russia, where it has already introduced its smoothies and juices. In order to do so, the firm could design a survey aimed at understanding drinking habits and devise an appropriate customer acquisition strategy. In this respect, the company would want to ensure that they talk to people who have never tried their products before. Therefore, the opening question in their questionnaire (see Chapter 12 for more information about questionnaire design) would be something along the lines of: Have you *ever* drunk an Innocent Drinks smoothie or juice before? Respondents selecting 'yes' would then have to be excluded from the research, as they would not qualify to take part in it. Similarly, people who have not tasted the company's products before but who only consume still soft drinks (as opposed to carbonated) would have to be identified and left out from the sample, i.e. another screening question would be needed. This process should be repeated for any other parameter used to define the target population in the first place.

Advanced: Honest Respondents, Please!

With more marketing research being conducted by organisations and students alike, it is fair to assume that many of us have been filling in questionnaires, giving answers to interviewers, registering on online panels, and so forth, on a fairly regular basis. These are indeed reasons for concern in research because re-using respondents and participants might result in them wising up, a situation whereby they could provide biased responses or information influenced by previous experiences (Waters, 1991).

Furthermore, some subjects – remember that organisations are ultimately made up of human beings, too – can be considered 'professional' in their approach to participating in studies, as they try to evade the screening questions by lying about their actual knowledge and possible competence about a topic. In this case, it would be appropriate to devise a set of termination questions around the frequency of participation in marketing research, personal interests and work experience. The latter is a particularly sensitive subject because people working in the marketing field would indeed not be useful to researchers in many instances; however, they should certainly be considered when experts are needed, which is often the case for large consumer studies and in qualitative research. While it is not ethical to trick respondents, it is important to select them carefully.

At this stage, we should issue a word of caution to underline the fact that no difference exists in relation to whether a qualitative or a quantitative piece of research is being undertaken. Every researcher should strive to choose good respondents as assessed by their ability to contribute to knowledge generation.

The sample size

Determining the correct sample size from a target population is a function of a series of factors linking back to some of the topics covered in previous chapters of this book. In fact, the overall research paradigm adopted by a researcher would be a sensible starting point as its various components tend to influence the end result: a sample should be 'as large as necessary, and as small as possible' (Sarantakos, 2013: 183). The nature of the study is a defining initial determinant as topics immersed in subjectivity and whose epistemology is interpretive tend to require smaller samples. This is also justified by the fact that depth is preferred to breadth in an attempt to apply inductive reasoning to qualitative data and possibly drive the discovery of particular patterns, which may ultimately be crystallised into a theory (refer to 'Building theory' in Figure 6.3).

If a study is informed by a precise understanding of the reality surrounding us in the form of a more precise 'model' or conceptual framework, there is a strong likelihood that a positivist epistemology will be adopted, together with the application of deductive reasoning to quantitative data. In this case, a researcher would need a large sample as breadth becomes more important than depth when statistically sound generalisations are sought (refer to 'Verifying theory' in Figure 6.3).

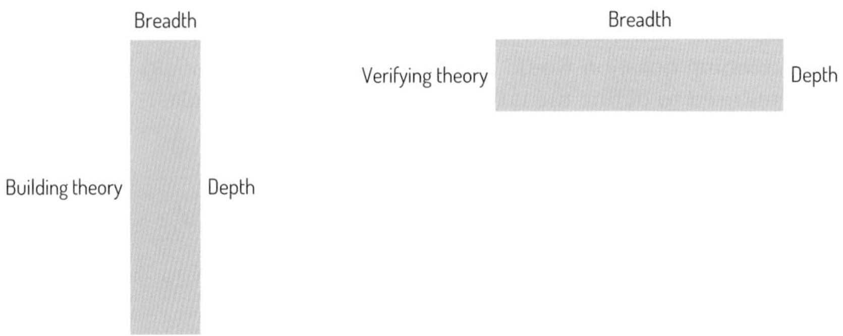

Figure 6.3 Sample breadth and depth

Eventually, we need to come up with a number of cases that satisfy our parameters and start to find appropriate participants and respondents to build our sample.

Samples for qualitative research

Determining sample sizes in qualitative research has been a hotly debated topic for a long time; there is some agreement that 'the guiding principle should [ultimately] be the concept of saturation' (Mason, 2010). This idea is conceptually simple: as data are collected and topics investigated, a picture emerges until a researcher is satisfied that everything has been adequately covered. However, in many instances it is overlooked in favour of widespread practices and rule-of-thumb judgement; practitioners with years of experience would probably choose a sample size based on what they have learned from previous studies and in similar circumstances (see Tables 6.2 and 6.3).

To illustrate this, let's take the development of characters and storylines for a Netflix series; this is based on the understanding of modern audiences (Weisman, 2014). As a form of entertainment, comedy appears to be based on 'territory' (cultural background) so interviewees might be sourced in different key areas, such as a US state or city. Samples need to be small in order to ensure a quick turnaround and for the information to be disseminated almost in real time, to give writers the time to develop the next episode(s). This is typically a situation where a fixed number of interviews need to be carried out without perhaps achieving saturation for the topics under discussion.

Table 6.2 Qualitative samples for academic projects

What	Average	Range
UG dissertation	12	8–15
PG dissertation	20	15–25
PhD thesis	50	40–60

Source: Baker and Edwards, 2012

Table 6.3 Qualitative samples for practitioner research

What	Average	Range
Expert views	5	2–8
Customer need recognition	25	20–30
Cognitive dissonance	80	60–100

Source: Adapted from De Paulo, 2000

It is strongly recommended that you consider the epistemological underpinnings of your qualitative research as well as its limitations and external influences; a safe way to proceed is to find out about best practice in a specific area (see Tables 6.2 and 6.3) and for a specific data collection method before making any decision based on averages or an individual's past experience.

Samples for quantitative research

A **confidence level** is the level of certainty relating to the expectation that samples actually include the true population parameter

Besides the general factors mentioned above, calculating sample sizes for quantitative research also has to take into account that 'we can only infer things about psychological, societal, biological or economic processes based on the models we build' (Field, 2009: 32). In other words, the number of cases we have to include in a sample is influenced by how precise one's explanation of a problem, issue or phenomenon needs to be. Huawei's decision to hold the worldwide launch of the P6 Ascend handset in London's Roundhouse could have been motivated by the need to improve recognition and acceptance of a Chinese brand by consumers in Europe. A decision such as this would have been supported by factual evidence to a specific confidence level.

Acceptable levels for quantitative research are typically set at either 95% or 99%; this means that for any parameter (variable) observed by Huawei before introducing the P6 Ascend there might have been a 99% probability that the measured value would actually be within a specified confidence interval.

In the case of social influence, defined as the extent to which others believe the respondents should consider the P6 Ascend handset, if 60% of people had answered 'definitely not', the researcher might attach a 99% confidence level to a pre-determined confidence interval, say plus or minus 3%. In other words, they would conclude that it is very likely that the respondents' true answers would actually fall between 57% and 63% (for the 99% confidence interval, there can never be absolute certainty!). Ultimately, these values allow us to establish the size of a sample for a quantitative piece of research, starting from the sample population of interest (see Table 6.4).

Table 6.4 Sample size table

Population Size	Confidence Level = 95%			Confidence Level = 99%		
	Margin of Error			Margin of Error		
	0.05	0.025	0.01	0.05	0.025	0.01
10	10	10	10	10	10	10
20	19	20	20	19	20	20
30	28	29	30	29	30	30
50	44	48	50	47	49	50
75	63	72	74	67	73	75
100	80	94	99	87	96	99
150	108	137	148	122	142	149
200	132	177	196	154	186	198
250	152	215	244	182	229	246
300	169	251	291	207	270	295
400	196	318	384	250	348	391
500	217	377	475	285	421	485
600	234	432	565	315	490	579
800	260	526	739	363	615	763
1000	278	606	906	399	727	943
1200	291	674	1067	427	827	1119
1500	306	759	1297	460	959	1376
2000	322	869	1655	498	1141	1785
2500	333	952	1984	524	1288	2173
3500	346	1068	2565	558	1510	2890
5000	357	1176	3288	586	1510	3842
10000	370	1332	4899	622	2098	6239
25000	378	1448	6939	646	2399	9972
50000	381	1491	8056	655	2520	12455
75000	382	1506	8514	658	2563	13583
100000	383	1513	8762	659	2585	14227
250000	384	1527	9248	662	2626	15555

Population Size	Confidence Level = 95%			Confidence Level = 99%		
	Margin of Error			Margin of Error		
	0.05	0.025	0.01	0.05	0.025	0.01
500000	384	783	9423	663	2640	16055
1000000	384	783	9512	663	2647	16317
2500000	384	784	9567	663	2651	16478
10000000	384	784	9594	663	2653	16560
100000000	384	784	9603	663	2654	16584

It is also possible to consult one of many sample size calculators available online, for instance the Survey System. These also provide the tools to determine a confidence interval based on the desired confidence level and the sample actually obtained; it could be the situation that the researcher only has a limited amount of time to collect survey questionnaires. Over time, industry-accepted and acceptable standards for sample size calculation have also been developed; some ballpark figures are available in Table 6.5.

Table 6.5 Sample size guide for quantitative studies

What?	At least ...	Suggested
Identifying consumer trend or phenomenon	500	1,500
Solving marketing management problem	200	500
Testing marketing communications, e.g. online commercial	150	300

Source: Adapted from Malhotra and Birks, 2007: 409

The process of sampling requires a lot of reflection as it needs to be well integrated with all the components of a research project, thus presenting the researcher with a series of rather complex choices to make. 'Non-coverage' errors (see Figure 6.2a) can be addressed by improving the basic sample frame with data from other sources. 'Non-response' errors are normally due to respondents not being reachable or declining to take part in the data collection stage. In the case of the former, a possible solution is to arrange appointments or to have multiple ways to contact subjects, for example both at home and at their place of work. Increasing the number of participants who qualify for a study based on historic response rates (see the 'Research in Practice' box on p. 158) is another useful way to bypass this kind of problem. When respondents refuse to answer, it is harder to find an appropriate solution as questions of procedure and ethics arise – this may suggest that the information provided to the subjects is not enticing them enough to take part in a study and needs to be improved, such as providing clarification about the nature and importance of a study. 'Response' errors, instead, refer to inaccurate information as obtained during data collection due to poorly phrased questions, unsuitable surroundings for research purposes and a lack of necessary knowledge on the subjects' part. Finally, 'office' errors arise from imprecise or plainly wrong data editing, coding and analysis (see Chapters 10 and 12 for more detail on this).

Non-response error The lack of representativeness from some portion of the target population originally selected to be part of the sample

Reflective Activity

- What is the difference between population, sample and case?
- How would you explain the need for sampling in qualitative research?
- What is a 'sample frame', and why is it important in this context?

These errors are in fact rather common because there are several instances in the course of a marketing research project where they can manifest themselves, and they effectively account for the largest proportion of total error together with sampling error (see 'Sampling error' later in the chapter). Non-sampling error can ultimately be reduced by improving the forward integration of sampling and data collection for all the aforementioned aspects, and by eliminating potentially weak links, such as the training of field workers in relation to 'response' error. Ultimately, caution must be exercised as the purpose of a research project, its parameters and its constraints in many instances affect our ability to reach out to an ideal number of subjects. Likewise, their selection adds pressure to the validity, reliability and generalisability of a study's eventual output.

The sampling technique

With our sights firmly set on a specific population and having determined a suitable sample frame and calculated a sample size, the next step is to select cases accordingly; in other words, to identify useful respondents or participants to match the required number. Any practitioner will tell you how hard this is and students rarely get the right mix of people – this could happen when collecting data in busy shopping malls and not being able to speak with a sufficient number of subjects in a pre-determined age group.

Cross-Sectional Versus Longitudinal Studies

There is also a distinction to be made when selecting samples for a cross-sectional as opposed to a longitudinal study due to the additional complexity of keeping track of people over time. The Guardian Brand Aid Panel is a straightforward illustration of a modern type of cross-sectional study aimed at returning quick and useful feedback on creative execution for marketing campaigns running in print, online, mobile, tablet and social media from over 3,000 panel members from the *Guardian* and *Observer* readership.

In contrast, the Kenya Home Panel is an example of a longitudinal study, which, amongst other things, tracks different households to examine how brand performance changes over time. Longitudinal studies are challenging insofar as collecting data from the same subjects on multiple occasions, such as a 'fixed panel', raises concerns in terms of the information obtained, the variability in the actual composition of the sample and the ability to perform the various phases of such a project consistently enough.

Furthermore, single-method research that requires the collection of data at two distinct moments in time could sway from this particular typology to consider samples that actually do not necessarily follow the same respondents or participants, such as a 'repeated panel'. For instance, the traditional video game market in Japan has been contracting from its peak in 2007 to its lowest level in 24 years, indicating a generational shift away from consoles. This trend could have been picked up by monitoring heavy console users and by reflecting on what has been happening to young gamers across the country.

Irrespective of these considerations, the general rules for choosing a sample depend on whether the chances of a sample unit being included in a sample can actually be calculated – this would effectively give each sample unit the same probability of being selected from a given population of interest, or not. Sampling methods can therefore be categorised as per Figure 6.4.

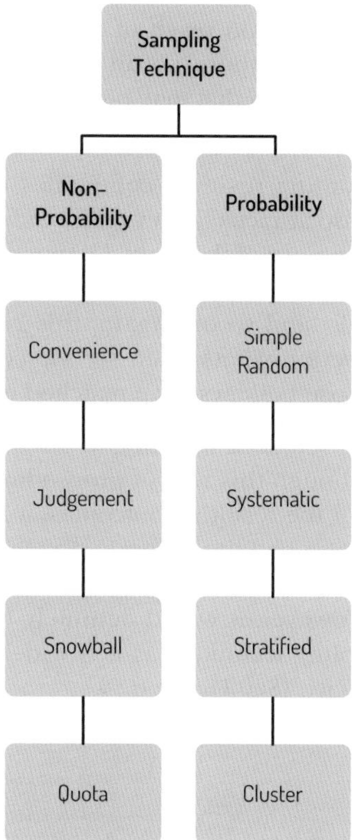

Figure 6.4 Sampling methods in a nutshell

Non-probability Methods

Choosing a sample using a non-probability method adds bias to the process due to the fact that an element of subjectivity is introduced in relation to who the decision maker is, as well as regarding how the when and where decisions about sample selection are taken.

Non-probability sampling is based on the arbitrary selection – i.e. without the existence of a sample frame – of units (or cases) from a target population

Let's assume that Metro, the German retailer, is looking to expand its product range in Pakistan, having by the end of 2015 operated nine cash-and-carry stores around the main metropolitan areas. Whatever the eventual sample frame and sample size, in principle, they could use any one of the following four approaches: convenience sampling, judgement sampling, snowball sampling or quota sampling.

Convenience sampling

Metro decides to collect data from people near its outlets, irrespective of the proportion of actual customers (Metro Card holders who can shop at their outlets), potential customers and indifferent customers. It does not distinguish between active and passive customers either. Therefore, subjects are included based on the 'convenience' of being able to access them easily as they happen to be within reach of a Metro at the time the information is needed. However, this means that all those not in the vicinity of an outlet are excluded, thus skewing the findings in a direction that may only paint a partial picture of what needs and wants the company should satisfy.

The same is possibly true of online reviews; companies like TripAdvisor have become extremely influential, but have also attracted heavy criticism from travel, tourism and hospitality operators around the world because of the limited dependability of opinions on particular portions of the population who are self-selecting themselves to leave comments about their experiences with airlines, hotels, and so on. Again, this could be considered convenient because there is in fact no selection whatsoever, so one could expect less satisfied users to be more vocal than those whose holidays have matched or exceeded their expectations.

Sometimes organisations use convenience sampling to discuss ideas with their staff before a full-scale study is launched. Although this way of proceeding is debatable and creates concern in relation to the validity of the resulting outcomes, it has the advantage of providing an inexpensive approximation of a real-life scenario. Exploratory research designs tend to favour convenience sampling as a method; likewise, qualitative data collection is commonly associated with this method. However, it would definitely be reductive and unwise not to take a critical view of this sampling technique as it is widely adopted by practitioners and academics for its relative simplicity. (See Figure 6.5.)

Judgement sampling

Going back to Metro's product development plans, the German retailer could instead decide to take an 'educated guess' as to who, within the overall target population, would constitute good, representative subjects to research. In this respect, the researcher, or team, in charge of the project would select cases from the sample frame deemed to offer a comprehensive description of the target population. The Marketing Research Society of Pakistan (MRSP) has adopted the ICC/ESOMAR International Code on Market and Social Research, which establishes key principles including the disclosure of technical information, for instance the sampling method, to enable clients to assess the validity of findings.

Often, companies utilise judgemental sampling as a purposive means of choosing participants for focus groups as they might favour a particular quality. This would be the case for Skol,

Figure 6.5 Assessing non-probability sampling

a popular brand of beer owned by AB InBev, wanting to understand customer behaviour in 18–24-year-olds, but only recruiting university graduates to ensure a high likelihood that they can articulate answers in a clear fashion. As there are still many young people without higher education degrees in the 12 countries where the beer is marketed and sold (Benin, Burundi, Central African Republic, Congo Brazaville, Democratic Republic of the Congo, Ethiopia, Guinea Conakry, Kenya, Madagascar, Rwanda, Togo and Uganda), this choice would not lead to a representative sample (even though it could still provide deep insight).

This method is employed by researchers both in qualitative and quantitative pieces of research. It should be noted that relying purely on experience and on one's knowledge of a market or sector is likely to introduce strong personal bias; however, if the sample size is small, this experience and knowledge could become an asset in identifying the best participants and eventually carrying out data collection, which could otherwise have proved impossible to achieve.

Snowball sampling

There is an additional technique which Metro could consider in its quest to obtain valuable information about product development. The starting point could either be determined by convenience or judgement; once a first group of subjects has been identified, the researchers ask them to name friends, acquaintances or colleagues who fit the parameters of the sample to continue with the selection process until the target number is achieved. This is a particularly worthwhile sampling method for research into specific topics, industrial environments or any other situation where experts are likely to make up the target population, so it would not be entirely advisable for Metro in this instance. It could however prove useful for Pfizer, a leading provider of pneumococcal vaccines that invests considerable amounts of money in innovation (research and development). In this respect, the company would be best off interviewing a narrow sample of medical specialists, starting with a group of people singled out by their sales team, and by asking each and every one of these professionals to refer another doctor with the same expertise. Although it is possible to see the advantages of using this kind of tactics, students should be warned that in mass consumer markets this practice might create a false sense of security as similar respondents would reinforce findings, even if the significance (*p*-value) of inferential quantitative analysis and testing (see Chapters 13 and 14 for more detailed information on statistics for marketing research) was consistent with the alternative hypothesis (also see Chapter 11). In other words, the composition of the sample would have the unwanted effect of presenting an opinion actually held by a rather distinct group of people within the sample frame.

Ethics: Researching Children in the Digital Era

The development of online research tools and techniques – these can entail filling in research documentation (e.g. a questionnaire) via a device connected to the Internet, participating in a live, qualitative one-to-one interview, or focus group or tracking web usage including collecting information from social networks – has made research with children fraught with potential pitfalls. For instance, researchers using social networks or fora must make their presence known and identify the organisation they work for and the nature of the project they are conducting; passive data collection is not allowed.

Furthermore, children (i.e. individuals younger than 16 years of age) may not participate in research unless explicit permission has been obtained from a responsible adult. The verification of this permission becomes crucial as no face-to-face contact may be possible. E-mail confirmations alone must not be accepted, so before data are collected researchers should get positive proof of identification and permission on the telephone or, preferably, via post (e.g. a signed form with a responsible adult ID). Like any other research subject, a child should then give consent to take part. Without the benefit of direct interaction between researchers and children, the data collection tool should avoid sensitive questions, which may prove hard for children to answer, or questions that might trigger unreasonable demands on the responsible adult; this could be the case for questions presenting specific products in an attractive manner.

Also, the language of the project should be fine-tuned to the particular capabilities of the children in the sample. With so much at stake, researchers should be extra cautious and seek specific advice from recognised bodies and organisations. A reflexive approach to research ethics must be emphasised to ensure dynamic and respectful relationships between researchers, children and their families.

Quota sampling

Finally, we can make the assumption that Metro understands the issue with product development well and, as such, wants to draw a sample with a specific composition. This would still require the researchers to decide which characteristics the participants, respondents or subjects should display. Things like a particular gender split – for example, 40% female to 60% male – and demographic types – for instance, 20% 'Affluent Achievers', 40% 'Rising Prosperity' and 40% 'Comfortable Communities' – could be considered (Acorn, 2014). It is important to note here that this way of proceeding is not comparable to building a probability, stratified sample (see 'Stratified sampling' later on in this chapter) as (a) no correlation might exist between the selected quotas and the behaviour of interest; (b) the selected quotas are not necessarily representative of the target population; and (c) the units within the sample are not selected randomly.

Spotify has made its music streaming and downloading services available in many countries around the world since it launched in 2008. Understanding consumption habits such as usage patterns is central to improving its offering, for example its website or app usability. If the company wanted to survey its customers in Malaysia, it could make choices with regards to the general composition of the sample by establishing quotas to ensure particular segments are included, even though this might not respect the actual proportions seen in the target population as a whole. For instance, if Spotify wanted to market to the over-55s, it could look at a sample containing 40% of this particular age group, although this would roughly make them over-represented in the sample by a factor of 3 to 1. In order to achieve this, the researchers would have to spend a relatively long period of time here as it could be hard to locate the right subjects quickly; this is the reason why, in some cases, some of the quotas might not be respected, especially when there are a few parameters to be taken into account. At times, this may result in quite a lot of bias and researchers should keep an eye on how the various quotas are 'filling up' while a piece of research progresses.

Reflective Activity

- Why does the use of non-probability methods require careful reflection?
- What are the potential pitfalls of 'judgemental' sampling?
- How does 'quota' sampling work – when could it be employed?

As stated earlier, non-probability samples are prone to a variety of potential pitfalls and shortcomings. If anything, it is more practical and less time-consuming to research friends and family, to conduct interviews in homes or to administer intercept surveys in a nice neighbourhood. Knowing and addressing these situations certainly contributes to the overall validity, reliability and, possibly, generalisability of a study. Alternatively, we can attempt to select samples more objectively using a different set of techniques which are explained below.

Probability Methods

The use of statistics in research has fuelled a lengthy debate on the merits of the 'justificationist' approach to science. In terms of sampling, probability methods provide a structure that allows a researcher to draw a representative sample from a target population (frame) for a chosen confidence level and confidence interval combination. This is a more complex and resource-intensive route to follow, and one which is much harder for students to understand and apply.

Simple random sampling

Probability sampling employs a systematic selection of units so that the probability of any one individual in the target population being included in the sample can be known and inferences made

Amazon has been extremely keen to grow its Amazon Prime service worldwide to ensure that many more items qualify for its guaranteed fast delivery to subscribers. Marketing mix (in this case, 'Product') decisions should typically be investigated in great detail, especially in the case of well-established businesses with a large customer base. In this respect, we can appreciate the importance of conducting an online survey in order to decide whether or not to take this step as well as to launch other features, such as streaming, photo storage or e-book borrowing, for Amazon Prime members.

The selection process for simple random sampling should start by defining the target population: all Amazon customers that can be described as regular or heavy users, but who have not yet switched to Amazon Prime. Based on the full list of these individuals at a specific moment in time, there will be a perfect match between the target population and the sample framework as the company holds data for each and every one of its customers. Moreover, they could be contacted directly via e-mail once a sample has been selected. The next step is to decide how the required cases should be singled out from the sample framework; this is where the research applies a 'random' rule, such as generating numbers using an appropriate statistical function in an electronic spreadsheet until the required total is achieved, while respecting the agreed confidence level and confidence interval parameters. An organisation like Amazon should also look at different countries independently as consumer habits and operational conditions could vary greatly, thus making it impossible for generalisations at a global level; this straightforward process should therefore be repeated within each country.

Research in Practice: Random Numbers and Response Rates

One of the most diffused misnomers in marketing research and sampling in particular is the idea that random effectively means anyone we want with regards to selecting subjects from a target population. On the contrary, there is nothing random about random sampling! Most of the confusion ensues from the rather different use of the word random in research as opposed to its common meaning: 'Made, done, or happening without method or conscious decision' (Oxford Dictionaries, n.d.). This book presents a strong case for planning and organising your work in a systematic way so that randomness is pretty much kept under control. In probability sampling, it refers to how to choose units from a sample frame while ensuring everyone has the same chance of being included in the sample. In the case of non-probability sampling, researchers instead draw from experience (judgement sampling) or work with ease of access in mind (convenience sampling) as they select units from a target population: this is still far from random.

At the same time, it is hard to imagine that the required sample size can be fulfilled at the first time of asking. In other words, more subjects should be identified initially to ensure that the target is reached. For instance, a shopping centre intercept study to understand the impact of location (GPS) services in driving footfall is likely to become particularly demanding if a very narrow target population is chosen, for example 18-year-olds (specifically school leavers without a university offer). Finding these subjects amongst a heterogeneous crowd of shoppers could prove extremely hard and a very low response rate – this being the percentage of valid respondents among those asked to take part in the study itself – is to be expected in this case.

On the other hand, if we conducted the study via e-mail (from a specific sample frame of school leavers), there could still be an issue with the response rate as we can't be sure how many people who qualify for the survey would actually complete it in full. This is a concern with both quantitative and qualitative research as it might slow down progress. Members of a focus group may decide not to show up, which could make it impossible for the data collection to take place, thus sending researchers back to the drawing board, having to re-recruit suitable candidates in order to organise a new focus group at a later date, resulting in a considerable waste of resources.

So precision and patience are necessary virtues during the research design phase of an assignment in order to define and implement all the components of sampling, irrespective of the preferred or preferable approach, and to avoid unwanted 'randomness' both in the process and in the results, as may be seen, for example, in a lack of 'symmetry'.

Systematic sampling

A slightly different procedure might be preferable to try and improve accuracy in the 'random' selection of cases for the same research project in the USA, Amazon's home market. Systematic sampling entails a two-step process: (1) choose a random start point in the sample frame (or the list of all known subjects for a specific target population); and (2) pick cases at regular intervals – the interval itself should be calculated as the population (N) divided by the sample size (n). So, if Amazon is looking at 200 million American customers who aren't yet using Amazon Prime and wants to survey 2,000 of them – this would give a confidence interval of 2.19% for a 95% confidence level – every thousandth (N/n) person in the sample frame should be surveyed after a first name has been chosen. However, this technique will only actually achieve better accuracy if the sample frame is ordered in a particular way, for instance in a descending order of average transaction value. In this way, Amazon researchers can put together a balanced sample, including heavy spenders, fairly heavy spenders, and so forth. A similar result could be achieved by using frequency (e.g. quarterly, monthly) as the discriminant variable in ordering the sample frame.

It is important to notice that systematic sampling would not yield any more accuracy than simple random sampling, should the sample frame be ordered in alphabetical order by customer surname. In case the elements are arranged following a cyclical or seasonal pattern and the selection interval is chosen using the same time lapse, systematic sampling does in fact reduce the accuracy of the survey as similar cases are indeed picked and biased results obtained. This could be a situation whereby Walmart decided to investigate customer service delivery on the shop floor by collecting data the same day of the week when satisfaction scores tend to be higher as there is a better staff to customer ratio, i.e. customers actually wait less time to be served.

Stratified sampling

One further problem with accuracy is that the larger the target population, the harder it becomes to achieve a reasonable level of precision. Stratified sampling helps with that, while providing a more effective way of selecting cases, too.

Let's now assume that Amazon wants to ensure that highly infrequent buyers, say people who order less than once a year, are definitely included in the aforementioned sample (n = 2,000), even though they only represent 4.5% of the overall target population. The organisation is trying to make them purchase more, or they have simply figured out that these people might subscribe and then not use the service, which is similar to widespread consumer behaviour in the case of gym membership.

Researchers would have to divide the population into different groups, one of them being made up of all the infrequent buyers; each person could only be part of one group. Because each and every group is now more homogeneous within itself than the overall target population could ever be, the overall sample size would eventually go down. The assumption being made is that with lower possible sampling error (see the next section on 'Sampling error') from each stratus (or layer), it is possible to achieve the same confidence level and confidence interval combination by surveying fewer Amazon customers. In the meantime, we know that the infrequent buyers will be sufficiently represented in the sample.

There is a final consideration to make in relation to the difference between proportionate and disproportionate stratified samples. The former refers to a correct match between the actual proportion of a group in the population and the number of cases picked as part of the sample. Put more simply, we would look at 4.5% of 2,000, or 90 respondents, for Amazon infrequent buyers. The latter, instead, makes a series of decisions in order to improve efficiencies by reducing the number of Amazon infrequent buyers needed for the survey – this, of course, is possible if there is evidence that variability of the estimated parameter(s) is reduced within one or more groups.

Cluster sampling

This final probability sampling technique is based on the idea of segmentation (clustering); a target population is divided into relevant, defined sets (clusters) which are then chosen using a 'random' procedure. However, clusters differ from strata in as much as they are homogenous between them and not within them.

In the case of Amazon, this could be achieved by treating zip codes (US postcodes) as clusters – the composition of each cluster would be heterogeneous, but every cluster would be similar to the next, containing a variety of possible respondents as per their defining geo-demographic, psychographic, behavioural and lifestyle characteristics. Once possible clusters are available, they need to be chosen by using a simple random or systematic sampling technique; clusters can finally be used in full (one-stage cluster sampling) or cases selected from clusters (two-stage cluster sampling). Of course, this way of proceeding might skew the results because, in this case, respondents within affluent neighbourhoods could eventually contribute to painting an unrealistic picture of how Amazon-infrequent buyers think and/or feel about Amazon Prime.

Cluster sampling focuses on efficiency by decreasing costs more quickly than accuracy or, in other words, by realising economies, but not at the expense of precision. This is a result of the fact that researchers focus on some clusters, ignoring others completely and, if possible, pick them in their entirety (one-stage cluster sampling) without any additional investment (time, money, etc.) The key points to bear in mind are:

(1) Go for as many clusters as is feasible.

(2) Maintain a balance between large and small clusters.

(3) Select a constant number of subjects from each cluster (this is in case you are adopting two-stage cluster sampling).

Reflective Activity

Looking back at the opening 'Snapshot' about IBM and Hofstede:

- What are your thoughts with regards to using specific organisational data to draw generalisations about national culture?
- What kinds of considerations might researchers have made when building the data bank for the research conducted by Hofstede?

More generally:

- What could influence the way a group of people is selected for a large-scale study? And what about for an undergraduate dissertation, instead?

No matter what principles are applied in the selection process, researchers using any of these sampling techniques are interested in knowing the statistical probability of any population element included in a sample, as this builds a rigorous platform for generalisability in marketing research. Likewise, probability sampling allows researchers to estimate the sampling error, the difference between the sample results and the actual results that could have been obtained by researching the entire target population, such as a census.

Sampling Error

A **sampling error** is an error due to the fact that a sample is not fully representative of the target population

Making inferences from a sample to a target population presents a series of issues of which researchers must be aware. Besides considerations about the process of sampling, or non-sampling errors, the units we actually select from a population using probability sampling techniques affect the precision of our research outcomes. In an ideal world, we would aim to draw more than a single sample from a population to observe how any chosen parameter varies, depending on the units that have been included.

This is not common practice and it does not matter because researchers know that the sampling distribution for samples larger than 30 cases is normally distributed with any parameter mean equal to that of the target population and a standard deviation of:

$$\sigma_{\bar{X}} = \frac{S}{\sqrt{N}}$$

Where $\sigma_{\bar{X}}$ is the standard deviation of a parameter mean, S is the sample standard deviation and N is the size of the sample.

So if Infiniti, the car manufacturer, wanted to collect information about brand associations, they could choose a sample of Infiniti owners in each of their 52 countries of operation, and measure parameters like positioning, trustworthiness, pride (of ownership), using bipolar scales, for example from downmarket to upmarket for positioning. Respondents in Qatar might say that the brand is very close to upmarket; if Infiniti had used a 10-point scale, that could be represented by an average value of 8.9. This would in turn mean that the distribution of the actual answers obtained from the sample displays high frequencies for values close to the average itself, thus making the results more reliable. Reducing the number of points on the scale also tends to reduce the amount of sampling error. Likewise, increasing the sample size pushes the margin of sample error down, making eventual determinations more precise and reliable.

Chapter Summary

Within the broader picture set for a marketing research project (see Chapters 2 through to 5), sampling needs to be equally well thought-out, as our ability to answer a particular research question is very much linked to the choices we make with regards to:

- defining the target population
- determining the sample frame
- calculating the sample size
- choosing the sampling technique
- implementing the sampling process.

First and foremost, a researcher should be able to specify the target population that seems most likely to provide useful insight into an issue, a problem, a phenomenon, and so on. If different audiences qualify to help, you might have to restrict your investigation to just one or two groups. It is reasonable to say that the intersection of various theoretical and empirical pieces of evidence, such as the conceptual framework, should provide enough wisdom to arrive at a decision here.

The following steps are more technical, starting from the identification of a sample frame; often there is no reliable list to refer to, which effectively excludes probability sampling as an approach. In fact, a lot of research projects, from module assignments to international surveys, are limited by this problem, and researchers should tread very carefully when presenting results, or, in other words, attempting to make generalisations from data (see Chapter 15 for more information on discussing marketing research findings). By the same token, we tend to use experience and best practice to decide on a specific sample size both for qualitative and quantitative research – in the case of the latter, this effectively means that we can estimate confidence levels and confidence intervals only retrospectively.

Ultimately, the implementation of sampling is influenced by the overall blueprint of a given piece of research and, in turn, influences the validity, reliability and generalisability of its findings. It is advisable to take a thorough, methodical look at the general elements surrounding sampling within the philosophical and practical boundaries set by the research paradigm.

Case Study: Online Research Panels

Online research panels have been growing in importance as consumers and businesses around the world tend to be available on a 24/7 basis. There are however some critical issues with creating and managing panels, such as:

a. self-selection – this is a problem associated with a lack of control in the selection of who registers for online panels; as a result of this, some segments might not be represented in a panel
b. professional respondents – some people tend to register for many panels, thus becoming 'professional' in the way they address questions, and end up providing doctored views on topics, and so on
c. speeders – respondents who are interested in the reward, be that guaranteed or otherwise, associated with a piece of online research; they rush through answers as their goal is to take part in as many projects as possible
d. openness – many respondents aren't necessarily honest when taking part in online panels as there is a lack of face-to-face contact.

The findings and outcomes of research might therefore be hard to generalise, even when a probability sampling technique has been used.

For these reasons, it is important to ensure that respondents are authentic, i.e. there is a multi-step validation process (contact information, double opt-in, IP verification). Also, panellist engagement should be assessed by examining the behaviour and participation history of subjects to exclude bad or inactive ones. The more sophisticated panels employ digital fingerprinting software to detect and de-dupe databases to integrate efforts to avoid over-sampling, i.e. to avoid interviewing the same people repeatedly. The resulting rules are reviewed to reduce the incidence of bias from all of these elements and, at the same time, replace panellists.

Because of the resources needed to create and maintain such conditions, there is a sizeable difference between what a company-run panel (e.g. the Microsoft.com Research Panel for the USA and Canada) and one managed by a global market research agency (e.g. the YouGov MENA Omnibus) can achieve. The former is a 25,000-strong panel that primarily collects feedback on products and services via online surveys – there is some initial screening to ensure that candidates are deemed useful, although one can always bend the truth. The latter comprises 434,000 dedicated panellists across the Middle East, North Africa, Pakistan and India, who take part both in regular and 'ad hoc' quantitative and qualitative research projects – this allows for the collection of data at a particular moment in time (cross-sectional) and between two or more points in time (longitudinal) with standard and sponsored (dedicated) questions.

For instance, members of online panels can share general information about what they buy, where and for how much. As a tool for data collection, panels generate a comprehensive view of consumer behaviour, opinions and attitudes, and can be integrated with other sources, such as point-of-sale (POS) data, in order to compile reliable views in many sectors. They have also proved to be effective and efficient instruments for reaching groups in remote locations or those who would otherwise be impossible to research within a given time frame. The more expensive ones are indeed extremely accurate as they employ statistically sound probability sampling techniques from a known sample frame, thus guaranteeing result generalisability. Furthermore, customised panels can be put together by specialist organisations to help achieve a comprehensive understanding of certain segments of interest. The minimum specifications required to

(Continued)

(Continued)

build and manage a 'private' panel include country, target audience profile, sample size (and composition), confidence level and confidence interval, timeline to completion and complexity, for instance length of questionnaire or duration of interview.

Multi-national FMCG giant Procter & Gamble has been leading the efforts to set guidelines for online research panels, which organisations should need to commit to, such as objectivity and transparency. This is to respond to situations whereby an apparently genuine set of responses would instead be found to be generated by a so-called 'intellectual sweatshop', an organisation hiding IP addresses so they can earn money by filling in multiple panel surveys posing as different people (Reitsma, 2010). Companies providing marketing research services must indeed be aware of the general and specific needs in relation to creating and selling online panels to other parties.

Case study questions:

1. What would you regard as the biggest threat to sampling when putting together an online panel, and why?
2. How do the various stages of sampling (refer to Figure 6.1) affect the way an organisation commissions an 'ad hoc' online panel if:
   - they want to reach out to a small group of highly knowledgeable respondents in a particular field, as opposed to...?
   - they want to attain a narrow confidence interval for a large target population, e.g. residents of Kuala Lumpur, Malaysia?
3. What viable alternatives exist in order for an online panel to address respondents belonging to particular target segments?

End of Chapter Questions

These questions should help you reflect on your understanding of this chapter:

1. What is the impact of a research paradigm on sampling, and vice versa?
2. What are the key steps of sampling, and what do they entail?
3. How can a sample frame influence the way researchers draw conclusions from a research project?
4. What kinds of issues are there to be considered when selecting cases from a target population?
5. How do the various sampling techniques relate to qualitative and quantitative research?
6. What is the fundamental difference between non-probability and probability sampling?
7. What are the pros and cons of non-probability sampling techniques?
8. How would you apply randomness in the context of probability sampling?

Checklist

After studying Chapter 6, you should now be familiar with these key concepts:

1. The definitions and principles of sampling
2. How to sample consumers and organisations for qualitative and quantitative research
3. The application of non-probability and probability methods
4. The characteristics of sampling and non-sampling errors
5. How to draw samples from target populations

Further Reading (in sequence from beginners to advanced)

Marketing Research Society of Pakistan (n.d.) Homepage. Available at: www.mrsp.com.pk/index.html

Research Rockstar (n.d.) Homepage. Available at: http://researchrockstar.com

De Keulenaer, F. (2008) Panel survey. In P. J. Lavrakas (ed.), *Encyclopedia of Survey Research Methods*. Thousand Oaks, CA: Sage Publications.

Southern Cross University (n.d.) Ethical research involving children. Centre for Children and Young People [online]. Available at: http://childethics.com

Griffin, A. and Hauser, J. R. (1993) The voice of the customer. *Marketing Science*, 12 (1), pp. 1–27.

Yang, Z., Wang, X. and Su, C. (2006) A review of research methodologies in international business. *International Business Review*, 15 (6), pp. 601–17.

Bibliography

Aaker, D. A., Kumar, V., Day, G. S. and Leone, R. P. (2011) *Marketing Research*, international student edition (10th edition). Hoboken, NJ: John Wiley & Sons.

Acorn (2014) The Acorn user guide: the consumer classification [online]. Available at: http://acorn.caci.co.uk/downloads/Acorn-User-guide.pdf [Accessed 5 May 2015].

Amanolahi, S. (2005) A note on ethnicity and ethnic groups in Iran. *Iran and the Caucasus*, 9 (1), pp. 37–42.

Baker, S. E. and Edwards, R. (2012) How many qualitative interviews is enough? *National Centre for Research Methods* [online]. Available at: http://eprints.ncrm.ac.uk/2273/4/how_many_interviews.pdf [Accessed 28 April 2015].

BBC News (2016) Georgia profile: overview. *BBC News World* [online, 22 January]. Available at: www.bbc.co.uk/news/world-europe-17302106 [Accessed 27 July 2016].

Betros, C. (2014) Organic food movement in Japan progressing slowly. *JapanToday* [online, 11 August]. Available at: www.japantoday.com/category/executive-impact/view/organic-food-movement-in-japan-progressing-slowly [Accessed 16 April 2015].

Bryman, A. and Bell, E. (2011) *Business Research Methods* (3rd edition). Oxford: Oxford University Press.

Bush, A. C. and Burns, R. F. (2014) *Marketing Research* (7th edition). Harlow: Pearson Education.

CAMEO Mexico Analysis (n.d.) Customer and market insight with CAMEO Mexico. *Callcredit Information Group* [online]. Available at: www.callcredit.co.uk/products-and-services/consumer-marketing-data/segmentation-analysis/cameo-global-classifications/cameo-americas/cameo-mexico [Accessed 22 March 2015].

Careers360 (2015) Top 100 universities in India 2014. *Team Careers* [online, 8 April]. Available at: www.university.careers360.com/articles/top-100-universities-in-india-2014 [Accessed 16 April 2015].

Coca-Cola Journey (2014) Coca-Cola to invest $8.2 million in Mexico by 2020. *Unbottled Our Blog* [online, 17 July]. Available at: www.coca-colacompany.com/coca-cola-unbottled/coca-cola-to-invest-82-billion-in-mexico-by-2020 [Accessed 11 March 2015].

Dane, F. C. (2011) *Evaluating Research: Methodology for People Who Need to Read Research*. Thousand Oaks, CA: Sage Publications.

De Paulo, P. (2000) Sample size for qualitative research. *Quirk's Marketing Research Media* [online, December]. Available at: www.quirks.com/articles/a2000/20001202.aspx [Accessed 5 June 2015].

Del Rey, J. (2015) Amazon relents on key merchant policy so prime members can get better selection. *Recode* [online, 14 May]. Available at: http://recode.net/2015/05/14/amazon-relents-on-key-merchant-policy-so-prime-members-can-get-better-selection [Accessed 16 May 2015].

European Commission (2014) What is an SME? Enterprise and Industry [online, 5 December]. Available at: http://ec.europa.eu/enterprise/policies/sme/facts-figures-analysis/sme-definition/index_en.htm [Accessed 16 April 2015].

Field, A. (2009) *Discovering Statistics Using SPSS* (3rd edition). London: Sage Publications.

General Statistics Office of Viet Nam (2014) Statistical Handbook of Viet Nam 2014. Released Publications [online]. Available at: file:///C:/Users/ab5750/Downloads/NGTK%20tom%20tat%202014.pdf [Accessed 5 June 2015].

guardianmedia (n.d.) Brand aid ad effectiveness testing. Available at: http://advertising.theguardian.com/brand-aid-ad-effectiveness-testing [Accessed 2 May 2015].

Hofstede, G. (1983a) National cultures in four dimensions: a research-based theory of cultural differences amongst nations. *International Studies of Management & Organizations*, 13 (1–2), pp. 46–74.

Hofstede, G. (1983b) The cultural relativity of organizational practices and theories. *Journal of International Business Studies*, 14 (2), pp. 75–89.

Innocent Drinks (2015) Things we make. Available at: www.innocentdrinks.ru/things-we-make [Accessed 25 April 2015].

Kantar Worldpanel (n.d.) Kantar Worldpanel Kenya Centre. Available at: www.kantarworldpanel.com/global/Countries/worldpanel/Kenya [Accessed 2 May 2015].

Malhotra, N. K. and Birks, D. F. (2007) *Marketing Research: An Applied Approach* (3rd European edition). Harlow: Pearson Education.

Mason, M. (2010) Sample size and saturation in PhD studies using qualitative interviews. *Forum: Qualitative Social Research* [online], 11 (3), Art. 8. Available at: www.qualitative-research.net/index.php/fqs/article/view/1428/3027 [Accessed 25 April 2015].

Microsoft (2015) About Microsoft: voice your opinions and make an impact on Microsoft products and services. [online]. Available at: www.microsoft.com/mscorp/marketing_research [Accessed 23 May 2015].

National Geographic (n.d.) Rural area. Encyclopedic entry [online]. Available at: http://nationalgeographic.org/encyclopedia/rural-area [Accessed 27 July 2016].

Osawa, J. (2013) Huawei set to launch new smartphone. *Wall Street Journal*, Tech [online, 17 June]. Available at: www.wsj.com/articles/SB10001424127887323566804578550454231397288 [Accessed 28 April 2015].

Oxford Dictionaries (n.d.) Random. *Language Matters* [online]. Available at: www.oxforddictionaries.com/definition/english/random [Accessed 23 May 2015].

Pfizer (2015) Vaccines. Health & Wellness [online]. Available at: www.pfizer.com/health/vaccines/index [Accessed 2 May 2015].

Pitcher, J. (2015) Japan's console and video game sales hit 24 year low. *IGN News* [online, 7 January]. Available at: http://uk.ign.com/articles/2015/01/08/japans-console-and-video-game-sales-hit-24-year-low [Accessed 2 May 2015].

Reitsma, R. (2010) The online panel quality debate continues. *Forrester* [online, 26 April]. Available at: http://blogs.forrester.com/reineke_reitsma/10-04-26-online_panel_quality_debate_continues [Accessed 13 June 2015].

Sarantakos, S. (2013) *Social Research* (4th edition). Basingstoke: Palgrave Macmillan.

Tesseras, L. (2015) How to stay on the right side of the rules when researching children. *Marketing Week*, 3 March.

Waters, K. (1991) Designing screening questionnaires to minimize dishonest answers. *Quirk's Marketing Research Review* [online, May]. Available at: www.quirks.com/articles/a1991/19910504.aspx [Accessed 25 April 2015].

Weisman, A. (2014) Here's how involved Netflix is in the production of its series. *Business Insider* [online, 24 June]. Available at: www.businessinsider.com/how-involved-netflix-is-in-production-of-shows-2014-6#ixzz3YaNwYd1d [Accessed 28 April 2015].

YouGov (2015) YouGov MENA Omnibus [online]. Available at: http://research.mena.yougov.com/en/services/omnibus [Accessed 23 May 2015].

Find journal articles and multiple choice questions online at: **https://study.sagepub.com/benzo** to support what you've learnt so far.

Part II introduced the theory and practice of planning marketing research and a system for identifying the correct tools and techniques to help best address a research question. Part III of the book focuses on the qualitative dimension of market research, but it is useful to remember that most questions may need to address both quantitative and qualitative aspects of the research problem in order to reach the best possible solution. Nevertheless, qualitative research is increasingly becoming the preferred method for social researchers and the next four chapters examine the reasons for this and the advantages of taking this approach.

Chapter 7 introduces the topic of qualitative market research and the justification for its existence. It considers its characteristics and gives advice on how to develop a good qualitative research design, taking into consideration the philosophical, methodological and technical dimensions of research.

Chapter 8 provides a toolbox for qualitative research, describing the methods and techniques that a researcher has at their disposal. It also examines two popular data-gathering techniques: 'observation' and 'interviews'.

Chapter 9 takes the topic further and demonstrates the merits of adopting a mixed-design methodology, illustrated through two research methods, action research and case studies, that may use qualitative and/or quantitative types of information.

Chapter 10 draws on the concepts and practice of the previous three chapters, illustrating how to develop a qualitative research project, from its earliest stage, establishing the aims of the project, through to the selection of relevant theories, methodology and carrying out data analysis, before addressing some key dimensions associated with the preparation of the report (or thesis).

PART III

Qualitative Research in Marketing

CHAPTER 7

Qualitative Research Methods: Elements of a Good Design

LEARNING OBJECTIVES

The key learning objectives of this chapter are:

1. To understand qualitative research in the context of marketing
2. To introduce the qualitative research methods available to researchers
3. To identify the key principles underpinning qualitative research
4. To explore how to design qualitative research
5. To determine how to assess quality in qualitative research

KEY CONCEPTS

By the end of this chapter, the reader should be familiar with the following concepts:

1. The philosophy of qualitative research
2. Qualitative research methods
3. Qualitative research tools
4. The concepts of validity and reliability
5. The quality of qualitative research

Chahid Fourali

Introduction

This chapter introduces qualitative research and the advantages it provides to market or social researchers. It reviews the research options available and highlights the philosophical as well as the methodological dimensions that relate to qualitative research and why this approach is particularly attractive. The chapter starts by offering guidance on how to determine whether a qualitative research approach is the right one to choose over alternatives, and subsequently how to ensure the process and outcomes of the research are sound, meeting the needs of the organisation sponsoring it.

For many years, qualitative research was criticised by 'scientists' for its lack of objectivity. Part of the problem stemmed from the fact that researchers used to believe that if you wanted to conduct proper research, you had to adopt the experimental methods favoured by the exact sciences, with their quantitative measurements and their ultimate aim of making precise predictions of phenomena based on hard scientific evidence. However, this type of approach to research has been deemed inadequate for problems that do not satisfactorily lend themselves to such experimental manipulation and objectivity.

Consider a researcher who wants to determine how a person decides what product they favour. They may of course surreptitiously watch customers, via cameras, making decisions about which products appeal to them most, but this does not inform the researcher about the exact reasons for their choice. Nowadays, the methodology debate has moved on from 'Which method is more scientific?' to 'How do you determine which is the most relevant method to help resolve a particular issue or problem?'

The aim of research is to ensure that there is a match between the research problem/question and the method adopted. This sounds like a truism, but many researchers focus too much on methodology, trying to match the problem to the method rather than the other way around. This is akin to a mechanic saying 'OK, now I have a hammer, let's see what the problem with this car's engine is'. Obviously, this approach is not helpful as it fails to select the appropriate tool based on the diagnosis and has been termed by some critics as 'methodolatry'. Hence, the issue of identifying a problem should come first rather than being relegated to a secondary stage after a method has already been selected.

Snapshot: Setting the Scene – Love Your Skin

This project won the prestigious Health Service Journal (HSJ) award of 'Best Social Marketing Project' for skin cancer prevention. The award was shared by NHS Devon and Exeter College who were partners in the project.

Social marketing is a fairly new development within the discipline of marketing. It emerged as a field of study, aiming to capitalise on the powerful techniques of marketing to address social problems. Instead of focusing on developing a product with a view to achieving commercial profit, social marketing aims predominantly address issues in society and highlight diverse problems such as drinking and driving, drug addiction, obesity or domestic violence, to mention just a few. Hence, social marketing integrates both social research and marketing research to provide compelling solutions to social problems.

This mini case reflects a social marketing issue: skin cancer. In the UK, the rate of skin cancer has quadrupled over the last 30 years as a result of changing lifestyles. Although the risk of cancer tends to increase with age, the most dangerous form, known as malignant melanoma, is disproportionately high for the 15–34 age group. This type of cancer is largely preventable if the right healthy habits are adopted, including preventing sunburn, avoiding sun beds, using SPF15 (or higher) sun cream, staying in the shade during the hottest parts of the day and covering up with adequate sunglasses and clothing.

Devon County Council discovered that incidents of all kinds of skin cancer amongst young people in the community, as well as its mortality rate, were much higher than the national average. Additionally, it found that the cost of diagnosing and treating skin cancer amounted to almost £3 million per year. Devon therefore identified skin cancer as a key health priority for the council.

Researching the challenges and determining the strategy

The council decided to take a social marketing approach to tackle this problem, which meant adopting marketing techniques, including marketing research.

It decided to undertake qualitative research techniques, such as focus groups and interviewing, to understand the attitudes, perceptions and preferences of its young population and look for opportunities to change unhealthy behaviour.

The research identified six priority audiences to target with the study: mothers of young children, parents of school children, teenagers, outdoor workers, sports and leisure participants and older people (for early diagnosis). Through the use of qualitative research, it identified a number of high-risk attitudes such as: 'skin cancer is something that happens to others', 'sunburn is not serious', 'sun beds are less harmful than the sun because you are in control', 'you need to burn to get a tan', 'tanned skin is more attractive than pale skin', 'sun cream is too expensive or difficult and messy to apply', 'the UK has less sun so it is best to make the most of it when it appears'.

Action and results

As a result of these findings, a four-fold strategy was adopted to help change unhealthy habits, which involved educating the targeted groups, designing an environment to minimise the problem and improve the distribution of resources, providing support when needed and healthy alternatives, and developing regulations/policies to support the aims.

As a result of the campaign, involving multiple agencies, the results showed a heightened sense of awareness and change of behaviour towards sun protection and avoiding sun beds. Since this study, NHS Dorset has also undertaken a campaign called 'Brilliant Futures' and, based on the research findings, piloted an appearance-based intervention strategy using ultraviolet light to demonstrate the results of sun damage and providing a safer alternative through fake tan application. The project was shown to be effective in changing short-term attitudes.

Source: Adapted from NHS (2011) and NHS (2012)

Market researchers are faced with a variety of techniques to help them understand various market phenomena. It is customary to contrast qualitative and quantitative research primarily to highlight their differences rather than set them up as either/or contenders. Indeed, in many cases, several techniques, quantitative and qualitative, are used by the same researcher to study the same phenomenon, as both can provide valuable insights into the issue being addressed.

What is Qualitative Research?

There is no easy way of defining qualitative marketing research (QMR). One approach is to start with a popular general definition of qualitative research (QR) before looking more specifically at qualitative marketing research.

Denzin and Lincoln (2000) offer the following definition in their *Handbook of Qualitative Research*:

> Qualitative research is a situated activity that locates the observer in the world. It consists of a set of interpretive, material practices that makes the world visible. These practices ... turn the world into a series of representations including field notes, interviews, conversations, photographs, recordings and memos to the self. At this level, qualitative research involves an interpretive, naturalistic approach to the world. This means that qualitative researchers study things in their natural settings, attempting to make sense of, or to interpret, phenomena in terms of the meanings people bring to them. (2000: 3)

This definition is quite inclusive and appears to cover the researcher's (the observer) position (natural setting), the tools (such as interviews and field notes) and the role of the researcher (i.e. to interpret phenomena) simultaneously, hence the label 'interpretivist' model. Another way of putting it is to argue that in qualitative research the inquirer makes knowledge claims based on constructivist, advocacy or participatory perspectives; these strategies tend to adopt matching 'speculative' methods such as grounded theory, ethnography or phenomenology and the derived data are by nature 'open-ended' with a view to helping develop them further (Galt, 2008).

From a market research perspective, the UK's Association for Qualitative Research (AQR) states that qualitative market research is:

> Research designed to help organisational decision making, focusing on understanding the nature of phenomena and their meaning, rather than their incidence. It tends to have the following characteristics: direct face-to-face contact between the primary researchers and those being researched; in-depth examination of small-scale samples or small numbers of observations; unstructured interviewing guides which are responsive to context and may be amended throughout the project; the researcher and his/her interpretative input is key to the process. (AQR, 2013)

QR appears to expressly or tacitly include the following characteristics:

- is naturalistic, interpretative with a view to understanding meanings which people assign to phenomena (actions, decisions, beliefs, values, etc.) based on their social worlds

Constructivism/Constructionism These concepts are generally used interchangeably. Constructivists believe that the world/outside reality can only be accessed via human constructions of knowledge based on one's own experience and interactions with other humans. The concept has been adopted by many researchers in fields as wide as education, sociology and psychology. Some writers differentiate 'constructionism' from constructivism, arguing that the former may be seen as the attempt to help others (e.g. students) build cognitive constructions and frameworks (also known as schemas) that can be explicitly described and criticised. This is an important part of the learning process. In a business situation (and especially the entrepreneurial world), such explicit rendering of a student construction is important to avoid unwarranted conclusions about the merits of a business idea, thereby saving time and money.

Causality The principle that every event that takes place is caused by another event or process. It is important to question the "direction of causality" as a researcher may make the false interpretation that one event (X) is caused by another event (Y) when the later may actually be the result of the previous one (if not caused by a third event (Z) or a combination of events).

- highlights the importance of the participants' frames of reference
- adopts a flexible research design guided by purpose
- provides a rich/complex perspective
- focuses on developing meaningful explanations through analysis and interpretation
- produces 'findings not arrived at by statistical procedures or other means of quantification'. (Strauss and Corbin, 1998, p. 11)

Qualitative research can be used for a variety of purposes; it may help define a problem, support a quantitative research approach through helping clarify directions of causality (see definition box) or simply be used as a fully satisfactory approach in its own right. In terms of links between interpretation and theory, researchers have long pointed out that once an interpretation has been 'accepted', that is, when it becomes an established theory, its influence can become quite potent as it will help filter out experiences that do not fit within it. This factor has been at the heart of debates by several constructionists and philosophers of science (e.g. Kuhn, 1970).

Reflective Activity: An Enjoyable Experience

Working in pairs, take it in turns to describe an enjoyable 'shopping' experience; and with the support of each other find out as much detail as possible about the context that helped shape the experience.

Having considered the definitions and characteristics of qualitative research given above, it might appear obvious that QR is an ideal tool to gain a close understanding of the most important subject of interest to the marketer: the customer. However, this has not always been the case, as we'll discover when we look back at the history of QR in the next section.

Qualitative Research in Marketing: A Chequered History

Up until a few decades ago, research was considered credible only if carried out through a logical empiricist/positivist approach (i.e. based on observable reality; see also Parts II and IV) and theory testing carried out through quantitative analysis. This view was dominant despite early arguments by some established thinkers (such as the philosopher Immanuel Kant and the sociologist Max Weber) who recognised that there are ways of knowing about the world *other* than direct observation and that people use these all the time.

Advanced: 'Marketers aim to understand customers better than they understand themselves'

Marketing research aims at a deep understanding of customers, but one of the obstacles it faces is the reliability of its findings. For instance, some studies use psychological techniques, including using

(Continued)

(Continued)

projective tests. These tests allow the researcher to identify unconscious motivations about different issues by inviting those taking part in the research to comment on a series of ambiguous stimuli, such as ink blot pictures that can be perceived differently by different people, depending on their current subjective interests. More recently, another method of marketing research was presented by Zaltman and Zaltman in a book aptly titled *Marketing Metaphoria* (2008). Using this method, the research goes beyond the stated reasons to uncover deeper causes of consumer behaviour. The method seems to make assumptions about its effectiveness without enough empirical evidence.

Such approaches, which can be classified by the label 'depth psychology', have not been convincing in addressing the criticism of their lack of rigour or reliability. Nevertheless, there is plenty of psychological research that comes under the banner of 'cognitive psychology', which has been pushing the boundaries of knowledge about consumer behaviour through studies linking customers' thinking and beliefs to their buying behaviours. One field that has particularly benefitted from these types of studies is that of branding.

Positivism A philosophical movement that rejects the study of events that may not be subject to objective testing through experimentation or logical inference. Hence, this movement rejects the study of metaphysical questions such as 'Why is there something, rather than nothing?' or 'Is the universe finite or infinite?'

By the 1970s, however, positivism and the legitimacy of social research based on the 'scientific method' began to be debated, although concerns had already arisen in the 1960s about applying a 'scientific approach' to social research. Denzin and Lincoln (2000) identified three crises associated with taking a positivist approach to qualitative research. The first they labelled a crisis of representation, a crisis which highlights the conspicuous gap reflected in the researchers' inability to formally address and report on the lived experiences of the subjects being studied.

A second crisis, referred to as one of legitimation, reflects the problem of what can be considered justifiable as a focus of research. Positivist research has established criteria for what can be considered 'robust research', such as validity and reliability (discussed below), which in turn are backed up by quantitative and other methods of analysis. Qualitative research does not always find such positivist criteria helpful, or the methods to back them up. Qualitative research can use a number of criteria for robustness and there does not appear to be a consensus (or limitations) on what may be considered legitimate for the researchers to focus their attention on. Nevertheless, this does not mean 'everything goes', as a strong rationale, backed up by some form of empirical support, has to be provided.

The third crisis, identified as a crisis of praxis (or practice), builds on the previous two crises and addresses the question of the unwieldy number of 'written reports' and how to decide what merits attention, with a view to taking action and 'changing the world'. This crisis also reflects the challenges of moving from the traditionally detached researcher's role, whose aim is to 'simply shed light on the phenomenon being studied' (at times, in an artificial environment), to a role of researchers who are part of the complex world they are trying to understand. This means that they need to work with a multiplicity of variables and stakeholders, to help find solutions to the real problems being faced and the practical urgency they reflect.

In light of the weaknesses of the positivist paradigm, outlined above, a number of challenges were identified (Ritchie and Lewis, 2003):

1. The unrealistic expectation of scientists to achieve unambiguous results and the need to accommodate the uncertainty of the findings (see also Fourali, 1997).
2. The lack of ability to 'control' subjective human variables under study as required by 'rigorous' scientific studies.
3. The irrelevance of neutralising contextual dimensions which are decisive in explaining human behaviour.
4. The importance of the meaning and purpose of behaviour in controlled experimental studies which tend to be done away with as 'unscientific' interferences.
5. The limited relevance of overarching theories and aggregated data to account for the lives of individuals.
6. The need for social researchers to immerse themselves in the reality they are studying to discover meanings and explanations, rather than adopting a detached, rigid hypothesis-testing perspective that may miss crucial insights into the phenomenon studied.
7. The importance of research is not solely as a tool for explaining 'reality' but also a tool for improving the human condition.

Although an improved version of positivism, known as post-positivism, was put forward to address the issue of external factors that might impede or influence researchers (e.g. background, knowledge and values as well as the theories they may subscribe to), it did not fully address all the reservations listed above. In particular, post-positivists still believed that there are 'universals' (abstract, general rules), external to the researcher, that could be discovered using the scientific method to guide practice. Hence, social researchers began to see that a more interpretivist perspective was better suited to their needs.

By 'interpretivism', researchers mean a perspective that recognises the human agency in interpreting/making sense of reality through social constructions that mediate 'language, consciousness, shared meanings, and instruments' (Myers, 2008, p. 38). As a result, interpretivism became a byword for qualitative research. Researchers see interpretivism as a development emanating from the previous two stages of research models – positivism and critical theory. Consequently, qualitative research provided a valuable alternative to overcoming the limitations of positivism and soon started to be used and considered as a credible research approach in the social sciences, including market research.

In this chapter and the following chapters dealing with qualitative research, when we refer to positivism we also include post-positivism, as, fundamentally, these two perspectives reflect the same outlook on reality.

The Market Research Context

Until recently, qualitative research tended to be overlooked or, at best, downplayed, in many market research books. There seemed to be a certain reluctance by market researchers to embrace a qualitative (i.e. interpretivist) perspective, as market research tends to focus almost exclusively on quantitative research techniques. One might say this is surprising for, whilst there will always be some contexts best addressed through quantitative analysis, many, if not the majority of marketing research situations, require at least some interpretation of data via qualitative analysis. This statement becomes even more relevant

Figure 7.1 Objectivism and the marketing researcher

when we consider that marketing is primarily about understanding the wants, desires and intentions of customers. Qualitative research can help provide a deep understanding of purpose and takes into consideration moral and social dimensions that may not initially have been obvious to the researcher. Despite its complexity, qualitative research offers a rich perspective that complements a quantitative approach, providing a more realistic insight into the situation a researcher is presented with.

Some researchers, for example Malhotra and Birks (2007), went further in specifying the various contexts a researcher might deal with, by identifying key information to help choose suitable research techniques, illustrated by the following questions:

- 'Is the targeted information publicly available or is it confidential or personal?'
- 'Is it communicable? (e.g. is there a lack of means of communication?)'
- 'Is the customer aware of the availability of the information?'
- 'What type of information is being targeted (e.g. underpinning reasoning, intuition or unconscious)?'

Like any explorer, a researcher wants to first be aware of what they are looking for, determine where they may find it and then set out to look for it.

Philosophical Assumptions and the Researcher's Toolbox

Researchers classify three broad stages or steps when determining the research methods they are going to use:

- Step 1: Determine the philosophical assumptions.
- Step 2: Determine the strategies of enquiry.
- Step 3: Determine the relevant research methods for data gathering.

We have already covered Step 1 in the previous section, so we will now focus predominantly on Steps 2 and 3.

As a researcher, it is important to take time to think about the precedents that help demonstrate the soundness of your choice. There is a wealth of literature on qualitative and quantitative methods, ranging from positivistic to interpretive approaches, as discussed above. The question any researcher needs to address is: How do I choose whether my method is qualitative or quantitative? Or, to put it in a more philosophical frame, would an interpretivist (qualitative) or positivistic (quantitative) approach be more appropriate?

In fact, this question appears to assume that the answer has to be one or the other. We will discuss this view later when we address the issue of fuzzy logic, a method that arguably combines both quantitative and qualitative perspectives. Nevertheless, the question remains: How do we select a research method?

There are several views about how a researcher can justify their research approach. Most would agree that there is a need to link a researcher's worldview to the chosen design based on the techniques available (see Figure 7.1).

Worldview An understanding of the 'tangible' reality based on personal beliefs and assumptions either derived from one's own or others' experiences

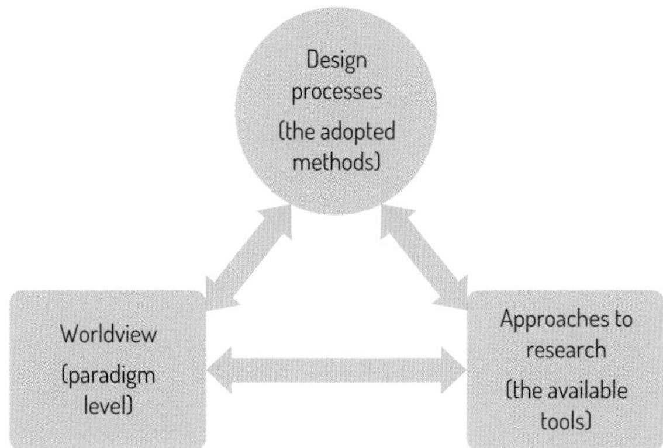

Figure 7.2 Dimensions of a research method

Source: adapted from Cresswell, 2003

Figure 7.2 suggests that there is an iterative process involving three dimensions that help in reaching a final decision about which research method to adopt. This iterative process may be encouraged by a deep understanding of the phenomenon at hand and feedback from other researchers about how best to address it. At each stage of the design process, the researcher needs to ask questions such as 'Have I adopted the right method?', 'Are there more appropriate methods available to me that match my target phenomenon more closely?', 'Does my approach match my worldview of reality (is it out there to discover or is it constructed)?'

Although marketing researchers – particularly practitioners as opposed to academics – do not tend to routinely consider, philosophically, the 'nature of reality' or knowledge explicitly, reflecting in this way is key to determining a consciously-driven research perspective. This consideration is at the heart of justifying a chosen method and its associated research tools. Such issues are primarily addressed by philosophers of science (including the social sciences).

One of the most detailed presentations available on qualitative marketing research, which starts from a philosophical perspective about the world to inform the choice of which research methods and techniques to adopt, is the one provided by Carson and colleagues (2005). Figure 7.3 provides an interpretation of their views.

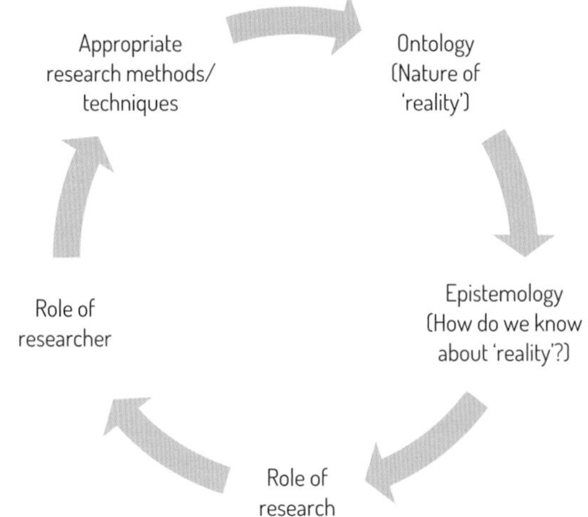

Figure 7.3 Diagram reflecting the link between worldview and research method

Source: adapted from Carson et al., 2005

As reflected in Figure 7.3, a savvy researcher will need to ground their approach by building arguments about the nature of the world (ontology), the justification for our knowledge (epistemology) and how to select a method of knowing that meets the requirement for valid justifications (i.e. methodology). Based on this perspective, we derive a quick algorithm to help decide what method would be most suited to our research, depending on the above precedents:

Research in Practice: Algorithm for Selecting a Method That Matches a Researcher's Perspective

The following list of questions should help a researcher identify a research perspective that matches their worldview. Depending on the number of positions selected for each question (in terms of positivistic, P, or interpretative perspective, I), researchers will be in a better position to understand their perspective and select the most helpful approach for carrying out their project.

Question 0: What is my view of the world? Is the world understandable?

Answer 0.1: If yes, move to next question.

Answer 0.2: If no, there is no point in doing your research if you believe the world is not understandable.

Question 1: Do we have direct access to physical external reality?

Answer 1.1: Yes, humans have direct access to external reality (positivism). (P1)

Answer 1.2: No, there is no direct access to the external world (interpretivism). (I1)

Answer 1.3: 'Not sure' —> Clarify your perspective and go back to Question 1.

Question 2: How many realities are there?

Answer 2.1: Only one reality (positivism). (P1)

Answer 2.2: Multiple realities (interpretivism). (I1)

Question 3: How do we gain knowledge about reality?

Answer 3.1: By working from theory and hypothesis testing and seeking to generalise findings. (P1)

Answer 3.2: By working with several 'realities' to understand specific contexts. (I1)

Answer 3.3: Both 3.1 and 3.2. (P1 & I1)

Question 4: What is the aim of research?

Answer 4.1: It aims to describe and explain reality as it is, with a view to predicting future occurrences. (P1)

Answer 4.2: The aim is to understand and interpret specific realities as they are now. (I1)

Answer 4.3: 'Not sure' —> Clarify your perspective and go back to Question 4.

Question 5: What is the position of the researcher?

Answer 5.1: The researcher aims to be neutral and objective by being detached from the phenomenon he/she studies. (P1)

Answer 5.2: The researcher is aware of and assesses his/her 'contribution' to reality. (I1)

Answer 5.3: 'Not sure' —> Clarify your perspective and go back to Question 5.

Question 6: Which primary techniques does the researcher tend to make use of?

Answer 6.1: Primarily quantitative methods with a view to minimising subjectivity. (P1)

Answer 6.2: Primarily non-quantitative. (I1)

Result: Depending on the number of P1s and I1s, the responses will range from a fully positivistic perspective (maximum of 7 P1s) to a fully interpretivist perspective (maximum of 7 I1s). If the number is a mixture of P1s and I1s, this may reflect an approach where a mixed methodology is favoured.

Strategies of Enquiry

After determining the appropriate philosophical assumptions for a research project, the next stage is to try and determine which strategies of enquiry to adopt which match the marketing researcher's worldview. There are three categories of research strategies: quantitative, qualitative and mixed, as illustrated in Figure 7.4.

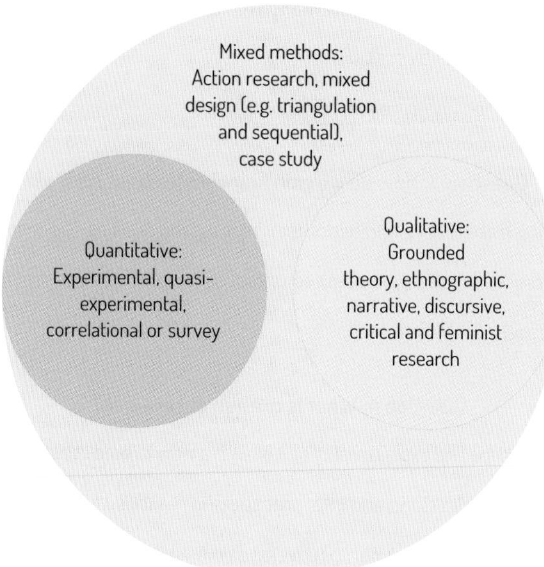

Figure 7.4 Categories of strategies of enquiries

Although there is general agreement amongst researchers about the different strategies, not all researchers tend to regard them in exactly the same way. For example, some researchers classify 'action research' (see Chapter 9) as a purely qualitative method of enquiry, but this is considered by some to be a reductionist view, since action research can make use of both qualitative and quantitative methods. As suggested in Figure 7.4, there is a variety of qualitative research methods and many of them overlap. Chapter 8 takes a closer look at a number of the best-known methods, including grounded theory.

Irrespective of which method of research is used, the aim of all research is to 'derive' new knowledge through one of three processes:

- deduction: moving from general models or theory to hypothesis testing based on empirical research
- induction: drawing general statements or explanations based on systematic observations of some cases
- abduction (refer back to Chapter 5 for a more detailed explanation and illustration).

The concept of abduction originated from Charles Peirce and is generally used to reflect situations where both induction and deduction are used in the iterative process of analysing the data and revising the theory. The aim of the abduction process is to present opportunities to make new discoveries, whilst retaining sufficient rigour to be able to justify it. Hence, abduction is more about an attitude of being open and ready to review old views in the light of new information. Given that this situation tends to apply to most research, the term abduction has become increasingly popular with researchers. The word 'abduction' (i.e. forcibly taking someone against their will) can be very misleading in this context. The word 'dinduction' would be a more straightforward and recognisable term to describe the concept.

Research Methods for Data Gathering

Once a researcher has decided on the most appropriate strategy of enquiry, the next step is to determine which research methods to use to gather the necessary information needed to answer the research question. The four research tools mostly associated with qualitative research and the most commonly used methods of data collection in qualitative inductive enquiries are:

Interviewing: a formal, face-to-face meeting with a view to elicit the meanings that an interviewee attaches to certain events or issues.

Focus group: a small sample of people associated with a particular event or issue selected with a view to obtaining their opinion on a selected topic.

Observation: direct or indirect recording of events as they happened live, such as when recording the behaviour of customers during their selection of the products.

Document/audio/visual material analysis: a systematic analysis of material with a view to understanding the communication in order to derive themes and trends.

When making a decision about which of the four tools to select for any specific research project, you are strongly advised to consider the advantages and disadvantages of each method. Chapter 8 reviews several qualitative research methods and advises on the pros and cons of data-gathering techniques that researchers can use.

Note that researchers have an ethical duty to inform the research participants about the purpose of the study, to ensure confidentiality and, where appropriate, to warn participants that their views will be disseminated (see also the Ethics box overleaf). These ethical considerations should be set out clearly in any final research project report, dissertation or assignment.

Generally, research subjects are reminded, right at the outset of any data collection context (e.g. interview or focus group), of the aims of the study and, in the case of a focus group, are given the opportunity to introduce themselves. Short, informal activities or conversations at the start can help to break the ice and establish rapport among the participants – they can even be linked to the research topic.

Ethics

Marketing is frequently criticised and seen as the culprit behind irresponsible business practices, whose main aim is to push their products or services without any concern for either society or the environment. It is true that many corporations do not seem to worry too much about the effect of their marketing activities on society, for example as a result of the aggressive marketing of alcoholic drinks or foods that are high in fat or sugar. However, it is also important to remember that marketing, like other disciplines, offers tools that can be used for social good. For instance, many governmental projects make use of marketing techniques to help address drinking and drug-related problems, domestic violence and car accidents, to mention just a few. Nevertheless, market researchers should always be aware of the consequences, both short and long term, associated with the products or services they are studying. Recent studies suggest that a community's choice of products is also influenced by the degree of responsibility associated with a product or the company producing it. So, it makes both moral and business sense to be aware of these issues.

Figure 7.5 Challenges of interviewing

Research in Practice: Example of an Interview Schedule

Possible questions when seeking advice from a successful entrepreneur:

- How do you select a winning idea? Could you illustrate this, using examples?
- Can you tell me if you have any general principles that guide you in selecting and running your businesses?
- How do you translate these ideas into day-to-day activities?
- Can you elaborate more, taking into account the marketing perspective?
- What advice would you give a budding entrepreneur?

Understanding the Key Principles Underpinning Qualitative Research: Validity and Reliability

All research needs to refer to agreed quality checks that ensure that sufficient rigour was involved in reaching conclusions that either support current views or provide new 'knowledge' on a particular issue. When doing so, researchers tend to refer to three key principles or their equivalent in a qualitative context:

1. Validity – whether an account or an instrument accurately represents what it sets out to measure
2. Reliability – whether a research tool can be relied on to produce consistent results
3. Generalisability – the ability to reach conclusions or recommendations that can be generalised or extended beyond the context addressed by the study.

The last principle, generalisability, is not considered as important as the first two in the context of qualitative research. Indeed, many social studies do not claim to apply their conclusions to other contexts, be it industries, countries or situations. However, it is useful to note here that although validity and reliability are separate concepts, they are mutually dependent. For example, if we consider a brand personality test, the more its components target exactly (and measure accurately) the key dimensions of a brand personality, the more agreement there will be between the different researchers. The more ambiguity there is surrounding the key dimensions being measured, the less accurate the test will be, resulting in less agreement between different researchers.

Some qualitative researchers have contested the relevance of the word 'reliability' (given that it is hard to replicate the results of unique situations) and prefer to use words like 'credibility', 'confirmability', 'consistency' or 'neutrality' (Lincoln and Guba, 1985). The concepts of validity and reliability are, arguably, at the heart of the debate between various research traditions. For instance, the positivist tradition argues that with adequate scientific instruments we should be able to objectively, logically and reliably measure the reality that is out there. In comparison, in qualitative studies, the 'conclusions' cannot be separated from the context of the occurrence of the phenomena, which are considered unique. Even if practitioners find certain research outcomes relevant to their own context and relate them to their own situation, they should always remember that they may not apply to their specific context. Hence, a qualitative research report may produce general guidelines that can help people dealing with similar cases, but these guidelines are not prescriptive.

Qualitative researchers seek alternatives to concepts used by positivist researchers, or at least aim to make them more flexible to accommodate their concerns. They suggest that validity should be linked to the quality of inferences or 'trustworthiness' of a study, rather than conforming to any formal rules or standardised procedure. In addition, the concept of reliability may be linked to the concept of triangulation (see point 6 below).

Triangulation This concept reflects a research approach that involves using multiple sources of information (e.g. different participants in different settings) and research techniques (e.g. surveys, interviews, observation in natural settings) to back up interpretations. For qualitative researchers, triangulation enhances the credibility of their findings and, consequently, the respectability of qualitative methods. The variety of sources also provides a fuller picture about the event being researched that helps *derive robust conclusions and increase the degree of success of the recommendations for business managers.*

Maxwell (2013), supported by other studies, suggests a number of strategies to back up the validity of qualitative research. The following is based on his classification:

1. Sustained involvement in the context of the study – there is no surprise here since the longer one spends interacting with a situation and working on alternative hypotheses that may explain it, the clearer and more valid the interpretation. This means that longer-term studies tend to reflect more accurately the phenomena of study.
2. Richness of data – as a consequence of point 1 above, sustained involvement leads to a richer variety of information and minimises researchers' bias by helping to provide a more detailed account of the phenomenon being studied, rather than selected clips that may say more about the researcher's idiosyncrasies. Researchers should take as many notes and details as possible (including transcription of videotapes) to provide a strong grounding to their conclusion.
3. Validating respondents' views – this type of validation, also known as 'member checks', involves verifying the accuracy of the derived data and conclusions with the participants that took part in the research. However, it is not clear why this later check should have more validity than the original responses, for example in an interview.
4. Use of informal interventions – given that qualitative research does not make use of 'formal treatments' as in an empirical approach, informal procedures for verifying an alternative interpretation are often used. An example of this type of intervention is Goldenberg's (1992) study of the effect that a teacher's expectation of and behaviour towards a pupil has on their progress in reading. In this study, the researcher, having shared his interpretation to account for one student's failure to meet the teacher's expectation, noted that this led to the teacher's change in behaviour which, in turn, led to a change in the student's reading ability. Additionally, Goldenberg provides a description of the process describing how the change took place which, according to Maxwell (2013), was more convincing than a correlation index.
5. Searching for discrepancies among evidence – this is similar to Popper's (1963) idea of falsifiability. The aim of this approach is to weigh up evidence supporting or disconfirming the suggested interpretation to either review the interpretation or account for the discrepant data. As part of this process, a researcher may seek fellow researchers' opinions to minimise personal bias. Clearly, there may be situations where it may not be easy to draw a conclusion either way. In this case, it is best for the researcher to report the discrepant cases and leave it to the research community to decide for themselves or determine new avenues.
6. Triangulation – Miles and Huberman (1984) argue that there is nothing new about triangulation as it is used on a daily basis in several professions, for example by police inspectors, mechanics or GPs. These professionals weigh up the evidence from a variety of sources to arrive at the most likely cause of a problem. Likewise, researchers are encouraged to make use of various sources, individuals or settings to avoid the errors/biases associated with one source of information. Another metaphor for this type of study is the old adage 'do not put all your eggs in one basket'. Although it is likely that all sources may be subject to an element of bias, using more than one source of 'evidence' makes it much easier to accept an argument.
7. Quantitative backup – traditionally, quantitative evidence has been associated with positivistic studies. However, it is hard to imagine a full report without reference to the 'occurrence', 'rarity' or 'frequency' of a particular phenomenon. If any such allusions

are made, it is important to back these up with evidence, in the form of a quantitative index (e.g. a percentage or number). For example, consider shoppers being observed buying a loaf of bread after marketers changed the packaging; how many observations or interviews seem to suggest that the new packaging is an influential factor in buying that loaf of bread? Numbers are also key to providing details of the context of the study so that other researchers may either try to replicate the procedure or simply understand it better. Fourali (1997) demonstrates that researchers should even try and accommodate how they measure responses by ensuring human uncertainties are taken on board (see Chapter 10).

8. Comparisons – similar to offering quantitative evidence, drawing comparisons is not exclusive to quantitative/positivistic studies. Comparisons, without necessarily invoking empirical concepts such as 'control groups', are generally necessary to try and make the causality case. This has been one of the key objections to the credibility of qualitative studies, especially if the study involves looking at different cases at different times and places from different perspectives. In this situation, the nagging question is 'How can it be demonstrated that the presumed cause, of any outcome, is the most potent one in the light of other potential explanations/scenarios?' (Shadish et al., 2002). This question, if not addressed, may constitute a breach of validity. Maxwell (2013) cites an example where the focus was on the characteristics of 'best teachers', without contrasting with another group of, say, 'not so good teachers'. However, the researcher did away with this need for a 'control group' by contrasting her findings with the literature of less helpful teachers, as well as encouraging contributors to the study to contrast the list of characteristics of 'best teachers' with those of less successful ones.

Determining the Research Design

By now it should be evident that the aim of qualitative research is to offer a flexible alternative to conventional research traditions, where research tools have to be aligned with the purpose of the study. This means that a design with a structure that is too fixed is not recommended. Indeed, various authors have suggested several models that are all appropriate. Although they differ slightly, they all agree that a minimum number of 'ingredients' need to be included, as shown in Figure 7.5.

Figure 7.5 reflects the main elements of a design described by several researchers; yet, whilst there is some initial linearity (e.g. aims, questions, conceptualisation and method), after each draft of these elements there needs to be an iterative process that moves backwards and forwards to verify what went before and link with what comes after. The research principles are at the heart of the diagram as these principles represent the basis for the arguments at each stage of the research. Although validity is key, other dimensions are also relevant. For example, transparency and practicality are included, which are close to the principles of verifiability and parsimony.

Using Figure 7.5, we can decide how to structure our study.

Quality in Qualitative Research

In a way, the concept of quality is very similar to that of validity, albeit slightly broader. Consequently, if a study and its conclusions are judged as having a high level of validity,

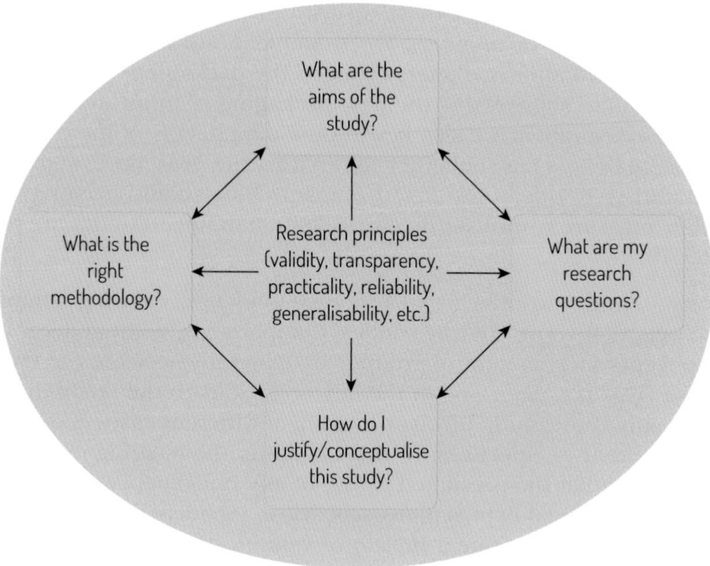

Figure 7.6 Design ingredients for a qualitative study

Source: adapted from Maxwell, 2013

Herd psychology is a concept used by psychologists to explain how imitation may affect the behaviour of humans. It argues that humans use the behaviour of others to determine what is considered acceptable to guide their own behaviour. This can be extended to researchers who may be 'induced' to adopt research approaches that constitute the traditional (acceptable) way of undertaking research, thereby limiting their options in trying to match the research problem to the research method

then this would mean them being of high quality, too. Qualitative criteria may include broader measures such as epistemological fit, coherence and integration. These factors also enable us to consider the whole enterprise of research. How much of it is influenced by human nature? Is it about 'herd psychology', where 'established' research methods are being adopted willy-nilly, or is there a genuine attempt at determining the purpose and needs of the study and deriving the relevant tools after thoughtful reflection?

Table 7.1 lists a number of quality criteria that researchers should adhere to, presented in the form of questions.

Table 7.1 Dimensions that qualitative researchers are interested in to ensure research quality

1. Do the identified categories of analysis fit the data?
2. How integrated is the suggested theory with the supporting analysis?
3. How reflexive/self-reflexive has the researcher been?
4. How adequate is the sampling in addressing a variety of competing explanations to the emerging theory?
5. Has the researcher been sensitive to alternative explanations, especially from the participants?
6. How much of the report/account is documented?
7. How transferable is the study or its outcomes to other situations beyond the current one?

Reflective Activity

- Based on the guidelines on the previous page, select a topic or study and develop a mind map that identifies the dos and don'ts that a quality qualitative research report should demonstrate, and illustrate examples of arguments developed to meet each of the guidelines. Are there aspects that may have been overlooked?
- Select an article associated with an area of interest to you and analyse it in terms of the above guidelines. Does the article satisfy all of the guidelines? If not, clarify the exceptions and decide how the outstanding issues may be addressed.

Chapter Summary

This chapter introduced the concept of qualitative research in marketing.

It described why some researchers have reservations about this method but argued in favour of market researchers who try to get as close as possible to understanding the customer's views and feelings about a product or a product idea before developing it. The chapter explained the need to be led by the aims of the research project and associated questions in choosing the research tools that will most likely help address the questions. It also addressed the need to link the researcher's worldview and associated assumptions to the most acceptable approaches. For example, a positivistic perspective aims to maximise the objectivity of the research tools, whereas a qualitative researcher argues for the need to focus on the subjective dimensions of the research area.

The chapter differentiated between qualitative, quantitative and mixed methods and the tools (or techniques) that make up these methods (e.g. experimental, survey, ethnography, critical). It also highlighted the importance of the two principles of validity and reliability in arguing for the accuracy and trustworthiness of both the research process and the results when conducting qualitative research. Associated with these principles are criteria that help improve the quality of qualitative research, which were outlined in Table 7.1. Finally, the chapter presented the main steps involved in identifying the aims of the study, determining the research questions and conceptualising the methodology and associated tools.

Case Study: Qualitative Research as the Basis of Innovation – The Kellogg Way

Kellogg's is considered to be the world-leading company for cereals. Its products are manufactured in 18 countries and sold in 180. Its stated focus for over 100 years is to produce nutritional products while catering for the variety of tastes of its customers. Kellogg's adopts a customer-focused approach to developing its new products; this means that rather than being product orientated by producing products before looking for a relevant market, Kellogg's prefers to consult extensively with its existing and potential consumers to find out about and anticipate their needs to inform product development.

(Continued)

(Continued)

One of the most successful products Kellogg's launched in the UK was Crunchy Nut Cornflakes in 1980. The current value of this product is £68 million. At the beginning of the new millennium, Kellogg's wanted to capitalise on the success of the Crunchy Nut brand and create a brand extension to it. Its objective was 'to provide a new flavour and texture for consumers, helping Kellogg's extend its share of the breakfast cereals market' (Business Case Studies, 2016, p. 1).

In order to fulfil this objective, Kellogg's became engaged in an expensive and time-consuming research exercise to directly interact with consumers and gather the necessary information. It used different methods of data collection, such as street interviews, focus groups and questionnaires. Focus groups were particularly useful as they enabled the researchers to allow subjects to taste prototypes and provide feedback in terms of flavour and texture. In addition, quantitative data were gathered in order to get an idea about the level of recurrence of views. Particular use was also made of qualitative data to collect opinions, feelings and attitudes.

As a result of this research, Kellogg's was able to discard some ideas, refine and develop others, and select some for further testing. Following this early stage of research, the researchers selected the most successful ideas and produced pictures showing what they would look like and provided a description of them. These were put on boards that were shown to large groups of representative consumers who were asked to rate the ideas using specific scales to help differentiate between the various options.

Based on the above, the idea that gained most support was to produce a new product called Crunchy Nut Bites. This idea showed potential for a significant increase in market share. During the tasting stage, Kellogg's food technologists developed a number of versions of the selected product based on consumers' 'eating experience'. Subsequently, Kellogg's also tested the package design for the prototypes.

The company also added one final test, known as the 'In home usage test', before launching the new product to market. In this test, consumers were given the product to use for several days to get as close as possible to how they would interact with it in real life. Part of this test involved participants completing a full questionnaire to show what they thought of the product during those few days of use. This allowed the researchers to identify more accurately how appealing the product is and the probability of customers actually buying it.

Kellogg's made use of the findings to help with other business issues, such as forecasting likely demand, setting budgets for organising the supply chain and scheduling food production.

Case study questions:

1. Identify the types of qualitative research methods that Kellogg's made use of, or can make use of, to help with addressing the issues associated with developing a new product.
2. Imagine you are a market researcher for a chocolate company that discovered that its customers are starting to lose interest in its products. What steps would you advise the company take to develop a new chocolate product?
3. Are there ethical issues that food producers need to take into account? What are they and why should these be considered?

End of Chapter Questions

These questions should help you reflect on your understanding of this chapter:

1. Why is qualitative research necessary for most market research?

2. Why are both concepts of validity and reliability necessary for a sound qualitative research project?
3. How does marketing qualitative research relate to the marketing concept? Give examples.
4. Why is the quality of qualitative research essential in helping address marketing problems effectively? Give examples.
5. Do researchers have to choose between qualitative and quantitative methods? Why?
6. Is it always necessary to use qualitative research? Why?
7. What steps do you need to take to determine if qualitative research is needed?
8. What are the main arguments against qualitative research and how would you counter them?
9. What is the link between worldview, methodology and research techniques?

Checklist

After studying Chapter 7, you should now be familiar with these key concepts:

1. The difference between worldview, method and research technique
2. The difference between deduction, induction and abduction (or dinduction)
3. Validity and reliability in qualitative research
4. What constitutes quality qualitative research

Further Reading (in sequence from beginners to advanced)

Denzin, N. K. and Lincoln, Y. S. (eds) (2000) *Handbook of Qualitative Research* (2nd edition). Thousand Oaks, CA: Sage Publications. Although this book is a bit old, it does provide useful clarifications about what qualitative research involves.

Carson, D., Gilmore, A., Perry, C. and Gronhaug, K. (2005) *Qualitative Marketing Research*. London: Sage Publications. This book demonstrates the link between the philosophical perspective about the world and the adopted research methods and techniques.

Creswell, J. W. (2003) *Research Design: Qualitative, Quantitative, and Mixed Methods Approaches* (2nd edition). Thousand Oaks, CA: Sage Publications. This book provides a useful overview of the research approaches covering quantitative, qualitative or mixed.

MRS (2011) MRS guidelines for qualitative research including observational, ethnographic and deliberative research. Available at: www.mrs.org.uk/pdf/2012-03-19%20Qualitative%20 Research%20Guidelines.pdf [Accessed 4 July 2016]. This is a guidance document that provides useful advice based on the MRS Code of Conduct for undertaking qualitative market research.

Fourali, C. (2016) *The Promise of Social Marketing: A Powerful Tool for Changing the World for Good*. London: Gower. This book provides a good introduction to social marketing and the types of action research it advocates.

Elliot, R., Fischer, C. T. and Rennie, D. L. (1999) Evolving guidelines for publications of qualitative research studies in psychology and related fields. *British Journal of Clinical Psychology*, 38 (3): 215–29. This is a very useful article that provides guidelines to researchers about the characteristics of good quality research.

Bibliography

AQR (2013) Qualitative research glossary. Available at: www.aqr.org.uk/glossary [Accessed 8 September 2013].

Becker, H. S. and Geer, B. (1957) Participant observation and interviewing: a comparison. *Human Organization*, 16 (3), pp. 28–32.

Bryman, A. (1988) *Quantity and Quality in Social Research*. London: Unwin Hyman.

Business Case Studies (2016) New products from market research: a Kellogg's case study. Available at: http://businesscasestudies.co.uk/kelloggs/new-products-from-market-research/introduction.html#axzz4MPjWXHz7 [Accessed 7 October 2016].

Carson, D., Gilmore, A., Perry, C. and Kjell Gronhaug, K. (2005) *Qualitative Marketing Research*. London: Sage Publications.

Catteral, M. and Clarke, W. (2000) Improving the interface between the profession and the university, *International Journal of Market Research*, 42 (1), pp. 3–15.

Chamberlain, K. (2000) Methodolatry and qualitative health research. *Journal of Health Psychology*, 5 (3), pp. 285–96.

Creswell, J. W. (2003) *Research Design: Qualitative, Quantitative, and Mixed Methods Approaches* (2nd edition). Thousand Oaks, CA: Sage Publications.

Denzin, N. K. and Lincoln, Y. S. (eds) (2000) *Handbook of Qualitative Research* (2nd edition). Thousand Oaks, CA: Sage Publications.

Elliot, R., Fischer, C. T. and Rennie, D. L. (1999) Evolving guidelines for publications of qualitative research studies in psychology and related fields. *British Journal of Clinical Psychology*, 38 (3), pp. 215–29.

Ellis, A. (1994) *Reason and Emotion in Psychotherapy*. (Revised and updated) New York: Birch Lane Press.

Eriksson, P. and Kovalainen, A. (2008) *Qualitative Methods in Business Research*. London: Sage Publications.

Fourali, C. (1997) Using fuzzy logic in educational measurement. *Evaluation and Research in Education*, 11 (3), pp. 129–48.

Fourali, C. (2013) Action research and social marketing: the joining together of two potential allies. *Value and Virtue Conference*, York St John University, 9–10 July.

Fourali, C. (2016) *The Promise of Social Marketing: Changing the World for Good*. London: Gower.

Galt, K. (2008) An introduction to mixed methods research. Creighton University. Available at: http://spahp2.creighton.edu/OfficeOfResearch/share/sharedfiles/UserFiles/file/Galt_MM_slides_CU_092309.pdf [Accessed 29 June 2013].

Goldenberg, C. (1992) The limits of expectations: a case for case knowledge of teacher expectancy effects. *American Educational Research Journal*, 29 (3), pp. 517–44.

Hammersley, M. and Atkinson, P. (1995) *Ethnography: Principles in Practice* (2nd edition). London: Routledge.

Henwood, K. L. and Pidgeon, N. F. (1992) Qualitative research and psychological theorizing. *British Journal of Psychology*, 83 (1), pp. 97–112.

Herr, K. and Anderson, G. L. (2005) *The Action Research Dissertation: A Guide for Students and Faculty*. Thousand Oaks, CA: Sage Publications.

Keller, K. L. (2012) *Strategic Brand Management: Building, Measuring and Managing Brand Equity* (Global Edition). Hoboken, NJ: Pearson.

Kuhn, T. S. (1970) *The Structure of Scientific Revolutions*. Chicago: Chicago University Press.

Lahire, B. (ed.) (2001) L'économie du sociologue ou penser (l'orthodoxie) à partir de Pierre Bourdieu. In *Le travail sociologique de Pierre Bourdieu: Dettes et critiques* (Revised and updated) (pp. 255–314). Paris: La Découverte.

Lincoln, Y. S. and Guba, E. G. (1985) *Naturalistic Inquiry*. London: Sage Publications.

Malhotra, N. K. and Birks, D. F. (2007) *Marketing Research: An Applied Approach*. London: Prentice Hall.

Maxwell, J. (2013) *Qualitative Research Design* (3rd edition). Thousand Oaks, CA: Sage Publications.

Miles, M. B. and Huberman, A. M. (1984) *Qualitative Data Analysis: A Sourcebook of New Methods*. Thousand Oaks, CA: Sage Publications.

Mishler, E. (1990) Validation in inquiry-guided research. *Harvard Education Review*, 60 (4), pp. 415–42.

Myers, M. D. (2008) *Qualitative Research in Business and Management*. London: Sage Publications.

NHS (2011) *Devon Skin Cancer Prevention Strategy 2011–14*. Exeter: Devon County Council/NHS.

NHS (2012) *Love Your Skin: Annual Public Report 2011–12*. Exeter: Devon County Council/NHS.

Papert, S. and Harel, I. (1991) *Constructionism*. Norwood, NJ: Ablex Publishing Corporation.

Piaget, J. (1936) *La Naissance de l'Intelligence Chez l'Enfant*. Paris: Delachaux et Niestlé.

Plutynski, A. (2011) Four problems of abduction: a brief history. *The Journal of the International Society for the History of Philosophy of* Science, 1. Available at: 155.97.32.9/~plutynsk/HOPOSproofs.pdf [Accessed 19 May 2017].

Popper, K. (1963) *Conjectures and Refutations*. London: Routledge.

Reicher, S. (2000) Against methodolatry: some comments on Elliott, Fischer and Rennie. *British Journal of Clinical Psychology*, 39, pp. 1–6.

Ritchie, J. and Lewis, J. (eds) (2003) *Qualitative Research Practice: A Guide for Social Science Students and Researchers*. London: Sage Publications.

Shadish, W. R., Cook, T. D. and Campbell, D. T. (2002) *Experimental and Quasi-experimental Design for Generalized Causal Inference*. Boston, MA: Houghton-Mifflin.

Strauss, A. L. and Corbin, J. (1998) *Basics of Qualitative Research: Grounded Theory Procedures and Techniques* (2nd edition). Thousand Oaks, CA: Sage Publications.

Stringer, E. (2007) *Action Research*. London: Sage Publications.

Willis, G. (2007) *Foundations of Qualitative Research: Foundations of Qualitative Research – Interpretive and Critical Approaches*. London: Sage Publications.

Zaltman, G. and Zaltman, L. (2008) *Marketing Metaphoria: What Deep Metaphors Reveal about the Minds of Consumers*. Cambridge, MA: Harvard Business School Press.

Find journal articles and multiple choice questions online at: **https://study.sagepub.com/benzo** to support what you've learnt so far.

CHAPTER 8

Determining a Robust Qualitative Research Approach: Reviewing the Methodological and Data-Gathering Options

LEARNING OBJECTIVES

The key learning objectives of this chapter are:

1. To introduce qualitative research methods used in marketing research
2. To discuss the main data-gathering techniques associated with qualitative marketing research
3. To explain how observation methods can be used in qualitative research
4. To describe how interviewing techniques are used in qualitative research

KEY CONCEPTS

By the end of this chapter, the reader should be familiar with the following concepts:

1. The difference between research methods and research techniques
2. Qualitative research methods and associated concepts (action research, case study, grounded theory, ethnography, narrative research, discursive research, feminist and critical race research, critical research, phenomenology, hermeneutics)
3. Data-gathering techniques and associated concepts (questionnaire, observation, focus group, interview)
4. The process of selection of appropriate method/s of study
5. The process of selection of appropriate data-gathering techniques

Chahid Fourali

Introduction

Chapter 7 reflected on the elements of a good qualitative research design and differentiated between paradigm, methods and techniques. In this chapter, we will start by presenting the main qualitative methods in more detail, together with the data-gathering techniques available to the market researcher. Subsequently, we will focus on two techniques of data gathering. The first technique, observation, can provide either an overt or unobtrusive approach to gathering information. The second technique, interviewing, provides the opportunity to look beyond appearances by using direct questioning techniques to unravel the reasons behind observed customer behaviour.

As discussed in Chapter 7, a researcher may subscribe to a particular worldview which, in turn, informs their perception of their role as a researcher and also their methodological preference. Their methodological preference may be for a quantitative, qualitative or a mixed-design approach. It is important that the researcher differentiates the data-gathering procedures from the research methods that guide the data gathering. Hence, a questionnaire is only a method of obtaining data but should be guided by the preferred research method, matching both the researcher's worldview and the problem at hand. Once the research method has been chosen, the researcher needs to develop a design that targets the information needed to make a decision about the business problem faced. The design development process is revisited in Chapter 10, with examples of the steps that the researcher goes through from problem formulation/ conceptualisation to writing up.

Snapshot: Sweet Positioning – Revitalising the Nestlé Chocolate Market

The title of this case study should remind us that the success of a product or service is not just attributed to its physical qualities. Marketers need to be mindful of the perception of a product, which is affected by a multiplicity of factors, such as new competitors entering the market, changes in the population makeup, changes in social tastes, and so on. Additionally, marketers know that most successful products go through a product life cycle reflecting different stages of interest, from early interest and curiosity following its introduction, to a peak in interest and, eventually, a decline in or loss of interest, unless marketers intervene. Hence, most businesses need to continuously review their marketing positioning and decide whether they are still viewed positively by their target customers or whether they need to take action. The confectionary industry is no different in this respect. In fact, as well as having to address the challenge of new perceptions, they face the extra challenge of needing to address changes in social tastes. Take, for example, one of Nestlé's best-known product lines, Smarties. In the 1990s, the company undertook several new developments in response to changing tastes in the market and to stimulate interest in what was an established product. These developments included the introduction of 'blue smarties', printing on sweets, the introduction of green chocolate, a change to the packaging and launching Smarties ice cream and Mini-Smarties.

Nestlé is one of the most successful brands in the UK and Kit Kat is now the UK's bestselling chocolate bar. However, this success was not always reflected in the company's sales numbers. In the 1990s, the volume of sales began falling steadily and statistics showed that the most significant loss was registered in the 12–20 age bracket. How did Nestlé face this challenge to not only stem the loss but also reverse the situation?

Cometh the challenge, cometh ... market research

To better understand the situation, Nestlé undertook a wide-scale market research project called 'Project Tyson'. The research targeted customers with the following characteristics:

- regular consumers of chocolate bars
- 17–20 years old
- of diverse ethnic origin
- from a variety of geographic locations in the UK
- a mixture of students and non-students.

The research considered a number of qualitative factors, including whether the product fitted with the target group's lifestyle, was considered innovative and exciting, and raised interest. When considering preferred chocolate 'tastes', the study looked at preferences in relation to the number of fingers (one or two) as well the most popular flavours (caramel, peanut butter, orange jelly, chocolate layers, etc.). Additionally, the research investigated the types of packaging that might attract consumers.

The researcher made use of focus groups as well as pairs of young people who were invited to give their views about the areas under consideration.

Findings, actions and results

The research confirmed that the idea of a single chunky finger generated a lot of interest, since the two-finger bar competed with Kit Kat's own four-finger variety. It also found that there was an opportunity to promote the view that Kit Kat is the ideal snack for any type of break, in order to increase the number of sales. Kit Kat was also encouraged to be more innovative in the count line (chocolate bar) market. In terms of promotion, the research showed that marketing communications would be more effective if they focused on aspirational associations, as it was found that the younger teenage age bracket (12–14) was attracted by behaviour attributed to older teenagers (17–18).

As a result of these useful insights, Nestlé launched 'Kit Kat Chunky', which proved to be one of the best marketing success stories in recent times. Within the first few weeks, over 50 million bars were dispatched. Almost immediately, Kit Kat became the bestselling count line and its success story has continued ever since.

Obviously, this example does not consider social responsibility in terms of an adverse health effect on the population with the increased sale of Kit Kats. Nevertheless, it demonstrates the strategic importance of marketing research – and more specifically qualitative research – in helping derive effective business decisions.

Source: adapted from www.businesscasestudies.co.uk

Approaches to Qualitative Methods

The qualitative researcher has many methods at his disposal. These can be summarised as follows.

Action research (AR)

This is a method predominantly used to resolve a practical situation or problem faced by a practitioner (a teacher, a marketer, etc.) who may use a number of techniques to unravel the issues at hand. Given the increasing importance of AR, this method will be dealt with in more detail in Chapter 9.

Case study (CS) research

Case study research does not represent a different research method as such, but it is unique in its focus on trying to understand a particular phenomenon (e.g. customer satisfaction) within a particular situation (e.g. a restaurant). Like AR, case studies can involve a variety of methods.

Like AR, and partly because of the similarities between CS and AR, case study research will also be addressed in more detail in the next chapter (Chapter 9).

Grounded theory research

This method of study has wide appeal within business research. It was originally put forward by Glaser, Strauss and Anselm (1967). As an approach, it constitutes a challenge to the hypothetico-deductive method.

Hypothetico-deductive method Starting with a hypothesis and testing it using a design that targets the relevant variables

It lends itself particularly well to qualitative research. For instance, one type of research question that can be addressed via this method is: 'What are the ways of developing relationships with customers?' After some early analysis of 'these ways', the researcher may detect some kind of chronology of steps ranging from 'weak relationships' to 'strong relationships'. This realisation may lead the researcher to revise the focus of the study to: 'What are the steps leading to a strong relationship?' Grounded theory involves a relentless iterative process of moving from the (coded) data to categories of recurring themes that will help describe the various types of relationships that can occur between a marketer and a customer.

Ethnographic research

Ethnography refers to two Greek terms – 'ethnos', which stands for a people or cultural group; and 'graphic', which means to write or represent. It is part of the broader field of anthropology which is the social science for understanding different ways of human life. Hence, the aim of ethnographic research is to describe and understand a particular group of people, which makes it the primary approach for studying cultures. For some, ethnography is not considered 'a method' but rather an approach of doing research that enables a researcher to understand the social meanings and activities of a target group through direct involvement, participation and observation of the group. An example of ethnographic research might be a researcher wanting to understand a fan club, for example the 'Star Wars Fan Club' or 'Harley Davidson Fans'. These groups of people tend to share meanings and symbols as well as consumption behaviours. This approach will be reviewed later in this chapter in the context of the data-gathering tool, participative observation.

Narrative research

A narrative can be defined 'as an organised interpretation of a sequence of events'. This involves relating the characters in the narrative to each other in some way and inferring causal links between the events. In its classic form, a narrative is an account with three components: a beginning, a middle and an end. The keyword associated with narrative research is 'story'. Broadly speaking, such narratives can take a variety of forms, ranging from 'personal narratives' to 'collective narratives' to 'grand narratives'. The latter reflects cultural beliefs that are globally shared. From a business perspective, narratives provide the opportunity for customers to define themselves, clarify the continuity in their lives and share it with others. Data used for narrative research can take a number of forms, such as narrative interviews and conversations, oral histories, journals, letters and field notes. In a narrative research report, the researcher guides the reader from empirical data to build an account (or story) that balances their voice with that of others.

Discursive research

This method focuses on the cultural meanings associated with experiences, people, events or artefacts. It makes use of a variety of theories associated with fields that include linguistics, anthropology, psychology, sociology and critical studies. In discourse theories, language is social and is therefore linked to social and historical contexts. Additionally, given that discourses imply knowledge claims and may reflect a particular position, this makes them prime candidates for analysis in terms of political (ways of influencing) and power relations.

Eriksson and Kovalainen (2008) argue that there are three types of discourse analytic research: the Foucauldian, social-psychological and critical discourse approaches.

Foucauldian approach

Foucault's primary interest was studying how the production of 'truth', including scientific knowledge, was systematically justified by the discourses that people produce, use and eventually institutionalise. Foucault implied that the meaning of discourses is governed by the rules and regulations of the discourses themselves. Consequently, he considered that some categories of words have been influenced by historical contexts. This means that there are a number of concepts we use whose meanings reflect the outcome of various stages of socio-economic environments. The impact of such influence affects both meanings and value judgements associated with such concepts. He includes in this distinction the generally perceived difference between reason and madness (Foucault, 1961). Foucault's work is very relevant to marketers who at least share in the responsibility of building images/brands and encouraging behaviours and in how such images and behaviours may impact on different sections of the population.

Social-psychological approach

This discourse type of analysis is very relevant to marketing as one of its primary focuses is how 'identities' are constructed and, consequently, how this affects positioning vis-à-vis other groups and objects (e.g. products and services). This type of analysis is heavily influenced by constructionist and social psychology. Social psychologists suggest that reality is negotiated through our interactions with others. In this respect, consider the identity that a customer portrays by insisting on buying only luxury items or the corporate reality implied by the hierarchical structure of a company.

Critical discourse approach

Developed in the 1980s, critical discourse analysis (CDA) is one of the latest additions to the social science researcher's research arsenal. Despite there being a variety of CDAs, one popular view describes the aim of CDA as demonstrating how social life, whilst constrained by social structures, is also a powerful agent for change. If we consider the hierarchical structure of a company, it may have become established as a result of a new (emergent) discourse that became dominant (hegemonic) and therefore resistant to any objections or suggestions for change. Subsequently, this dominant discourse became reflected (re-contextualised) in the reality of relations/communications between other parties and within the organisation itself, and its implementation (operationalisation) resulted in the 'adoption' of the company's hierarchical structure.

Feminist and critical race studies research

Feminist and critical race research are two fields of study that take a fairly similar approach, in that they do not use any particular method of research, but are positioned at the junction between postmodernism (the existence of several 'truths'), post-colonial and critical studies. Both of these research works are particularly relevant to marketing as a discipline, given its use of communications and consumer behaviour.

A number of authors have argued for the adoption of more so-called feminist values, such as caring and self-reflection which, arguably, are reputed to make us all happier. This argument may have some intuitive value or face validity, but there is a danger of justifying prejudice through counter prejudice. Many policy makers have made the argument repeatedly that just because someone is black or female, it is not guaranteed that they will discriminate any less against similar traditionally disadvantaged groups. This argument was particularly reflected in the work of Frantz Fanon in his evocatively named book *Black Skin, White Masks* (1952).

Figure 8.1 Feminism

Critical research

Like some of the other 'methods' we have already discussed, this type of research is more a philosophical approach to research rather than a separate method. However, because of its broader scope, it is relevant to all the approaches we have explored so far. In critical research, at least 4Cs can be identified (Eriksson and Kovalainen, 2008):

- Critical theory
- Critical thinking
- Critical realism
- Critical management studies.

Critical theory focuses on highlighting the links between values, knowledge and politics and consequently rejects positivism. It has, as its aim, human emancipation by identifying the causes of oppression with a view to eliminating them. *Critical thinking* differs from the other three types of critical research as it is primarily a process of self-reflection that may or may not be guided by any theory, including critical theory.

Critical realism provides an alternative to positivism and/or postmodernism, as it recognises that, while reality exists, it is significantly affected by social structures. *Critical management studies* has evolved as a result of critical theory's attempt at emancipating the human condition. This emergent branch of critical studies encourages the use of fairer and more democratic approaches to business, so that management is more accountable to those affected by its decisions.

Phenomenology

Phenomenology is described by its main supporters as the 'science of the subjective'. Phenomenology, rather than focusing on the independent nature of phenomena in the world, is more concerned with how these phenomena are reflected in our consciousness.

Most qualitative research in social science can be classified from a phenomenological perspective. Hence, Carson et al. (2005) list social constructionism, naturalistic enquiry and interpretative sociology as phenomenologically led approaches, which is why a phenomenology focus has such clear relevance to marketing. As an example, marketers aim to increase the value perceived by customers to maximise the chances of them choosing a particular product or service over another. Marketers have long realised that in many cases it is not necessarily the product itself that determines value but rather the whole experience, including the quality of the product along with other contextual factors. Take, for example, a customer who selects a particular restaurant not for one specific reason, such as a particular dish on the menu or the cost of drinks, but because of the overall ambience and dining experience, which could include the décor, the lighting, the quality of service and the music.

Hermeneutics

This approach is akin to the phenomenological approach, involving a particular focus on the influence of language and culture (beliefs, theories, myths, ideologies, etc.) for determining how we experience people or texts we are trying to understand. It is therefore important for social researchers to be aware of these influences when trying to understand the subject of study and aim to get as close as possible to their experienced reality.

Qualitative Data-Gathering Techniques

Having introduced the different qualitative methods, the next step is to determine which qualitative data-gathering technique to use.

Before moving on to focus on two techniques – observation and interviewing – we will consider the main data-gathering techniques.

There are many data-gathering methods, some of which are used for deriving both qualitative and quantitative data. For example, quantitative data-gathering techniques may include observation or questionnaires. A qualitative approach may make use of these techniques, in addition to others such as focus groups and interviews. Table 8.1 lists the main techniques used in qualitative research together with their advantages and disadvantages.

Table 8.1 Pros and cons of qualitative data-gathering techniques

Technique	Description	Pros	Cons
Questionnaire	Written or oral delivery, following a set of written questions with associated options	Seen as more objective and offers opportunities for statistical analysis	Preset answers do not allow flexibility Not very helpful for qualitative analysis
Observation	Direct/formal or informal collection of information through observation as in field trips	Provides contextual and behavioural information	Generalisation is limited, can be expensive and depends on trust of observee in observer
Focus group	A small sample of people associated with a particular event or issue selected with a view to obtaining their opinion on a selected topic	Help analyse attitudes linked to complex/interactive situations A good source of ideas	Limited time to cover all issues at hand Issues of restriction in views as well as power relations
Interview	A formal, face-to-face meeting with a view to elicit the meanings that an interviewee attaches to certain events or issues	Allows the interviewer to capture the perspectives of project participants Provides flexible in-depth information Helps build relationships	They are intrusive, expensive and information may be open to manipulation
Indirect sources (document and audio-visual analysis)	These may be existing records and documents written or taped	Can be economically accessible Useful for determining values, interest, attitudes and historical trends or procedures	Information may not be valid, reliable or authentic Analysis may require help from local expertise
Projective techniques	These are techniques that may make use of pictures or direct questioning to probe for deeper/subconscious reasons	Can provide access to subconscious information not available through other means	Requires expertise Needs supporting evidence from other sources

Observation and its dimensions

Observation is a method of collecting empirical data by watching participants in a particular setting, relevant to the topic of study. Information can be collected in various ways, including by human, mechanical, electrical or electronic means. Observations may differ, according to a number of characteristics. Eriksson and Kovalainen (2008), Flick (1998) and Cooper and Shindler (2001) identified many dimensions that reflect these characteristics and the context of the observation which can be represented along a continuum.

For instance, the observation may differ depending on whether the researcher is a participant or a non-participant in the setting being studied; whether the researcher is hidden from the participants (obtrusive or non-obtrusive observation); whether the observation takes place in a natural setting or a contrived/artificial environment; or whether it is a structured (using a checklist) or a non-structured observation.

Table 8.2 lists the dimensions identified and includes an additional dimension to take into account the level of use of technology for recording observed events. As an example of this, an observation may be combined with interviewing; this can be the case where one

Table 8.2 Dimensions of observation

Dimensions of observations	Full existence of characteristic	Complete absence of characteristic
Level of participation	Researcher is fully part of the environment he/she is studying	Researcher is not part of the environment being studied
Level of overtness	Researcher openly acknowledges his study to the target group	Research is covert
Level of naturalness	Research is undertaken in the natural setting where event normally take place	Research takes place in a simulated environment
Level of structure of observation	Fully structured according to pre-determined criteria	Unstructured and ad-hoc
Type of data	Quantitative	Qualitative
Purpose	Descriptive	Explanatory
Timeline	Brief	Long-term
Level of focus	Highly focused	Unfocused
Type of targeting	Direct/live	Indirect
Level of inclusion	Others	Self, others and micro/macro elements
Level of technological use	No technology	Full use and multilevel recording
Level of combination with other data-gathering techniques	Pure observation	Combined with several other techniques (e.g. interviews, tests)
Level of avoidance pre-empting bias	Selected observer/s	Non-selective

Source: adapted from Eriksson and Kovalainen, 2008

or more researchers observe, interview and record one or more subjects while they undertake a task, such as cooking or washing, in their natural setting. Such scenarios can lead to a better understanding of how certain products, for example soap powder or washing machines, are used.

Observations can be a very useful tool for marketing researchers as they help identify what customers actually do as opposed to what they say. One of the main justifications for the need for data on customer actions is that studies have shown that past behaviour is the most reliable predictor of future behaviour, compared to geo-demographic or psychological characteristics. In fact, in many cases researchers need to make use of all three categories of information, as the latter may help enhance the predictability of future behaviour.

Issues for consideration by observers

Simpson and Tuson (2003) and Cohen et al. (2011) highlight a number of areas that should be considered by researchers using the observation technique. These have been adapted and presented in the form of the following 15 questions:

1. What is the focus of the observation?
2. What is the purpose of observation (is it about understanding how a situation develops, looking for similarities, or looking for patterns, etc.)?
3. What research questions does the observation aim to address? This should be derived from question 2.
4. What is the scope of the observation (what to include and exclude)?
5. Where to observe (social contexts/places that will be observed)?
6. What to observe (specific objects, people, events, etc.)?
7. Whom to observe (the key people to focus on)?
8. What are the characteristics of the observer(s) (demographics, language, ethnic group, etc.)?
9. How often to observe (number of people, objects, settings)? This is equivalent to sampling.
10. What is the process of observation (is it systematic, descriptive, etc.)?
11. What is the unit of observation (individual people, pairs or group(s))?
12. How will the observed phenomena be recorded?
13. What level of support is needed (number of observers, video, audio, supporting material, templates, etc.)?
14. What potential obstacles should be avoided?
15. How will the information obtained be processed and analysed?

In a way, the questions above are examples of the specific questions that a researcher focusing on Table 8.2 should ask. By considering each question, you will be able to refine the dimensions of your research to a greater extent and thus be able to 'standardise' the various situations you may encounter and minimise errors. This clarification will also enable future researchers to repeat the study in similar or different contexts, to allow comparisons.

Observation: from field data collection to reporting

Having clarified the above dimensions of the research, as a researcher you will need to make notes of anything you judge to be important. Once the above has been clarified, four steps, ranging from pure description of observations to analysis and reporting, should be followed, as shown in Table 8.3. Broadly speaking, Stage 1 is the in-field observation. In this first stage, it is important that the observer differentiates actual events from interpretations. This could be helped by having a margin in the notebook where comments and early ideas/hunches are reported. In the second stage, the researcher takes the time to elaborate on the gathered notes, clarifying raw data/observations as well as reflections and impressions about them. In the third stage, the researcher undertakes in-depth analysis of the data before reporting on the results in the fourth and last stage.

Table 8.3 Steps of field research

	Stage 2: Recording information			
Stage I: In the field observations	**Follow up elaborations of the field notes (note that some of these may occur during observation)**	**Supporting evidence**	**Stage 3: Analysis**	**Stage 4: Reporting**
Mental and jotted notes	Raw data (descriptions of situation and quotations of conversations with place, date and time) Reflections, second thoughts and memories Early ideas and inferences (e.g. early themes) Personal feelings and emotional reactions Planning next stages (to collect missing information or moving to the next stage of research)	Audio, video, photos, sketches, memory notes	Primary analysis	Written report which will be disseminated to key stakeholders and the community of researchers at large

Source: adapted from Gray, 2014

Participant ('ethnographic') observation

Table 8.2 above referred to the level of participation of the researcher in the phenomenon being studied. This ranges from a position where the researcher is completely external to the phenomenon being studied, to a position where he/she is a fully immersed member (insider) of the context being studied. The latter position was historically influenced by the work of ethnographers whose aim was to understand cultural phenomena and how they influenced the thinking, feeling and behaviour of ethnic groups within their environment. This type of research was briefly introduced in an earlier section but we will say a bit more about it here as it has been taken up by most qualitative researchers in the social sciences. Indeed, marketing research has identified areas where ethnographic skills may come in very handy, such as when trying to understand the significance of use of a new product in a particular family or what differentiates a group holiday organised by two rival holiday companies. Whilst originally ethnographic studies meant spending an extended period of time, which could last months or years, observing a phenomenon, more recently the period of study has become much shorter. Rand (2006) talks about mini-ethnography to account for a method that capitalises on the skills of ethnography within a short period of time (a programme of up to eight weeks).

In order to undertake 'ethnographic' participant observation fieldwork, Gray (2014) advises following a few guidelines, in particular:

- Bear in mind that the research problem may not always be clear enough at first to decide on the most appropriate context of study. In this situation, it is possible to try a broadly relevant research context that may lead to further clarification of the research problem, following the collection of data.
- Consider both formal and informal avenues for gaining access to the environment being studied (e.g. the manager of a fan club as well as members who may facilitate the acceptance of the 'new member').
- Obtain consent – it is generally considered good practice to inform the target group about the research and its purpose, whilst also taking into account how the presence of the researcher may influence the reactions of the members. There may be situations where it may not be possible to negotiate consent from the group, for example if joining a large community, such as football supporters.
- Balance the insider and outsider positions – this means that while the researcher should aim to integrate both physically and emotionally into the group/community being studied, they should also keep a professional distance. Take, for example, a researcher studying a group of gang members. Matching the researcher's age as closely as possible to that of the gang members they are studying can make the experience more relevant for both parties, but being mindful of their position as a researcher will keep the focus on the study in hand. Maintaining a level of professionalism should also prevent the researcher from breaching ethical standards.
- Inform the community being studied about the schedule of research and allow enough time for closure towards the end of the session – this is necessary to minimise the negative effect of an abrupt 'getting out' and the emotional turmoil it may create for both the researcher and the members of the community being studied.

Reflective Activity

Individually or in pairs, think about a holiday you've taken in a foreign country and compare what you learnt from your experience of living alongside people from that country. Identify a number of themes (e.g. level of individualism; what constitutes happiness; food preferences). Provide evidence (e.g. observations made or produced statements) supporting your arguments.

Advanced: Ethnography, Netnography and its Critics

The field of ethnography is continually expanding to accommodate new circumstances and theoretical challenges. As a critical tool of qualitative research, it has already broadened to include autoethnography, an autobiographical form of investigation and writing that connects the personal to the social/cultural dimensions of one's culture and is routinely used by marketers in various fields including the IT industry. As early as 2006, Sirius radio contracted a team of ethnographers and designers as consultants to help them compete with the listening figures of a rival radio station. The consultants spent four weeks shadowing 45 people in Nashville and Boston in order to understand how they listen to music, watch TV and browse gossip magazines. On the back of the advice they received, Sirius radio developed a portable satellite-radio player that was easy to use and load with music to playback later. This device, the S50, which enabled a listener to save up to 50 hours of broadcasting, became one of the holiday season's hottest sellers. Sirius says it has helped the company sign up more subscribers than its rival during the season. This solution was not unique as ethnographers were also used by other companies such as Marriott International Inc. (MAR) and Intel Corp. (INTC) to design user-friendly lobbies at hotels and a cheap PC designed to run in rural Indian villages on a truck battery in a 113-degree temperature, respectively. The ethnographers were able to determine these innovative solutions by identifying what was missing in people's lives and work with designers and engineers to produce suitable products and services to satisfy those needs.

Current discussions around ethnography tend to make use of modern sources of community information thanks to social media. Marketers have become aware of the wealth of information generated in virtual/Internet-based communities that needs to be taken into consideration when studying consumer behaviour. Indeed, the Internet made it easier for 'communities' to meet, discuss with, inform and influence each other about products, brands, people, and so on. This information is of vital importance when helping companies learn about the perception of their products and fish for new innovative ideas with a view to developing better strategies for designing, communicating about and selling their products. Every source of information should be targeted (within legal boundaries), be it chat rooms, newsgroups, independent websites or any e-networks that can provide a platform for the exchange of information about products/services. The concept of netnography, coined by Kozinets (1998), was created to account for studies focusing on e-communities. Kozinets defines netnography as a 'new qualitative method devised specifically to investigate the consumer behavior of cultures and communities present on the Internet' (1998: 366).

Like ethnography, netnography follows a similar process of research, covering planning, joining the target group(s), collecting data, analysis/interpretation, ethical considerations and reporting. However, netnography can provide much more detailed information which is culturally and geographically specific. Depending on the effectiveness of supporting software analysis tools, this information can be very rich, including both qualitative and quantitative elements, such as types of stakeholders and their respective influence. As an example, the United Nations monitors discussions about current themes such as food security, ethnic and gender equality and sustainability. These discussions may take place across any of its associated organisations.

As part of the process of delimiting the scope of the research, the researcher may choose to identify one of the following contexts (Majewski, 2012):

- Channel selection: the researcher may opt to focus only on information sourced from Facebook, micromedia/Twitter, blogs and mainstream news.
- Demographics: the researcher may decide to focus on one particular language and geographical region.
- Contexts: this involves the selection of one or more topics of interest (e.g. online discussions on human rights abuse associated with a region).

(Continued)

(Continued)

- Actors: this involves the selection of entities being monitored such as a number of specific United Nations organisations.
- Data collection: here the researcher needs to select keywords that maximise the selection of all discussions associated with the selected topic/s.

Clearly, the analysis and outcome will depend on the systematic selection of what is deemed relevant information. If this process is not appropriate, it will affect the validity of the subsequent results.

Criticism of ethnography

It is important to realise that ethnography, despite being a powerful technique, is not without its critics. As several critics highlighted the importance of history in explaining the current ways of seeing and evaluating our present world, Said (1979, 1989) suggested that current anthropological techniques, such as ethnography, may still carry a conceptual framework originally shaped by colonialism and imperialist domination. He demonstrated how such techniques not only contribute to presenting a Eurocentric perspective of the phenomena studied but even help support colonialist ideology through providing narrow explanations that overlook the historical and power structures behind the observed phenomena. Carspencken (1996) in particular warns that research and thinking are mediated by power relations that are socially and historically located; that facts and values are inseparable; and that language is central to perception (see Reflective Activity box for challenging claims of validity). Hence, researchers using ethnographic techniques are not only advised to be aware of and minimise any source of bias, but they are also encouraged to advise on how any issues of injustice, that they may come across, may be addressed. At the same time, interpretations such as these and subsequent advice should be left open to consideration, to allow plenty of opportunities for alternative interpretation. As we will see in the next chapter, the nature and values underpinning action research provide a context that supports the importance of focusing the light on the researcher as well as the researched, in addition to highlighting the social responsibilities of researchers. This kind of approach is particularly welcome in marketing, where there have been too many accusations levelled against the discipline's lack of social responsibility.

Reflective Activity

When can you rely on received information?

Habermas (1984) advises that when judging a statement's validity, one should consider several dimensions: whether the information is comprehensible; whether the statement is accurate; whether the speaker is the right/authoritative source; and, finally, the speaker's sincerity. Consider a PR apology offered on behalf of an organisation, preferably a global one, that addresses an event that could have serious repercussions for the reputation of the company. What was your view about the event before listening to the statement? Did the PR statement help change your views? Why?

This activity may refer to any source (e.g. a newspaper or a video available online) that presents the PR statement.

Interviews: a powerful technique for unravelling causes

Interviews are another data-gathering technique providing market researchers with the opportunity to test their understanding of a situation, and the ethnography researcher's toolbox would be incomplete without this important technique. By definition, interviews reflect the need to seek a variety of opinions on a topic from two or more stakeholders. Interviews are an ideal method for gathering information that reflects the richness of human communication, including what is said directly or indirectly, consciously or unconsciously and spanning the verbal, non-verbal, emotional and behavioural dimensions.

Interviews can take different forms, ranging from the most structured, such as administering a questionnaire (see Table 8.1 above), to the most informal conversational type of interview, as illustrated in Figure 8.2. While a conversational style has the advantage of being more natural and flowing more easily (as in interviews), it can lack comprehensiveness and comparability. The reverse also applies, as pre-set answers do not allow flexibility for further qualitative analysis. It is therefore important that the researcher undertakes a cost–benefit analysis, based on the questions and situations targeted.

Least planned	Some planning		Most planned
Conversational interview	Use of interview guide	Standardised; open-ended	Closed/fixed questions and responses
	Nature		
Questions emerge as the discussion progresses	Topics pre-determined but interviewer decides about the timing and sequencing	All questions are asked in the same order	Questions and alternative answers are pre-determined and fixed
	Pros		
Can be adapted to situation and people	Interviews are conversational although the key dimensions are more comprehensively covered	Makes comparability and analysis easier than above two interview types	Easy to administer, analyse and compare responses
	Cons		
May miss important elements Difficulty of analysis	Some topics may be missed and there may be a reduction in the comparability of responses	Words may not relate equally to different interviewees/ situations	Wording may be irrelevant and unnatural Options may not be appropriate

Figure 8.2 Types of interviews

Source: Patton (1980)

Reflective Activity

You need to interview a number of children to find out what kind of toys appeal to them. What interview style would you adopt and what topics would you include?

Conducting an interview: the steps

There are many aspects that any interviewer needs to take into account to ensure they are adequately prepared for an interview and that it runs smoothly. These are presented in chronological order by the following steps:

Step 1: Preliminary considerations

Leading questions Questions that encourage a respondent to respond one way as opposed to another

All research has a purpose, reflected in a number of objectives, which in turn translate into key questions that guide the design of the interview schedule. The researcher needs to identify the people they want to target for the interviews, the format of the questions which need to match the specific queries they are hoping to clarify as well as the timing and location of the meeting. The latter should aim to provide a comfortable/secure environment that minimises distraction. Regarding question format, it is very important to avoid leading questions.

Step 2: Conducting the interview

Building the relationship: the interviewer should decide what kind of relationship they need to develop. Research has shown that the first impressions of a person and the associated decision, such as whether or not to recruit them, can be made within the first few seconds of meeting them. Although it is not clear exactly what determines these early impressions, a person should always aim to stack the odds in their favour by adopting a professional, respectful, friendly and interested attitude.

Kvale (1996) highlights a number of dimensions that guide the flow of an interview. He suggests that the interviewer introduces the topic before eliciting responses from interviewees. The interviewer may need to probe and seek further clarification, including illustrating a question with an example, as needed. Depending on how they interpret the responses, the interviewer may need to ask further questions directly, to avoid ambiguities or gaps in the information. It is also important to paraphrase or summarise information for the interviewee at the end, to ensure the message is understood as intended.

Step 3: Transcribing

Transcription The conversion of information from one type of communication such as oral to a written version

As suggested for the observation technique, the interviewer can make use of recording devices. Video recording provides rich data but is time-consuming to analyse. Because of the very nature of transcription, some aspects of the data can be lost in translation, so it is important that the interviewer locates the discussion in a particular context to help the reader better understand the implied meanings. As well as noting the actual content of a response, the transcription should also note the tone of voice, pace of delivery, mood, interruptions and any other aspects that were of significance when the comment was made.

Step 4: Analysis

The aim of analysis is to determine patterns that help provide meaningful ways of interpreting information needed to address the questions that are the focus of the project. This involves organising the wealth of information that is gathered and is generally achieved by some form of coding that enables information from several sources to be compared. It also helps justify the arguments supporting one interpretation as opposed to another. Miles and Huberman (1994) suggested several techniques to help make sense of the transcribed material, including identifying themes, counting frequencies, clustering sections of information into meaningful groups, and creating metaphors by moving beyond the actual words to help organise aspects of information according to commonalities of meanings. An alternative analysis technique involves unpacking broader meanings to identify specific aspects; the researcher relentlessly looks for possible meanings and relations between potential variables with a view to building evidence that helps develop theories to explain the observed responses. Whilst being sensitive to different possible relations, the researcher has to remain cautious that any contradictory information is not overlooked. Once themes have been elicited and tested (e.g. via independent judges), Hycner (1985) advises writing a summary of each interview transcription to reflect the themes identified.

Step 5: Reporting

The research report is then written to reflect the nature of the information collected, with the aim of providing responses to the questions derived from the objectives of the research. Although there is a general degree of consensus as to the sections that are expected to be included in the report (such as research rationale, literature or methodology), there are disagreements concerning the most appropriate structure to adopt as well as content to include, especially as qualitative research can address controversial subjects or make use of new sources of information, such as projective techniques. As a general guideline, a researcher should aim to include the following sections:

1. An introduction showing the aims of the research, the main themes addressed and the sections covered in the report.
2. A description of the methodology followed (design and conduct of the interview, transcription and how analysis was conducted).
3. A description of the findings showing analysis, interpretation of observations and verifications of interpretations.
4. A discussion of the findings, which may link to other research outcomes and theories, and clarification of any assumptions being made. It is also important to avoid the 'reification' of interpretations or the advanced theorising of others. By doing this, the researcher is able to keep an open mind about alternative interpretations or explanations.
5. A conclusions, issues and implications section (or recommendations in a commissioned report) should also be added to summarise the findings and advise on a way forward based on the 'adopted' interpretations of the findings. Some authors, rightfully, object to the word 'conclusion' as it suggests finality. Hence, it is always important to present the conclusions as tentative and only to help argue for the follow-up implications.

Reification Treating something abstract as 'final' and real

Research in Practice: Videography as an Asset for Qualitative Research

Videography has given a big boost to qualitative research. The old adage 'a picture is worth a thousand words' is very well respected among the marketing community. So, how about a moving picture ... with sounds? A video. This is very much the idea behind the increasingly popular technique of videography as a research tool. Research of this kind makes use of audio-visual material to represent as accurately as possible the natural environment where observation and interviews take place to gather research on patterns of consumption. Researchers use this method not only to register details of the event being studied but also as a means of analysis and reporting. At the reporting stage, researchers edit the audio-visual clips, very much as they would edit the written word, to provide richer (and more accurate) information about the market phenomenon being studied. This approach is gaining popularity not only among marketers but also among their corporate funders who are increasingly requesting that research makes use of video material for clarity, richness of information and persuasiveness of outcome.

Acontextual speculation Political or social speculation devoid of any consumption context

Nevertheless, researchers realise that if this method of communication is to be adopted by the academic community as a credible source of information, it needs to meet a number of criteria. Kozinets and Belk (2006) suggest four criteria, the four Ts, to justify videographical use:

Topicality: the topics featured should focus on consumer research and avoid getting side-tracked into acontextual speculation.

Theoretical understanding: the material should increase our understanding of the target phenomenon to help us develop more robust theories.

Theatrical demonstration: the material should produce an interesting 'story' that demonstrates complex forces at play and a meaningful conclusion.

Technical standards: the material has to be designed in such a way that it is clear, audible and makes sense. This means that anyone using this medium should demonstrate editing skills to improve the clarity and logic of the message.

Videography has already enriched several fields of study, including medical and oceanic studies. It provides a vicarious experience, enabling the observer to empathise or identify with some of the participants depicted (Belk, 2006).

Videography, netnography and the future

In the light of fast-moving developments in new digital media as a source of information and method of communication and their subsequent integration within one platform (e.g. Facebook combines networking, video conversations and multimedia attachments), researchers are already finding ways to include new sources of evidence to back up their theories. Hence, while videography has gained in popularity over the last two decades, the future of consumer research is much more complex. This was alluded to above when we referred to netnography. A researcher choosing a particular discussion forum is not just restricted to recording the proceedings, but can also access videos produced by targeted subjects or record live discussions, for example via Skype, webinars or direct interactions with certain products. An example of this is a computer game that involves an international group of subjects playing live and interacting online. As a consequence, accessing such a broad range of sources requires highly technical and ethical standards.

Matching Methods and Research Techniques

This issue relates to the question of what constitutes a good research design. The answer to this question is addressed in detail in Chapter 10. However, Chapter 7 also provides the links between the various components of a research design. Broadly speaking, all dimensions of a research design should match each other, including methods and research techniques. In particular, the following aspects should be addressed:

1. A clear conceptualisation of the targeted issues, reflecting the (business) problem being addressed, the aim of the study and associated questions. This step will inform the next step.
2. Determination of an adequate approach of study (quantitative, qualitative or mixed design). This step will inform the next step.
3. Selection of adequate method(s) linked to the adopted approach. This step will inform the next step.
4. Selection of the technique(s) used to access the targeted information (e.g. via observation, survey, interview). As seen above, all steps of the research design derive from the targeted problem, including the selected method and associated data-gathering techniques.

Ethics

Qualitative methods such as ethnography allow access to people's inner reasons for assuming certain behaviours. As such, it is important that the trust gained by the researcher is respected and the source of the information kept confidential. Even if the interviewee agrees that their identity can be revealed, the researcher should still consider any possibility of risk to the individual before doing so. In the case of ethnography, there is also the added challenge of ending a relationship that may have been nurtured over a period of months, if not longer. It is important to show consideration when preparing to end the relationship, by doing so in as gentle a manner as possible, rather than suddenly and abruptly informing the research participants: 'OK, I have finished my study. Thank you and goodbye!' Ending researcher–participant relationships without warning can lead to painful adjustments, as humans develop emotional bonds that can be hard to break. Outcomes such as these can be minimised if the researcher prepares everyone from day one. As the research starts winding down, the researcher should inform the participants that they are nearing the end of the project, and suggest issues for discussion that may arise as a result. Encouraging an open discussion like this can help ensure a better sense of 'closure'.

Recent developments surrounding the availability of digital information adds to the complexity of ethical dimensions. In particular, netnographic studies raise a number of questions, as highlighted by Sixsmith and Murray (2001) in Table 8.4.

The researcher needs to balance the values involved and determine, with arguments, the best way forward. This approach is advisable in the absence of clear guidelines in new research areas. Generally, it is best to consider the following questions when aiming to determine whether or not an action is ethical (Carrigan and Kikup, 2001; APA, 2010):

(Continued)

(Continued)

1. Does an action violate the law?
2. Does an action violate any generally accepted moral obligation (justice, beneficence, integrity, respecting rights and dignity)?
3. Is the action likely to result in a harmful consequence (direct or indirect)?
4. Is the action likely to produce more good and less harm than any alternative action?

Table 8.4 Ethical issues linked to the Internet

Issue	Dilemmas
Whose voice is being heard?	It is important that the researcher makes sure to reflect the views of all voices of stakeholders associated with a dilemma, although these may be too many or hard to reach
Should the researcher inform the target of observations?	This is not an easy one. On the one hand, researchers should aim to 'come clean' about their purpose (e.g. when being part of a chat room), whereas providing such information may affect the dynamics and create a more superficial outcome
Should information be considered private?	If the information appears in a discussion post, it may be considered public although the intention may not have been to make it available to all
Should the source be kept private?	Like the second point above, removing information may remove important dimensions significant to the research issues
Should interpretation be checked?	This may not always be possible and there is always the issue of authenticity, as some Internet users are quite savvy and may not reflect their genuine opinion (e.g. a representative of a company selling a product, claiming it is the best thing they have ever used)
Should ownership be retained and the message kept in its original format?	Although in principle this should be respected, it is not always possible to know the origin of a post or whether it has been copied from elsewhere. However, there is an argument for keeping a message received from any source in its original format for comparative purposes

Source: Sixsmith and Murray, 2001

Reflective Activity

- Based on the guidelines above, select a topic or study that might be best investigated using an observation method of data gathering. Develop a table identifying the dos and don'ts of the study and illustrate this with examples of how each requirement will be met. When ready, exchange the results and make comments about areas that may have been missed by each group.

- Select an article written by a fan of a sports team and analyse it in light of the guidelines discussed in this chapter. Does the article satisfy the guidelines for a quality ethnography study? If not, clarify the exceptions and decide how the outstanding issues can be addressed.

Chapter Summary

This chapter described the tools and techniques associated with qualitative research in marketing. It clarified the difference between qualitative research methods and techniques of data gathering. It subsequently listed the most common methods used in qualitative research as well as the key methods associated with data-gathering techniques. The chapter looked in detail at two techniques of data gathering: observation and interviews. It highlighted the links between participative observation and ethnography methods, which are successfully adopted by modern marketers due to the richness of data that they can provide by observing the day-to-day lives of target groups. Finally, the chapter highlighted the key ethical dimensions associated with qualitative methods and data-gathering techniques.

Case Study: Mobile Ethnography and Party Planning – The Kraft Foods Way

Market researchers are aware that consumers may not always be conscious of the real reasons behind a decision they make. They often provide 'justifications' that are very different from the real grounds for their decisions. As argued by Fourali (2016), behavioural economics has long confirmed this situation, based on numerous experiments. To make marketers' findings more trustworthy, there is a need to limit the direct response scenario that enables subjects to rationalise their decisions after the event, but also to provide more opportunities for observations and illustrations of the events being referred to, as they happen.

Kraft Foods, supported by the research agency BrainJuicer, wanted to study what is involved when hosting and entertaining. The company considered traditional ethnography (i.e. observations carried out by trained researchers) but realised that it would be limited by the information available, the researcher's interpretations, their intrusion (and potential effect on the observee) and, not least, the very expensive nature of such an approach. The researchers for Kraft discovered that mobile ethnography (ME) could provide more reliable and live information. It enabled project researchers to directly access the target consumers' behaviour via their own mobile devices. ME allowed the researchers to directly observe the situations that subjects were experiencing 24/7, as well as to listen to commentary to help explain emotions, meanings and reactions. An opportunity such as this made the data more credible as it minimised any unsupported interpretations of decisions (or ex post facto justifications).

The study invited hosts to apply to be part of the study and attracted over 150 applications. The researchers selected 28 participants from 13 US states. The selected entertainment scenarios ranged from 'hanging out with friends' to 'the celebration of a 3-year-old's birthday'. The study focus started with the pre-event preparations stage (e.g. shopping) and extended to the cleaning-up stage after the event. To start with, the participants were introduced to the study and asked to become the ethnographers of their own story.

(Continued)

(Continued)

After the study, some of the participants were invited to take part in a follow-up study to help document Thanksgiving preparations, which contributed more information to the research.

As a result of this study, Kraft Foods was able to systematically map out the whole entertaining process. It derived 16 themes associated with the process and provided more consumer insight than would have been afforded by traditional ethnography. These insights formed the basis of a useful strategy for Kraft to design new products that address new identified needs. Additionally, the extensive information gathered (1000 items comprising pictures, video and written documents) enabled the development of a library of information that researchers could review for insights each time new questions arose.

Finally, although ME has plenty of advantages, it is always useful to consider its weaknesses. For example, there may be situations where it is not possible for the host to illustrate a particular event if they are occupied with other activities. Another challenge is that consumers often lack the training needed to make an observation more relevant or to probe deeper, which may result in gaps in the information gathered.

Case study questions:

1. What makes mobile ethnography attractive to market researchers? Illustrate with examples.
2. Contrast traditional ethnography and mobile ethnography and determine their advantages and disadvantages.
3. Select a study that has been undertaken and determine how it could have been improved with a mobile ethnography.
4. Discuss the duration of relevance of the Kraft Foods study based on a number of factors (e.g. time, location, culture).

Source: Hunt (2014)

End of Chapter Questions

These questions should help you reflect on your understanding of this chapter:

1. Identify and clarify the difference between the various qualitative methods of investigation.
2. Identify and clarify the difference between the various data-gathering techniques of qualitative research.
3. What is the difference between a qualitative method and a data-gathering technique?
4. Why does ethnography provide rich information about target populations that may result in the development of innovative products or services?
5. Why is it important for market researchers to heed ethical principles?

Checklist

After studying Chapter 8, you should now be familiar with these key concepts:

1. Qualitative research methods
2. Qualitative research techniques of data gathering

3. The difference between 1 and 2 above
4. The relevance of ethnography to market research
5. Ethical principles as applied to qualitative research

Further Reading (in sequence from beginners to advanced)

Eriksson, P. and Kovalainen, A. (2008) *Qualitative Methods in Business Research*. London: Sage Publications.

Belk, R., Fischer, E. and Kozinets, R. V. (2013) *Qualitative Consumer and Marketing Research*. London: Sage Publications.

American Psychological Association (APA) (2010) *Ethical Principles of Psychologists and Code of Conduct*. Washington, DC: APA.

Cohen, L., Manion, L. and Morrisson, K (2011) *Research Methods in Education*. London: Routledge.

Gray, D. (2014) *Doing Research in the Real World*. London: Sage Publications.

Sixsmith, J. and Murray, C. D. (2001) Ethical issues in the documentary data analysis of internet posts and archives. *Qualitative Health Research*, 11 (3), pp. 423–32.

Bibliography

Ambady, N., Bernieri, F. J., Richeson, J. A. and Zanna, M. P. (eds) (2000) Toward a histology of social behavior: judgmental accuracy from thin slices of the behavioral stream. *Advances in Experimental Social Psychology*, 32, pp. 201–71.

Ambady, N. and Rosenthal, R. (1992) Thin slices of expressive behavior as predictors of interpersonal consequences: a meta-analysis. *Psychological Bulletin* 111, no. 2: 256–274.

American Psychological Association (APA) (2010) *Ethical Principles of Psychologists and Code of Conduct*. Washington, DC: APA.

Anderson, K. (2009) Ethnographic research: a key to strategy. *Harvard Business Review*. Available at: https://hbr.org/2009/03/ethnographic-research-a-key-to-strategy [Accessed 31 December 2014].

Ante, S. E. and Edwards, C. (2006) The science of desire. *Bloomberg Businessweek Magazine*. Available at: www.businessweek.com/stories/2006-06-04/the-science-of-desire. [Accessed 31 December 2014].

Baines, P., Fill, C. and Page, K. (2011) *Marketing* (3rd edition). Oxford: Oxford University Press.

Belk, R. (2006) *Handbook of Qualitative Research Methods in Marketing*. Cheltenham: Edward Elgar.

Belk, R., Fischer, E. and Kozinets, R. V. (2013) *Qualitative Consumer and Marketing Research*. London: Sage Publications.

Bernieri, F. J. and Petty, K. N. (2005) The influence of a handshake on personality perception accuracy. Paper presented at the meeting of the Midwestern Psychological Association, Chicago, IL, May.

Brown, S. (1995) *Postmodern Marketing*. London: Routledge.

Carrigan, M., and Kirkup, M. (2001). The ethical responsibilities of marketers in retail observational research: protecting stakeholders through the ethical 'Research Covenant'. *The International Review of Retail, Distribution and Consumer Research*, 11 (4), pp. 415–35.

Carson, D., Gilmore, A., Perry, C. and Gronhaug, K. (2005) *Qualitative Marketing Research*. London: Sage Publications.

Carspencken, P. F. (1996) *Critical Ethnography in Educational Research*. London: Routledge.

Cohen, L., Manion, L. and Morrisson, K. (2011) *Research Methods in Education*. London: Routledge.

Cooper, D. R. and Schindler, P. S. (2001) *Business Research Methods*. New York: McGraw-Hill.

Danemark, B., Ekstrom, M., Jakobsen, L. and Karlsson, J. (2002) *Explaining Society: An Introduction to Critical Realism in the Social Sciences*. London: Routledge.

Ellis, C. S. and Bochner, A. P. (2002) Autoethnography, personal narrative, reflexivity: researcher as subject. In N. K. Denzin and Y. S. Lincoln (eds) *The Sage Handbook of Qualitative Research* (2nd edition), pp. 733–68. Thousand Oaks, CA: Sage Publications.

Eriksson, P. and Kovalainen, A. (2008) *Qualitative Methods in Business Research*. London: Sage Publications.

Denzin, N. K. (1999) Interpretive ethnography for the next century. *Journal of Contemporary Ethnography*, 28 (5), pp. 510–19.

Fairclough, N. (2005) Peripheral vision: discourse analysis in organization studies – the case for critical realism. *Organization Studies*, 26 (6), pp. 915–39.

Fanon, F. (1952) *Peau noire: Masques blancs*. Collection: la condition humaine. Paris: Les Éditions du Seuil.

Flick, U. (1998) *An Introduction to Qualitative Research*. London: Sage Publications.

Foucault, M. (1961) *Madness and Unreason: History of Madness in the Classical Age*. New York: Routledge.

Fourali, C. (2016) *The Promise of Social Marketing: Changing the World for Good*. London: Routledge.

Gergen, K. J. (1995) Relational theory and the discourses of power. In D. M. Hosking, H. P. Dachler and K. J. Gergen (eds) *Management and Organization: Relational Alternatives to Individualism*, pp. 29–51. Aldershot: Avebury.

Gladwell, M. (2007) *Blink: The Power of Thinking without Thinking*. New York: Back Bay Books.

Glaser, B., Strauss, G. and Anselm, L. (1967) *The Discovery of Grounded Theory: Strategies for Qualitative Research*. Chicago, IL: Aldine.

Gray, D. (2014) *Doing Research in the Real World*. London: Sage Publications.

Habermas, J. (1984) *The Theory of Communicative Action*. Boston: Beacon.

Hunt (2014) [to add] Hunt, A. (2014) Mobile ethnography let Kraft capture the highs and lows of party planning and hosting. Available at: https://www.quirks.com/articles/mobile-ethnography-let-kraft-capture-the-highs-and-lows-of-party-planning-and-hosting (Accessed on 12 July 2017)

Hunt, A. (2014) Mobile ethnography let Kraft capture the highs and lows of party planning and hosting. Available at: www.quirks.com/articles/mobile-ethnography-let-kraft-capture-the-highs-and-lows-of-party-planning-and-hosting [Accessed 12 July 2017].

Hycner, R. H. (1985) Some guidelines for the phenomenological analysis of interview data. *Human Studies*, 8, pp. 279–303.

Jordan, S. and Yeomans, D. (1995) Critical ethnography: problems in contemporary theory and practice. *British Journal of Sociology of Education*, 16 (3), pp. 389–408.

Kelly, G. A. (1955) *The Psychology of Personal Constructs*. New York: Norton.

Kozinets, R. V. (1998) On netnography: initial reflections on consumer research investigations of cyberculture. In J. Alba and W. Hutchinson (eds) *Advances in Consumer Research*, 25, pp. 366–71. Provo, UT: Association for Consumer Research.

Kozinets, R. V. and Belk, R. W. (2006) Camcorder society: quality videography in consumer and marketing research. In R. W. Belk (ed.) *Handbook of Qualitative Research Methods in Marketing*, pp. 335–44. Cheltenham: Edward Elgar.

Kvale, S. (1996) *Interviews*. London: Sage Publications.

Lester, S. (1999) An introduction to phenomenological research. Taunton: Stan Lester Development. Available at: www.rgs.org/NR/rdonlyres/F50603E0-41AF-4B15-9C84-BA7E4DE8CB4F/0/Seaweedphenomenologyresearch.pdf [Accessed 31 December 2014].

Majewski, S. (2012) Monitoring stakeholder conversations in social media: a United Nations case study. Submitted in partial fulfillment of an MA & MSc in International Marketing Communications, London Metropolitan University, January.

Miles, M. B., and Huberman, A. M. (1994) *Qualitative Data Analysis: An Expanded Sourcebook*. Thousand Oaks, CA: Sage.

Murray, M. (2007) Narrative psychology. In J. Smith (ed.), *Qualitative Psychology: A Practical Guide to Research Methods* (2nd edition), pp. 111–32. London: Sage Publications.

Patton, M. O. (1980) *Qualitative Evaluation Methods*. Beverley Hills, CA: Sage.

Rand, J. (2006) Mini-ethnography: a multi-method approach in an ESOL IT class. *Reflecting Education*, 2 (1), pp. 85–102.

Said, E. (1979) *Orientalism*. New York: Vintage Books.

Said, E. (1989) Representing the colonised: anthropology's interlocutors. *Critical Enquiry*, 15, pp. 205–25.

Schor, S., Van Buskirk, W. and McGrath, D. (1994) Caring, voice and self-reflection: feminist values and organizational change. *Journal of Organizational Change Management*, 7 (6), pp. 34–48.

Simpson, M. and Tuson, J. (2003) *Using Observations in Small-Scale Research: A Beginner's Guide*. Revised edition. University of Glasgow: The SCRE Centre.

Sixsmith, J. and Murray, C. D. (2001) Ethical issues in the documentary data analysis of internet posts and archives. *Qualitative Health Research*, 11 (3), pp. 423–32.

Find journal articles and multiple choice questions online at: **https://study.sagepub.com/benzo** to support what you've learnt so far.

CHAPTER 9

The Merits of Mixed Design Research Methodology: Illustration through Action Research and Case Studies

LEARNING OBJECTIVES

The key learning objectives of this chapter are:

1. To introduce the concept of mixed design research methodology
2. To consider the types of mixed design research methodology
3. To discuss the merits of mixed designs as a valuable research option
4. To discuss action research as a useful example of a mixed design method
5. To present case studies as another useful context for a mixed design method

KEY CONCEPTS

By the end of this chapter, the reader should be familiar with the following concepts:

1. The nature of mixed design approaches
2. Concepts that enhance the credibility of mixed design methodology (e.g. triangulation)
3. Visual models and how they help develop mixed designs
4. The nature of action research as a mixed design methodology
5. Action research as part of the development of social research paradigms
6. The case study as a context for a mixed design methodology
7. The varieties of focus of case studies

Chahid Fourali

Introduction

In Chapter 7, we introduced qualitative research and described the elements that make up a good design. Then, in Chapter 8, we introduced a variety of research methods available to researchers, particularly marketers, and focused on two important data-gathering research techniques: observation and interviewing.

In this chapter, we go one step further by looking at what has become an increasingly popular method among market researchers: using a number of techniques, both qualitative and quantitative, within the same research design, known as a mixed-design methodology. We illustrate this by focusing on two particular methods, action research and case studies, demonstrating their relevance to marketing research. Despite the fact that researchers use different labels for research designs, for example multi-method, mixed or simultaneous, it is important to remember to keep looking for opportunities to make adjustments to a design in order to maximise the degree it matches the research problem at hand. Taking this approach may even result in a 'hybrid design' that combines characteristics from several established types of designs. At this point, you may like to revisit Chapter 5, to consider some of the design options available and the possible contexts in which they may be adopted, before reading this chapter.

As outlined in Table 9.1, this chapter presents three dimensions: an introduction to the concept of mixed design, an introduction to the action research method and, finally, an introduction to the case study method.

Table 9.1 Three main dimensions of this chapter

Topic of focus	Illustrating examples
Mixed-design methodology (Introduction)	Action research
	Case study

Snapshot: Kraft Foods Inc. – A Journey from Unwarranted Assumptions to Learning to Listen

The story

Kraft Foods' flagship brand, Oreo, had a turbulent time establishing itself in the Chinese market. Although the company was operating in China as early as 1996, its sales were disappointing against forecasts. For some reason, the company kept this status quo for almost 10 years before realising that sales were predicted to drop further, despite an increase in customer spending in what was a fast-growing market. Shawn Warren, Regional Head of Biscuits and his team, realised that Oreo faced a definite threat and radical changes were needed to prevent this. The problem seemed to stem from the fact that Kraft did not carry out systematic research of the market before making a decision to enter it, nor in the first years of trading there. The company did not have a tradition of carrying out marketing research and made the assumption that if a product is successful in the USA, it will most likely be successful anywhere else.

Finding itself in dire straits, the company decided to undertake marketing research to assess the situation and, based on established research traditions at Kraft, the research sought the views of hundreds of Chinese consumers over many months and took into account local tastes, appearance, price and packaging. It included information on demographics, competition, product attributes, brand preferences and competitive imagery, together with awareness and recall. This complex study required the use of a number of research techniques (including questionnaires and focus groups), as well as types of information including cognitive and emotional data. Indeed, as argued by Clements et al. (2013), unless there is emotional attachment developed over many years, as is the case with the American consumers, 'the taste and shape of the cookie could be quite alien'.

Research revealed that Kraft's strategy of replicating the US approach was at the root of bad decision making, including overlooking local/Chinese preferences around the product (e.g. the Chinese prefer a less sweet biscuit), the type of advertising and packaging used and the pricing structure. These insights led to a number of radical changes, such as introducing wafers as well as a less sweet version of Oreo, more targeted marketing communications, smaller packets and a readjustment of distribution channels to include convenience stores.

Results and insights

As a result of these changes, sales rocketed from $20m in 2005 to $400m in 2012. The moral of the story is: *Do not assume that if a product is successful in one market it will necessarily be successful anywhere else.* Decisions should be evidence-based whilst focusing on the needs and preferences of the target population.

Whilst there are many situations when perhaps a simple questionnaire or a focus group may be enough to address a particular problem, in general marketing researchers need to look at a problem from a variety of perspectives to attempt to make sense of the 'reality' they are facing. They may need to look at the number of times a phenomenon occurs, how it is perceived and the variety of perceptions from a number of stakeholders or groups of people affected by the phenomenon. This is well illustrated in the snapshot above. Kraft Foods made a classic mistake of 'making unwarranted assumptions' about what the customer wants. It was only after managers set out to objectively test their assumptions that they discovered that they were wrong and their business decisions were the source of their loss. Once they understood how their target groups felt about their product and its meaning for them, they were able to make adjustments to their product offering which turned around the results of the company. This was only made possible through the company's flexibility over its sources of information (quantitative and qualitative), thereby demonstrating the use of the mixed-design methodology. As argued previously in Chapters 7 and 8, the methods/techniques used for gathering and organising data may differ but the purpose remains the same: to address a business challenge by understanding the target groups within their environments.

Source: adapted from Magwood (2011), Clements et al. (2013) and Reddy and Sproule (2013)

What are Mixed Designs?

If you asked a researcher the question 'Should researchers be restricted to the use of only one research tool, just questionnaires, for example?', their response would be understandably dismissive. A question such as this would be akin to asking any problem investigator to only look in some places and not others. Indeed, several breakthroughs in research made use of new insights emanating from other fields, illustrated by the story of James Watson and Francis Crick, who discovered the structure of DNA as a result of a combination of physics and knowledge of genetics. The same applies to the methods and paradigms of research.

Although generally research methods tend to broadly refer to two options, with mixed methods as the third methodological movement, you could argue that there are in fact four options: quantitative, qualitative, critical studies and a mixture involving various elements of all three, labelled a mixed-method approach. The critical dimension is included as it tends to be distinctive for having a normative aim (human emancipation) and, therefore, goes beyond a simple instrumental goal, such as developing happier customers. Emancipation is an ideal goal that all research should aim towards. However, research is often restricted by a number of factors, such as a lack of resources, or restrictions imposed by companies commissioning the research. Hence, research, like most human activities, is affected by a variety of influences and may not always align itself with the values of every stakeholder associated with the study.

Emancipation Freedom from exploitation

Incommensurability is a concept in the philosophy of science (popularised by Kuhn, 1962) that denotes a situation where it is impossible to compare research theories as they do not have a common basis that allows comparison as they belong to two different research traditions. This idea is usually attributed to Fleck, a medical researcher who developed his ideas in Poland. He argued that truth is relative and that it depends on the degree of acceptability of the language and concepts by a community of researchers/scientists. This idea has subsequently been taken up by the social constructionist movement. A similar concept was also used by Foucault in the form of 'episteme'

There are many definitions of the expression 'mixed design'. A simple definition is one provided by the *Journal of Mixed Methods Research*. It defines mixed research as any 'research in which the investigator collects and analyses data, integrates the findings, and draws inferences using both qualitative and quantitative approaches or methods in a single study or program of inquiry' (JMMR, 2015).

Whether a researcher adopts any of the four methodological options outlined above will depend on their worldview (ontological and epistemological), as discussed in earlier chapters, but consider the following question carefully: As each research method is underpinned by a worldview and associated paradigm, can a mixed method be adopted without undermining the agreed paradigm? This question makes the following two assumptions:

1. Qualitative, quantitative and critical-methods approaches reflect different paradigms that cannot be compared. The reason for this is that they do not share an agreed common basis (in terms of language or concepts) about what they consider to be rigorous. Philosophers of science use the expression 'incommensurability' to reflect this inability to measure and compare different views/theories. From this perspective, qualitative and quantitative approaches are not seen as complementary to each other. A method purist would support this argument, but it is not robust because, although quantitative researchers argue that their approach is objective and proceed through testing previously formulated hypotheses, in fact all approaches involve a good degree of creativity and subjectivity in their analysis and interpretation of findings. In turn, qualitative research can also contribute to the testing of theories.

2. There is an assumption that research methods must carry consistent ontological implications, a position that is not easy to sustain given the variety of tasks that the methods can be used for. For example, a questionnaire, usually associated with a *quantitative* approach, can also be used to gather views on meaning (e.g. through Likert-scale techniques), which reflects a *qualitative* research perspective (Bryman and Bell, 2015).

In light of the above, a purely qualitative or quantitative approach is not only logically but also pragmatically unsustainable, as reality is diverse and needs to be viewed through a variety of lenses to provide a more comprehensive representation of it.

A **method purist** is researcher who, believing that there is an epistemological divide between quantitative and qualitative methods, decides to opt, exclusively, for either of the two traditions. Such an approach would mean that the researcher would overlook any benefit that the 'alternative' method could provide

Consider a study on the habits of different ethnic groups with the aim of understanding the behaviour, emotions and meanings associated with various products/services and how these products and services are best positioned to have the greatest appeal to certain groups of people. A study like this could make use of in-depth interviews, direct observations of interactions with the product or service and multi-dimensional scaling and concept mapping (to help organise information in terms of areas of influence). The information could highlight significant motivators that the marketer can use when positioning their products, making this option of using mixed methods very compelling.

The benefits of mixed methods put forward by researchers include:

1. Triangulation: the purpose of this approach is to enable researchers to use more than one method (e.g. numbers and opinions through observation and interviews) to compensate for the weaknesses of each. As a result, combining approaches will provide a more robust view of the reality than a separate perspective.
2. Complementarity: using more than one type of data can provide complementary information (e.g. numbers versus meanings or macro versus micro), which increases understanding and helps design more relevant solutions to a business problem.
3. Development: using one type of information can lead to the development of and inform further studies. For example, quantitative analysis may identify certain geographical areas that reflect the adverse effects of cigarette smoking more strongly than the general population. This can result in more precise targeting of the group needing special attention, with support from a qualitative perspective.
4. Problem clarification: combining several methods can help identify the reality of a problem more clearly and provide opportunities for understanding and resolving any contradictions. For example, simply looking at the number of people selecting a particular item at a shopping centre may lead to a misleading interpretation. However, combining this quantitative data with more qualitative information gained through interviews or focus groups gives much more valuable data.
5. Relevance: a combination of methods is key to providing both quantity and quality to help determine whether an outcome/solution may be applicable elsewhere. The introductory example of Oreo demonstrates the need not just to refer to past results but also to understand each context and type of customer separately to be able to determine a tailored solution.

Although we've seen that a multi-method and multi-level perspective can help provide richer information than a single approach, enabling the researcher to better understand the phenomenon at hand and in turn suggest appropriate solutions, there is still a need to systematically weigh up various dimensions associated with the phenomenon to help

Figure 9.1 An inspector's use of triangulation

refine the researcher's choice. The researcher first needs to understand the characteristics of the problem being addressed:

- Is the information publicly accessible?
- Will the target population be able to express its views on the issue and is the information provided reliable?
- Is the phenomenon a conscious one?

They will then need to determine the purpose of the study:

- Is the aim to explore a new phenomenon with a view to describing it more accurately?
- Is the researcher interested in understanding a particular context, such as a classroom or an SME company?
- Does the researcher want to select one or more samples to study the phenomenon, or does he/she want to follow up one sample and collect information from them on more than one occasion to see if views have evolved or changed?

See the Research in Practice box for an illustrative scenario.

Once these questions are clarified and, based on the above identification of the four research design options, a mixed design may take five different forms depending on the level of focus of the research:

1. A *quantitatively driven research design* supported by qualitative and/or critical positioning methods
2. A *qualitatively driven research design* supported by quantitative or/and critical positioning methods

3. A *critical study design* supported by qualitative and/or quantitative empirical backup
4. A *partial equal status design* offering equal emphasis on two of the three possible research traditions
5. A *full equal status design* offering equal emphasis on all three traditions (quantitative, qualitative and critical).

So, as we can see, research designs are not only classified according to three orientations but should also consider the various dimensions of design (quantitative, qualitative and critical) and contemplate their relevance and the benefits or risks that could occur if the research adopts or ignores them.

Research in Practice

A researcher was interested in the following question: 'How do people select their political candidates in England? An exploration of possible influences'.

Based on the purpose and context of the study, the researcher listed the dimensions that needed to be addressed in order to determine the characteristics of the research design. Table 9.2 considers, on the one hand, the type of problem/phenomenon faced and, on the other, the possible types of methodological design that might match the purpose of the study.

Table 9.2 Preliminary considerations for the selection of a research design

Type of Phenomenon (Choose 1 for first column and 2 for second column)		**Decision**
Public (1)	Private (2)	2
Communicable (1)	Non-communicable (2)	1
Conscious (1)	Subconscious (2)	1
Directly accessible (1)	Indirectly accessible (2)	1
	Total	5
Characteristics of Research Design (Choose 1 for first column and 2 for second column)		
Exploratory (1)	Conclusive (2)	1
Descriptive (1)	Causal (2)	1
Cross-sectional (1)	Longitudinal (2)	2
Single (1)	Multiple (2)	2
	Total	7

Source: adapted from Malhotra and Birks, 2007

(Continued)

(Continued)

The researcher reviewed the key dimensions of context and purpose, then selected from the options available in Table 9.2.

Based on the type of phenomenon, they selected the following:

- This is *private* information that cannot reliably be accessed indirectly.
- This is *communicable* information if the subject is prompted to provide it.
- The subject is *consciously* aware of this information.
- The information can be *directly accessed* from targeted individuals (if the information was archive-based, as is the case with past material, digital or otherwise, then it would be indirectly accessible. This dimension is added in as it helps clarify the research context).

In terms of the methodology, they selected the following research design elements:

- This is an *exploratory* piece of research (perhaps preparatory for a larger study).
- The exploration aims to better understand and *describe* the phenomenon before putting forward hypotheses (e.g. about the direction of effect).
- This used a *longitudinal* design that gathered data on two separate occasions from two groups of subjects located in different parts of the country (*multiple*). On the first occasion, information was gathered on the factors that influenced their choice of political candidate (based on ranking and/or relative weights/importance of each factor). On the second occasion, following election day, the subjects were asked to determine whether the previously stated influencing factors and suggested steps for the candidate selection process were followed closely.

Note that in Table 9.2, the higher the total number for type of phenomenon or characteristic of design, the more challenging it may be to develop an adequate research design. This is because the dimensions attracting a '2' (i.e. in the second column) present the researcher with a situation where it can be difficult to access the information or carry out the investigation.

It is worth remembering at this stage that the selection of the type of research design, and the associated qualitative or quantitative methods, will primarily depend on whether these methods:

1. maximise the chance of providing valuable information, and
2. minimise the cost of accessing this information.

Once the researcher clarifies the context and aim of study, using Table 9.2, they can start considering potential sources of information and how best to access them. In the example above, questionnaires might have been a useful tool to determine the influences and frequency of the choices. However, given that some of the subjects might have forgotten how they actually arrived at their decision (months or years ago), the researcher decided to back up their findings with interviews immediately after election day.

The exploration stage revealed that a high percentage of the influences were beyond direct conscious awareness. This may be the case if there is an incongruence between the stated (i.e. conscious) influences and the process of decision making, on the one hand, and the 'actual' (derived) decision-making process, supported by final voting decisions. Subsequently, the researchers might set out to discover whether the subjects changed their views or whether they were simply not aware/conscious of the full process of candidate selection. The study may review the procedures for the next, more 'conclusive' stage when it will add another source of information to go beyond surface-level answers and help provide the deeper reasons for voters' selection process. As such, in-depth techniques may be recommended to enable deeper probing of subconscious influences. Among these techniques may be direct probing and, if relevant, developing and using a test that is administered to probe these influences.

Note that research manuals sometimes restrict researchers when choosing their options. For example, a manual may advise that if you choose an 'exploratory' aim, then you need to specify whether your choice is qualitative or quantitative (i.e. not both). Additionally, a research guide may advise the junior researcher to refrain from qualifying their aims as descriptive or causal since, they argue, choosing 'exploratory' precludes these aims.

We feel that these are unwarranted restrictions (and, in the context of mixed design, irrelevant) that limit the options available to the researcher and, consequently, the effectiveness and efficiency of the research process and outcomes. Indeed, exploratory research may be carried out with a view to attempting an early description of a phenomenon, or the identification of possible causes of the phenomenon at hand, that may need looking at closely. Hence, it is argued that mixed-design research tends to be more relevant to business research (over the mono-method design) as it provides rich information combining several perspectives, multiple data types, methods, positions and paradigms.

Importance of Visual Representation

As we've seen, a mixed-model approach uses a mixture of techniques targeting different stakeholders to help progress the aims of a project. Ivankova et al. (2006) advise making use of visual models to determine the dimensions and steps involved in a mixed-model framework. They suggest that the design should include the phase of the study, the procedure used for data gathering and the type of data obtained. Crump and Logan (2008) propose adding a fourth dimension in the form of targeted samples of stakeholder groups. Table 9.3 shows a potential layout of the four dimensions with associated information, based on likely steps for a research framework used to advise a company on how to respond to a crisis.

Table 9.3 Visual representation of a likely sequence of research steps for determining a successful response to a crisis

Research phase	Data-gathering procedure	Outcome (e.g. forms of data)	Sample used
Step 1 (quantitative analysis) – fact finding	Survey seeking information including how many people are aware of a crisis and changed their mind about loyalty to brand	Numerical data	Stratified sample covering the whole spectrum of population
Step 2 (qualitative) – zooming into reasons	Interviews – determining reasons behind decisions	Text data (transcript of interviews)	Interviews with those remaining firmly loyal and those who changed their allegiance as a result of crisis

(Continued)

Table 9.3 (Continued)

Research phase	Data-gathering procedure	Outcome (e.g. forms of data)	Sample used
Step 3: (qualitative)	Focus group – what should the company do to demonstrate its social responsibility?	Text data Development of alternative response scenarios	Focus groups with a representative population of (degree of allegiance groups) 'loyal', 'undecided' and 'switched allegiance' groups considering effectiveness of different response scenarios
Step 4: (quantitative)	Survey (online) seeking information on newly developed simulated responses in the form of three video scenarios	Numerical data	Stratified sample covering the whole spectrum of population
Step 5: (Connecting quantitative and qualitative)	• Selecting five reps from each of three types of allegiance groups to form a focus group • Developing discussion/prompt questions	Cases (n=6) Focus group questionnaire	
Step 6: (qualitative)	• Individual in-depth interviews	Text data Image data (photographs)	Six representatives of the three allegiance groups
Step 7 (final) – integrating quantitative and qualitative data	Interpretation and explanation of the quantitative and qualitative results	Discussion Implications/ recommendations Future research	

Source: adapted from Ivankova et al., 2006; Crump and Logan, 2008

Using a visual representation like this can help to manage the complexity of a design that draws from a variety of sources of evidence at a number of levels.

Action Research: A Primary Candidate for Mixed-Design Methodology

Action research (AR) has been classified under various labels, including a technique, a qualitative method, a mixed method or even a philosophy of research. Here, we regard it as a mixed methodology that also reflects a philosophical position.

Advanced: Variety of Action Research Models

Action research should be seen as a family of approaches rather than a single approach to practice-based research. Such a family of approaches is continually expanding. Perhaps among the more known orientations we may list the following:

- **Action science**: this approach argues that traditional social science is inadequate as it portrays a researcher detached from the 'experiment' they are undertaking. Such an approach differentiates between the researcher's openly espoused theories and (covert) theories that actually guide their actions. This would lead to rich information that helps view problems from various perspectives and produce more learning.
- **Cooperative/collaborative enquiry**: this approach advocates the need to work 'with people' rather than 'on people'. Such an approach involves an iterative cycle of evaluation that includes propositional, practical and experiential knowing that should lead to creating new 'corroborated' knowledge and skills.
- **Participatory action research**: this approach is heavily influenced by Paulo Freire's work on critical pedagogy (1970). It aims to democratically involve all sections of society with a view to creating new knowledge that leads to improvements in social conditions.
- **Developmental action research enquiry**: the aim of this approach is to take into consideration all dimensions associated with the research. It considers three levels of focus: the *researcher*, the second person *relationships* in which the researcher engages to carry out their research and, finally, the third person *institutions* that are being focused on.
- **Living educational theories**: this approach highlights how both the researcher and the research process affect the subject studied. It encourages researchers to be honest about, on the one hand, any bias that may affect their perspective and, on the other hand, how the experience of researching affects them in turn.

A rigorous AR is useful at two levels, improving the researcher's perspective, either professionally or educationally for example, as well as the situation they are addressing. In many cases, research focuses primarily on improving an external situation, without due regard for the researcher's, or even the project manager's, influence on the studied situation. AR recognises the input of every stakeholder involved and, above all, that of the researcher since it is often carried out by an 'insider' or somebody directly linked to the situation being studied. Referring back to the Kraft Foods example, AR can advise on the best way to address a business problem and help those leading the research to avoid making unwarranted and costly assumptions, not to mention raising awareness of any power dynamics present in the organisation that may lead to destructive decisions.

This form of AR, with its dual focus on researcher and problem, regards no aspect of the research as off-limits when it comes to addressing a problem. Ethics is of constant concern to action researchers and taking a critical approach is regarded as positive AR practice.

Given the variety of definitions of AR, one fairly comprehensive definition, despite its age, is the one offered by Rapoport (1970, 499): 'Action research aims to contribute both to the practical concerns of people in an immediate problematic situation and to the goals of social science by joint collaboration within a mutually acceptable ethical framework'.

Because AR's natural inclination is to be practical and solution-focused, it generally makes use of a methodology that encourages an iterative interplay between reflecting, planning, acting and observing. An alternative, slightly modified version (see Table 9.4) is the one offered by Susman's action research model (1983): diagnosing a problem, action planning (looking for alternative courses of action), taking action (selecting one option), evaluating (the consequences) and specifying the learning/findings.

Both of these models are iterative as the researcher will keep going back through each step until satisfied with the outcome. The main difference between the two models is primarily the fact that Susman specifies the acquired learning (the final step of each round of iteration).

Table 9.4 Comparison between two perspectives on the AR stages

Kemmis and McTaggart (1988)	Susman (1983)
Reflecting	Diagnosing
Planning	Action planning
Acting	Taking action
Observing	Evaluating
	Specifying learning

Susman's model also starts with a problem identification stage which is important if we are to argue for the practicality of AR. Yet, both models seem to assume that reflection tends to occur primarily at stage one of the process. Given that reflection is pervasive to all these stages, one possible improvement might be the model in Figure 9.2.

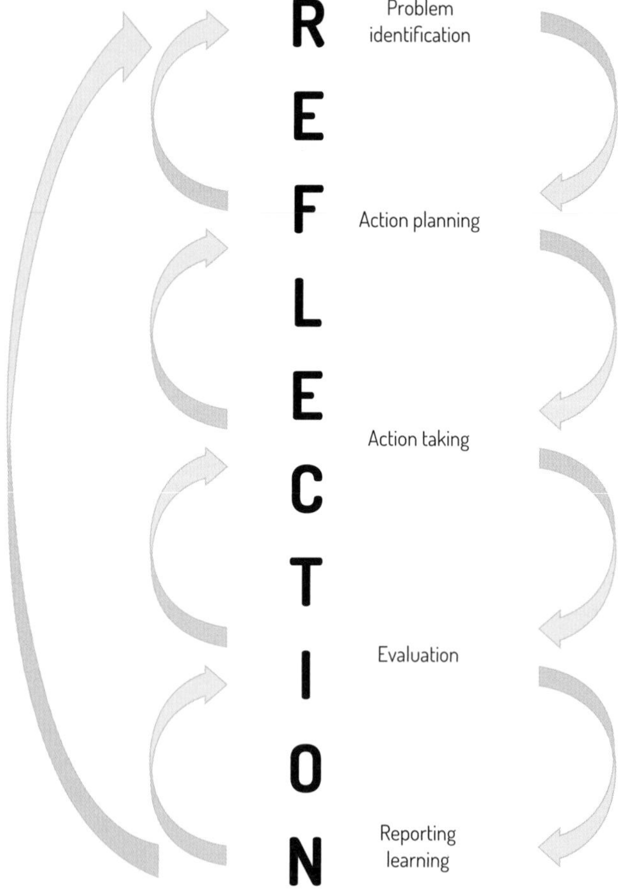

Figure 9.2 Steps in action research

Source: Fourali, 2016

Here, the model (Figure 9.2) recognises that reflection is a pervasive activity associated with every step. The researcher should still ensure there is direction to the research process and that each iteration learns from and subsumes earlier insights, associated with previous phases. In other words, whenever a researcher moves to a new stage of analysis, either a full cycle or a single step, they need to take into account the information gained in the previous stages.

Research in Practice

A new Head of Marketing Communication, recently appointed to an overseas branch of a global company, is asked to determine and implement the best way of advertising a new product in a new country. 'Best' in this case means an advert that maximises interest from the target population while ensuring the material is sensitive to the new environment. An action research project starts by gaining an in-depth understanding of the new environment, including carrying out some marketing research to understand local interests and cultural differences. As a result of this research, a plan of action is designed, taking into account the information received. The plan is tested with selected groups representing the local population, and, after making adjustments, the final advert is aired (action stage) on a popular TV channel. Reactions to the advert are closely monitored, looking for opportunities to make improvements, and, depending on the general feedback, the lessons learned (together with any suggestions for improvement) are reported to the management of the company. The management will, in turn, either decide to stick with the new ad or, if there are any problems, advise the marketing team to work on the issues highlighted at the evaluation stage before a new version of the ad is produced. This leads the Head of Marketing Communication to start a new cycle of the research.

McNiff and Whitehead (2006) argue that social research paradigms developed through a number of steps (see also the earlier treatments of the concept of paradigm in Chapters 4 and 7):

Stage 1 – Positivistic approach (technical/rational): Researcher aims to avoid the research field to maintain objectivity and ensure knowledge is not contaminated by human contact – uses quantitative analysis.

Stage 2 – Interpretative: Researcher observes people in their natural settings to describe and explain what they are doing – uses qualitative analysis.

Stage 3 – Critical theoretic research: At this stage the researcher recognises that research is never neutral and that social situations are created by people. These can be deconstructed and reconstructed. There is an interest in analysing power relationships.

Stage 4 – Action research: 'How can a situation be understood, maintained or improved?' AR emphasises both understanding and action. This stage considers both the external situation (e.g. the explicit external problem) and the internal, no-less influential dimensions (the researcher's effect), the short and long term as well as local and global perspectives. In other words, the AR should become more routinely geared towards taking into account all these dimensions and, if it chooses not to consider any of these aspects, should be upfront with this decision and its potential effect on the robustness (reliability and meaningfulness) of the findings.

You could argue that the next paradigm stage (stage 5) is one that ensures that the action research makes a difference to society. This means the focus should be on 'critical action research' where purpose, process and outcome of research go beyond resolving just the business problem to offer solutions that are concentrated around a long-term, inclusive social concern.

However, and not withstanding arguments about the nature of paradigms, as proposed by Kuhn (1962), perhaps the most likely way forward is towards a 'conceptually consistent eclecticism'. This idea borrows from Dryden (1987) who similarly argued for the use of 'theoretically consistent eclecticism' to enable counsellors working within a theoretical framework to still consider using a variety of psychological techniques developed within other psychological theories (i.e. eclecticism), as long as such tools do not necessarily clash with the practitioner's chosen theoretical model. Accordingly, it is possible to argue that while there are clear advantages in being technically eclectic (in our case, making use of a variety of research methods and techniques, depending on the needs of the study, underpinned by a business problem), it is still incumbent on the researcher to develop a conceptualisation (or argument) that justifies such an eclectic approach. For example, many successful companies carry out studies to help them identify products that, in turn, help them compete better. They may, for instance, be working to develop a new strawberry or tomato that is more robust in resisting the elements (using a positivist paradigm). However, they still need to ensure that these are 'tastier' than existing ones and do not attract adverse publicity (interpretive, critical theoretic and action research) if they aim to launch them in the marketplace (as genetically modified products are prone to do). Hence, both 'hard' and 'soft' experimental approaches can inform each other. Of course, several 'philosophical purists' may argue that paradigms are incompatible and cannot work with each other but, as the example indicated, this is perfectly possible. As each new product has an effect on humans, it is not surprising that all the other dimensions will be implicated in deciding on how such a product will fare. Accordingly, the outcome of research (or dimensions of research) would be the result of interplay between the various perspectives, as shown in Figure 9.3.

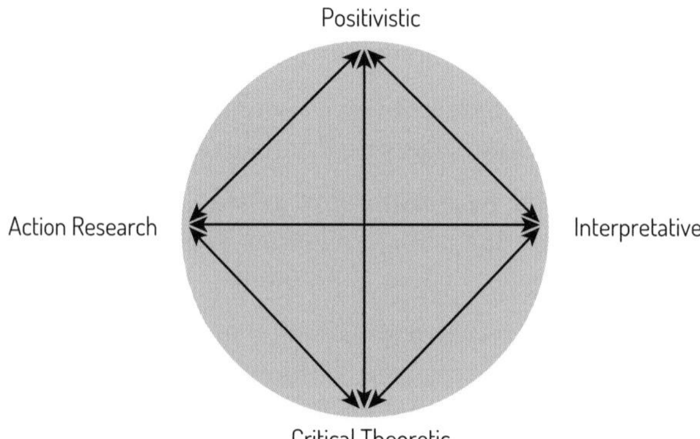

Figure 9.3 Mutual influence/benefits of the various research traditions in a mixed-design action research scenario

Introduction to Case Studies: Separating the Unique from the General

A very good metaphor for the difference between case studies and other broader studies was provided by Gerring:

> There are two ways to learn how to build a house. One might study the construction of many houses – perhaps a large subdivision or even hundreds of thousands of houses. Or one might study the construction of one particular house. The first approach is a cross-case method. The second is a within-case or case study method. (Gerring, 2007, p. 1: Gerring, J. (2007) *Case Study Research: Principles and Practices*. Cambridge: Cambridge University Press.)

When selecting a research method, researchers need to consider the scope of the research they are undertaking and select either extensive (expansive) coverage or an intensive focus (Swanborn, 2010). An expansive, wide scope considers large populations and geographical areas with a view to determining generalisable models or theories about how certain phenomena link to a set of explanatory variables. This approach tends to adopt a more standardised perspective, using definitions, surveys and statistical modelling. When adopting this expansive approach, any result that does not match a generally adequate explanatory model may be regarded as an 'error fluctuation' or attributed to unique contextual differences (e.g. cultural). For example, a researcher studying brand marketing may come up with variables that explain why customers select certain brands over others. However, they may discover that the model does not apply in certain areas that exhibit unique cultural characteristics, as these regions may focus on other dimensions, deemed less relevant by the researcher. This type of unique scenario may benefit from a more intensive or focused approach to research (a case study) to help unravel the unique characteristics. Having said this, a case study may reveal dimensions that require confirmation through additional, broader studies. For example, a study about the infamous debacle of Enron may highlight a key finding that the main cause of failure of business leadership was the lack of transparency. In turn, this may become a 'hypothesis' for further studies, with a view to generalising this finding.

Case studies are usually appropriate to consider as a research method if the researcher is interested in a phenomenon that is either new, misunderstood or where the boundaries between the occurrence of the phenomenon and its context are not clear. Case studies are particularly appropriate if the focus is about understanding the 'how' or 'why' of an event or a situation. In the Kraft Foods scenario shown earlier, the interest was not simply in how people buy its products and what age they are – a simple survey would have answered this question. Rather, the researchers wanted to find out the reason for the lack of interest in the product and 'how to make the product more attractive to the Chinese market'. The purpose was to derive learning to help the company make effective decisions to turn things around. Most learning organisations adopt this strategy to maximise their chances of survival and also to enable them to thrive.

The object of focus in a case study can be varied and may be an individual, a job role, an organisation, a community (e.g. a tribe), a region, a country, a process, a crisis or an event (Gray, 2014). The actors involved in a case study may reflect individual (micro-level), organisational or institutional (meso-level) or national or regional (macro-level) dimensions. Contextual restrictions may dictate what a case consists of. For example, many psychotherapy publications focus on just one individual case study (i.e. a patient), whereas in marketing and business studies the focus may be at more than one level – for example, moving between micro and meso levels when undertaking brand marketing studies where individual associations may account for how decisions affect companies with different brand positioning.

From this perspective, a case study can also be classified as action research, especially if it follows a number of cycles that alternate between identification of a problem, fact-finding, planning action, implementation and, finally, taking stock of the outcomes and considering whether the suggested solution is adequate or needs improving by going through another cycle.

A case study may have more than one aim but Stake (1995) identified three broad categories when considering the aims of a case study:

1. Intrinsic case studies that focus primarily on understanding the particularities of a situation or an event.
2. Instrumental case studies that aim to clarify broader issues and/or challenge unwarranted generalisations.
3. Multiple or collective case studies that work in concert to try and understand a general phenomenon.

Researchers have several types of case study at their disposal and may find it useful to position their study in relation to them. Five types identified in the current literature (Yin, 2003; Bryman and Bell, 2015) are:

1. The unique case or extreme case (known for its individual characteristics).
2. The revelatory case, which, as its name suggests, offers the opportunity to study an event that was previously inaccessible. However, this may be a misnomer as 'inductive researchers' consider all studies as revelatory.
3. The representative or typical case, which aims to explore a situation that may be representative of certain types of events or organisations.
4. The longitudinal case, concerned with how a situation develops/changes over time.
5. The critical case, used to review situations where a certain hypothesis or model may or may not hold, given the uniqueness of the case at hand, as suggested earlier.

The above section may be illustrated by a two-way table that can help researchers position their case study projects along the two dimensions of 'aims' and 'types'. Table 9.5 facilitates this process as it identifies the dimensions and allows a degree of overlap between different elements of the dimensions.

As we discussed in the section on mixed design frameworks, the choice of case should be based on the twin aims of maximising valuable information and minimising the cost of accessing it.

Reflective Activity

Consider a case study (based on your research project or a paper you have read) and complete a copy of Table 9.5 to determine its aim(s) or type(s).

Table 9.5 Positioning the case study along the dimensions according to aim and type

		Aims of case study		
		Intrinsic case study	**Instrumental case study**	**Multiple/Collective case study**
Type of case study	Unique/extreme case			
	Revelatory case			
	Representative/typical case			
	Longitudinal case			
	Critical case			

Once researchers are clear about the aims and type of case study they want to adopt, they will need to clarify the following:

1. The number of cases to focus on (e.g one or more companies)
2. The unit of analysis (e.g. an individual or a company)
3. The criteria to be used for selecting the units
4. The timing and frequency of occurrence of the observations
5. The number of techniques of data collection they judge helpful (e.g. type of interviews, archives, observation).

Empirical Moving from hypotheses to experimentation to conclusions

As advised earlier, it can be very helpful to both the researcher and readers of the eventual report, to develop a visual representation of the steps involved in the research, based on the selected characteristics above. Research studies do not have to be positivistic or empirical in nature as the route observed (inductive or deductive) depends on the purpose and context of the study. In turn, the purpose should influence the structure of the report. Gray (2014) identifies three possible ways of organising a report:

1. A linear analysis structure – this is particularly appropriate for theory building research. In this case, the traditional research steps of statement of a problem, literature review, methodology, findings, analysis and conclusions/recommendations are followed.
2. A comparative report – based on the same case and seen from a number of perspectives, or two or more cases studies that contrast different views to help explain or understand the phenomenon in question. Here, the author first provides answers to the issues addressed and then proceeds to provide a background (of the phenomenon) together with alternative explanations.
3. A chronological report – this refers to successive events, or critical incidents, associated with aspects of a business. The events are not necessarily linked, could deal with wide-ranging issues from product, communication, health and safety to HR, and may be presented in any order. The focus of the researcher is to advise the company why different incidents occurred and to make recommendations for the future about whether similar events should be encouraged or avoided.

Case study research can involve a large amount of data which may confuse the researcher and affect the reporting. One suggestion to manage this complexity is to construct case records about each case. This involves the researcher gathering all the raw data/information about each case before proceeding to organise and edit it all, so that it makes sense. They can then produce a condensed 'summary' version for each record, for example a report or an interview associated with a key contributor to a situation. Following these three steps, the task of producing a case study report, involving all studied cases, should become more manageable.

Note that when multiple cases are used, each case may be undertaken to feed information into the next case. For example, a company may decide to investigate why the numbers of its customers are dwindling. The marketing researcher may start with a number of possible ideas and decide to select a number of retail outlets selling its product for examination. After investigation and interpretation of the findings for each outlet, new views are formed about the possible reasons. These reasons are then 'tested' against the views of the next outlet, and so on and so forth, until a more robust interpretation is reached accounting for the findings gathered from all of the outlets. For example, although the first interpretation may have reflected the economic recession, subsequent interpretations may involve new competitor products, that are more effective and cheaper, or a high level of staff turnover leading to inexperienced sales and communication skills.

One recurrent criticism of case studies involves the issue of rigour and how this affects reliability, replicability and validity. However, as argued by Bryman and Bell (2015), the relevance of these particular concepts depends on the researcher's assessment, as it may be argued, with evidence, that they do not apply to a case study context. In addition, the very nature and strength of a case study comes from its focus on deriving findings that apply to the particularities of a specific case. As such, case studies are not concerned with generalising findings to other contexts, even if the findings may provide useful ideas for similar situations. Borrowing a famous metaphor, you could say 'if it walks like a duck, and talks like a duck, then it's probably, but not necessarily, a duck'.

Ethics

Overall, there are no specific ethical aspects that apply exclusively to mixed designs. The ethical issues raised in Chapter 8 are also relevant here and it may be advisable to go back and briefly review Table 8.4: Ethical issues linked to the Internet. However, there is always the possibility of encouraging a more comprehensive approach to ethics, one that goes beyond the work of a researcher to cover the whole organisation. Figure 9.4 builds on the advice of Laczniak and Murphy (2006), but presents it in a format that can apply at either an individual or organisational level, in addition to focusing on both social and environmental responsibilities. The figure considers marketing research ethics as part of the broader ethical considerations that should be assumed by socially and environmentally responsible organisations, be that a global commercial organisation or a small market research agency.

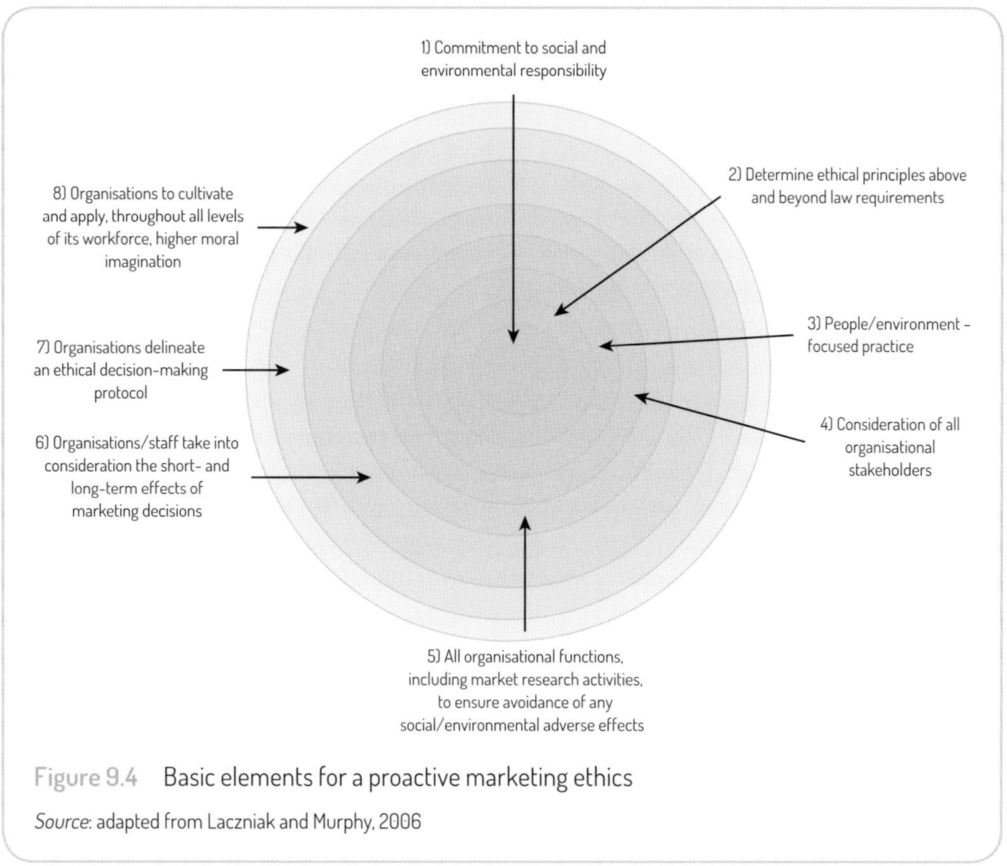

Figure 9.4 Basic elements for a proactive marketing ethics

Source: adapted from Laczniak and Murphy, 2006

Chapter Summary

This chapter introduced the mixed-design research approach and showed its relevance to business research, over the 'mono-method' design; it discussed how using mixed methods in research provides rich information, combining several perspectives, multiple data types, methods, positions and paradigms.

Two mixed-design methods, action research and case studies, were introduced and demonstrated with illustrative examples. It was argued that different situations require different designs, especially given the variety of available designs within both action and case study research. In considering the various options, the researcher should aim to maximise the chances of obtaining valuable information and minimise the costs of obtaining it, while heeding the ethical advice presented in the previous chapter.

Case Study: Being Global Means Being Local as Well – The Value of Case Studies in Making Business Decisions

McDonald's regional business decisions are underpinned by case study research that involves focusing on all dimensions that affect the target consumer's buying decisions. These influences can address regional as well as national differences, which, in turn, reflect economic, cultural, political as well as local taste and psychological factors. McDonald's capitalises on insights gained from local studies (case studies) to adjust its offerings to match local interests and values. Examples of this are:

- India: McDonald's, aware of local taboos regarding the consumption of pork and beef, decided to adjust the menu in India. Instead of the usual hamburger, it introduced chicken, lamb and fish burgers, more suited to the Indian palate. The menu includes *McCurry Pan, McSpicy Paneer burger, Pizza McPuff* and *Masala Grill Burger, made* exclusively from either chicken or potato soya.
- China: in accordance with Chinese traditions, chicken burgers use thigh filler rather than breast meat. At Chinese New Year, McDonald's serves *Grilled Chicken Burgers* with fries in the shape of the 12 animals of the Chinese zodiac.
- Egypt: *McFalafel* was a product introduced to the McDonald's menu based on the falafel dish said to have originated in the country.
- Morocco: *McArabia*, wrapped in Arabic-style pita bread, is the local product offering. During the Islamic month of Ramadan, a special menu is offered for breaking the fast, including milk, dates and a local soup known as *Harira*.
- Italy: *McItaly*, using 100% meat produced in Italy and local ingredients such as extra-virgin olive oil and bresaola, was adapted for the Italian market, as well as other local dishes, such as pasta salad.

These successful initiatives by McDonald's demonstrate the advantage of understanding each target market (case study) and not carrying out large-scale global studies that do not take into account local differences, thereby missing out on huge business opportunities.

However, it is not always easy for companies to address all sources of concern. As an example, McDonald's is still struggling to adequately deal with health-related claims associated with how its products increase obesity, as well as political issues, such as the 'boycott McDonald's' movement. As an example of the latter, a recent decision showing McDonald's' sensitivity to international concerns (not to mention law) came when the company refused to build new branches in occupied Palestine areas. This rule followed an earlier decision by Burger King to pull out of another occupied territory. These examples show that companies that are truly global cannot simply rely on tailoring their goods or services to the country they are operating in. Given increased global access to communication, a company's reputation can be made or broken as a result of a simple piece of news based on insensitive practices. Hence, while companies are encouraged to be sensitive to local interests, customs and trends, they still need to ensure that values, such as human rights and transparency, are upheld anywhere they do business. This could be regarded as a minimalist approach, as currently causal marketing is encouraging organisations to proactively support social or environmental issues (through a selected non-profit NGO) to help strengthen their brand in the eyes of their target population.

Case study questions:

1. Considering the case study, determine what makes case studies attractive in helping to understand and develop effective solutions to business problems.
2. Given the new product ranges listed above, demonstrate how case studies can help organisations be more creative.

3. Looking at the example above, what are the potential risks facing organisations and how can they be avoided when adopting a case study approach to address or pre-empt a business problem or look for new, potentially attractive, products or services?
4. Select any of the new McDonald's products above and suggest how they could be reviewed or even improved on. Consider the stages that a researcher could suggest.

Sources: Anon (2013); Verma et al. (2014)

End of Chapter Questions

These questions should help you reflect on your understanding of this chapter:

1. Identify and clarify the difference between mixed design and other more traditional designs.
2. Determine the objections against adopting a mixed-design model and address their validity.
3. Why is it important for marketing research to routinely consider adopting a mixed-design research framework?
4. What are the options available in adopting a mixed-design model and what are the advantages and disadvantages of each mixed-methods approach?
5. Identify and clarify the differences and similarities between an action research and a case study research design.
6. Should critical studies be considered a bonus in mixed-design research? Argue your answer.

Checklist

After studying Chapter 9, you should now be familiar with these key concepts:

1. What constitutes a mixed-design approach
2. The advantages that may be provided in employing mixed-design methods in marketing research studies
3. Action research and how to differentiate it from other methods
4. Case studies (intensive) versus extensive/expansive methods

Further Reading (in sequence from beginners to advanced)

Malhotra, N. and Birks, D. (2007) *Marketing Research: An Applied Approach*. London: Prentice Hall.

Bryman, A. and Bell, E. (2015) *Business Research Methods*. Oxford: Oxford University Press.

Coghlan, D. and Brannick, T. (2013) *Doing Action Research in Your Own Organization*. London: Sage Publications.

Ivankova, V., Creswell, J. W. and Stick, S. L. (2006) Using mixed-methods sequential explanatory design: from theory to practice. *Field Methods*, 18 (1), pp. 3–20.

Bryman, A. (2006) Integrating quantitative and qualitative research: how is it done? *Qualitative Research*, 6, pp. 97–113.

Bibliography

Anon (2013) A McDonald's restaurants case study: the marketing process. *The Times 100 Business Case Studies*. Available at: http://businesscasestudies.co.uk/mcdonalds-restaurants/the-marketing- process/introduction.html#axzz2H1cP5Y9Z [Accessed 2 July 2015].

Belk, R. W. (ed.) (2006) *Handbook of Qualitative Research Methods in Marketing*. Northampton: Elgar.

Bohman, J. (2015) Critical theory. In E. N. Zalta (ed.) *The Stanford Encyclopedia of Philosophy*. Available at: http://plato.stanford.edu/archives/spr2015/entries/critical-theory

Brorson, S. and Andersen, H. (2001) Stabilizing and changing phenomenal worlds: Ludwik Fleck and Thomas Kuhn on scientific literature. *Journal for General Philosophy of Science*, 32 (1), pp. 109–29.

Bryman, A. (2006) 'Integrating quantitative and qualitative research: how is it done?', *Qualitative Research*, 6, 97–113.

Bryman, A. and Bell, E. (2015) *Business Research Methods*. Oxford: Oxford University Press.

Clements, S., Jain, T., Jose, J. and Koellmann, B. (2013) *Smart Cookie*. London: London Business School.

Coghlan, D. and Brannick, T. (2013) *Doing Action Research in Your Own Organization*. London: Sage Publications.

Creswell, J. W., Fetters, M. D. and Ivankova N. V. (2004) Designing a mixed methods study in primary care. *Annals of Family Medicine*, 2 (1), pp. 7–12.

Creswell, J. W. and Plano Clark, V. L. (2011) *Designing and Conducting Mixed Methods Research*. Los Angeles, CA: Sage Publications.

Creswell, J. W., Plano Clark, V. L., Guttmann, M. L. and Hanson, E. E. (2003) Advanced mixed methods research design. In A. Tashakkori and C. Teddlie (eds) *Handbook of Mixed Methods in Social and Behavioral Research*, pp. 209–40. Thousand Oaks, CA: Sage Publications.

Crump, B. and Logan, K. (2008) A framework for mixed stakeholders and mixed methods. *The Electronic Journal of Business Research Methods*, 6 (1), pp. 21–8.

Dryden, W. (1987) Theoretically consistent eclecticism: humanizing a computer 'addict'. In J. C. Norcross (ed.) *Casebook of Eclectic Psychotherapy*, pp. 221–37. New York: Brunner/Mazel.

Fetters, M. and Freshwater, D. (eds) (2015) *Journal of Mixed Methods Research*. London: Sage Publications. Available at: www.uk.sagepub.com/journals/Journal201775 [accessed 24 June 2015].

Foucault, M. (1966) *Les Mots et Les Choses* [*The Order of Things*] (in French). New York: Vintage.

Fourali, C. (2016) *The Promise of Social Marketing: Changing the World for Good*. London: Routledge.

Freire, P. (1970) *Pedagogy of the Oppressed*. New York: Herder & Herder.

Gerring, J. (2007) *Case Study Research: Principles and Practices*. Cambridge: Cambridge University Press.

Gray, D. (2014) *Doing Research in the Real World*. London: Sage Publications.

Greene, J. C., Caracelli, V. J. and Graham, W. F. (1989) Toward a conceptual framework for mixed-method evaluation designs. *Educational Evaluation and Policy Analysis*, 11 (3), pp. 255–74.

Hartley, J. F. (1994) Case studies in organizational research. In C. Cassell and G. Symon (eds) *Qualitative Methods in Organizational Research: A Practical Guide* (pp. 209–29). London: Sage Publications.

Ivankova, V., Creswell, J. W. and Stick, S. L. (2006) Using mixed-methods sequential explanatory design: from theory to practice. *Field Methods*, 18 (1), pp. 3–20.

Johnson, R. B. and Christensen, L. B. (2014) *Educational Research: Quantitative, Qualitative, and Mixed Approaches* (5th edition). Los Angeles, CA: Sage.

Johnson, R. B., Onwuegbuzie, A. J. and Turner, L. A. (2007) Towards a definition of mixed methods research. *Journal of Mixed Methods Research*, 1 (2), pp. 112–33.

Kemmis, S. and McTaggart, R. (1988) *The Action Research Reader* (3rd edition). Geelong, VIC: Deakin University Press.

Kilts, J. M. (1990) Kraft Foods Inc. *The Journal of Consumer Marketing*, 7 (3), pp. 39–45.

Kuhn, T. (1962) *The Structure of Scientific Revolutions*. Chicago: Chicago University Press.

Laczniak, G. and Murphy, P. (2006) 'Normative perspectives for ethical and socially responsible marketing', *Journal of Macromarketing*, 26 (2), p. 157.

McNiff, J. and Whitehead, J. (2006) *All You Need to Know About Action Research*. London: Sage Publications.

Magwood, J. D. (2011) Kraft Foods Inc.: marketing and managing the customer relationship. *Customer Think*. Available at: http://customerthink.com/kraft_foods_marketing_and_managing_customer_relationship/ [Accessed 22 June 2015].

Malhotra, N. and Birks, D. (2007) *Marketing Research: An Applied Approach*. London: Prentice Hall.

Reddy, S. and Sproule, K. (2013) Kraft changed its biscuits for China. *Financial Times Case Studies*, 3 June. Available at: www.ft.com/content/6bcc1c00-c886-11e2-8cb7-00144feab7de [Accessed 22 June 2015].

Rudolph, L. (2013) *Qualitative Mathematics for the Social Sciences: Mathematical Models for Research on Cultural Dynamics*. London: Routledge.

Rapoport, R. (1970) Three dilemmas of action research, *Human Relations*, 23 (6), pp. 499–513.

Stake, R. E. (1995). *The Art of Case Study Research*. Thousand Oaks, CA: Sage.

Susman, G. (1983) Action research: a sociotechnical systems perspective. In G. Morgan (ed.) *Beyond Method*. Beverly Hills, CA: Sage Publications.

Swanborn, P. (2010) *Case Study Research: What, Why and How*. London: Sage Publications.

Teddlie, C. and Tashakkori, A. (2009) *Foundations of Mixed Methods Research: Integrating Quantitative and Qualitative Approaches in the Social and Behavioral Sciences*. Thousand Oaks, CA: Sage Publications.

Verma, A., Gupta, A. and Nangia, G. (2014) Study of various adaptation policies by companies to compete at a global scenario. *Global Journal of Finance and Management*, 6 (7), pp. 615–18.

Yin R. K. (1993) *Applications of Case Study Research*. Applied Social Research Series, Vol. 34. London: Sage Publications.

Yin R. K. (2003) *Case Study Research: Design and Methods* (3rd Edition). Applied Social Research Series, Vol. 5. London: Sage Publications.

Find journal articles and multiple choice questions online at: **https://study.sagepub.com/benzo** to support what you've learnt so far.

CHAPTER 10

From Theory to Practice: Illustrating the Qualitative Research Process

LEARNING OBJECTIVES

The key learning objectives of this chapter are:

1. To demonstrate the importance of qualitative research to marketers and businesses in general
2. To discuss the key steps involved in marketing research and the issues associated with each of those steps
3. To illustrate qualitative marketing research through some practical examples
4. To advise new researchers on existing techniques for qualitative research and the added value of researching and adopting technological tools that are available
5. To provide tips on how to position a research report

KEY CONCEPTS

By the end of this chapter, the reader should be familiar with the following concepts:

1. Crafting the steps of market research
2. Iteration and its particular relevance to market research
3. Pervasive relevance of conceptualisation to market research
4. Research problem conceptualisation
5. Theoretical framework
6. Methodological framework
7. Analytical framework
8. Safeguarding against unwarranted influences in the analysis of information
9. Using software to support analysis
10. Development of a research report

Chahid Fourali

Introduction

The purpose of marketing research is to minimise the uncertainty of a business environment through clarifying the factors influencing its target groups and facilitating decisions that maximise the chances of business success. To do so, the researcher needs to clarify and formulate the problem/opportunity the business is facing and move through a number of crucial steps before producing a likely solution/recommendation.

This chapter builds on previous ones and focuses on how to organise a qualitative research project, starting from the formulation of the aim, the selection of relevant theory, methodology and data analysis through to the presentation of the research report (dissertation/thesis). Although the focus of the chapter is primarily on the qualitative approach of marketing research, the principles, steps and examples presented can also reflect a mixed model. As we've seen earlier, a mixed approach can offer certain advantages over an exclusively quantitative or qualitative perspective.

Snapshot: Redbull – A Brand with Marketing Wings

Introduction

For a long time, marketers and, in fact, any successful business, have known that value is not necessarily reflected by the direct, functional benefits of individual components of a product or service, but is largely dependent on the associations that customers have with the brand. How else could a beverage consisting of 'humble brown carbonated water, caffeine and vegetable extracts' have reached a global value of $190 billion for corporate giants such as Coca-Cola and PepsiCo? This argument also applies to the popular energy drink, Red Bull, the main difference being that the latter contains a much higher level of caffeine.

The story

Red Bull was launched in 1987 by Dietrich Mateschitz, its key founder, who came across a popular energy drink when visiting south-east Asia, known in the Thai language as 'Red Bull'. Having noticed the drink's success, he quickly realised the huge potential for a similar drink in Europe and other parts of the world. Mateschitz approached the owners of the brand at the time and they agreed to set up a company. The rest, as they say, is history. Today, Red Bull employs more than 10,400 people in over 167 countries, selling over 5 billion cans a year.

Although Red Bull likes to be seen as 'the anti-brand' and tends to 'conspicuously' dismiss a marketing approach, this does not mean the company does not adhere to marketing principles. On the contrary, the brand is very much guided by marketing principles, particularly qualitative research. A brief look at its website reveals the following statement about the role of the Consumer Insights Manager:

> The Consumer Insights Manager is a part of the Red Bull national brand marketing team based in Santa Monica, CA. The position is responsible for the development, execution and analysis of consumer research and insight projects for Red Bull's US business. The position serves as one of the consumer experts within Red Bull US marketing and is responsible for establishing an in depth understanding of the Red Bull consumer and consumer segments to help grow the user base and increase brand relevancy. The position will work closely with US marketing cross functional stakeholders, international brand marketing and US business unit brand managers to ensure an aligned approach to research and consumer understanding. (Red Bull, 2016)

The role described above is a good example of the objectives needed by a market researcher, aiming to have a deep understanding of the Red Bull US national and international market. As well as quantitative data gathering, the Red Bull qualitative researcher's role includes stimuli development, marketing concept and communications testing, expertise in sourcing syndicated research in FMCG and utilising existing Consumer Insights resources.

Insights and positioning

Red Bull realised at a very early stage that one of the most potent ways of beating the competition in the soft drinks market was to create what came to be known as an 'anti-brand'. It portrayed itself as being anti-establishment, thus attracting a generation of rebellious young people, aged 16 plus, generally, interested in extreme sports such as hang-gliding, bungee jumping, F1 racing and, more recently, the highest ever free-fall parachute jump from 39 kilometres above the Earth. These associations were reinforced by an early system of exclusivity surrounding its distribution, making use of brand representatives at places such as university campuses and night clubs. A certain sense of mystique grew up around the brand and its supposed effectiveness as a stimulant for supporting extreme activities and all-night partying. As a result, the brand attracted a number of 'edgy' nicknames such as 'liquid cocaine' and 'liquid Viagra'.

The strategy seemed to work and embodied the brand's strapline 'The Drink That Gives You Wings'. The company made huge profits and managed to ward off many challenges from copycat products introduced by global brands such as Coca Cola and Pepsi. Despite this success, more recent research suggests that there are increasing health concerns amongst the drink's young demographic plus a shift in taste preferences. This has led Red Bull to develop new types of energy drinks such as Sugar Free and Zero Calories as well as three energy drinks with a different flavour from the original. In 2016, Red Bull also began capitalising on its brand value, extending it to selling merchandise such as jackets, shoes and head gear.

In light of the above, it is clear that the so-called 'anti-brand' is not, in fact, anti-marketing but very much pro-marketing, inspired by in-depth analysis of its target demographic and cultural trends that clearly make full use of qualitative research tools and techniques.

Sources: adapted from Kumar et al. (2005) and Red Bull (2015)

Conceptualisation

As explained earlier, in this chapter we will look at the main steps that a marketing researcher needs to undertake, discussing them from a qualitative marketing research perspective. Broadly speaking, most research, including qualitative research, needs to address a set of five recurrent stages, covering problem conceptualisation, uncovering relevant theories, determining and implementing a suitable methodology for addressing the study's focus, then collecting and analysing data towards developing a discussion of outcomes and writing up.

This suggests that there is only one 'conceptualisation' stage. Yet, conceptualisation is a pervasive stage; it is simply the process of specifying what we mean by a term and each concept carries within it a number of sub-concepts or associations which the conceptual analysis clarifies.

Conceptualisation can apply to the formulation of the research problem or to the theoretical or methodological arguments involved and, as such, is relevant to all stages of research – not just the first one. For this reason, we can differentiate between the initial 'problem exposition stage' conceptualisation, where the researcher presents the problem being addressed, and subsequent conceptualisations. The latter derive from the initial conceptualisation and integrate previous stages, always linking back to the original conceptualisation. In this way, the steps of the research become an integrated whole, showing the beginning and end as a 'story'. To achieve this, the researcher can make use of any conceptual tool, discursive as well as visual representations that help clarify their position at each stage. Table 10.1 illustrates this further, presenting each step and clarifying how conceptualisation is important to all of them.

Advanced: Mind Maps – Tools for Clarifying Communication and Strengthening Reasoning

The qualitative research reports have, on occasions, overtly or covertly encouraged students to make use of diagrams or, as they have become known, mind maps. The reason is that many advanced researchers find it very useful to present their ideas visually via a diagram. These diagrams help the researcher to quickly represent an argument or a perception of a situation they may be facing. Such 'maps' are then constantly reviewed as new information is forthcoming or as a result of reflection that produces richer information. They may be used at any stage of the research process. They could represent the components of the business problem at hand, the theoretical dimensions relevant to it, the methodological steps and even the broad picture of the final report and its components. A mind map provides a more flexible way of representing dimensions of the perceived reality that circumvents the language limitations due to their complexity, ambiguity and linear nature. There are many mind-map tools (many of them freely available online) that students could play with to decide which ones may help them better represent their ideas.

Taking the reasoning above into account, we end up with five levels of conceptualisation as follows:

Step 1: Problem conceptualisation framework – this initial stage focuses on the presentation of the problem/opportunity and the associated research framework (including associated questions) that will help address it.

Step 2: Theoretical exposition/conceptualisation – at this stage, the researcher identifies the relevant theories and models that could help clarify or solve the phenomenon at hand. Here, the researcher provides a conceptual framework that links the various dimensions of the problem/opportunity to the relevant theories.

Step 3: Methodological framework conceptualisation and its implementation – here, the researcher reviews several research designs associated with studying the problem/opportunity at hand, in light of the theoretical review, and selects one based on its characteristics and the principles of good research practice. This stage integrates (i.e. organises) the previous two into a meaningful whole.

Step 4: Analytical framework conceptualisation and its implementation – here, the researcher sets out the steps the analysis will undertake, taking into account the previous ones (e.g. research questions, relevant theoretical issues and methodological restrictions), and implements these steps. The analytical stage needs to follow on smoothly from the previous research stage. The interpretations of the findings are used as the basis for the recommendations made to resolve the initial business problem or for advice on how to pursue a business opportunity.

Table 10.1 Research steps and the pervasiveness of conceptualisation

Step in research	The focus	Type of conceptualisation required	Illustrative question: ***Would the introduction of a restaurant serving a lesser known ethnic food be successful in London?***
Step 1: Problem conceptualisation framework	Statement of the marketing practical business problem being addressed	This conceptualisation of the research framework formulates the main problem and associated questions and unravels the various concepts associated with the problem. It also provides the rationale for undertaking such a study. The rationale, although problem focused, may also target theoretical and methodological elucidations which would be elaborated on below.	This question would need unpacking in terms of 'What type of food? Where? Pros and cons? How likely is it to succeed? Resources/Costs involved? etc.' Determine importance of this question for addressing the immediate business proposal problem but also its potential in addressing similar questions, thereby helping to develop the methodology for addressing these problems or developing existing associated theories, etc.
Step 2: Theoretical exposition/ conceptualisation	Reviewing the literature	In this section, the researcher reviews all relevant literature and determines the 'state-of-the-art' of the subject associated with the problem being tackled. The conceptualisation of the problem is reflected in the derived insights from the theoretical review. Hence, a conceptualisation will need to be designed towards the end of this section to show how the stipulated problem statement in Step 1 links up with the derived wisdom of the theoretical review. This presentation will identify any gap in theoretical knowledge that may benefit from addressing the problem at hand.	Based on the above identified problem, the researcher may review several theories. Among topics reviewed may be factors affecting consumer behaviour, customer satisfaction models, innovation success and any model/theory about taste development for new products. Additionally, any study associated with the restaurant industry may come in handy. The researcher will develop a clear idea about established models/theories, what might be missing and what the key determinants are that may be decisive for the success (or failure) of such an initiative.
Step 3: Methodological framework conceptualisation and its implementation (i.e. 'data' gathering)	Developing a fit-for-purpose methodology	Here the researcher identifies the methodological framework within which the research will be carried out and provides justifications for it. The selected methodology will take into account the nature of the problem being addressed. At this stage, the conceptualisation will revisit the targeted problem and associated questions and demonstrate how the selected methodology will address all questions systematically and synoptically.	If we consider the above problem, the researcher is supposed to help gain a practical solution to the identified problem. The researcher may go for an action research methodology combining quantitative (how many restaurants exist serving similar dishes, how many people may be interested in such an initiative, etc.) and qualitative methods (is the taste of the new dishes appealing to any target group? How to position the new restaurant, etc.) that can systematically help address the identified questions and help provide a business decision.

(Continued)

Table 10.1 (Continued)

Step in research	**The focus**	**Type of conceptualisation required**	**Illustrative question:** ***Would the introduction of a restaurant serving a lesser known ethnic food be successful in London?***
Step 4: Analytical framework conceptualisation and its implementation	Developing a systematic scheme of analysis of the received information	In this section, the conceptualisation is reflected in the steps that will be undertaken to address each of the dimensions of the target problem. It will be largely derived from the conceptualisation associated with the methodological framework.	In order to address the qualitative dimensions of the research (e.g. would the new ethinc taste appeal to the target group?), the researcher may interview a number of people living in a potentially targeted geographical area. These interviews are subsequently analysed with a view to identifying recurrent themes that may help advise the decision about the business proposition. The analysis may also provide advice on future methodology of such research and may help develop theories and models further, although these latter aims are less of a concern to a researcher primarily interested in addressing a business proposition.
Step 5: Writing the report (conceptualisation, design and production)	Developing a well structured report that tells 'the story'	In this section, the conceptualisation is reflected in organising the material into a structure that maximises clarity in content and argumentation.	The report will produce the information broadly following the above steps. However, the presentation should be interesting and rationally designed to maximise impact and provide clear recommendations on how to respond to the business proposition.

Step 5: Writing the report (conceptualisation, design and production) – at this last stage, the researcher becomes the creator of a 'meaningful story' that integrates all the stages above and provides a logical interpretation of the problem or opportunity that was identified initially. The 'story' has to heed the agreed research protocols in order to be convincing and valid. As argued earlier, although various dimensions of the research are drafted and reviewed throughout the study, once the research has completed all dimensions, the researcher may need to go back to examine the steps to maximise clarity, the effectiveness of argumentation and the impact on the reader.

It is important to remember that the steps are rarely linear. Indeed, the researcher may move between steps iteratively depending on new insights at any step that in turn affect the other steps. Nevertheless, the research report must demonstrate an integrated whole. You could think of a research project report (or dissertation/thesis) as a whole structure or building that is developed cumulatively from the original problem and associated questions, linked to relevant theories and selected methodology which, in turn, lead to the analysis and final recommendations that answer the research question(s). Clearly, the research outcome may be the beginning of a new cycle of questions leading to more research, as suggested by most research methodologies (including that of action research as presented in Chapter 9).

How to Conceptualise a Research Problem/Opportunity

In many ways, conceptualisation is at the heart of the whole research enterprise as it tacitly includes both ontological (worldview) and epistemological (the accessibility of the phenomenon being addressed) perspectives. It is also pervasive to the whole project as each step has to refer back to the original conceptualisation or statement of the research problem being addressed which is, in turn, refined further, based on the focus and information provided by subsequent stages of the research (see Table 10.1).

In a way, a conceptualisation becomes a visual representation of the link between the various issues and concepts addressed at each step and how they relate to the original statement of the problem. It is also this link that iteratively leads the researcher to revisit prior steps following new observations further down the line. If, for instance, the theoretical or methodological steps highlight new insights, this may lead to a reformulation of the problem and associated questions.

The problem-focused conceptualisation is reflected in the research aim and questions. The resulting framework will help guide the subsequent literature review and the organisation of the relevant theoretical concepts. A marketing researcher, commissioned by a company, will need to use any type of representation (discursive, networking of ideas, matrix format, charts and graphs) to help conceptualise and clarify the relevant dimensions of the issue being studied.

From a business or marketing perspective, the purpose of the research might be to gather any of the following types of intelligence to help make an informed decision (Montgomery and Weinberg, 1979):

1. Defensive opportunities (depending on change in the business environment, be ever ready to protect the company from any new threats) – using the Red Bull example, the company may decide to take action when it hears that some of its competitors in the energy drink market are introducing healthier versions. It may decide to carry out research to look at effective ways of addressing the threats.

2. Offensive opportunities – in this case, the company may realise that its brand is quite strong and want to find out if it can use this advantage for brand extension purposes, such as selling other merchandise apart from drinks.
3. Industry performance comparison – in this case, Red Bull would keep track of its performance compared to that of its competitors.

An entrepreneur needs to focus first on point 2, before addressing point 1, as their priority is to set up a business that capitalises on an existing unserved need (point 2) before considering ways of protecting it from potential competitors or copy-cats, thus ensuring its sustainability (point 1). For example, their idea needs to include some unique features that are difficult to copy and which can be patented.

Industry performance comparison
Continually compare a company's achievements with similar companies to understand how it is performing and look for areas of improvement

Part of the process of conceptualisation is to narrow the scope of the research and determine the aim of the study together with the associated objectives. Many students come up with several projects which are very broad in focus, for example 'the importance of brand image'. Try to identify specific aims applying to a particular context so that the research becomes more manageable and the business advice resulting from the exercise more credible. The aim establishes the direction and contextual area of the research interest, whereas the objectives home in on specific aspects that are of interest or relevance to the business (or organisation commissioning the research) in order to achieve the aim. Take a look at the Research in Practice box below.

Research in Practice

The aim of this research is to study the London restaurant scene with a view to considering opportunities for setting up an Algerian restaurant.

This topic is very much an opportunity-based research question that calls for an 'action research' type methodology to help the researcher provide advice on whether it would be recommended to set up an Algerian restaurant in the London area and, if so, where the best location would be.

In this example, the following objectives associated with the aim are identified:

- First, identify all restaurants on a London map.
- Undertake analysis to determine the nature of each restaurant (e.g. type of ethnic group, fast food versus full service, premium) and the local demographic. Note any gaps in the market or opportunities.
- Based on the previous stage, identify selected areas for further analysis.
- Obtain the perspectives of key stakeholders (such as restaurant managers, customers) from the selected areas to determine how well businesses are doing and whether there may be a need for another restaurant. Target areas with successful ethnic dining options similar to Algerian cuisine (e.g. Moroccan or Turkish) for further analysis, to find out what makes them attractive.
- Seek the perspective of local government to find out what plans are in place for other restaurants and the requirements for establishing a new one.
- Once an area has been targeted, undertake tasting sessions to decide which recipes appeal most to the demographic.

Although the topic above gathers quantitative information on local restaurants and local residents, the actual decision about whether or not to go ahead with setting up the new restaurant is reliant on whether there is an appetite for Algerian cuisine, a qualitative dimension, assuming there is not a large Algerian community in the area. In addition, the researcher should try and discover the types of setting, brand positioning and services that would be attractive to the target demographic. These, too, are qualitative dimensions that require a qualitative methodology to help determine the positive characteristics associated with the new 'concept'. It is important to note that each of these added dimensions may need unpacking (in terms of specific objectives) and might become the subject of the research focus. The clarification of a research aim can be illustrated by a tree-like structure, showing the aim, broad objectives, specific objectives and sub-specific objectives:

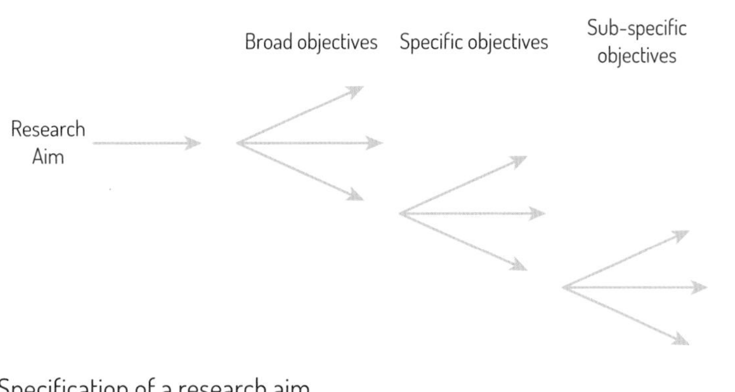

Figure 10.1 Specification of a research aim

How to Provide a Theoretical Framework that Matches the Research Problem/Opportunity at Hand

At this second step of the enquiry, the research statement associated with the relevant aim and objectives – that is, the problem-focused conceptual framework – becomes the main source for determining the models and theories to use. The researcher should identify all concepts associated with the problem exposition statement and review the latest literature related to each concept. As we've already noted, the problem exposition statement itself may need reviewing, having studied the relevant literature.

It is important to realise that reviewing literature is not just listing down relevant theories; it involves a critical evaluation of these theories, contrasting the different perspectives and identifying areas of agreement as well as points of contention. From this critical evaluation, a synthesis can be derived that may help improve the identification of the research problem/opportunity and research question(s).

Given that marketing research revolves around real-life problems faced by a business to help determine the optimal decisions, the theoretical section will need to be supplemented by research on the relevant environmental context, with a special focus on the industry situation. This context provides valuable environmental information about the industry, including its history, value and influential players within, as well as current and predicted trends.

Illustration of the Theoretical Investigation Stage

Consider the following social marketing, problem-based research topic:

> 'How can we conceptualise the process behind smoking to develop a strategy for minimising its prevalence among the population in the East London area?'

Some of the relevant concepts that may need unravelling include:

- theoretical concepts: conceptualisation, smoking theories, strategy, teenage psychology/motivation
- environmental/industry context: demographic picture of prevalence, smoking industry, East London.

The theoretical investigation associated with smoking within the target group may pin-point several influences. As a result, the researcher may draw a framework to help summarise them (see Figure 10.2). The influences may also be ranked according to the weight of each influence, based on previous research evidence. Subsequently, this framework may help guide the primary research and associated methodology, with the added possible advantage of rank-ordering the influences by importance.

	Input	Process	Output
External influence ↕ **Internal influence** ↕ **Consumer behaviour**	• Marketing effort (4 Ps) • Socio-culture environment • Other situational factors (PESTLE)	• Decision-making steps • Psychological precedents • Past experience	• Behavioural adoption (trial) • Post-behavioural adoption (evaluation/decision)

Figure 10.2 Factors of behavioural change/influence

Source: Fourali, 2016

There are benefits from learning more about the smoking industry and any influential stakeholders associated with it, such as trade industries, health organisations, community representatives, government, educational institutions and professional bodies, especially those associated with marketing or social marketing. This type of analysis may end up integrating the framework above with associated stakeholders.

Later on, primary analysis will help determine the most influential factors affecting the population of East London. This would help inform the process of providing smokers with a compelling healthier offer in the form of an attractive social marketing mix (e.g. an attractive, healthier alternative to the self-destructive smoking behaviour, persuasive messages) that could defuse the predisposing factors in smoking.

Reflective Activity

Building on the previous example about setting up a new restaurant in London, consider the following research project:

The aim of this research is to study the London restaurant scene with a view to considering opportunities for setting up a restaurant serving specialities from a particular ethnic group.

- Try to identify a gap in the market by considering a cuisine that is highly regarded, but also currently under-represented in London.
- Identify potentially helpful concepts associated with consumer behaviour theories as well as the dimensions of the restaurant industry context which you will need to research to help give advice to the lead project researcher.

How to Construct a Methodological Framework that Matches the Problem/Opportunity Being Studied

Having defined a worthwhile business problem/opportunity and the associated research literature, the next stage is to determine a method of investigation that is fit for purpose. As stated in Chapter 7, the research project should *never* assume a particular research method. This type of approach has become known as 'methodolatry' (Chamberlain, 2000). The selected methodology should be problem-focused and the researcher will need to systematically review the research problem and expected outcomes before determining an optimal methodology (see Table 10.2). Students who do not feel at ease with this stage may find it useful to review Chapter 7, which explains the links between worldviews and preferred research methods.

Table 10.2 The research methodology framework: interaction between nature of research problem, expected research outcomes and matching research design

Research problem considerations	Research outcome considerations	Research design considerations
• Aims of research • Information required • Nature of target population • Complexity of the context (theoretical and industrial aspects) • Data availability	• New knowledge? • New methodology? • New practical solution to the problem? • Importance/urgency of outcome • Evaluation of outcome • Format of reporting	• Philosophical position (ontological and epistemological assumptions) • Research method(s) • Research technique(s) • Sources of data/information • Sampling (see Chapter 6 on sampling) • Type of analysis and any supporting tools

As discussed earlier, since most research is not undertaken in a linear fashion, it is normal to expect a number of iterative reviews during the process alongside suggested considerations until a balanced, holistic overview is achieved. Chapter 8 listed 11 qualitative research methods and six data-gathering techniques which should be referred to, to determine an appropriate research design.

Reflective Activity

Consider the previous social marketing problem concerning the prevalence of smoking among teenagers in East London.

- What research methodology would you adopt? (Refer to Table 10.2, to help with identifying relevant information; then Chapter 8, to review qualitative research methods and data-gathering techniques.)

How to Undertake a Qualitative Analysis that Matches the Problem/Opportunity Under Study

Once the researcher has selected the appropriate methods of gathering data and meticulously implemented them via data collection, the next step is to consider ways of analysing the data collected. Qualitative marketing research data analysis can take any form based on the sources of information, as discussed in Chapter 8.

Researchers have identified a number of procedures involved in the analysis stage. Despite the variety of approaches, fortunately the steps making up the procedures tend to be similar. To illustrate the variety of procedures, consider the five types of data analysis listed here:

1. Lindlof (1995) proposed four aspects of analysis:
   i. *Process* – the continuous process of analysis and reanalysis throughout the study
   ii. *Data reduction* – comprising the coding of data and conceptual reduction through the development of structures
   iii. *Explaining* – reflecting the subjects' interpretation of actions, goals and motives
   iv. *Theory* – the context of the explanation of data.
2. Morse (1994) also suggested four processes covering:
   i. *Comprehending* – in-depth understanding of the setting, culture and topic before undertaking the research
   ii. *Synthesising* – through research, linking themes and concepts and integrating them into a generalised explanation
   iii. *Theorising* – through inductive reasoning, producing a number of alternative explanations and homing in on the most appropriate theory following the testing of explanations
   iv. *Recontextualising* – this involves an attempt at testing the explanatory power of the favoured theory in other contexts and with other people to look at opportunities for generalisation.

3. Quinlan et al. (2015) suggest that data analysis predominantly goes through four stages covering:
    i. *Description* – simply describing what is seen in the data
    ii. *Interpretation* – attaching possible meanings to the data
    iii. *Conclusion* – broadly drawing 'intermediary stage' conclusions/findings that will contribute to the major conclusions
    iv. *Theorisation* – or contribution to knowledge described in the literature review.
4. Braun and Clarke (2006) suggest six phases of thematic analysis:
    i. *Familiarisation* with the data
    ii. *Coding*
    iii. *Searching for themes* – reflecting patterns relevant to the topic at hand
    iv. *Reviewing themes* – checking relevance to the current focus and the whole data set
    v. *Defining and naming themes* – after producing a detailed definition, analysis and story produced by each theme
    vi. *Writing up* – producing a persuasive story interspaced with supporting material and framed within the context of existing literature on the topic.
5. Glaser and Strauss (1967), the creators of the grounded theory method of analysis (see Chapter 8) which favours the inductive method, suggest[1] five main stages of analysis:
    i. *Identifying* categories of events – to subject to analysis
    ii. *Comparing* incidents linked to each identified category – this stage is similar to the conceptualisation stage where the various concepts arising from the data are clearly specified
    iii. *Integrating* the categories and dimensions – for instance, taking into account the demographic dimensions of the subjects being studied
    iv. *Identifying the boundaries* of the theory – identifying the key dimensions of the theory and dropping the least relevant cases
    v. *Writing the theory* – translating the derived theory into discursive reasoning and sharing it with the research community.

The inductive method of analysis is an approach that starts with a reflexion on the raw data with a view to deriving some conceptualisation to account for what may be happening. This is seen as a bottom-up approach, as opposed to the theory/hypothesis-driven approach that starts from the broad perspective and tries to determine whether the theory is being borne out by the data

Despite the variations among each suggested procedure above, most data analysis tends to reflect the following four stages:

- description of the information available (as objectively as possible)
- interpretation of the information

1 The authors suggest four stages but if we separate the preliminary 'identification of categories of focus', as a further stage, then they add up to five.

- extracting a summary of what has been learnt
- considerations for generalisation.

So, irrespective of the concepts used by the qualitative researcher, the above stages should be accounted for one way or another.

Special Cases in Qualitative Research Analysis

Researchers are advised that, like most things in life, tools of analysis should be adapted to the context of the study. Again, the adage 'horses for courses' applies here. For example, Quinlan et al. (2015) argued that models such as the steps described above, tend to apply more to thematic analysis. They listed a number of other contexts where thematic analysis needs adjusting, for example:

Narrative analysis: in this type of analysis, the focus is on describing and interpreting the various narratives, or stories, from the data collected rather than the themes exhibited, for instance, by customers providing accounts of their interactions with a particular brand.

Semiotics: here, the focus is on identifying the signs, known as denotative data, used in communicating their variety and meaning, or connotative dimensions. The example of symbolism is relevant here, for example in relation to a company name or logo.

Image-based data: given the rich nature of images, these can be analysed using any of the methods referred to above (by theme, narrative, textual, semiotic or content analysis), depending on the aims of the research and methodological interest. Consider a list of images produced by an advertising company to help promote the 'right' associations in the minds of their target audiences; a researcher could ask representatives of these audiences to provide narratives about how they reacted to the images and check whether they achieved their aim.

Phenomenological approaches: given that the focus of this method is on understanding the subjects' lived experience of an event, the methodology follows a different process involving first isolating the subjects' beliefs and assumptions in regard to a particular event – a process known as 'bracketing'. Next, the researcher identifies and organises all the significant statements in the data into meaningful units – a process known as 'horizontalisation' of the data. Finally, the researcher builds up a picture of how the phenomenon was experienced, based on the resulting meaningful units. This is tested on each of the participants before developing a more detailed description of what it was like experiencing the event.

Consider a holiday company wanting to gain a better understanding of how and why certain customers appear to enjoy package holidays more than others. Understanding their beliefs and what they perceive as meaningful events are a necessary part of appreciating why they were particularly pleased with the overall experience of the holiday. This information is extremely valuable to the company and will help it improve the experience and position itself appropriately to its customer groups.

Guarding Against Unwarranted Influences

Qualitative researchers are acutely aware of the 'baggage' they bring with them to research, in terms of past experiences or long-held attitudes or values. Although this baggage affects almost all research, it applies even more so in the social sciences, as the subjects of study are human beings in all their complexity and influenced by their own thoughts and experiences, past or present, conscious or subconscious.

Because of this, advice may be needed to guard against undue influence and maximise the relevance and accuracy of analysis. Braun and Clarke (2006; Clarke and Braun, 2013) recommend adopting the following safeguards:

- Acknowledging assumptions, beliefs and values: immediately before starting a new research topic, researchers are encouraged to think about any assumptions, values or experiences that may shape their reading or interpretation of the topic at hand, as well as their feelings about it. Just as a psychologist aims to remove any 'automatic', if not subconscious, response to an event, especially a self-destructive one, so should the research aim.
- Familiarisation before coding: when facing the task of coding the collected data, there can be a temptation among student researchers to look for themes before any objective examination of the data at hand. This approach reflects a superficial analysis and presents generic themes that do not accurately reflect the real data. As suggested, following the 'familiarisation' stage, students could attempt a draft of a mind map of themes and sub-themes they identify within the text. This approach encourages deeper processing of the material and its nuances, resulting in more robust themes. If in doubt, these themes always benefit from the second opinion of an interested colleague.
- Widening discussions on draft theme structure: researchers are encouraged to work in groups, to determine the structure of their themes and then invite feedback on the material from other groups. These wider discussions and comparisons of structures should encourage the researchers to notice their individual characteristics and help make the material more relevant. The purpose is to encourage a clarity of definitions of themes and their relevance and address any weaknesses.
- Process issues: researchers should be encouraged to share the process of developing the themes. Has a 'bottom-up' approach been taken with themes derived from the data without any pre-conceived ideas and theories? Or are researchers using a 'top-down' approach, by working from a theory and looking for confirmation in the data?

Determining a Convergence Among the Analytical Orientations

The above arguments on how to conduct a robust qualitative analysis suggest that qualitative analysis is as much an art as a science as there is no one way of conducting the analysis. However, most qualitative data analyses undergo a preliminary stage of qualitative data processing, common to all qualitative data, whether derived from interviews, observations or biographical narratives. This process transforms the raw information into a format for in-depth analysis. Three broad steps are involved (Quinlan et al., 2015):

Step 1: *Coding the information.* Coding refers to the task of organising individual pieces of data in meaningful coding units, thereby making the information retrievable at a later stage if and when further analysis is required. Any detail can be coded, including settings, events, meanings or relationships. The way the material is coded may be naturally visible, for example sentences, paragraphs or sections of articles, or derived through analysis such as when trying to develop a vision, a mission and the objectives of two companies, based on some of their publications. The coding units may be either theory driven (where the coding units are guided by a previous theory) or they may be openly coded without any assumed theory-led categorisation. For example, a researcher interested in persuasion techniques used in the communication practices of two companies, may identify broadly emotional or rational arguments. In turn, each of the emotional dimensions can be 'unpacked' further. For instance, the researcher may identify emotional messages in the form of anger, sadness, happiness, anxiety, hope, trust, and so on; and rational messages in the form of logical analysis, empirical arguments or practical benefits.

To illustrate this stage, a researcher looking at relationship marketing may consider the various factors that lead people to become loyal Red Bull drinkers. They may also make use of the ladder of customer loyalty (that is, the levels of relationship that a customer goes through before becoming a loyal customer) to help understand the degree of loyalty to Red Bull. The researcher could ask the following: Tell us about how you perceive Red Bull.

An example of a script produced from one response may be organised as shown in Table 10.3.

Step 2: *Memoing.* Coding can involve more than just structuring the data, such as text, to reflect selected coding units or concepts. The verb 'memoing' is a form of the word 'memo'. Writing memos is a very useful way of clarifying, commenting on or offering early interpretations of data. Notes or memos can be added to explain what the coding label or concept stands for, minimising ambiguity. Notes can also comment on operational aspects of the study, when clarifying the context/circumstances of data gathering that may affect its collection or interpretation, for example, or may suggest ideas for future data collection. Such notes can help improve validity, such as procedural validity, or reliability issues. Finally, notes can provide early interpretations or observations about meanings of concepts, links between them and/or an early theoretical proposition. This kind of information can be useful during the next stage of research. As an example of memoing, a researcher looking at Table 10.3 might decide to add two notes, the first one stating that 'loyal Red Bull drinkers may not like the taste initially' and the second one that 'customers who reach the stage of complete loyalty may still slide back to a less loyal stage'.

Ladder of customer loyalty A ladder presenting different levels of relationships that a customer goes through before becoming a loyal customer. The levels show that customers develop from being simply a prospect to becoming loyal customers and even advocating for a company and its products. The aim of each organisation is to try to lead each potential client to move up the ladder

Fuzzy logic (FL) is a concept that rejects the Aristotelian view that either a characteristic applies or does not apply. For example, the concept of 'height', like 'competence' and 'psychological health', may be reflected in a continuum ranging from one extreme to another (e.g. from 90 cm to 2.5 m), and having to say tall or not tall would mean different things to different people. Smithson (1988) offers the following event to clarify the relevance of FL; he argues that if we assume that the probability that it will rain tomorrow is P(A) =1/2, this could mean that the probability that it will rain P(A) and the probability that it will not rain P(B), are equally likely, or it could mean that we are utterly ignorant of the likelihood of A or B. In addition, probability is incapable of capturing any ambiguity or vagueness about the event. In the rain example, there still remains some ambiguity about whether the rain is a mist or a drizzle, moderate or heavy. These are fuzzy uncertainties of a qualitative nature which can be dealt with by FL. Fuzzy neural networks have been used for over two decades to help calculate indices combining uncertainty and iterative dimensions

Step 3: *Concept mapping.* At this stage, the researcher spends a lot of time 'playing' with the concepts derived from the information obtained, in an attempt to identify relationships between them. This step is reminiscent of a cognitive schema whereby a researcher develops

Table 10.3 Example of an interview transcript for a Red Bull study with suggested coding

Example of script	Coding
Ehm...Red Bull is a great drink that I discovered at a great event when I went to University during the rave days.	Context: university, rave party
There was a mystery about it and it sounded almost a forbidden fruit as there were a few things going on at those raves that one would not feel proud to tell their parents about. Nevertheless all my mates were having it and it was also like a macho thing. There were rumours that it would help give you lots of energy in various departments. Eventually it seemed like part of the whole image thing...being unconventional, macho and cool would mean holding a can of Red Bull.	Advantage: forbidden fruit, energy (non-tested), social (friendship, macho, image, macho, cool)
Actually initially I did not find the taste appealing but after a few atttempts I developed a taste for it....supported by all these associations.	Histoy: developed taste – incentive
I developed from a 'discoverer' of the drink to somebody who was having it on various occasions (at parties, to keep up with sleepless nights; and during exam revisions)	Advantage: fights sleep, exam revisions
It cost me a fortune as I believed that nothing else will do	Disadvantage: costly
I developed from a 'discoverer' of the drink to somebody who was having it on various occasions (at parties, to keep up with sleepless nights; and during exam revisions) It cost me a fortune as I believed that nothing else will do and seemed to advise colleagues about the effectiveness of the drink. Gone are these days. I no longer tell the world about the greatness of the drink but I still occasionally enjoy a can of Red Bull.	Loyalty ladder chronology: 1) discovery, 2) regular, 3) nothing else will do, 4) advocate, 5) now (non-regular drinker).
	Memoing notes: 1 *"loyal Red Bull drinkers may not like the taste initially"* 2 *"customers that reach the stage of advocacy may still slide back to a less loyal stage".*

a diagram that reflects links between the various concepts. For instance, following the analysis of many interview scripts, such as the one shown in Table 10.3, a researcher interested in determining the brand dimensions of Red Bull can derive four broad recurrent themes which could be the subject of closer analysis, for example, in terms of their links, respective weights, predominance among Red Bull drinkers and associated models, such as brand personality models, that could help shed some light on how to organise/interpret the data (see Figure 10.3). Although the example suggests a fairly linear layout, in reality the links may reflect an iterative picture, thereby demonstrating that any change of opinion at any level may affect not only some of the other sub-concepts but also the whole brand perception.

For example, if an existing loyal customer finds out that Red Bull is being less than candid about the effect of the drink on sexual energy, as this was not proven through studies on its ingredient, Taurine, this may affect their decision to trust the company in the future in relation to any health claim, overt or implied. This in turn may erode the customer's loyalty to the brand. In fact, the iterations of most concepts make them amenable to measurement via a fuzzy logic analysis which marketers should consider making use of (Smithson, 1988 and Fourali, 1997, 2009).

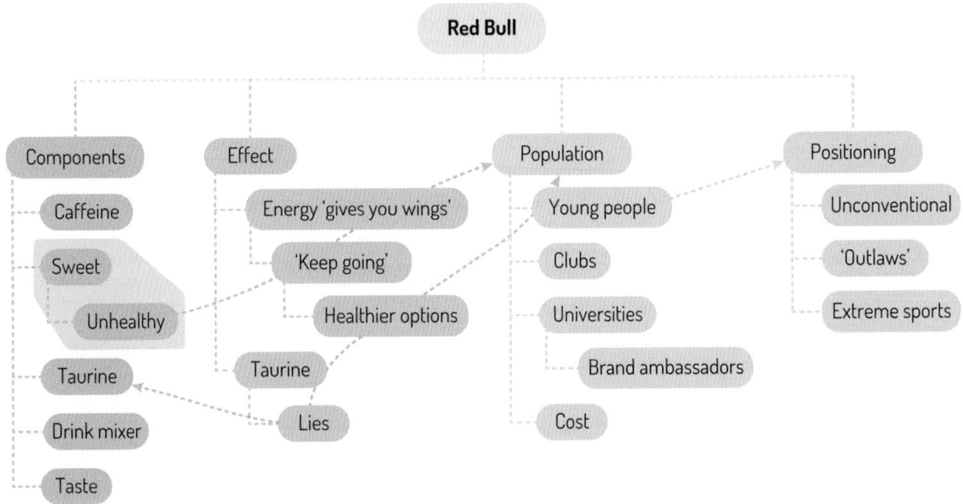

Figure 10.3 Possible concept mapping for Red Bull brand

Another example of the benefits of qualitative marketing research can be illustrated by a topic which is seldom addressed: the 'reputation' of different religions relating to whether or not they are seen to promote violence. Although this is an issue that should be handled sensitively, it can still be addressed using a marketing perspective since reputation is particularly relevant to marketers. Indeed, reputation is relevant to a broad range of 'products' or subjects, covering individual personalities, groups of people, companies, countries or, as in this case, even different religions. For instance, a researcher may be particularly interested in the sources or causes of the 'reputation' of two religions within a certain community or geographical area. The author may refer to various 'sources' of the so-called reputation, one of which may be the religious texts of each faith. For example, they may look at the reputation of Christianity and Islam within a certain community and decide to look for textual sources on the matter. The author may opt to adopt two stages of analysis, first contrasting the 'violence' theme by referring to *The Bible* and *The Quran* respectively and, second, referring to articles written about both religions.

Addressing the first part of the analysis, a software engineer, Tom Anderson, developed software that enabled him, through text analytics, to compare the New International Version of both the Old and New Testaments with an English version of the Quran from 1957 (2016; Bowden, 2016). He categorised words into eight emotions (joy, anticipation, anger, disgust, sadness, surprise, fear/anxiety and trust) and plotted the occurrence of these emotions in both religious sources; he identified words such as 'destroy' and 'kill' and phrases such as 'suffer vengeance' as having violent connotations. Among some of the calculated indices, the author noted that (Anderson, 2016):

- Of the three texts, the content in the Old Testament appears to be the most violent. He clarified that killing and destruction are referenced slightly more often in the New Testament than in the Quran (2.8% versus 2.1%), but the Old Testament is a clear leader with 5.3% – more than twice the number of violent references to destruction and killing than the Quran.
- Whilst the New Testament was found to be highest in 'Love', the Quran was highest in 'Mercy'.

Obviously, a critical researcher could argue that calculations such as these could be regarded as very crude and not consultatively derived. Additionally, the system used seems to categorise the results as being either within or outside a category, in an Aristotelian way. The calculations also do not take into account the context for each use of a word. These are all very valid points that should be addressed during close analysis of approaches such as these. Nevertheless, the results support the view that many presumptions about a particular religion, or group of people, are not supported by evidence and it doesn't take a great deal of close analysis to support this. Types of studies such as these can be very helpful as a prelude to fighting prejudices, which is at the heart of social marketing.

The example above combined both codifying of material (a qualitative task) and derived a statistical analysis (a quantitative approach) demonstrating that both approaches may be necessary to research a question.

At a later stage, some researchers may decide to go a step further and find out about the sources of influence on a social bias. They may decide to demonstrate the influence of media on prevailing social views about a religion. They may review a number of sources of texts or other media concerning each religion selected. As perceptions can be framed under different categories of themes, the researcher's first step is to derive as many of those themes as possible from prior reading – in the region of 20 articles – so that these form the basis for the subsequent coding of the material. The researchers define the sources consulted for the study according to strict criteria, for example type of medium, relevance of topics, country, size of audience of the medium, period of publication, context/events referred to, types of argument used, credibility of the medium among the masses, and so on. They then come up with an initial list of coding categories open to further refinement. The definitions help other researchers to identify any weak or unclear area of the study and also enable them to verify or build on its findings.

The researchers may also seek to check the codifications with other colleagues, especially those from a different background. This ensures consistency and helps to minimise bias. Additionally, the researchers can talk openly about their background, as it may affect their views (perception and interpretation) of the events they are studying.

Reflective Activity: Codifying Information

Personal branding is becoming increasingly important as a research concept studied by marketers.

- Work in groups and select two well-known personalities; they could be politicians, CEOs of a famous/infamous company or figures in the public eye. Identify 12 themes/categories you could use to compare them (e.g. trustworthiness, responsibility, representing the common man/woman). Each group member should source a number of articles online and see what themes the articles evoke.
- Adjust any of the 12 themes if necessary to ensure that they are a good tool for organising the sources you consulted. Finally, compare your 12 themes with the 12 archetype themes of Purkiss and Royston-Lee (2012). How similar are they?

Research in Practice: What Characteristics do Successful Viral Ads Share?

A research agency gathered a lot of data based on interviews with various people to gauge the characteristics that account for a successful viral advert.

The researcher reviewed the preliminary steps of the data-gathering exercise: the original problem formulation and any background theoretical considerations that may have informed the study. The researcher also clarified the methodological approach (see Chapter 8), which determined whether both the method and the data-gathering tools matched the problem. If the researcher found that this wasn't the case, they would have to consider whether to use other sources of data as supplementary evidence to compensate for any weaknesses associated with the data obtained.

The researcher then undertook an evaluation of the information, according to any of the qualitative analysis methods described above in the 'How to Undertake a Qualitative Analysis' section, including how to determine the various themes (characteristics).

Once the researcher had derived a list of themes and cross-checked them with different colleagues, they proceeded to verify whether these themes were sufficient to evaluate any existing or new advert. They tested this against three types of advert: a failed advert, a mixed result advert and a very successful advert, defined in terms of frequency of recognition and its effect on generating sales of the company's product. They were then able to see if there was a convergence of opinions (level of agreement) about the identified characteristics of each advert and its level of success. If this exercise had shown any missing characteristic (e.g. humour), they would have needed to add it before finalising the results.

What Software to Use for my Qualitative Analysis

Unlike quantitative research, which routinely makes use of an ever-increasing armoury of statistical software, for several decades qualitative analysis tended to be undertaken without the support of any software. However, as technological tools developed, researchers increasingly started to undertake more complex studies that necessitated the development of qualitative analysis software, as it increased the accuracy of analysis and helped save a tremendous amount of time. Such technological developments are even affecting the way we learn. It is difficult for any research methodology lecturer to ignore the advantages that new technological tools offer to make learning more accessible, flexible and tailored to different needs and learning styles. Only a few years ago, lecturers delivered the majority of their courses or modules face-to-face with their students, without the support of a qualitative data analysis (QDA) package, but new Learning Management Systems (LMS), such as Blackboard or Moodle, are now commonplace on many learning programmes.

Nowadays, data analysis tools are routinely expected in research methodology teaching, ranging from statistical analysis packages to help determine indices associated with fairly complex theoretical models, such as multi-level modelling, to qualitative information analysis packages that make the researcher's life much easier. Nevertheless, it is not obligatory for all researchers to make use of a qualitative data analysis tool; some are still happy undertaking a 'paper and pencil' analysis. In addition, it is highly advisable for new researchers to have a go at undertaking analysis without the support of any software, to get a feel for and understand the principles, as well as potential weaknesses, associated with this approach. However, the advantages of using QDA tools are clear and many are freely available or provide a trial version. Here are a few that a qualitative researcher may come across (Babbie, 2016; CAQDAS, 2016):

1. AnSWR
2. Atlas.ti
3. Dedoose (mixed methods)
4. DRS
5. Ethno
6. Ethnography
7. HyperResearch (transcription and analysis)
8. MAXQDA
9. NVivo
10. QDA Miner
11. Qualrus
12. QUIRKOS
13. TAMS (Transcription and analysis)
14. TRANSANA
15. Weft

This is not an exhaustive list and you may well like to consider others, but the examples above are an ideal place to start to consider the functionalities that QDA tools offer. While researching these tools, it is worth accessing the Computer Assisted Qualitative Data Analysis (CAQDAS) website (www.surrey.ac.uk/sociology/research/researchcentres/caqdas), which provides useful advice on the adequacy of QDA tools. Go ahead and try a few, perhaps as part of an exercise you've been asked to undertake or using improvised data associated with a research plan you are working on.

In fact, selecting the most appropriate package for your needs, including looking for comparative reports, could be considered an opportunity in itself to demonstrate qualitative research skills. Consider the next reflective activity.

Reflective Activity: Wading through the Maze of Qualitative Research Tools

Select up to five qualitative research packages and identify a list of characteristics that qualitative researchers should look for when choosing a new package. Read about the various packages (organise your sources, such as application website versus other sources, e.g. independent user forums) and identify themes associated with their advantages and disadvantages.

- Is there a different weighting you would give to some characteristics as opposed to others? What advice would you give, based on your research, which may be fairly limited?

How to Write a Qualitative Report

This will be covered in more depth in Chapter 15, but it is important to remember a few points at this stage.

Importance of design

Like all projects, writing the report, whether a business report, dissertation or thesis, should be preceded by a design structure that takes into account the target audience. Some reports (probably most marketing reports) are produced for the purpose of addressing a business problem that requires practical implementable solutions. Others, as well as addressing this issue, may adopt an academic style that requires producing new knowledge or procedures. This may need thorough analysis in the context of existing literature on a particular subject and offer a methodology, with as much detail as possible, to enable independent testing/replication or applications in a similar or different context. Whatever the case, the report should not only weave a coherent narrative, derived from the analysis of information obtained, but also aim to provide convincing arguments for adopting a possible way forward that could maximise the chances of marketing and business success.

Hence, the structure of a qualitative research report can differ, depending on the approach followed and the type of evidence used: quantitative, qualitative or mixed (see Table 10.4).

Table 10.4 Example of types of structures of research

Quantitative research	Quantitative and qualitative structure (mixed)	Qualitative structure (can be for mixed research)
• Introduction • Theory and hypotheses • Methods • Results • Discussion • Conclusions • References	• Introduction (with aims and objectives) • Review of literature • Methods • Presentation of main themes • Interpretation/Discussion • Implications • Conclusions • References	• Introduction • Context • Aims and concerns • Justification and context for the research • Previous situation supported by data gathering • Options faced and actions taken to improve the situation • Monitoring results • Selecting procedure of analysis • Analysis and interpretation of results • Preliminary conclusions and testing of their validity • Modification of practice in the light of evaluation • Significance of and implications for results

Source: Bryman and Bell, 2015; McNiff, 2016

Importance of the assessment framework

The framework that is referred to for assessing the quality of the report is a key determinant of the content and style of the research. This framework may be in the form of a client research brief or a regulatory body setting the standard expectations. For example, the UK

Quality Assurance Agency for Higher Education, known as QAA, determines three possible requirements for a doctoral thesis to be eligible for success, in the form of original contributions to knowledge, methodology or practical solutions to a recognised issue. Hence, each researcher needs to clearly identify at the outset, not only the target audience for the report but also the set regulatory requirements referred to for judging the adequacy of the report.

Importance of reflexivity

Perhaps the most pervasive tacit enabler and requirement of all research is the importance of reflexivity. This could be regarded as the jewel in the crown of academic learning, as ultimately the purpose of a university education is to push the boundaries of teaching and learning, going beyond simply reproducing facts and other people's views and arguments. Although these are important pre-requisites, the ultimate achievement of a university education is to enable learners to become confident and independent thinkers, who can receive a new piece of information or advice and be able to scrutinise it using logical, experimental, critical and practical lenses. For example, an argument may be logically and experimentally robust but the consequences of adopting it could create problems, for example disquiet in a society as a result of granting undue powers to a select group of people. The ability to openly, and consultatively, determine a 'balanced argument' is perhaps one of the most hotly debated issues among researchers.

Reflective Activity

Research on smoking has found the highest smoking trends among ethnic groups in the Bangladeshi population, where up to 40% are smokers.

What type of research structure do you think would be most relevant to a study that aims to understand the causes of this trend? Consider the list of factors of behavioural change shown in Figure 10.2.

Ethics: A General Statement

Qualitative research, unlike other types of research, is particularly vulnerable to the bias resulting from a researcher's world outlook. This is because the targets of the study are humans with values and philosophies that may be similar to or different from those of the researcher. Hence, researchers are reminded to be as transparent as possible regarding their particular influences, including, as highlighted above, recognising aspects of their background that may lead them more readily into certain unwarranted conclusions.

This is why researchers should not only demonstrate the strength of character to challenge their own views but also look for every opportunity to seek a second (and third or beyond) opinion to determine whether other likely interpretations are available. Also, when seeking other opinions, researchers should favour those with a close understanding of the event and context in question, rather than seek the opinion of like-minded individuals. Finally, opportunities for 'testing' views should be sought wherever possible.

As shown in the previous chapter (see Figure 9.4, page 239), qualitative research can be affected by factors beyond an individual researcher's control. Hence, identifying and using models for flagging sources of bias/unfairness is a worthwhile activity for any researcher.

Chapter Summary

The journey undertaken over the last few chapters in relation to qualitative or mixed design research approaches offers a rich and varied landscape reflecting the variety of interests and worldviews and demonstrating how these areas remain a 'contested' field. Denzin and Lincoln (2011) talk about the qualitative confederacy. This metaphor is explained by the variety of qualitative researchers who are continuously involved in friendly debates about how to get as close as possible to the human experience they want to understand. In this respect, there is a tradition that includes the social and health sciences and has roots that go as far back as Herodotus and Thucydides in Greece and Sima Qian in China. Another expression that has been used is 'the qualitative tapestry' to reflect the variety of perspectives that aim to address and integrate the various research concerns. Despite the variety of perspectives, qualitative researchers share a common ground in the form of a 'commitment to theoretically and conceptually formulating an engagement with the world that produces vivid descriptive accounts of the human experience' (Preissle, 2011, p. 688).

Nevertheless, the main thrust of the position adopted in this book is that the decisive factor in choosing qualitative, quantitative or mixed design should be an approach that is led by the research problem and question(s). This will remain a focal fact, for past, current and future developments of the field of research.

Case Study: The Roles of a Mother – the Saatchi and Mumsnet Perspective

A reliable market research study should aim to avoid simplistic answers such as 'segment the population and target a group of consumers with a quick survey or a few interviews'. This approach may result in significant weaknesses, for example surveys may miss the 'whys' and opportunities to discover important associated factors about consumer decisions. On the other hand, as early as the 1960s, research started showing that a high percentage of face-to-face interviewees may be reluctant to reveal certain information about themselves. For example, it was found that only 17% of interviewees were willing to admit in an interview that they had borrowed money from a bank. In either case, the information can be either inaccurate or misleading. On the back of this, more recently, Saatchi and Saatchi discovered that only 1 in 5 of British mothers surveyed identified with the way they were portrayed in adverts. It was also argued that marketers are primarily interested in functional roles (what customers do), and these in turn are reflected in marketing campaigns which tend to omit personal perceptions of these roles. Saatchi and Saatchi decided to focus more closely on mothers' self-perceptions with a view to identifying their emotional roles and aspirations (Vince, 2016). As a consequence, they undertook a study in 2016 combining four sources of information:

- a UK national survey of 1,022 mums
- a week-long mobile ethnography (i.e. a study where consumers, in this case mothers, using their mobile phones, capture via photo and video, aspects of their environment) to understand their home and their direct environments
- listening to and interacting with a large community of mothers who are part of a large forum known as Mumsnet (www.mumsnet.com); the community has around 8 million unique visitors monthly, including both mothers and fathers
- two Mumsnet panel surveys with 1,800 parents.

Despite some criticism associated with the study, which thought the study missed the opportunity to address the role of women more generally rather than just 'mothers', the study revealed some very interesting findings. In particular, it identified eight broad emotional roles:

- a carer who provides love and comfort
- a provider of a safe house
- a playmate/entertainer
- a friend who is understanding
- a role model/hero who encourages others with her success
- a coach that can help with experience/knowledge
- a fan that can feel proud and inspired
- a rule-breaker who can be rebellious and fun to be with.

The findings provided huge opportunities for marketers who capitalised on these different roles and, by associating with them, sought to appeal more to their target groups. It is also interesting to see that studies such as this demonstrate that what may have been seen in the past as the domain of statistical analysis is no longer the case. For instance, in the past, marketers routinely made use of complex statistics, such as factor analysis, to categorise data into simpler dimensions. This was done, for example, in studies on brand personalities. This study demonstrated that qualitative approaches can be very helpful in trying to summarise a diversity of opinions.

Case study questions:

1. What were the problems faced by previous studies on understanding mothers and how did the Saatchi/Mumsnet study seek to improve on them?
2. Given that many companies are interested in what a person does or did (behaviours), would such information be enough for the marketer to ascertain what people might do in the future and why?
3. In what way could understanding people's role perceptions be helpful to marketers?
4. What are the challenges/risks associated with the Saatchi/Mumsnet approach (social perceptions, methodological, etc.) and how can a marketer address them?

Sources: Saatchi & Saatchi (2015); Vince (2015, 2016); Jobber and Ellis-Chadwick (2016)

End of Chapter Questions

These questions should help you reflect on your understanding of this chapter:

1. What are the key stages in a credible qualitative marketing study?
2. How do you conceptualise a research problem?
3. How do you develop a theoretical framework to match the aims of your research?
4. How do you develop a methodological framework that addresses the objectives of your research?
5. How do you choose suitable methods and techniques to use in marketing research?

6. How do you develop an analytical framework that maximises your understanding of the findings?
7. What do you need to take into consideration when developing your research report?

Checklist

After studying Chapter 10, you should now be familiar with these key concepts:

1. The key steps for designing a market research project
2. The relevance of conceptualisation to each step of the market research design
3. The problem-based nature of market research
4. The need to consider theories and models to help inform the business issue
5. How to develop a robust, problem-focused methodological framework
6. How to ensure the development of a credible analysis
7. How software should be selected to support analysis
8. How to develop a research report that presents a meaningful 'story'

Further Reading (in sequence from beginners to advanced)

Lofgren, K. (2013) Qualitative analysis of interview data: a step-by-step guide. Available at: www.youtube.com/watch?v=DRL4PF2u9XA

Gibbs, G. (2014) Alan Bryman's 4 stages of qualitative analysis. Available at: www.youtube.com/watch?v=rs8L_xzU2_U

Quinlan, C., Babin, B., Carr, J., Griffin, M. and Zikmund, W. G. (2015) *Business Research Methods*. Andover: Cengage Learning.

Babbie, E. (2016) *The Practice of Social Research* (14th edition). Boston, MA: Cengage Learning.

Bryman, A. and Bell, E. (2015) *Business Research Methods* (4th edition). Oxford: Oxford University Press.

Zuber-Skerrit, O. and Fletcher, M. (2007) The quality of an action research thesis in the social sciences. *Quality Assurance in Education*, 15 (4), pp. 413–36.

Bibliography

Aaker, J. (1997) Dimensions of brand personality. *Journal of Marketing Research*, 34 (3), pp. 347–56.

Anderson, T. H. C. (2016) Text analysis answers: is the Quran really more violent than the Bible? Available at: http://odintext.com/blog/text-analysis-quran-bible-3of3 [Accessed 6 March 2016].

Babbie, E. (2016) *The Practice of Social Research* (14th edition). Boston, MA: Cengage Learning.

Bowden, G. (2016) Bible and Quran text analysis reveals 'violence' more common in Old and New Testament. *Huffington Post.* Available at: www.huffingtonpost.co.uk/2016/02/09/bible-and-quran-text-analysis_n_9192596.html [Accessed 6 March 2016].

Braun, V. and Clarke, V. (2006) Using thematic analysis in psychology. *Qualitative Research in Psychology*, 3, pp. 77–101.

Bryman, A. and Bell, E. (2015) *Business Research Methods.* Oxford: Oxford University Press.

CAQDAS (2016) Choosing an appropriate CAQDAS package. Available at: www.surrey.ac.uk/sociology/research/researchcentres/caqdas/support/choosing/index.htm[Accessed 16 March 2016].

Chamberlain, K. (2000) Methodolatry and qualitative health research. *Journal of Health Psychology*, 5 (3), pp. 285–96.

Clarke, V. and Braun, V. (2013) Teaching thematic analysis: overcoming challenges and developing strategies for effective learning. *The Psychologist*, 26 (2), pp. 120–3.

Collis, J. and Hussey, R. (2003) *Business Research: A Practical Guide for Undergraduate and Postgraduate Business Students.* Basingstoke: Palgrave Macmillan.

Denzin, N. K and Lincoln, Y. (2011) *The SAGE Handbook of Qualitative Research.* London: Sage.

Fourali, C. (1997) Using fuzzy logic in educational measurement. *Evaluation and Research in Education*, 11 (3), pp. 129–48.

Fourali, C. (2009) Tackling conflict: a beyond opposites approach. *Counselling Psychology Quarterly*, 22 (2), pp. 147–69.

Fourali, C. (2016) *The Promise of Social Marketing: Changing the World for Good.* London: Routledge.

Glaser, B. G. and Strauss, A. L. (1967) *The Discovery of Grounded Theory: Strategies for Qualitative Research.* Chicago: Aldine.

Jobber, D. and Ellis-Chadwick, F. (2016) *Principles and Practice of Marketing* (8th edition). London: McGraw-Hill Education.

Kumar, N., Linguri, S. and Tavassoli, N. (2005) *The Anti-Brand Brand.* London: London Business School.

Lindlof, T. R. (1995) *Qualitative Communication Research Methods.* Thousand Oaks, CA: Sage Publications.

McNiff, J. (2016) *Writing up Your Action Research Project.* London: Routledge.

Montgomery, D. B. and Weinberg, C. B. (1979) Towards strategic intelligence systems. *Journal of Marketing*, 43, pp. 41–52.

Morse, J. M. (1994) Emerging from the data: the cognitive processes of analysing in qualitative enquiry. In J. M. Morse (ed.) *Critical Issues in Qualitative Research Methods*, pp. 23–43. Thousand Oaks, CA: Sage Publications.

O'Dell, W. F. (1962) Personal interviews or mail panels. *Journal of Marketing*, 26, pp. 34–9.

Preissle, J. (2011). Qualitative futures: Where we might go from where we've been. In N. K. Denzin, & Y. S. Lincoln (eds.) *The Sage Handbook of Qualitative Research* (4th edition), pp. 685–98. Thousand Oaks, CA: Sage.

Purkiss, J. and Royston-Lee, D. (2012) *Brand You: Turn Your Unique Talents into a Winning Formula*. Harlow: Pearson.

Quinlan, C., Babin, B., Carr, J., Griffin, M. and Zikmund, W. G. (2015) *Business Research Methods*. Andover: Cengage Learning.

Red Bull (2015) Milestones 2015. Available at: http://energydrink-uk.redbull.com/history-of-red-bull [Accessed 5 December 2015].

Red Bull (2016) Consumer Insight Manager, Marketing. Available at: http://jobs.redbull.com/us/en-US/santa-monica-consumer-insights-manager-017999#qualitative-and-syndicated-research [Accessed 22 February 2016].

Saatchi & Saatchi (2015) Less of a housekeeper, more of a rule breaker. Available at: http://saatchi.co.uk/en-gb/news/less-of-a-house-keeper-more-of-a-rule-breaker [Accessed 17 November 2016].

Smithson, M. (1988). Possibility theory, fuzzy logic, and psychological explanation. In T. Zetenyi (ed.) *Fuzzy Sets in Psychology*. North Holland: Elsevier Science Publishers.

Vince, L. (2015) Motherhood is not a job. Saatchi & Saatchi, London. Available at: http://saatchi.co.uk/uploads/142676674036405/original.pdf [Accessed 17 November 2016).

Vince, L. (2016) Stop faking it: creating meaningful connections with mums. Available at: www.mumsnet.com/pdf/mumstock-2016-saatchi-research.pdf [Accessed 17 November 2016].

Wolcott, H. F. (1990) On seeking – and rejecting – validity in qualitative research. In E. W. Eisner and A. Peshkin (eds) *Qualitative Inquiry in Education: The Continuing Debate*, pp. 121–52. New York: Teachers College Press.

Zippel, K. (2015) *Research Methods*, Chapter 4 (Conceptualization and measurement). Available at: www.atsweb.neu.edu/zippel/courses/321/classnotes/ch4.pdf [Accessed 29 December 2015].

Find journal articles and multiple choice questions online at: **https://study.sagepub.com/benzo** to support what you've learnt so far.

Having covered the qualitative approach to conducting marketing research and its related methodology in Part III, Part IV focuses on quantitative research. As a more numeric-based and statistically engaged approach, it does not compete with qualitative research on answering the same research questions. Rather, it tackles different dimensions of a research problem and can be used to complement qualitative research as it can be carried out either before or after it, depending on the research aim and objectives. Accordingly, Chapters 11 to 14 explore various dimensions and aspects of planning and implementing quantitative marketing research, from research approach to design, to methodology and choice of data collection methods, and then onto data analysis and discussion of the research results.

Chapter 11 starts off by discussing hypothesis testing to provide a better understanding of an element of quantitative research that young researchers may find challenging; this involves explaining when and how to formulate hypotheses, and the underlying dimensions and types of hypothesis, with examples. The chapter also delves into how hypotheses are tested and decisions are systematically made as to whether to accept or reject each of them, with implications for the research outcomes.

Chapter 12 moves on to an exploration of quantitative research methodology, investigating quantitative research design and methods, benefits and constraints in conducting quantitative research, and how to select the optimal method for data collection. The chapter then progresses in depth onto a discussion of a key and most popular quantitative research method: survey research, discussing its typologies and different means of questionnaire administration.

Chapter 13 takes survey research methodology further into a discussion of questionnaire design and development, offering tips constituting dos and don'ts in constructing an efficient and effective questionnaire. The chapter also explores the next step in the research process following quantitative data collection: data preparation for analysis through examining 'coding' and data cleaning, paving the way for a discussion of quantitative data analysis in Chapter 14.

Finally in Part IV, Chapter 14 delves into data analysis using descriptive and inferential statistics. The chapter covers the univariate statistical methods used in exploring and summarising the data, and further explains parametric and non-parametric data analysis techniques, offering tips for choosing the right technique as appropriate to a research project's specific objectives. The chapter concludes by unveiling the importance of interpreting data analysis results and synthesising the hypothesis testing outcomes towards answering the key research question set forth at the start of the research project.

PART IV

Quantitative Research in Marketing

CHAPTER 11

Hypothesis Building and Testing

LEARNING OBJECTIVES

The key learning objectives of this chapter are:

1. To define the notion of a hypothesis and to understand when and how to formulate hypotheses in conducting research
2. To understand how a hypothesis relates to research variables and research objectives
3. To determine hypothesis-testing procedures and the steps involved
4. To explore how to make decisions on whether to accept or reject research hypotheses

KEY CONCEPTS

By the end of this chapter, the reader should be familiar with the following concepts:

1. What a hypothesis is
2. When to develop a hypothesis
3. Null and alternative hypotheses
4. Types of hypotheses
5. Hypothesis-testing procedures
6. Significance level
7. Type I and type II errors
8. Accepting and rejecting hypotheses

Marwa G. Mohsen

Introduction

This first chapter in Part IV covers a key concept which researchers extensively use, one that students may find it quite challenging to understand and synthesise: *hypothesis formulation and testing*. It explains what is meant by a hypothesis in conducting research, when to formulate it and how to develop it, as well as key steps and considerations in carrying out hypothesis-testing procedures. The relationship between specific hypotheses, specific research objectives and research variables is explored and explained. Finally, the results of hypothesis testing are studied to identify how to interpret the findings from hypothesis tests on the way to accepting or rejecting the hypothesis in question.

Learning about hypothesis formulation and testing is vital in conducting all types of research and in using various types of research approach. It is given that a hypothesis can be:

1. An outcome in some studies – for instance, hypothesis formulation can be the resulting output of qualitative research studies (as indicated in Part III).
2. The basis of other studies – namely quantitative studies – where a hypothesis is formulated at an early stage, based on existing literature (some of which can be previous qualitative/exploratory studies in the same domain), towards systematically testing it through collecting and analysing data to establish whether the data supports or falsifies the developed hypothesis. This process will be extensively discussed in this chapter.

Thus, it is important for researchers at all levels to acquire proper knowledge and comprehension of what a hypothesis is, when it is developed and how, its various interactions and relationships with the research objectives and variables, its types and forms, hypothesis-testing procedures, interpreting hypothesis test findings and, lastly, how to make sense of such findings.

In essence, it is imperative to recognise what a hypothesis *is NOT* before an appreciation can evolve as to what it *is*. A hypothesis is NOT just a guess that directs the course of a research project. It is also NOT a wished-for result that the researcher concludes their research with or builds a study on. Furthermore, it is a NOT a complicated set of sentences that pulls variables into proposed complex relationships. Such ways of thinking about or conveying a hypothesis are misguided and confused and can also endanger the research process if endorsed. Without proper support at its backdrop, a hypothesis becomes unscientific and a weak base for any further systematic research work. In view of this, it is critical that a proper comprehension and application of the concept of hypothesis transpires. Towards this end, this chapter delves in detail into what a hypothesis encapsulates as a notion and helps you, as the researcher, get a better grasp of this important concept.

Snapshot: Setting the Scene – Nutella: from an Infrequent Treat to a Breakfast Food

Nutella was a well-known and successful brand in the UK. However, unlike in the rest of mainland Europe where Nutella was a staple of breakfast, most people in the UK saw Nutella as a treat. This was a particularly firmly held view amongst mums. Prior to a repositioning of the brand, mums' perceptions of Nutella were mainly associated with 'indulgence' and 'treat'.

No wonder then that 75% of mums claimed that they 'would try to limit their child's consumption of Nutella'. They might allow Nutella occasionally, as a special treat for the weekend, as a treat for birthday parties or for a special occasion like Pancake Day.

Seen from the perspective of owner, Ferrero UK's ambitious plan to double the volume sales of Nutella in three years, this 'pigeon-holing' of the brand was a real challenge.

Identifying the volume opportunity and the keys to unlock it

With Nutella being part of the breakfast ritual in many countries, the breakfast opportunity in the UK was thoroughly explored. Although there are many more breakfast occasions than treat occasions, initially these opportunities seemed well beyond the reach of a brand that was so strongly associated with being a treat. That was until Ferrero UK's rigorous research and audit of the brand showed a way forward.

The research revealed that people's perceptions of the brand were based on incorrect ingredient information. Most people misunderstood Nutella as a chocolate spread, when in reality it is a hazelnut spread. Understanding the product truth of hazelnuts could start a positive chain reaction for the brand. Hazelnuts communicated a number of positive benefits, especially that of slow release energy, and slow release energy had a clear value at breakfast time in advance of the day ahead. Clearly, this new information about hazelnuts needed to be the content of any new communication about the brand. In research, mums claimed that this content would persuade them to think differently about the brand and even to start giving Nutella to their kids at breakfast.

But, as we all know, behaviour claimed in the experimental conditions of research does not always translate into actual behaviour in the real world. To ensure that we went beyond 'belief change' and converted beliefs into actual behaviour, we took one further strategic step. This was to frame the new information we were communicating in a specific context. That context was

> families' breakfasts where toast already features; perhaps spread with jam or peanut butter. Put another way, we were targeting those mums who were already comfortable with giving their family toast with something on it. *Our hypothesis was that switching from jam or peanut butter on toast to Nutella on toast was a smaller, and therefore more likely to be taken, behavioural step than asking mums to include Nutella in a breakfast that didn't include toast with something on it, currently.*

The above scenario is borrowed from an existing advertising case study that reflects research in practice. It reflects an exploratory study by Ferrero UK which led to some data that was used to build a hypothesis for practical testing. The hypothesis is grounded in existing facts about the target audience of the product – in this case, mothers who make breakfast decisions for their families/children. For academic research purposes, the proposed hypothesis can be expressed or reworded as follows:

> A behavioural shift towards adopting Nutella is more likely for parents who offer 'toast plus a topping' for breakfast versus mothers who offer other breakfast options, not involving toast and topping.

Source: adapted from *Nutella – Wake up to Nutella* (White et al., n.d.)

By Malcolm White and Isabelle Leveque of Krow Communications, with Nick Pugh of Billetts Marketing Investment Management; Bronze, IPA Effectiveness Awards 2009

What is a Hypothesis?

A hypothesis (plural: hypotheses) can be considered an educated claim; it is primarily an informed assumption about a certain phenomenon, predicting a factor or interpreting an observation. Nevertheless, it is not yet empirically examined. According to Oxford Dictionaries (n.d.), a hypothesis is 'a supposition or proposed explanation made on the basis of limited evidence as a starting point for further investigation'.

In other words, a hypothesis is a conjecture that is grounded in background support originating from secondary research, hence the word 'educated claim'. Accordingly, it is a statement built on the foundation of a tentative argument assembled from existing literature; it then requires empirical testing and scientific evidence to support whether or not it holds as true through conducting primary research within the context of the study.

The development of a hypothesis is contextual as it relates to the situation, phenomenon or condition under which it is formulated within a research project. For example, in a study on organic food consumption behaviour in the UK, the researcher can put forward the hypothesis that: 'Females are more likely to *routinely purchase* organic food than males'. In collecting and analysing data to examine the likelihood of accepting this hypothesis, it is important to remember that:

1. It is only relevant for consumers in the UK at this point in the study.
2. It is based on what 'organic food' means to this stated consumer population.
3. Findings may be limited to the types of organic foods on which data are collected.
4. It is operational on the grounds of what 'routine purchase' signifies for the consumer sample under consideration.

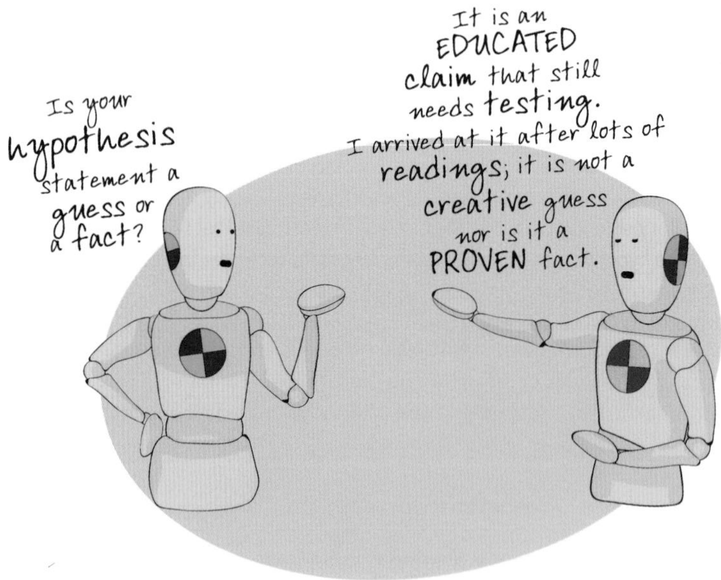

Figure 11.1 What a hypothesis is and what it is not

Hence, in interpreting the results, the context in which the hypothesis is formulated is crucial to acknowledge so that generalisations are only made within systematically controlled boundaries and only where the sample and methods used permit generalisation. Accordingly, the wordings of a hypothesis have to be carefully designed before it is ready for empirical examination. *Hypothesis testing* coins this process of systematic scrutiny; it involves testing the educated claims – hypotheses – made about a population through collecting data on the variables involved from a selected representative sample of the target population. Through analysing the primary data collected and examining proposed relationships or differences, the hypothesis can be accepted as supported, partially supported or otherwise rejected as false.

Notably, despite a hypothesis being an important part of conducting empirical research, it is not necessarily developed in every study. Some research designs necessitate the early formulation of one or more hypotheses, whereas other study designs can start with a set of propositions that can be explored, though not as hypotheses, as is explained next.

When to Develop a Hypothesis in Research

The starting point for any research project is to determine clearly the research aim and the key question the study intends to answer. The research objectives then pave a way to follow as they relate to a set of specific and more detailed questions corresponding to the study's variables. At this point, assumptions may emerge and you may have some initial ideas about the direction of the anticipated answers. However, the experienced researcher needs to guard against approaching the study with preconceived stereotypes or ready-made ripostes with no scientific base. The research objectives and questions, thus, should emanate from an impartial front and in response to a clearly defined research problem, be it a challenge or an opportunity, for which information of consequence is desired to inform decision makers.

After reviewing and scanning the relevant studies, and depending on how much secondary data exist regarding the research question, a decision is made as to whether hypotheses can be developed. On the one hand, when the topic has been tackled in previous studies from a different perspective, investigated in other countries and/or explored using another set of variables, intelligible arguments can be built into plausible hypotheses. In this case, extending lucid arguments into a proposed hypothesis essentially embeds the research in the extant studies and highlights the research gap to be bridged. A conclusive research design (descriptive, explanatory or causal research) is suitably in place then, where a proposed hypothesis can be investigated and statistically tested.

If, on the other hand, there is insufficient secondary data due to the topic being novel, a domain that has received insufficient research attention or scant information has been published on the phenomenon at hand, developing a hypothesis is unlikely to be possible. In this instance, an exploratory research design is more appropriate and any available literature can provide research *propositions* as bases for an exploratory investigation; this calls for qualitative research considerations. In this case, hypotheses cannot be formulated upfront but will rather become a byproduct of the study, expected to emerge at the end within the research findings and implications. In sequence again, the latter ensuing hypotheses can be taken forward to a future/new study cycle aimed then at investigating further identified research gaps.

Research in Practice: Research Designs and Hypothesis Formulation

Research that starts with hypothesis formulation

Dan is conducting a study on how individual time orientation influences purchase intentions for new technological devices, comparing a sample of students and professionals. Through a detailed scan of literature on time orientation, Dan found many established and contemporary studies in marketing and sociology conducted in different countries. A comparison of the time orientation of students and professionals and its relationship to intentions to buy innovative products has been investigated in many countries but not in the Middle East where culture plays an important role that may affect findings. Using results from the existing literature, Dan can develop informed hypotheses and then test them through collecting data during his research visit to the UAE. A descriptive research design would be appropriate in supporting his planned study; results can then be linked back to prominent literature to reflect on the similarities and differences among countries.

Research that concludes with hypothesis building

Sian is interested in *neuromarketing* and how marketers can use it to investigate consumer behaviour where traditional research methods (such as surveys and interviews) fall short of bridging the intention-behaviour gap. However, studies on neuromarketing are still in their (relative) infancy. Hence, Sian is unable to find enough literature to build an intelligible hypothesis for empirical examination through the data she collects. Her research is exploratory and she will collect data through expert interviews with neuromarketing experts and marketing research academics and practitioners. Accordingly, Sian's research is of a theory-building nature and the limited studies already available will help in developing the interview guide. Findings from her subsequent analysis of the data collected will result in new insights that can evolve into hypothesis statements. Future research can build on her hypotheses for further conclusive investigations.

Neuromarketing The study of consumers using neuroscience. It involves researching responses to marketing and advertising stimuli through technology-based brain activity measurement, such as brainwave monitoring and eyeball tracking

Where applicably formulated, the importance of developing research hypotheses is to keep the research purpose and direction on track. Hypotheses provide a research focus, operationalising the objectives and proposing a point of departure for answering the research question. A hypothesis provides a logical conjecture on how the key research variables can be linked. Accordingly, it assists in deconstructing the study's theoretical framework, stating and illuminating its elements, and showing the proposed relationship(s) among its main constructs, as explained in more detail next.

Hypothesis, Research Objectives and Research Variables

Research objectives constitute the operational backbone of research. They create the key research question and aim from a strategic top level to a more specific operative grounding. The hypothesis expounds the probable relationship between the research elements; it breaks down the research objectives into fundamental parts that have a certain direction and focus.

For example, a study can start with this key research question:

> To what extent are opinion leaders on social networks influential in driving purchase intentions for and against brands?

You would aim to investigate the significance and power of opinion leaders on social networks in swaying consumer intentions to purchase a specific brand name (e.g. Samsung).

Subsequently, the research objectives/specific questions that ensue could be articulated as:

1. Identify how opinion leaders take part in brand discussions on Samsung official web pages or non-official blogs/forums/chat rooms.
2. Determine how significant are the views of opinion leaders vis-à-vis other contributors on these social networks.
3. Articulate whether the expressed views of opinion leaders have the power to translate into purchase intentions for Samsung products.

Based on existing studies, you can build a logical argument using literature sources for support that lead to the emergence of specific hypotheses. For instance, the hypotheses for the above example may be stated as:

1. The credibility of the opinion leader is related to their perceived level of expertise.
2. The credibility of the opinion leader is influenced by perceived trustworthiness.
3. The significance of the influence of opinion leaders on purchase intentions is related to the combined effect of expertise and trustworthiness perceived by the target audience.
4. Opinion leaders as a power source can influence consumer attitudes but not purchase intentions for Samsung products.

These hypotheses spell out a number of variables and advocate the probable relationships that may exist among them. In the above example, the key variables are:

Variables are measurable characteristics or properties of people and/or things that can take on different values

A: Perceived expertise

B: Perceived trustworthiness

C: Perceived credibility

D: Purchase intentions.

The proposed relationships are between A and C, between B and C, and the influence of A and B in relation to D.

Types of Hypothesis Formulation

In the first phase of a study, you can search through and explore the extant literature and decide on the gap to investigate; this gap involves some factors which have received attention in other studies as well as other factors whose relationships with or influence on others are yet to be scrutinised. These factors become research variables that are the keywords of the study and the researcher then starts to fit them together like the pieces of a puzzle, positioned first then checked for appropriateness. Adjusting the puzzle pieces, based on a pre-study of the likelihood of their places being right, is like formulating a hypothesis towards further empirical checking. In research, the suggested relationships among variables can be visually and/or verbally illustrated through *conceptual frameworks* that model variables in a form fit for systematic investigation.

The association among variables can take on a variety of forms, transpiring into different types of hypothesis formulation. Three main types of formulation are explored here: a *correlation-based* hypothesis, a *causation-based* hypothesis and a *difference-based* hypothesis. All such types of formulation can be *directional* or *non-directional*.

Correlation-based hypothesis

In a *correlation-based* hypothesis, the link between two variables is expressed in *association* terms. For example, it can be suggested that 'The perceived expertise of online opinion leaders is systematically related to/associated with perceived trustworthiness', using variables from the illustration explored in the previous section. In other instances, the link proposed can be framed in *effect* terms; extending the earlier example about online opinion leaders on social networks and consumer purchase intentions for/against brands, the hypothesis may be formulated as 'The perceived credibility of online opinion leaders systematically affects/influences the consumer purchase intentions of Samsung products'.

Hypotheses postulating a potential relationship or a possible influence can be *non-directional* or *directional*. Proposing that variable A systematically relates to variable B or that variable A influences variable B, with no specified direction, is a *non-directional* hypothesis formulation. The above examples are thus non-directional hypotheses.

To reshape them into *directional* hypotheses, you can advance a more specific dimension involving a *positive* or *negative* tendency; hence, a directional hypothesis can postulate a positive or a negative relationship or influence. For instance, proposing that 'The perceived credibility of online opinion leaders is *positively related* to purchase intentions' is a directional hypothesis suggesting a positive association between these two variables. Alternatively, hypothesising that 'The perceived credibility of online opinion leaders *negatively influences* purchase intentions' is suggestive of a probable negative effect, also referred to as an *inverse* relationship between the two variables. A positive relationship or influence designates that when the value of variable A increases, the value of variable B increases in turn. Conversely, a negative/inverse relationship or influence indicates that when the value of variable A increases, the value of variable B decreases in turn.

Causation-based hypothesis

A second type of hypothesis can be *causation-based*, advocating that variable A (the independent variable) causes variable B (the dependent variable). An example of a causal hypothesis is 'Online opinion leaders' perceived credibility causes improved consumer purchase intentions'. A causation-based hypothesis can also be directional or non-directional. However, caution has to be taken when investigating causality as it is the hardest thing to establish; establishing causality requires control over all other possible factors in order to scientifically determine the percentage of the independent variable's casual effect on the dependent variable. For this reason, a causation-based hypothesis can only be proposed in more advanced research where it can be empirically scrutinised using a complex causal research design that involves rigorous and advanced data analysis tools.

Difference-based hypothesis

The third type of hypothesis formulation is *difference-based* hypothesis, which advocates a difference between two levels of an independent variable (e.g. age groups) for a dependent variable (e.g. organic food consumption). For instance, a non-directional form of a difference-based hypothesis may be expressed as 'Age impacts on the level of organic food consumption in the UK'; if developed in a directional form, the hypothesis may put it forward that 'Older consumers are more likely to consume organic food relative to younger consumers in the UK'. In the opening 'Snapshot: Setting the Scene' at the start of the chapter, the hypothesis about mothers who offer 'toast plus a topping' for breakfast being more likely than mothers who offer other breakfast options to have a behavioural shift towards adopting Nutella is a difference-based directional hypothesis.

The various types of hypothesis discussed here are all developed based on existing secondary data sources; a critical literature review is indispensable in supporting the construction of a study's hypotheses towards subsequent empirical examination. The variation in the types of hypothesis only stems from how the key variables under study are expressed in relation to each other. In essence, this will correspondingly reflect ensuing variation in the statistical methods used in testing these hypotheses (see Chapter 14 for further details). Furthermore, articulating hypotheses entails paying attention to the form in which they are presented for systematic testing, as explained next.

Forms of Research Hypotheses

A hypothesis is formed as a declarative statement of a predictive nature, reflecting a possible answer to the study's research questions. This answer can highlight that what is proposed as a relationship, an influence, a causation or a difference among variables is true – thus supporting the proposed hypothesis – or is false, hence calling for a rejection of it.

Two forms of hypothesis can be developed: the *null* hypothesis and the *alternative* hypothesis. The null hypothesis (H_0) is often the hypothesis that is tested and so it is what any statistical investigation sets out to test by default; it advances an indifferent proposition whereby empirical data examination results in no statistically significant association, influence or difference between the two research variables in question. It means that any statistical difference or consequence detected is happening merely by chance and is not systematic for the specific relationship under investigation.

If H_0 is accepted as true, no action or change planned as an implication of the research transpires; thus, no new notions supplement existing knowledge. The key notion in testing a hypothesis is to presume that the null hypothesis is true until statistical evidence invalidates it. For example, in a study testing the H_0 that there exists no significant difference between male and female consumers on their attitude to the celebrity endorsement of perfumes, attitudinal data are collected for both genders and analysed. If no systematic difference is detected, H_0 is retained as true.

If, however, the null hypothesis is rejected as untenable, the *alternative* hypothesis (H_1) is accepted as true instead. H_1 is the reverse of H_0; H_1 is in fact the statement originally proposed by the researcher as the suggested answer to the research question. It is defined in *The Encyclopaedic Dictionary of Marketing* as 'a population parametric, taking on a different value from that stated in the null hypothesis' (Khan and Naved, 2006). Support for the acceptance of the alternative hypothesis is that if the occurrence of the relationship between variables is not due to chance, then it is scientifically noteworthy and, therefore, supported as true. Usually, this is how the null hypothesis (H_0) is developed, such that its rejection leads to the acceptance of the alternative hypothesis (H_1).

It is interesting to note that in setting out to test H_0, the default assumption is that it is correct. Henceforward, in refuting it as false through systematic data analysis, support is achieved for the other side of the coin – that is, H_1. The burden is on you as the researcher to disprove H_0 through the scientific process; otherwise, if H_0 is sustained, H_1 disintegrates.

Reflective Activity: The Null Hypothesis and the Alternative Hypothesis

In a study investigating the speed of adoption of fair trade foods among consumers in the USA, the literature on willingness-to-pay (W-T-P) for organic food suggests that people with a high income have a positive W-T-P attitude towards including fair trade foods in their weekly shopping basket. Based on secondary data, the researcher would formulate H_0 by default as 'Consumers with high income levels are unlikely to adopt fair trade foods more readily than consumers with low income levels'.

Accordingly, H_0 denies a possible systematic association between consumer income level and a positive inclination to adopt fair trade foods among the target population. If statistical tests find no significant difference between consumers with high and low levels of income in readiness to adopt fair trade foods, H_0 is validated as true.

Consider the alternative hypothesis H_1; can you express it in systematic terms vis-à-vis the null hypothesis H_0?

If data analysis indicates a significant difference in fair trade food adoption readiness among consumers based on income level, H_0 is rejected in favour of H_1.

Answer: H_1 – 'Consumers with high income levels are likely to adopt organic food more readily than consumers with low levels of income'.

Activity: Can you think of another formulation of a possible alternative hypothesis (H_1) for the above scenario?

Defining Key Parameters in Hypothesis Testing

Significance level

After data are collected from the population sample, analysis tools are selected and used for examining each hypothesis in light of the research objectives (this will be further investigated in Chapters 13 and 14). However, in all instances, the null hypothesis is the main statement under scrutiny. The aim is for the researcher to carefully check if the relationship, influence or difference between variables being investigated is only occurring due to chance or whether it is consistently and systematically in effect. It is important for this purpose to ensure that H_0 is guarded and only rejected if the findings are far from it.

For this purpose, a probability value is set for the statistical hypothesis test that is as small as possible so the researcher does not wrongly reject H_0 when it is true. Hence, a value is fixed as a probability value that is as extreme as, or more extreme than, what the observed value would be if achieved only by chance. *Level of significance*, denoted by alpha (α), in hypothesis testing refers to the probability of rejecting H_o wrongly if it is in fact correct. The significance level is set by you as the researcher, whereby if the statistical hypothesis test value obtained is at the significance level or less, H_o is rejected and, at that point, the proposed relationship, influence or difference is said to be *statistically significant*. Statistical significance is a term commonly used in hypothesis testing and can lead to accepting H_1.

Probability value

The *probability value*, denoted by *p*-value, is the probability of getting a test statistic that is far from the value observed by chance (if the observed test value is equal to the expected value, then H_o is true). Accordingly, the *p*-value equates the level of significance for which the researcher would only just reject H_o. The level of significance is usually set in hypothesis-testing statistical terms at 0.05 (i.e. $\alpha = .05$), so there is only 5% or less tolerance for H_o being false, or at 0.01 (i.e. $\alpha = .01$), so there is only 1% or less tolerance for H_o, or otherwise at 0.1 (i.e. $\alpha = .1$), where there is 10% or less tolerance for H_o being false. In any of these cases, the *p*-value is obtained from the data analysis test and compared with the level of significance set by the researcher; if p is $\leq$ the set α, the result of the statistical test is significant and H_o is rejected in favour of H_1.

For example, if $\alpha = .05$, and p is found in the data analysis results to be any value $\leq .05$, H_o is rejected. Hence, the smaller the *p*-value, the more likely that H_o is false, providing stronger support for refuting it and enhancing the probability of accepting H_o as correct. In the social sciences, the level of significance usually selected is set at $\alpha = .05$, signifying a level of confidence of 95% that the right conclusion is drawn, with only 5% chance of making a wrong conclusion about H_o.

Hypothesis-Testing Procedures

In conducting research, it is not often possible to collect data about the whole population of interest. This is especially the case when the population under study consists of individuals such as consumers, patients, employees, students, and so on. Thus, as a researcher you will have to select a sample of this population that represents its key characteristics and trends, to collect data from. In doing so, data collected from this group is considered to be representative of, and ideally applies to, the wider target population.

Accordingly, hypothesis testing is a systematic method of examining whether hypotheses about certain parameters of a group/sample of the target population are empirically supported. This is undertaken through identifying the sample frame (see Chapter 6) and then selecting the target sample from which to gather data, collecting the primary data needed and then systematically analysing it.

Hypothesis-testing procedures take the form of five main steps:

1. Develop a conceptual framework backed by a review of the relevant literature that highlights the key research variables – searching for and finding sources of existing information about the research topic are always the first highlights of progressing forward in any study. In understanding, explaining and critiquing what other researchers have done in academic sources and industry reports, you are able to focus on the gap in existing knowledge and to ensure a clear rationale for undertaking a research enquiry.

Research in Practice: Step 1 of Hypothesis Testing

Understanding customer complaining behaviour in Ghana

According to Keng and colleagues (1995), demographic factors such as age, gender and educational level play an important role in customer complaining behaviour. Many studies advance the notion that people with a higher education level file complaints more frequently because they are better aware of how to do it. Other research, however, points out that complainants from specific ethnic groups, such as Mexican-Americans, tend to have a lower level of education. Keng et al. (1995) posit that public complainers in Singapore are older, though other literature indicates how younger consumers file more complaints than the older.

In the comprehensive work of Keng, Richmond and Han (1995), six categories of psychographic parameters were developed, namely assertiveness, risk-taking attitude, conservatism, self-confidence and individualism, attitude towards complaining, and sense of justice; these categories are used to differentiate between complainers and non-complainers. However, a relevant study on engaging in complaining behaviour in Indonesia indicates dissimilar results (Phau and Sari, 2004).

Based on the above review of literature in relation to customer complaining behaviour, it can be postulated that such behaviour may vary by within-country consumer characteristics. The proposed research hence sets out to better explain the socio-demographic and psychographic variables as antecedents of the complaining behaviour of African consumers in Ghana.

The key independent variables to be examined are the demographic factors of age, gender, educational level, and psychographic factors of self-confidence and individualism. The dependent variable is customer complaining behaviour in the services sector among consumers in Ghana. The study's results will provide a new dimension when compared with similar studies undertaken in other geographic regions.

At this stage, it is vital to bring to light the key variables to be examined and to support the proposed links between such variables using secondary data inferences. This path, in contributing to learning, comprises a deductive approach to knowledge acquisition, starting with the general and moving on to the more specific in an upright funnel form. The general constitutes the claims which are built up based on existing knowledge towards new scientific examination, encompassed in the research hypotheses. The specifics that result are the outcomes of this systematic investigation, which produce new knowledge related to the particular context of the study.

2. Formulate the research relationships into null hypothesis and alternative hypothesis – once the grounding for a study weaves the literature closely with the research aims and objectives, the relationship between the research variables can be framed in hypotheses. The default formulation will be the null hypothesis (H_0), where it is assumed that any significant influence or difference in the observed data compared to the expected value in the population happens only due to chance. The associated alternative hypothesis (H_1) emanates from the conceptual framework developed in step one of the hypothesis-testing procedures. Guided by the secondary data, H_1 represents how the data may portray itself if H_0 is rejected as false.

Research in Practice: Step 2 of Hypothesis Testing

Understanding customer complaining behaviour in Ghana (continued)

With the aim of better understanding and explaining the socio-demographic and psychographic variables as antecedents of the decision to engage in complaining behaviour within the context of service settings in Ghana, the extant literature is used to develop hypotheses for empirical examination in the proposed study. The socio-demographic variables of age, gender and education level are investigated as potential antecedents.

Thus, it is hypothesised in this particular study that:

1. H_0: No significant association exists between consumer age and the decision to file a complaint against an unsatisfactory service provider in Ghana.

   H_1: There is a significant association between consumer age and the decision to file a complaint against an unsatisfactory service provider in Ghana. *(Non-directional hypothesis)*

2. H_0: No significant association exists between consumer gender and the decision of whether to file a complaint against a service provider in Ghana.

   H_1: Male consumers are more likely to engage with the decision to file a complaint against an unsatisfactory service provider in Ghana, than female consumers. *(Directional hypothesis)*

3. H_0: No significant association exists between consumer level of education and the decision to file a complaint against an unsatisfactory service provider in Ghana.

   H_1: Level of consumer education systematically and significantly influences the decision of whether to file a complaint against an unsatisfactory service provider in Ghana. *(Non-directional hypothesis)*

3. Select a representative sample of the population of interest to collect data in relation to the research objectives and determine the level of statistical significance – as covered in Chapter 6 – this step involves clearly identifying the population of interest, drawing a representative sample from this target population, defining a suitable sample size and deciding on the possible use of probability or non-probability sampling techniques as relevant to the study; this is linked to the research objectives and the possible access to the target respondents.

4. Analyse the data collected from the selected sample using appropriate statistical methods to determine the sample mean – the level of significance (α) is decided at this point. The level of significance can be determined as $\alpha = 0.01$ (confidence level is 99%), $\alpha = 0.05$ (confidence level is 95%) or $\alpha = 0.10$ (confidence level is 90%). For each hypothesis, based on the type of hypothesis formulated (correlation or effect, causation or a difference-based hypothesis), the relevant statistical analysis tools are selected and applied to the data to determine whether or not it supports H_0. More details on statistical analysis tools will be given in Chapters 13 and 14.

5. Compare the observed statistical values with the expected values and decide whether to accept or reject the null hypothesis(es) – having determined the level of significance (e.g. $\alpha = 0.05$), if the *p*-value $\leq .05$, H_0 is rejected; in this instance, the observed value (sample mean) is not equal to or close to the expected value (population mean) obtained if the relationship between the variables occurs merely by chance. Consequently, this leads to rejecting H_0 as false and can result in accepting the H_1 claim as supported by the data.

Research in Practice: Steps 3, 4 and 5 of Hypothesis Testing

Age and adoption of self-service technologies (SST) in the UK

A study was conducted to investigate the opportunities and obstacles for consumer engagement with self-service technologies (SST) in the UK, such as GP practices' self-booking and airport self-check-in. The research built on a literature review where studies posit that ageing consumers are reluctant to use online and technology-linked services due to anxiety and limited instruction in the use of computers. Hypotheses were developed from secondary data and the first null hypothesis proposed that:

> H_0: Older people are likely to adopt the use of self-service technology (SST) for check-in at GP practices and airports at the same adoption rate as younger people.

Using a level of significance of $\alpha = 0.05$, statistical tests were run to examine whether the test value indicates that this difference in age on rate of SST adoption takes place systematically or merely by chance. If the observed statistical test value is equal to the expected value (randomly due to chance), where $p > .05$, then H_0 is accepted and retained as true. Alternatively, if *p* is $\leq .05$ and the observed statistical test value is different than the expected value, then the difference between older and younger people on SST adoption rate would be statistically significant and H_0 would be rejected. H_1, in this case, can be expressed as:

> H_1: Older people are likely to adopt the use of self-service technology (SST) for check-in at GP practices and airports at a lower adoption rate then younger people.

Based on the statistical analysis conducted so far where H_0 was negated, H_1 is likely to be correct. Nonetheless, to further support accepting H_1 as true, the statistical test should highlight the *strength* and *direction* of the difference in age for adoption rate of self-service technologies; this means that a further statistical test value should be obtained to indicate the *effect size* of the significance (discussed in detail in Chapter 14) and the *direction* of the difference in terms of whether it is positive (i.e. as age increases, the SST adoption rate increases) or negative (i.e. as age increases, the SST adoption rate decreases).

Making Hypothesis-Testing Decisions

Hypothesis-testing procedures involve statistical analysis which thus incorporates the probability of statistical errors. The researcher's intention in testing the null hypothesis is to use the data collected to make the correct decision. This decision can either be to accept the null hypothesis or otherwise to reject it. However, given that the data collected is related to a sample of the population, statistical errors may occur if the test results for the selected sample do not correspond with what would be real for the population under study. In this case, the decision made, whether it is to accept or reject the null hypothesis, may be incorrect.

In view of this, four possible decision scenarios may take place for the outcome of hypothesis testing. These are:

1. To Accept the Null hypothesis when it is True.
2. To Accept the Null hypothesis when it is, in fact, False.
3. To Reject the Null hypothesis when it is False.
4. To Reject the Null hypothesis when it is, in fact, True.

Based on these decision scenarios, different statistical errors might ensue, as presented in Table 11.1.

Table 11.1 Decision scenarios following hypothesis testing where correct or incorrect decisions are made following analysis of the sample data collected

		Decision to accept H_o for the sample	Decision to reject H_o for the sample
Reality in the population under study	True	1. Correct Decision $1 - \alpha$	4. Type I Error Alpha (α)
	False	2. Type II Error Beta (β) Error	3. Correct Decision $1 - \beta$ (Power)

As noted in the Table 11.1 illustration, two decision scenarios reflect good situations; that is 1 and 3, where the decision to accept H_o is correct or otherwise the decision to reject H_o is correct, respectively. In the other scenarios, incorrect decisions are made. If the decision to reject H_o is erroneously made while it is true, **type I error** occurs. Alternatively, when the decision to retain H_o is mistakenly made when it is in fact false, **type II error** is in effect.

It is important to note that these decision scenarios are only probabilities. It is given that the reality in the population cannot be measured (otherwise we would not have used a sample in the first place!). Hence, these are only possible outcomes to determine the probable errors that may arise such that steps can be taken to reduce the possibility of type I and II errors taking effect. The best decision made, which is called the *power of hypothesis testing*, is where H_o is rejected and is actually false (decision scenario 3 in Table 11.1). The *power* here contributes to existing knowledge when H_1 is reinforced, given data analysis correctly and successfully disproving H_o.

Ethics: Procedural Ethics in Business and Practice

Inherent in the use of statistical testing is an understanding of the rationale behind its relevance to the marketing research aim and the key research objectives. Formulating hypotheses implies a prior exploration and critique of the extant secondary data as the backdrop for further progress in acquiring new knowledge.

(Continued)

(Continued)

Ethical considerations have to be explicitly tackled to ensure that procedures are followed along the consecutive steps of hypothesis testing. This is important, especially in deciding on the sample used as representative of the target population, given that the consequent data analysis relies on the assumption that the correct sample is selected. Sampling errors are part of the blunders to guard against as they nip at the base of the research framework and its consequent findings. Using a correct sample frame, a justifiable sampling technique and a suitable sample size, where all these elements are correctly reported in the study, is of crucial importance.

Avoiding type I and II errors may not be copiously possible in every study. Nevertheless, trying to minimise such errors in procedural practice, both in academic and applied research, is an ethical specification to concede in conducting the research and in reporting its findings and related limitations.

Type II error

Notably, H_o constitutes existing notions of reality regarding the variables under investigation. When accepted as true, H_1 is implicitly set aside as unsupported, hence whatever knowledge existed before the research took place is held to be enduringly correct. If an error occurred whereby H_o is accepted when it is in fact false, this results in *type II error*. A type II error, also known as a 'beta' (β) error, erroneously maintains a false H_o, causing a halt in knowledge progression where a new contribution through the H_1 is incorrectly falsified. Further analysis or a new study can take place afterwards which rectifies this error and the new truth can be re-established without error.

However, this does not mean that type II error should be taken lightly as it can inform bad decisions built on incorrect research findings. For example, if H_o posits that a positive brand image is not associated with high levels of customer retention and it is accepted as true whereas it is in fact false, then a correct relationship between the two variables is erroneously unsupported, affecting marketers' decisions and their relationship with consumers.

Further analysis, or increasing the sample size, can resolve type II error; however, the researcher may or may not conduct this latter step. In another example, if research carried out by policy makers advocates as H_o the notion that pricing does not influence consumer decisions to purchase ethically sourced products and type II error occurs and it is accepted as true, these policy makers may consider the ramifications of such an outcome too problematic to accept and hence decide to conduct further research in order to double-check the initial findings in case a β error incidentally occurs.

Type I error

At the start of any hypothesis-testing procedure, the H_o is assumed to be true. When data analysis indicates that H_o is false, this negates it in favour of H_1, so the decision made is to reject H_o. In this case, a claim made by H_1 that changes current knowledge is supported, thus amending existing reality with a new truth. If this decision is mistakenly reached whereby H_o is actually true but is rejected, *type I error* is in play. Type I error, also known as 'alpha' (α) error, erroneously accepts a false H_1, leading to an incorrect contribution to existing knowledge.

It can be postulated that making type I error is in fact a more serious problem than making type II error. However, the researcher regulates against making type I error in step 3 of the hypothesis-testing procedure when a level of significance is determined; this is why type I error is denoted by alpha (α). The notion behind deciding on an alpha (α) level is to guard against making this type of error. If, for instance, $\alpha = 0.05$, the probability of making type I error and rejecting H_o, when it is in fact true, is at a maximum of 5%; hence, the level of confidence in this case in making a correct decision about H_o is 95%. In comparing the *p*-value to α, if $p \leq .05$ then this negates H_o and it is rejected. If $p > .05$, H_o is accepted as true.

An example of the four decision scenarios for a tested null hypothesis is illustrated in Table 11.2.

Table 11.2 Example of decision scenarios following the empirical testing of a null hypothesis

		Decision Following Hypothesis Testing	
		Decision to accept H_O for the sample	**Decision to reject H_O for the sample**
H_O: Creativity in advertising has no association with building brand image	True	I. Correct Decision *Creative adverts have no significant influence on consumer-perceived brand image*	4. Type I Error/Alpha (α) error H_O is true but rejected, concluding that: *Creative adverts have a significant influence on consumer-perceived brand image* (H_I wrongly supported)
	False	2. Type II Error/Beta (β) error H_O is false but accepted, concluding that: *Creative adverts have no significant influence on consumer-perceived brand image* (wrong conclusion)	3. Correct Decision *Creative adverts have a significant influence on consumer-perceived brand image* (Power: H_I correctly supported)

Advanced: Minimising Statistical Errors

Despite statistical errors being an integral part of statistical analysis in hypothesis testing, researchers should attempt to reduce such errors where possible. A problem, nonetheless, faced is that reducing type I error (α) may increase type II error (β) and vice versa. It is given that reducing the level of α can lead to a greater probability of accepting H_o where in fact it is false, thus increasing the possibility of type II error. Alternatively, attempting to minimise the possibility of accepting H_o when it should be rejected may result in using a higher level of α and increasing the possibility of type I error occurring; choosing a level of α defines the probability of a type II error (β) for a study with a given sample size and critical effect size.

Recent research suggests that the key problem is that the level of significance is set capriciously at a fixed value, e.g. $\alpha = 0.05$, as a decision made by the researcher early on in the hypothesis-testing procedures. Setting a level of α determines the power ($1 - \beta$) to detect effects of specified sizes (the effect size is the magnitude

(Continued)

(Continued)

or strength of the phenomenon, i.e. the extent of the significance obtained, if any). As a result, deciding to use $\alpha = 0.05$, for instance, implies that an arbitrary decision was made about the strength of the effect size that the researcher will consider as 'significant'.

A study by Mudge and colleagues (2012) advocates the importance of calculating an optimal level of α that minimises any potential errors, whether type I or II, and leads to sound scientific inferences about the phenomenon being investigated. This can be realised by undertaking statistical tests via calculating the level of significance (α) associated with the minimum average of α and β at the critical effect size (the optimal level of significance to use $= (\alpha + \beta)/2$), relying on the assumption that the probabilities of H_0 and H_1 are equal.

Chapter Summary

This chapter is the first in a series of four chapters under Part IV, covering quantitative research in marketing. It presents a case for understanding and better explaining the role of hypothesis formulation and testing in marketing research. Developing and testing hypotheses apply in conducting theoretical and practical research and are linked with exploratory and conclusive research designs. Given that hypothesis testing involves statistical investigations, it is an essential part of employing a quantitative research approach.

Developing a hypothesis in its different types and forms depends on the conceptual research framework and the particular relationships among variables under examination. Although the null hypothesis is typically tested before the alternative hypothesis can be considered, only the alternative hypotheses are explicated in more detail in reporting findings of research-based studies. That is, the statistical tests undertaken are presented in the case when a significance association, difference or causal effect is found from data analysis; in such instances, the *power of hypothesis testing* is in effect and H_0 is rejected in favour of H_1. The rationale for this style of reporting findings is that if the null hypothesis is accepted as true, no new contribution of knowledge accrues, thus maintaining unchanged truth on the investigated phenomenon. If, instead, the alternative hypothesis is accepted and new knowledge is established with evidence supporting it, reporting effect sizes in detail is appropriate.

Having covered hypothesis formulation and testing in detail, Chapter 12 will discuss quantitative research methods, with a particular focus on the use of survey methods.

Case Study: Primark versus M&S – Fast Fashion Winning on the High Street?

The UK is a leader in the manufacturing of clothing and fabrics, where the clothing and fashion sector is very competitive and highlights the importance of speed of design, marketing and distribution. The UK high street apparel industry was worth over £47 million in 2012, where this sector generates around 8% of the GDP of the UK.

As is the case with all other sectors, the recession has influenced the clothing and fashion industry worldwide, with retailers complaining of stagnant sales as consumers cut their spending on most discretionary items. However, many fast-fashion retailers employ various strategies to keep up to date with consumer tastes and changing preferences and to stimulate demand worldwide and in the UK. In so doing, economy apparel has triumphed over premium apparel, where some fast-fashion retailers beat the more established high street giants. Primark is the buoyant example. With reported sales for 2013 to the end of September up 22% and operating profits growing at twice this rate, its success story continues. At a time when consumer spending remains stagnant, the popularity of Primark in the UK has established it among the main UK high street retailers.

Marks & Spencer (M&S), a long-standing name in the high street fashion industry, cannot claim the same glittering success. Despite changing designers and revamping store layouts, an impressive advertising campaign and heavy investment in a new women's collection, its sales plummeted in the lead up to Christmas 2013. M&S Simply Food is enjoying a success story, but not M&S clothes and apparel. Promising quality and targeting middle-class customers who can afford the high prices compared to those offered by fast-fashion Primark, M&S continues to aim for a small target market. Consumer loyalty, however, is compromised by the economic situation, immense consumer hyperchoice and evolving market trends.

A changing culture in the UK retail environment reflects a growing consumer base for Primark, with surging loyalty. Younger consumers continue to choose Primark, where M&S is still viewed as a store for the older and wealthier middle-aged and senior consumer. Segmentation plays an important role in a winning marketing strategy, as Primark is expanding among more diverse segments beyond the young generation using word-of-mouth (WOM) and choosing to stay away from advertising expenditure. Relying on fashion shows, product promotions in women's magazines and success that earns it WOM customer support, Primark does not need mass advertising. On the other hand, M&S's promotional spending using celebrity endorsement is focused, albeit expensive, and it has not succeeded, as yet, in attracting the younger generation.

Primark relies on a management approach that combines lean production with fast fashion and sells its products through its own outlets. Using a number of cost-saving strategies, it aims to offer on-trend women fashion products of style and quality at affordable prices; it is thus positioned at the price-focused end of the fashion retail market. The company has gained a broad customer base over the years in Germany, France, Switzerland, Ireland, Belgium and the UK. As Primark relentlessly strives to meet the challenge of bringing new trends and innovative designs to its stores at a fast pace that constantly keeps customers satisfied and in style, it is a highly demanding endeavour. Its store environment is lively and classier than it used to be. The M&S store environment is essentially still viewed by younger consumers as a place where their parents shop, but less so for them and only for limited items such as lingerie and tights.

With most companies challenged by the consequences of an unfavourable global financial situation, they need to collect up-to-date information on customer attitudes, usages and changes in preference. The goal is to find out whether customers prefer to purchase low/reasonably-priced women's fashion products frequently, or expensive, high-quality women's fashion items that they would purchase occasionally. Given that this may vary among different consumer segments with varied demographic, social, economic and psychological characteristics, marketing research can help the company gain fresh insights into this domain.

Accordingly, the management teams of both companies may decide to prompt the marketing research team to collect data to respond to the following research objectives:

- Identify the size of the women's fashion market in the UK and the different types of retailers competing in it.
- Examine the recent perceptions, attitudes, preferences and purchase intentions of female fashion consumers in the UK.
- Investigate the characteristics of different consumer segments in this market and determine which segment(s) can be tackled through which product offerings and related marketing programmes.

(Continued)

(Continued)

Case study questions:

1. Develop two non-directional H_0 for Primark, consistent with the proposed research objectives, which can be examined following data collection.
2. Can directional H_0 be formulated based on the information available in the case study on Primark? Why or why not?
3. Specify two different hypotheses for M&S. What type of hypotheses are these: correlation-based, causation-based or difference-based?
4. For each H_0 developed for Primark and M&S, what would H_1 be?
5. In testing the first H_0 developed in question 1, assume that data analysis using appropriate statistical tests results in $p = .085$ at a level of significance of $\alpha = .05$. Would the researcher accept or reject this H_0? Why or why not?

End of Chapter Questions

These questions should help you reflect on your understanding of this chapter:

1. What is the difference between a hypothesis and a research assumption?
2. When are hypotheses formulated in different types of research designs?
3. What are different forms of hypothesis formulation?
4. Which is more problematic: type I or type II error in hypothesis testing?
5. Can type I and type II errors be totally avoided in statistical testing?

Checklist

After studying Chapter 11, you should now be familiar with these key concepts:

1. What a hypothesis is and what it is not.
2. Hypotheses are directly formulated in relation to the research variable, phrased in line with the research objectives and research questions.
3. Types and forms of hypotheses.
4. The null hypothesis versus the alternative hypothesis.
5. The various scenarios associated with accepting or rejecting H_0.
6. Type I and II errors in hypothesis testing decision scenarios.

Further Reading (in sequence from beginners to advanced)

Schmarzo, B. (2013) Understanding type I and type II error: analytics, big data, mast data mgt. EMC², *InFocus, The Global Services Blog*. Available at: https://infocus.emc.com/william_schmarzo/understanding-type-i-and-type-ii-errors

Gaur, A. S. and Gaur, S. S. (2009) *Statistical Methods for Practice and Research: A Guide to Data Analysis Using SPSS* (2nd edition). London: Sage Publications.

Mudge, J. F., Baker, L. F., Edge, C. B. and Houlahan J. E. (2012) Setting an optimal α that minimizes errors in null hypothesis significance tests. *PLoS ONE*, 7 (2): e32734.

Tabachnick, B. G., Fidell, L. S. and Osterlind, S. J. (2013) *Using Multivariate Statistics* (6th edition). Boston, MA: Pearson.

Snyder, M. and Swann, W. B. (1978) Hypothesis-testing processes in social interaction. *Journal of Personality and Social Psychology*, 36 (11), p. 1202.

Bibliography

Babakus, E., Bligh, A. D. and Cornwell, T. B. (1991) Complaint behavior of Mexican-American consumers to a third-party agency. *The Journal of Consumer Affairs*, 25 (1), pp. 1–18.

Byrne, P. J., Toensmeyer, U. C., German, C. L. and Muller, H. R. (1992) Evaluation of consumer attitudes towards organic produce in Delaware and the Delaware region. *Journal of Food Distribution Research*, 2, pp. 29–44.

Canavari, M., Bazzani, G. M., Spadoni, R. and Regazzi, D. (2002) Food safety and organic fruit demand in Italy: a survey. *British Food Journal*, 104 (3/4/5), pp. 220–32.

Day, R. L. and Landon, E. L. (1976) Collecting comprehensive consumer complaint data by survey research. In B. B. Anderson (ed.) *Advances in Consumer Research*, Vol. 3, pp. 263–8. Cincinnati, OH: Cincinnati Association for Consumer Research.

Gad Mohsen, M. and Dacko, S. (2013) An extension of the benefit segmentation base for the consumption of organic foods: a time perspective. *Journal of Marketing Management*, 29 (15–16), pp. 1701–28.

Keng, K.A., Richmond, D. and Han, S. (1995) Determinants of consumer complaint behaviour: a study of Singapore consumers. *Journal of International Consumer Marketing*, 8 (2), pp. 59–76.

Khan, K. M. and Naved, K. M. (2006) *The Encyclopaedic Dictionary of Marketing*. London: Sage Publications.

Mudge, J. F., Baker, L. F., Edge, C. B. and Houlahan, J. E. (2012) Setting an optimal that minimizes errors in null hypothesis significance tests. *PLoS ONE*, 7 (2): e32734.

Oxford Dictionaries (n.d.) Definition of hypothesis in English. [Online] Available at: www.oxforddictionaries.com/definition/english/hypothesis

Phau, I. and Sari, R. P. (2004) Engaging in complaint behaviour: an Indonesian perspective. *Marketing Intelligence & Planning*, 22 (4), pp. 407–26.

Thompson, G. and Kidwell, J. (1998) Explaining the choice of organic produce: cosmetic defects, prices and consumer preferences. *American Journal of Agriculture Economics*, 80 (May), pp. 277–87.

Walker, R. (2013) Crunch time for M&S as Primark goes from strength to strength. *Euromonitor International* (November). Available at: Euromonitor.com. [accessed 11 June 16].

White, M. and Leveque, I., with Pugh, N. (n.d.) *Nutella – Wake up to Nutella*. Case study, IPA: Bronze, IPA Effectiveness Awards 2009.

Find journal articles and multiple choice questions online at: **https://study.sagepub.com/benzo** to support what you've learnt so far.

CHAPTER 12

Quantitative Research Methodology

LEARNING OBJECTIVES

The key learning objectives of this chapter are:

1. To learn how new knowledge is acquired through quantitative research
2. To understand the quantitative research methodology and its application in marketing studies
3. To discuss in-depth issues related to survey research
4. To introduce preliminary insights into how to design a survey and develop a questionnaire

KEY CONCEPTS

By the end of this chapter, the reader should be familiar with the following concepts:

1. Quantitative research methodology
2. Quantitative designs
3. Benefits and constraints in using quantitative research methodology
4. Quantitative data collection methods
5. The survey research method
6. Types of surveys
7. Introduction to questionnaire development and administration methods

Marwa G. Mohsen

Introduction

This chapter is the second in Part IV of the book, which covers quantitative research in marketing. It aims to explore quantitative research designs and methods, delving deeper into the survey research method. Studies taking the quantitative research path, as opposed to the qualitative, are usually guided by a different type of aim and objectives, have different research questions and start with a different level of existing information. First, the aim and the objectives are usually more focused and specific, arising from a more concrete backdrop. They are less exploratory and more explanatory, descriptive and/or cause-and-effect driven. Second, the key questions in quantitative research are particular and not generic, whereby they are looking for precise and micro-level answers rather than macro or theoretical constructions. Third, quantitative studies are built on an abundance of existing knowledge that contributes theory and practical dimensions as the bases on which the new study is launched.

While qualitative research springs from the specific and moves on to general building theories and conceptual frameworks, quantitative research advances from general theories and conceptualisations and proceeds to investigate the specifics and arrive at evidenced conclusions. Accordingly, quantitative research is not just about numerical data as its characteristics exceed the numbers it encapsulates. One of its key features relates to the use of hypothesis testing. The previous chapter explored and expounded the concept of hypothesis formulation and testing, discussing how hypotheses fit in for both qualitative and quantitative research designs. While qualitative research results in the building of theory and hypotheses, quantitative research uses hypothesis development as a point of departure to collect and analyse data and then check the level of accuracy of these hypotheses. Quantitative research asks explanatory, descriptive, comparative or causality questions such as 'how?', 'why?', 'how much/many/often?', 'to what extent?' and 'what is the cause of a certain effect?'. These are usually closed-ended and explicit questions associated with pre-built response options stemming from previous exploratory studies and existing literature.

Snapshot: Setting the Scene – 'Grow Wild': Selling Sustainable Foods in a Non-sustainable Business Environment

Societal awareness of ecological and environmental concerns has risen immensely over the last three decades. Nowadays, consumers not only pay attention to satisfying their own needs when purchasing products and services but are becoming increasingly engaged with where a product has been sourced, how it has been processed and how sourcing affects local communities and the environment in the producing countries (Torjusen et al., 2001).

Transporting food over long distances results in high energy consumption, and a growing world population raises concerns as to whether natural resources will be sufficient in the coming years. This indicates that the food sector faces a great challenge to offer more sustainable product choices and to convince sceptical consumers both now and in the future. The concept of sustainability can be traced back to the 1980s and 1990s when environmentally-conscious consumers became more sensitive to ethical issues.

As food companies face the pressure to enhance their competitiveness through better environmental performance and offering more sustainable food product choices, smaller companies emerge to take advantage of this market opportunity. An example is a UK firm set up in Scotland in 1998 by Lindsay Girvan with deep beliefs in the notion of eating the natural and sustainable. *Grow Wild* took off over the coming years, from distributing food locally as a part-time job to growing its own produce in bigger premises and producing food preserves. Rather than rely on intensive farming methods, *Grow Wild* opted for the philosophy of growing organic food using sustainable methods that preserve and support the environment. Its local organic growers and suppliers help supply it with fresh organic products that are passed on to customers in delivery baskets distributed through box schemes.

Successful over 15 years of selling to a Scottish market in Edinburgh, Glasgow, West Lothian and Central Scotland, despite premium prices and satisfying demand while maintaining its sustainability standards, the company was doing well. However, as the economic environment tightens consumer expenditure, consumers are starting to search for means to spend less on food and other daily consumption goods. Coupled with rising production costs, the company needs to continue to maintain and grow its sales and profit margins.

Acknowledging that consumers' attitudes, usage and preferences change, *Grow Wild* could undertake a marketing study aimed at better understanding the changing market trends and at better profiling its target segment(s); this would help it gain conclusive results to aid future decision making in terms of whether to focus on retail or wholesale strategies, and which customer groups to target, thus identifying which segments are lucrative and have market needs that coincide with the firm's offerings.

Given the nature of the aim and objectives of the study, a conclusive research design would be deemed appropriate. This would entail a deductive approach to acquiring knowledge through a quantitative study that tests hypotheses developed at the start, based on existing knowledge.

The company needs robust results based on an understanding and description of the market at large, using a large sample of the target population to draw representative conclusions. Hence, survey research is an appropriate method, through a questionnaire to be built around the study's objectives and hypotheses.

Taking this mini case study as an example, lots of research has explored the notion of organic food consumption, but there are specific research questions that remain unaddressed; some of these relate to specific companies such as box scheme delivery providers, and some have to do with specific variables such as adoption decision making and its antecedents in relation to distrust and value perceptions, for instance. In such cases, quantitative research is more likely to move beyond exploration to description, explanation and seeking causality among different factors.

This chapter will commence by introducing what quantitative research is, why such research designs are selected for use by researchers in marketing, when this is the case and how quantitative research methodology works. It will then explicate the associated research methods, looking more in-depth at the most commonly used method: surveys. Though extensively used by researchers, care needs to be taken in designing questionnaires to ensure they are efficient, effective, valid and reliable. Issues in the development of a survey will be considered throughout the course of the chapter, explaining its various types, together with their advantages and disadvantages and the criteria for selecting the appropriate survey administration method. Issues associated with survey research will be reflected on, focusing on the dos and don'ts and the blunders that young researchers may make. Finally, the chapter will conclude with how survey data can be primed after collection to arrive at useable data and how the completed questionnaires should be organised and used for the first steps of quantitative data analysis. The latter will then be taken up in the subsequent chapters – 13 and 14, in Part IV.

What is Quantitative Research?

Debates over the best way to acquire knowledge using research have gone on throughout the decades and will not cease as long as mankind seeks new additions to current knowledge. Every time a study is conducted, new information is gained and existing knowledge is changed or complemented by further evidence or through adding a new dimension, negating a previously supported perspective, opening up new ideas in other countries or cultures, or coming up with totally new phenomena and trends.

Quantitative research is original, systematic and objective research that collects numerical data and uses logic and statistical analysis to verify hypotheses

The way knowledge is attained is debatable because there are variations in the epistemological starting points of qualitative and quantitative research. The debate refers to how knowledge is theorised, what initiates knowledge that is considered to be valid and how best to achieve that knowledge (see Chapter 4 for more details). Understanding and deciding on which theory of knowledge acquisition to follow – the subjective/interpretivist or the realist/positivist/post-positivist – are not restricted to theoretical research or academic studies. Anyone who sets out to explore, explain, identify, define, compare, describe or in any way better understand, has to make a decision on how to acquire new knowledge, be it for applied research within a company, the government, an organisation, a research centre or at university or even school level. So, whether you call yourself a researcher, a detective or a scientist, the key purpose of undertaking research is to acquire knowledge, and there are some key common decision points to depart from in order to arrive at meaningful information.

The following constitutes a simple definition of quantitative research:

> It is original, systematic and objective research that uses numerically collected data to test a hypothesis through statistical analysis, which establishes the correctness or falseness of such hypothesis.

Breaking down the terms involved in this definition, being *original* is a key prerequisite to acquiring knowledge that makes a contribution. Studies that use quantitative research designs are *systematic* as they have a precisely stated aim, SMART objectives (objectives that are Specific, Measurable, Attainable, Realistic/Relevant and Time-specific), and follow the scientific process; that is, quantitative research is based on a conceptual framework, based on secondary research and built into a verbal or visual model with clear variables/constructs and relationships which will be empirically examined using mathematical and statistical tools.

Quantitative research is *objective* given that it does not rely on a human interpretation of observed reality; rather, it utilises reliable numbers and methodical logic, based on theories pertaining to existing phenomena, to explain why and how things happen, thus verifying hypotheses. It does not try to elucidate a meaning or allow humans to interpret in-depth observations through words, as qualitative research does. Thus, the human factor is mostly taken out of the equation in carrying out quantitative studies and is replaced with a method of inquiry that is solid and numerical. The large scale of data involved in quantitative studies adds to its objective dimension as it justifies the resulting conclusions.

Quantitative Research Designs

As a researcher, once you set a clear aim and objectives for a study, the next step is to decide on a research approach. This partly comprises the philosophy behind the study and its epistemological route to acquiring new knowledge about the phenomenon in question. Guided by the objectives and the research questions, a conceptual framework is also developed that helps define the key variables of focus and interest. Such grounding helps the researcher decide whether to take a qualitative or a quantitative approach forward. If it is clear that it is a quest for objective knowledge that aims to answer how or why questions that explain the study's domain, guided by a positivist perspective and following a deductive approach to testing theory, then all the quantitative boxes are thus ticked. In this case, a quantitative research design should be the one to go with.

A research design is a blueprint that sets the frame for constructing a research project. It provides details of the action plan to follow towards implementing the study at hand. These include the type of research to be conducted, the methodology, the nature of data to be collected and related data collection method(s), and subsequent data analysis procedures. Research designs follow from the objectives, as the latter determine how the research is developed in order to properly address them and answer the related research questions.

Quantitative research designs are conclusive in nature, given that they build on existing theory and secondary data with the purpose of arriving at more definitive results from the active investigation. The first element in setting the research blueprint as such is defining the key variables and the proposed relationships to be examined. The conceptual framework emanating from the literature review and the objectives should enlighten this step. If for instance the study aims to describe market characteristics, exemplar research objectives can be identifying the extent to which usage and attitudes of m-commerce users vary across sectors, defining profiles of sub-segments within the mature market for cruise packages, identifying the causes of customer dissatisfaction with self-service technologies in public service provision, and describing the behaviour of early adopters of smart phones in a growing market.

In each of these examples, the type of research conducted has the purpose of answering how, how different, to what extent and why questions. Designs suited to these studies are called conclusive research designs, which are studies with specific inputs going into their conceptual development – key variables and constructs – built from the extant literature as well as specific outputs expected to emerge from the primary data collection and analysis to follow.

Types of quantitative research design

Conclusive research designs are linked with a quantitative approach. The methodology and methods involved are associated with the collection and analysis of numerical data. There are three key types of conclusive research design: *descriptive*, *explanatory* and *causal*.

Descriptive marketing research is mainly concerned with research questions that aim to obtain information associated with an existing marketing phenomenon. It investigates relationships between variables (e.g. the relationship between perceived brand quality and brand loyalty) and differences associated with a variable or the manipulation of a variable

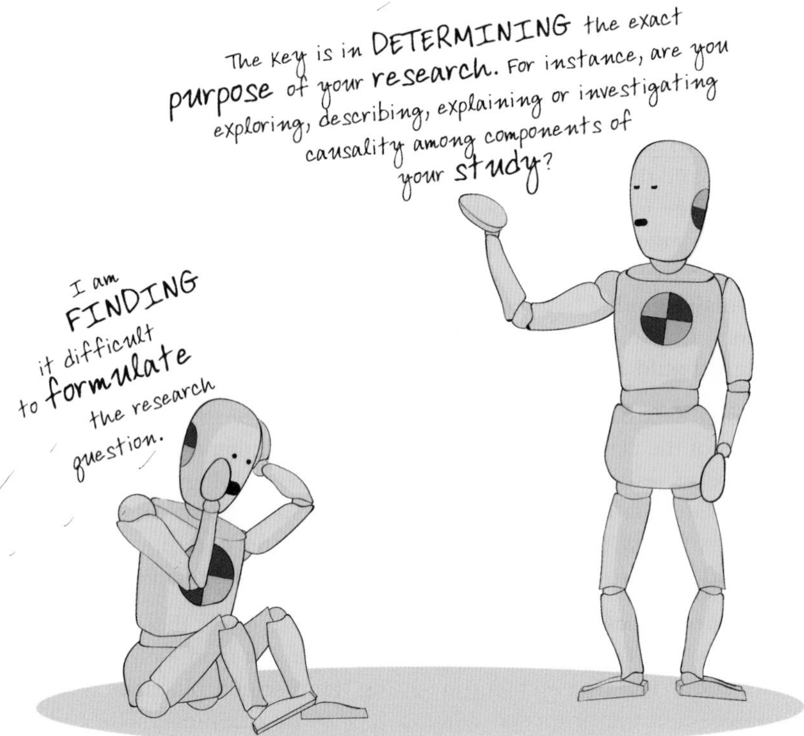

Figure 12.1 The key to formulating the research question

on another (e.g. the difference between young female versus young male attitudes towards dining in restaurants patronised by senior customers). Data collected under this research design describes such naturally occurring relationships and differences to then mathematically test whether they are systematic and significant in the population of interest, hence answering 'what is/was' questions.

Explanatory research design is controversial as it was conventionally used as a quantitative blueprint that aimed to explain, as opposed to describe, a phenomenon under investigation. In more recent times, explanatory designs have been linked with qualitative research designs, given that explaining requires the depth and probing associated with qualitative methods on a small target sample; in the sense that it takes exploratory research to the next level (Maxwell and Mitapalli, 2008). In any case, the researcher needs to be clear about the research direction and how the research design selected is supported by the appropriate research methods (may be implemented through mixed-method research – see Chapter 5) towards achieving the main research aim.

Causal research design is used in marketing studies that intend to create a better understanding of a phenomenon beyond description and possibly into the manipulation of variables to infer cause–effect relationships that are probabilistic. It is based on research questions where relationships between variables may go beyond the two-way arrows in correlation associations, to a one-way arrow in causal associations. The causal design is a more intricate form of conclusive research and thus involves different methods of data collection and complex data analysis. A key challenge in carrying out causal research is that Variable A, hypothesised as causing Variable B, may be only one of the possible causes, i.e. there is no way of proving with certainty that Variable A is the only cause of Variable B, and the causal association between them can only be inferred. It also means that the occurrence of A is not concretely or solely a reason for B to occur, but that – putting it scientifically – a research study can only put it forth that the occurrence of B is probabilistically increased with the occurrence of A.

For instance, a study may be carried out to investigate the causes of customer membership retention at Virgin Active health clubs when the variable price packages and membership options are considered, and whether the motivation levels of gym staff affect customer satisfaction with service quality; these are examples of causal research questions that could be pursued in a real-life case study.

Why and when to undertake quantitative research?

Research is generally initiated by interest in a certain domain and an inquisitive need for a better comprehension of it. Junior researchers conducting research as part of an academic degree, be it an undergraduate business project, a masters dissertation or a PhD thesis, are more likely than senior researchers to find it a challenge to decide whether to take the qualitative or the quantitative route. The key problem with this group of younger researchers is that some of them are motivated by subjective rather than objective rationales.

Some researchers are number-scared, worried about the mathematics and statistics, hence preferring to go qualitative just to avoid the numerical dilemmas they fear facing in the data analysis. Other researchers are driven by their knowledge of regression models and hence to use a quantitative approach to indulge in running regression models on a numerical data set. Alternatively, some researchers are warned that qualitative methods are not as structured as quantitative methods and take longer as they involve scrutinising data as it is being collected, with lots of reiterations between data collection and interpretation.

Research practitioners are also usually guided by what decision makers are looking for. The study is usually initiated for purposes of problem identification or problem solving in order to assist management in choosing a course of action; hence, the beneficiary of the research may dictate the form of information they want to obtain in the final report which for them is most likely to aid their decision making. There is nothing problematic about this, but an issue occurs when this managerial requirement forms the sole and main drive for the study's design.

In all these examples, the motivation for which research approach to take seems to have nothing to do with the topic itself or the specific research questions involved. Whether a research project is of academic or practical orientation, the choice of the research approach, design and subsequent methodology should be scientifically justifiable. Importantly, this choice should evolve directly from the research focus and objectives rather than from the researcher's preferences and inclinations.

Research in Practice: Quantitative Research Design – An Example

A study was conducted by a research agency in relation to the adoption of sustainable food trends. The aim of the study was to respond to a client brief seeking to identify whether a significant relationship exists between the level of education of the target market and the dynamics of decision making in adopting organic food into a consumption lifestyle. The company was facing a situation where positive usage and attitude studies with regard to healthy food consumption including organic food were not translating into actual adoption behaviours. Hence, there was an urgent need to determine whether to target consumers of a high level of education with distinct marketing communication efforts to bridge the attitude-behaviour gap.

The research agency explored existing studies to identify current views and found mixed indications; hence, the agency set out to investigate the systematic relationship between consumer education level and organic adoption. Thus, it was hypothesised that:

H_0: No significant association exists between consumer level of education and the decision outcome to fully adopt sustainable foods into the consumer's routine shopping basket.

H_1: Level of consumer education is systematically and significantly associated with the decision outcome to fully adopt sustainable foods into the consumer's routine shopping basket.

Based on $\alpha = 0.05$, researchers used one-way ANOVA to determine the adoption decision outcomes for consumers at five different levels of education, namely (a) less than high school; (b) high school; (c) college; (d) university – undergraduate; and (e) university – postgraduate. Analysis results confirm H_0, where no significant differences in organic food adoption behaviour were observed among varied levels of consumers at various educational levels. Accordingly, H_0 was supported; the decision was made to retain H_0. The findings are consistent with some extant literature while contradicting other studies.

By addressing the following questions, a researcher can decide whether or not a quantitative research design is the way to go:

1. How much information already exists around the phenomenon of interest?

In other words, is there sufficient secondary data that justifies building a conceptual framework, including hypotheses? If other studies have already done the exploratory phase of the 'what', then it is time for a conclusive research design (quantitative methodology) that takes the topic forward into the how and why.

2. What is the purpose of the study as specified in its aim and objectives?

Is the study aiming to go in-depth into an exploration of a phenomenon on a small but profound scale, or is it targeting a description of a trend, defining the relationships involved or its causes on a broader scale, albeit with less depth among the larger population of interest? If the latter, then a quantitative research design is appropriate.

3. What is the scope of the population of interest and how can the study's sample be accessed for data collection?

This is one of the basic considerations in setting the research blueprint and determining whether it takes a qualitative or quantitative direction. If the population of interest is limited in size (e.g. the big steel companies in Saudi Arabia, or the globally operating soft drinks companies), or it constitutes research subjects where the possible reach is limited (e.g. consumers who have volunteered for neuromarketing experiments, or early adopters of new Jaguar car releases), then the sample frame is narrow and only a small sample can be drawn from it. Collecting a small sample of data to be analysed quantitatively does not make sense as it will not allow for rigorous and valid results; statistical analysis tools mostly call for larger samples for rigour and accuracy. In such cases, a quantitative research design is a challenge to undertake.

Data measurement scales refer to how data for the various research variables is captured and the form they take towards analysing them through the use of appropriate analysis tools

4. Based on existing literature, what is the most common methodology for data collection in this field of study?

It is important that researchers scan the extant studies, not just in terms of the variables other researchers have investigated and their findings, but also in terms of the methodology and methods they employed. Established researchers who got their work published may have already set existing measurement scales and utilised certain research designs and approaches, providing a rationale for it. You should explore this as a researcher and decide whether to follow the same route or to take a new one – all with proper justification linked directly to the research objectives and questions.

5. Other considerations?

If the study is conducted for the purpose of supporting decision makers with managerial implications, this may influence the choice of the research design based on their needs. If the study is marketing research to be conducted in an applied setting with practical implications, then the decision makers may have an input based on the nature of the report findings that can support their decision-making process; some decision makers prefer numerical data and statistical figures to rely on, while others seek in-depth information based on themes and trends, numbers aside. The researchers in this case need to follow the required format while still advising the commissioner of the marketing research, based on the earlier requirements for conducting suitable and effective systematic research.

Reflective Activity: Adoption of Eco-friendly Products between Attitudes and Actions in the USA

Despite a rebounding economy and growing consumer awareness and acknowledgment of the need for sustainable consumption to protect an endangered planet, such positive beliefs are not lining up with purchase behaviours. Shelton Group's seventh annual Eco Pulse™ study, which surveys shifts in American consumers' sustainability attitudes and behaviours, found in July 2014 that there are more pro-environmental attitudes but fewer self-reported sustainable behaviours, such as in energy and water conservation, and in category purchases such as food products and personal care (Sustainable Brands, 2014).

This might be attributable to improving economic conditions distracting consumers from matters of conservation and social responsibility. Yet, green brands are becoming popular among consumers and so are companies endorsing sustainability agendas. The attitude–action gap may be the result of eco-friendly consumption being viewed at a more abstract, strategic level for consumers, who are unable to find ready

(Continued)

(Continued)

ways to operationalise it. Businesses may thus need to take up this initiative of leveraging green products and green consumption habits by bringing them closer in association with everyday lower-level needs.

To find out more about how to reach out to consumers in this manner, companies need to carry out research aimed at establishing the specific variables that are closer to consumers' cognitive and emotional needs, and pursuing them in their product design, promotion and distribution. The objectives of the study would be to determine the extent to which target customers find sustainability operationalised in altered product content (fewer chemical ingredients of concern), packaging (using recyclable packing alternatives) and/or place of purchase (distributed at reputable retailers who reduce waste and are environmentally responsible).

Activity: As a consultant for one of these companies, consider (individually or in groups) whether quantitative research is appropriate/inappropriate to use for such a study, justifying *why*, in line with the checklist of questions suggested in the earlier section. Which research design is suitable to use for this study?

Quantitative Research Methods

A coherent and systematic approach to conducting research means that a researcher cannot know early on in the process which research method will be used, especially at the very beginning when only a topic exists; many young researchers fall into the trap of deciding on the method before defining the objectives and before an appropriate research design is determined. Selecting a research method because it is the most common, most convenient, comfortably familiar or technically accessible is not a good point of departure. It can take the research in the wrong direction as it can cause inconsistency within the research process and affect the next critical stages of addressing the research question and its objectives.

A number of quantitative data collection research methods are commonly used in the fields of business and, more specifically, marketing. Each method is usually associated with a specific research design, as will be discussed next.

Types of quantitative research methods

Methods of data collection can be classified into direct and indirect methods. Direct methods are those where the researcher engages in direct data collection with respondents who are aware that data are being collected from them. These include survey methods and experiments. Indirect methods are those where the respondents are not aware of the data collection exercise as they are not directly taking part in the procedures. Such methods include structured quantitative observations and quantitative data compiled online using web-tracking techniques to monitor traffic and various online user activities.

Survey Research

One of the most established and commonly used methods of data collection in the social sciences is survey research. As a quantitative research method, it involves investigating a specific topic through administering a set of pre-arranged questions that measure the variables associated with the research objectives in a population sample. Though the term 'survey' is used in English to mean collecting information in general, pedagogically in research terms it refers to a quantitative approach usually resulting in the production of numerical data subsequently analysed mostly in statistical terms. This does not necessarily mean that all questions on a survey have to generate responses that are translated only into numbers; as we will explore in more detail later regarding types of survey and question types, some questions can still result in responses of a qualitative nature, i.e. in word form, which need to be analysed separately.

Survey research can be used to understand consumer attitudes, perceptions, opinions and intentions to buy different products or services. For instance, it can help answer research questions related to customer satisfaction, repeat purchase behaviour, perceptions of newly launched products or services, attitudes towards emerging trends and innovations or perceived brand image and usage patterns. Example research questions that survey research can answer include: 'What is the relationship between consumer lifestyles and perceptions of genetically modified foods?'; 'To what extent are consumers satisfied with the latest release of Apple phones?'; 'How do customers perceive e-services in the public sector domain offered through local councils?'; and 'Which benefits are female consumers seeking in consuming luxury brands in the fashion sector?', among others.

Differentiating the use of the term '**survey**' from '**questionnaire**' can better support researchers in using the right term for the right purpose. A survey corresponds to the wider notion of collecting quantitative data through a designed and controlled tool, where the latter tool is the questionnaire

It is important to note that another term used synonymously with survey is *questionnaire*. Despite not being a major problem to use the terms interchangeably, it is worth clarifying the difference between the two terms so that a researcher can use the right term in the right place for a more accurate meaning.

A *survey* covers the wider notion of collecting data within the scope of conducting a quantitative-based investigation, with all that the process involves in terms of planning the measurement scales to be used, the question format, the number and sequence of the questions, and how the questions will be administered to the target respondents (which will be discussed in the next few sections). The controlled tool on which the questions are formulated in a form suitable for administration to the target sample is the *questionnaire*. In other words, a questionnaire is a means of conducting survey research and represents the actual tool used.

Survey questionnaires can be administered in different ways and the level of structure of the questionnaire can vary, too, based on the researcher's choice in relation to how best to build an efficient and effective data collection tool. Administration to the sample of the target population can be done in writing where the respondent answers the questions themselves on paper; verbally, where the researcher fills in the questionnaire based on the respondent's verbalised responses; or on a computer, where questions are given online or via e-mail and the respondent directly answers them. The pros and cons of each of these methods of administration will be discussed in subsequent sections, with the aim of providing some insight as to when it is best to use the various methods of questionnaire administration.

Experimental Research

Just as the most commonly used data collection method is the survey for descriptive research designs (more on surveys later in this chapter), causal research can be applied to data collection through the common use of experiment-based research. As posited before, the causal relationship needs to be stated carefully and examined scientifically, given that the causal scenario examined is clouded by the existence of other possible causes. Experimental research involves the systematic manipulation of a certain independent variable (IV), while controlling for others, to infer causality of the former variable in relation to the dependent variable (DV). If a number of variables are to be examined, changing one variable at a time and observing the results is a good way of inferring statistical causality to avoid having a complicated experiment. This latter approach is called a *true experiment*. It involves controlling for other variables that may affect the experiment, in addition to randomly selecting the study's respondents before randomly allocating them between the sampling groups. The statistical analyses that follow can help come up with findings that guide decision makers via evidence-based predictions and recommendations. This book offers only a brief introduction to experimental research, and further resources on the subject for advanced researchers are suggested in the Further Reading section towards the end of the chapter.

Quantitative Observations

As discussed in Chapter 8, observations are usually associated with the collection of qualitative data on user behaviour, processes and workflows as an unobtrusive technique that complements other data collection methods within an exploratory research design. Observations can take place in real-world contexts or in controlled environments. Usually observations are unstructured and the researcher is open to exploration and flexibly identifying elements in the observation setting in relation to the phenomenon under study, with no fixed pre-determined themes against which data are collected.

A **natural setting** is a research environment representing a real-life context, where, in the case of observational research, subjects are observed spontaneously and naturally (e.g. in a shop, on a train)

A **contrived setting** is an artificial research environment where the researcher creates the situation where data collection takes place, so it is a controlled environment (e.g. laboratory-based)

Within the realm of quantitative data collection, another approach is the use of quantitative *structured observations*. This method is still indirect as observations are made in a *natural* or *contrived* setting without approaching the observed subjects with any direct questions. It involves systematically recording specific pre-defined behavioural elements related to individuals, events or objects in the observation context, where it is usually possible to count the observed behaviours/elements and obtain quantifiable data.

Structured observations have a pre-requisite of the researcher being able to set forth clearly the behavioural elements to be observed, the associated measurements to be used and the structure with which they will be recorded during the observation. Examples include observing the number of people browsing a particular isle in a supermarket, the number of products they examine in detail before picking up their chosen one, and possibly the number of store personnel available at any given section in the store at a specific hour of the day. Along these lines, *mystery shopping* is a popular form of quantitative observational research where the researcher poses as a customer in a store but in this case interacts with the personnel there in the role of a normal customer, to observe behaviours and determine service quality level and customer satisfaction/dissatisfaction-related factors.

Benefits of using quantitative research

In social sciences generally, including business and marketing, quantitative-based studies are carried out extensively as a key approach to enhancing theoretical and applied knowledge. The systematic and methodical nature of this approach has many advantages, including:

1. Variables are clearly defined and built into a literature-based hypothesis, so there is a higher degree of certainty for the researcher in terms of the direction of the investigation; if the study is carried out in an orderly manner, there should be no deviation from the research's focal aim and key constructs.
2. The research methodology increases the level of objectivity and reduces the chance of researcher or respondent bias, and the sample's statistical errors can mostly be calculated and accounted for; the objective nature of quantitative research is enhanced by the maintained distance between the researcher and the participants due to the anonymity of the data collection and the large sample size.
3. The results tend to be more accurate given that standard and approved validity and reliability measures are conducted; the data collected is numerical and the statistical analysis takes the sample size and errors into consideration.
4. The large sample size characteristic of quantitative research entails data generalisation and representation based on collection from a sample properly representative of the population of interest (there will still remain some limitations to representation when non-probability sampling is applied).
5. The methodical nature and inherent reliability of quantitative research allow a duplication of the studies and comparability to take place, as well as allowing for a meta-analysis of related studies to be conducted over time (a quantitative analysis of findings from a number of systematically selected studies on a certain topic).

Constraints in the use of quantitative research

Despite having many advantages, quantitative research receives some critique due to a number of limitations perceived as integral to its use. Some of these are:

1. In pursuing objective inquiry into knowledge, the human element is deliberately removed; it hence disregards the human dimension of the subjects through the quantification of variables into numerical data. Any reflexivity of the research analysts is also eliminated in the process of seeking methodical objective knowledge, informed solely by statistical analysis, with any subjectivity viewed as a 'must-avoid' bias.
2. Only limited details can be provided about the behavioural depth, emotional attitudes and human perceptions of respondents when using quantitative research, as the structured methods applied cannot probe into these softer dimensions. Unlike qualitative research methods, probing deeper through asking further questions is not possible as quantitative research methods have pre-designed questions and are not designed to be responsive to the direction taken by the data collected.
3. The pre-determined nature of the set of alternatives provided as optional responses to the closed-ended questions on questionnaires to select from, may push respondents into limited choices and to disregard other options.

4. The context of the administration of the research method does not feature in planning the data collection setting and is not a consideration in data analysis; the setting is usually controlled in experiments and considered unimportant in survey questionnaires (e.g. if a respondent is completing a questionnaire at home, by phone or online, the data collection environment is not reflected on as a factor of influence).

Which method is optimal to use in a quantitative study?

A key characteristic in conducting quantitative research is that all aspects of the study are designed and planned before collecting data. As a researcher defines the research paradigm and design and then progresses onto further planning of the methodology, the question of which research method is best to use calls for a justified answer; you need to provide a rationale for any decision made. The choice of a suitable quantitative research method extends deep beyond a method's name; it entails implications related to possible access to the sample of the population to be studied, the specific administration technique to be applied and whether one method is adequate in addressing the research objectives or the study necessitates combined methods; and, if the latter, the appropriate sequence of method administration necessitates a coherent and systematic arrangement.

In simple terms, the criteria for which method(s) to choose for a particular quantitative study involve determining the following:

1. Which type of research design is involved? A quantitative methodology means the research design is conclusive, but whether it is a descriptive or causal design, or whether it has an explanatory dimension, is a key determinant of the data collection method, as explained earlier. For example, a survey is not a suitable method to resort to when causal relationships are investigated, such as a study that aims to determine whether free and satisfactory product trial causes repeat purchase of the same brand.
2. Following on from (1), the relationship between/among the variables under examination is the second detail to consider in determining which method to adopt. If the proposed relationship is one of association/correlation/difference, then a survey is a possible way forward. For example, in determining whether female high earners are more likely to purchase luxury products compared to male high earners, a survey targeted at the correct sample of respondents is an appropriate data collection method. If the hypothesised relationship, however, necessitates manipulation of the independent variables and a simultaneous assessment of parallel relationships (for instance, the influence of mediating factors such as having children as opposed to single high earners on the purchase of varying luxury items), then an experiment is the better data collection method to embrace. If the study is related to observing actual behavioural variables as they take place, rather than retrieving self-reported data from the subjects of the study, a quantitative observation is the optimal data collection method in this case.
3. Access to the sample of the population to be investigated in the research is another important consideration. This is given that some of the quantitative research methods are direct (i.e. the subjects of the research are directly requested to respond to research questions, such as in surveys) and some are indirect (i.e. data are collected from the subjects of the research indirectly without asking them to directly respond to questions in relation to the study, such as in observations, experiments or analysis of Big Data). Moreover, the location where the sample is accessed determines the method of data

collection; if the research question entails data that comprise behavioural dimensions taking place in natural settings (observations) or artificial settings (pre-set experimental research in a controlled environment), this is different than if the data can be collected anywhere the respondents are willing to provide it (different types of survey research are to be explored in the next section). Accordingly, the decision on which method to use depends on access to the research respondents, where the data needs to be collected, and the time available to reach the required sample size.

4. Whether one or more quantitative data collection method is required is an important decision; if sufficient literature exists with established data measurement scales for the variables involved in the study, then a survey can be used without the support of another data collection method. If, alternatively, insufficient information is available in existing studies in relation to the variables to be investigated, then the survey may be preceded by a quantitative observation, for example (see Chapter 5 for more details on multiple-method research); the latter supports the development of the survey through providing knowledge that, once synthesised with secondary data, can support in building the skeleton of the pre-determined response options of the questionnaire questions.
5. Following on from (3), if a survey is the selected method of data collection, the next decision concerns the optimal survey administration technique to employ.

This turns our attention to a review of types of survey research and a deeper probe into various aspects related to this quantitative method of data collection.

Ethics: Ethical Approval for Social Science Researchers

The world of conducting research now is alert to the importance of considering and dealing with ethical considerations from the outset of planning a study and till its completion. Ethical approval procedures and codes of conduct are established and continuously being updated by research organisations, agencies and HE institutions to ensure every researcher follows a consistent ethical process in carrying out any study.

Accordingly, the researcher needs to think early while designing a research plan about ethical issues that may arise and how they will be dealt with. In higher education, universities require researchers, whether staff or students at various levels, to seek ethical approval before any data are collected for a research study; research agencies establish, for any study, the ethical code of practice related to the domain in which the study will be carried out and will also have their ethical approval processes before any interaction with respondents or data.

Ethical approval papers involve completing a set of questions related to the context of the research and its target respondents; the objectives are to determine whether the respondents of a study are vulnerable, if they may be subjected to any deceitful practices during data collection, whether they will be made aware of the purpose of the study, how they are going to be recruited and how the researcher will safeguard them against any negative implications or consequences of the study.

The ethical approval papers will thus include an information sheet which will be provided to respondents prior to data collection so that they are made aware of the research aim; a consent form also needs to be developed by the researcher and signed off by each participant in the study where they give permission to take part in whatever procedures the study involves (it may be consenting to recording an interview, to using their data for the study and beyond, to accepting it is anonymous and confidential, etc.).

(Continued)

(Continued)

Furthermore, an important element of the ethical approval process is ensuring that the participants are not subjected to any physical or emotional dangers or risks in taking part in the study, and ensuring that proper guidance and support are provided. Research subjects need to be aware of and agree to how the data collection procedures will be carried out and how the information generated will be used, stored and reported. Reassuring subjects of the confidentiality of the data they provide and its anonymity can make the difference between their consenting to participate or not, and also makes a difference between a study being ethical or unethical in implementing it practically; any promises made on the information sheet or the consent form are binding and the researcher(s) involved should abide by the code of conduct of the particular industry/sector within which the study is carried out.

An exit option and procedures should also be made clear and available to the study's respondents/participants; in other words, the latter should be aware from the onset that taking part in data collection is voluntary and that they have the right to stop or withdraw at any point, should they wish to. If they are completing an online survey, instructions about how to exit if they wish to should be made clear in the information sheet or in the introduction section of the questionnaire form.

More information on research ethics for social scientists can be found at www.ethicsguidebook.ac.uk

Survey Research Method: An Example

As one of the most commonly used methods of enquiry, this section will focus on survey methods by looking at types of surveys, questionnaire administration techniques and how to build questionnaires. The type of survey used in a study depends on its key research question and objectives, i.e. what data the study seeks to collect, the target audience from whom sample respondents will be drawn and their accessibility and availability, and the associated data collection costs.

Survey typology

Surveys can be classified into two main types: cross-sectional and longitudinal.

Cross-sectional surveys take place at a given point in time, where data collected represents a snapshot description or explanation of the phenomenon under study for the respondents at a given time. One questionnaire is developed and it can be used to collect data from one or more target samples at that point in time. This can also work well for comparative studies in international marketing research where more than one country is under study and the same questionnaire is administered to a sample in each of the countries. The survey may be repeated again for new samples at another point in time, but comparability will be limited as the sample units are not the same.

For example, if Samsung launches a new tablet and conducts survey research to identify consumer perceptions of it directly after its launch, this is a cross-sectional study that can be conducted on one or more samples simultaneously. If Samsung conducts the survey research again by administering the same questionnaire six months later using new samples representing its target audience, it will provide insights into generally evolving perceptions of the target audience over time. However, the results do not represent the changing perceptions of the same consumers as the sample(s) that completed the questionnaire the first time round is/are different to those in the second administration. If the survey is carried out only once, this is a special type of cross-sectional survey called the *ad hoc survey*. For example, if Skoda is facing a decline in sales in Egypt, it may decide to carry out ad hoc survey research there to find out at that point in time whether there is a decline in its brand image among its target consumers through a cross-sectional study.

Longitudinal survey methods can be used if the research objectives entail the collection of data on multiple occasions across multiple time periods to track alterations in behaviour or identify a change in attitudes or opinions, for example. This type of survey assists in obtaining repeated observations on the study's variables for the same sample units across time, thus turning the snapshot of cross-sectional research into a picture in motion as the same respondents are studied over time. It overcomes the problem of limited comparability in cross-sectional surveys, as the sample of respondents does not change. There are different forms of longitudinal studies, such as individual studies, panel surveys and cohort studies.

Individual studies are the simplest form, where a sample of individuals is surveyed at different points in time to track their attitudinal, opinion or behavioural changes over time. Panel surveys are very common and they involve recruiting groups of respondents who agree to provide data to the researcher continuously, frequently or intermittently at agreed intervals. A very common type is household panel surveys where the members involved are followed and data are collected from them over agreed intervals (such as the British Household Panel Survey [BHPS], carried out annually by the Institute of Social and Economic Research at the University of Essex). Those who are invited to the panels are profiled based on a number of questions, so that their characteristics (such as demographics, usage and attitudes, lifestyle, habits, values, preferences) can allow for proper targeting of the survey questionnaires. Those who agree to be part of the panel commit to providing data over an extended time period in return for rewards, such as monetary compensation, gifts, shopping vouchers or promotional coupons. Cohort studies are those where customers belonging to certain age groups are surveyed to track certain changes related to consumption attitudes, perceptions and/or behaviours as they age (e.g. as they move along the family life cycle from parenthood to post-parenthood or from one life stage to another, such as from provisional adulthood to first adulthood).

Examples of research questions that can be addressed through longitudinal surveys are: 'What is the influence of a celebrity endorsement campaign on consumer attitude towards a product over time, from its launch till six months after it ends?'; 'How did consumers' endorsement of electric cars change usage patterns and choices of automotive brands/models over a set number of years?'; and 'How does getting trial-free vouchers for shopping on a brand's online store influence teenagers' subsequent browsing and online shopping behaviour?'.

Theoretically, the essence of longitudinal studies is that there is no replacement of subjects in the panel so the same subjects are surveyed over time. However, problems occur when some members of the panel drop out due to moving location, loss of interest in cooperating/participating and/or mortality. These members may need replacement and can affect the smooth continuity of the data collection. The reduced response rate along the waves of the survey administration, for example between the first wave of conducting it and the fourth wave, is referred to as *panel attrition*. Conditioning of panel members can also become a problem as their behaviour and responses may be affected by having been on the panel for some time, thus leading to response bias where responses in later waves are coloured by experience in the early waves of the survey; this is referred to as *panel conditioning*. If new members join, there can also be discrepancy in the data between established members and new joiners, till the latter overcome the novelty factor.

Advanced: Challenges and Opportunities in Quantitative Research

Conducting quantitative research involves a number of stages which can become more complex in conducting research in international markets. Data collection procedures may differ as ethical considerations vary across cultures and countries; access to large samples can require different routes and approaches to reach a sample of female consumers in Saudi Arabia vis-à-vis Germany, for example (Saudi Arabia being a highly conservative culture where there are many restrictions on females mixing or dealing with males). Conducting research online can enable easier access and reach but it has its own challenges as the researcher needs to reduce the sampling errors and sample bias that result when some respondents who complete the questionnaire are not part of the sampling frame.

Moreover, in a digital age, use of mobile devices and smart phones can assist researchers in collecting large samples of quantitative data and in analysing it using advanced analysis software. Given that consumers are becoming more tech-savvy and search for products and services across multiple devices, data analytics and large-scale surveys can be used by marketing research and intelligence companies to analyse consumers' search behaviour and report back to decision makers, such as insurance companies, telecommunications providers and entertainment firms.

It is also possible for researchers to access survey responses through providers, such as Survey Monkey Audience, who have respondent banks that can become a 'targeted audience' depending on the targeting criteria of the research. Targeted audiences constitute respondents who become part of global contributing networks by voluntarily signing up with their profiles so that they can be invited to take part in surveys as needed and when they match the sample frame for a survey study (help.surveymonkey.com).

Questionnaire administration methods

In operationalising the survey methodology into a questionnaire, the key purpose is to translate the research objectives and the variables to be investigated into a set of questions that respondents can answer. These questions should inspire respondent co-operation by being specific, clear and at a language level that the research subjects can comprehend. At the backdrop, the questions should aim to minimise response error in providing the answers and in recording them. Given that the survey research method involves obtaining information by posing direct questions to a sample of the population of interest, this questioning can take place in writing, verbally or via the use of computers and technology. Depending on a number of factors, including the budgeted cost set for data collection, the time available and the required speed of data collection, the accessibility of the target sample and the accepted level of non-response, the researcher can choose from a number of methods, typified as:

- face-to-face questionnaires
- telephone-administered questionnaires
- self-completion/postal questionnaires
- web-based questionnaires (also known as online surveys or e-mail surveys).

Face-to-face questionnaires are conducted in person as the researcher asks the respondent the prepared questions, offering the pre-determined options, and then records the responses on paper, or on a device such as a computer or tablet (computer-assisted personal interviews [CAPI] is a term used to refer to paperless recording of face-to-face survey questions). Unlike

Figure 12.2 Considerations in deciding questionnaire administration methods

personal interviews, the researcher does not probe further based on the responses and is not supposed to clarify the questions to avoid interviewer bias (which is why structured surveys should have very clear, specific and pre-tested questions). There are advantages and disadvantages associated with personal administration, as with all other types. In terms of the positives, the respondent has control over who completes the survey and the context in which it is completed, ensures a response is provided for each question and can achieve high response rates. It is also suitable for complex topics as the researcher can explain the topic, or show any probes or images as part of the process, and the aim of the survey can be objectively explained prior to questionnaire completion. The disadvantages, however, include the high financial and time cost associated with a large sample size, especially if other researchers need to be trained to administer it to target respondents. Also, any clarification of questions by the administrator can pose interviewer bias; this is why face-to-face is considered the most personal form of conducting a survey.

Telephone questionnaires are administered by calling respondents using a database of phone numbers (which are usually residence-based and taken from local telephone directories) and asking them if they wish to take the survey. The respondent asks each question in sequence, offers the optional responses and waits for respondents' answers to record them. In the past, this recording took place on paper, but now it is usually computer-assisted using specialised software. This is referred to as computer-assisted telephone interviews (CATI). One advantage of telephone-administered surveys is that they are less expensive than face-to-face interviews, particularly given that there is a time saving and a large sample can be reached. Interviewer bias can be less as well, though voice impressions may remain a potential response bias if researchers are not careful. The negatives, however, are an inability to access respondents as people are more reluctant to answer survey calls, perceiving them as 'sales calls' or 'junk calls', and it may be difficult to control the sample as the person answering the call in the household might not be the target respondent. There is also the issue of the inaccuracy of telephone directories, in terms of missing out on some numbers or recording incorrect numbers. The questionnaire usually has to be short, otherwise people may lose interest and hang up.

Self-completion questionnaires are usually given out to respondents to complete at their own convenience and then give/send back to the researcher. It can be context-controlled, such as giving out the questionnaires to respondents at a café or restaurant and giving them the chance to complete and give them back there and then. In this case, the questionnaire needs to be short and respondents may need an incentive to encourage self-completion. One form of self-completion survey is the postal survey. In this case, the questionnaire is sent in the mail, asking respondents to complete it and send it back in the enclosed prepaid envelope. One advantage of postal surveys is that a large number of them can be sent out, though the response rate is usually low. Interviewer bias is removed, with a chance still to send probes in the form of visuals. As respondents complete the survey at their own convenience, the environment is not controlled and the target respondent in the household may not be reached. The questionnaire should be simple, clear and short, with an incentive to encourage not only completion of it but also the extra step of putting it in the post.

Web-based questionnaires are referred to as *online surveys* or *e-mail surveys*. These are very popular forms of survey administration in the new digital era. Online surveys are administered via the web, where respondents access a link on social media, on a company's website or on other forums online and the link connects them to a web set-up where the questions are administered sequentially. In e-mail surveys, the link is sent direct to respondents' e-mail accounts based on a researcher-accessible database of names and e-mail addresses, accompanied by an invitation to open it and take part in the survey. However, a sampling frame, constituting a list of e-mail addresses for the population of interest, is needed from which to draw a sample that will be e-mailed. In the case of either type of web-based questionnaire, the respondent answers each question by clicking the suitable response options or completing short questions. The researcher can tailor the application used to the question numbers and types, and modify its features such that a respondent does not move from a question to the next till a response is given (which guarantees that all questions are completed), or otherwise allow it to be flexible. Also, researchers can use 'Skip Logic' in web-based questionnaires where researchers can change the path respondents take by routing them to skip certain questions/pages and to go to specific ones based on their response to particular branching questions; this is also referred to as survey routing or branching.

The advantage of online surveys is that you can reach a large sample of respondents, regardless of their location, at a very low cost and especially where they are more likely to respond given heavy use of the web and technological devices. The application used for web-based questionnaires is usually user-friendly, systematic and easily tailored by the researcher. The disadvantage of online surveys is that there is less control over who takes part in the survey, so filter questions must be placed at the start (together with an introduction to clarify the aim of the survey and who should participate) to ensure compliance with the target sample characteristics; however, this filtering attempt is not always airtight (i.e. there is a risk that some respondents will take part who are not representative of the population of interest). An incentive for completion enhances participation, an example of which is offering respondents the opportunity to access the survey results after the survey is closed and the data are analysed; this incentive appeals mainly to those for whom the research topic is of interest. Another incentive is the chance to participate in a prize draw on completion;

however, this poses the risk of losing anonymity as respondents who want to take part in the prize draw have to enter their e-mail address, hence identifying themselves. Some may not be willing to do so, which weakens the value of the incentive. If the questionnaire is too long, respondents may drop out midway which can also happen if they lose interest or get distracted given that there is no context control.

E-mail surveys are sent to user accounts and hence target the sample of interest, and this may also encourage respondents to 'take it personally' and respond to the survey invitation by clicking on the link and answering the questions. Disadvantages of e-mail surveys are that the database may have errors, hence some e-mail addresses may be incorrect, and respondents may not respond if they feel their privacy is invaded when they receive the e-mail on their private account, or consider it 'junk mail'. Technically, the e-mail may itself get directed to the 'junk mail' folder of the respondent's e-mail account since it is coming from an unknown sender based on security settings, and therefore fails to get noticed in the first place. The lack of anonymity in the use of e-mail questionnaires may raise ethical concerns, although in most instances once respondents click the link and are directed to the survey, the researcher may be said to have brought it back to the confines of anonymity. Table 12.1 provides a summary of the various features of different methods of questionnaire administration.

Table 12.1 Features of different methods of questionnaire administration

Feature	Face-to-Face	Mail	Telephone	Web-based (online or e-mail)
Control over who completes the questions	Highest	Least	Some	Some (through filter questions)
Suitability for complex questions	Best suitable	Least suitable	Somewhat suitable	Less suitable
Cost	Usually highest	Relatively low (can increase if reminders are needed to increase response rate)	Lower than face-to-face	Lowest
Respondent ability to complete at own convenience	Least	Highest	Some (if pre-arranged)	High
Context control	Highest	Lowest	Low	Low
Researcher bias	Greatest chance	None	Some (possibility caused by voice inflection)	None
Respondent's bias	Least chance	Highest chance	Minimal chance	High chance
Use of visual aids	Best chance	Some chance	No chance	Some chance

(Continued)

Table 12.1 (Continued)

Feature	Face-to-Face	Mail	Telephone	Web-based (online or e-mail)
Cause of negative respondent reaction	Invasion of personal space and time	Perception as 'junk mail'	Perception as imposing 'sales call'	Invasion of online privacy
Time interval between soliciting and receiving response	Low (depending on sample size and geographic coverage)	Greatest	Least	Some (depending on effectiveness of reminders)
Response rate	High	Least	Low	It depends on interest level, incentive (and online location of the survey link)
Potential for collecting unusable responses	Lowest	High	Low	Relatively high
Need for research skills in administration	Most	Least	Medium	Low (mainly linked with planning logic and dynamic sequence)

Reflective Activity: Approaches to Questionnaire Administration

Working in pairs, discuss the following scenarios where a survey has been determined as the suitable research method of choice. What is the optimal and most appropriate method of questionnaire administration in each case, and why?

- A survey will be launched to collect data to describe consumer perceptions of ethnic group representation in mainstream advertising in the UK through a comparative study of two ethnic minority groups: Asians and Arabs in the age bracket of 25–45 who are resident in the West Midlands region.
- Apple decides to carry out a survey-based study of retailers' opinions on the diffusion rate of the iPad Air 2 since its launch in the Greater London region within non-Apple stores.
- Worcestershire Council for Voluntary Youth Services (WCVYS) needs to commission survey research to determine whether there is a need to provide consulting and training services to service providers dealing with children and/or youth (e.g. taxi firms, restaurants, leisure services, hotels) in relation to safeguarding policies.

Chapter Summary

This chapter was the second in a series of four chapters under Part IV, covering quantitative research in marketing. After discussing hypothesis formulation and testing in detail in Chapter 11, this chapter discussed quantitative research designs and methods, with a particular focus on the use of survey methods.

Furthermore, it explored and discussed quantitative research designs, methodology and methods. It provided a rationale for choosing a quantitative approach to conducting research and presented the possible advantages and disadvantages of taking such a path. It described and explained different types of quantitative data collection techniques, with a particular focus on the survey research methodology. Survey typologies and administration techniques were also visited, looking at the pros and cons of the various approaches to questionnaire administration. Questionnaire development was discussed at the end of the chapter, paving the way for further reflection on questionnaire design and the descriptive statistical analysis of survey data which will be covered in the next chapter.

Case Study: Skoda Auto – Value Perceptions and Cultural Variability

With its headquarters in the Czech Republic, Skoda Auto is one of the top five car manufacturers. It became a wholly owned subsidiary of the Volkswagen group in 1990. Prior to this, Skoda struggled in certain regions as its sales did not pick up or even declined. Customer perceptions of the technology it used, relative to other Western brands, were also not very positive. To secure an international competitive future, Skoda formed a joint venture with the Volkswagen group to become its fourth brand after Volkswagen, Audi and Seat.

Car manufacturers are currently facing challenges in maintaining and expanding their market share as developed markets are saturating; yet demand continues to grow in emerging markets. Automotive market demand was projected to grow by 3.2% in developed markets in 2014–17, while growth in developing markets is anticipated at 15.2% (McKinsey, 2014).

Although trade barriers have fallen and access to global markets has increased, it remains a challenge for organisations to successfully enter foreign markets. Many organisations have failed to transfer their success in existing markets to new markets and this is true in the case of Skoda. The company enjoys relatively large market share in some markets and relatively small market share in others, for instance 3% in Europe but only 0.5% in the Middle East.

In 2013, Skoda enjoyed worldwide sales of just over 1 million vehicles and overall profits increased on the previous year by 14%. Success has not, however, been replicated in some regions, such as the Middle East where sales growth remains relatively low at just 2.5% in 2013. In 2014, Skoda published its annual report with details of its upcoming 'Go East' strategy, wherein the company set out a clear aim to penetrate the markets of the Middle and Far East in 2014–2020. The United Arab Emirates was identified as a hub for growth and development in the Middle East, while China was identified as the growth centre for the Far East.

Skoda's success in maintaining its progressive presence in the various markets calls for marketing research of the specific value perceptions of target segments in each of its existing and new markets. With increasing opportunities in new markets, it is important for Skoda to develop a greater understanding of the consumer value perceptions that shape and form brand image in different regional or country contexts. This is given that value perceptions relate to brand image and preferences. The study can build on existing exploratory studies and market reports on the automotive sector, consumer motivation and associated value perceptions (Aaker and McLaughlin, 2007).

Case study questions:

1. Would you use a quantitative research methodology if commissioned by Skoda to carry out the above study? Justify your choice.
2. Identify the research design suitable for carrying out this marketing research study for Skoda, providing a rationale for it.

(Continued)

(Continued)

3. Which research method may be used for data collection – A survey, an experiment, an observation or combined methods? Why?
4. How would you administer the data collection tool – Face-to-face, by phone, by mail or online? Why? What would be the pros and cons associated with the chosen method of administration?
5. If, as the marketing researcher for Skoda, you decided to carry out a survey of the target market in China and the UAE, think of five questions that could be included on the questionnaire.
6. Advanced readers: Would you use the same questionnaire in China and the UAE, or are there key considerations and differences that you need to think about/adapt for each market?

End of Chapter Questions

These questions should help you reflect on your understanding of this chapter:

1. What is quantitative marketing research?
2. What are the different types of quantitative research design?
3. What are the different research methods that may be used within a quantitative research methodology?
4. When would a researcher opt for a quantitative study, and what are the benefits of quantitative research?
5. What are different questionnaire administration techniques, and what are their advantages and disadvantages?

Checklist

After studying Chapter 12, you should now be familiar with these key concepts:

1. The key features of quantitative research and how it differs from qualitative research
2. Types of quantitative research design
3. When to undertake quantitative research studies
4. Benefits and constraints in using quantitative research methodology
5. Key research methods that may be used in quantitative data collection and deciding on the optimal quantitative research method to use in a study
6. A survey typology, characteristics of different types of surveys and alternative questionnaire administration methods available to researchers

Further Reading (in sequence from beginners to advanced)

Lietz, P. (2010) Research into questionnaire design: a summary of the literature. *International Journal of Market Research*, 52 (2), pp. 249–74.

Carefoot, J. L. (1993) Modeling and experimental designs in marketing research: uses and misuses. *Marketing News*, 27 (12), p. H19.

Webb, J. (2000) Questionnaires and their design. *Marketing Review*, 1, pp. 197–218.

Betts, P. and Lound, C. (2010) The application of alternative modes of data collection in UK government social surveys. Office for National Statistics. Ref. SMB 67 9/10. [Online] Available at: www.ons.gov.uk/ons/guide-method/method-quality/general-methodology/data-collection-methodology/reports-and-publications/alternative-modes-of-data-collection/index.html [accessed 16 December 2016].

Institute of Education (n.d.) *The Research Ethics Guidebook: A Resource for Social Scientists.* London: IOE. Available at: www.ethicsguidebook.ac.uk

Yu, J. and Cooper, H. (1983) A quantitative review of research design effects on response rates to questionnaires. *Journal of Marketing Research*, 20, pp. 36–44.

Wilson, A. and Laskey, N. (2003) Internet based marketing research: a serious alternative to traditional research methods? *Marketing Intelligence & Planning*, 21 (2), pp. 79–84.

Bibliography

Aaker, D. A. and McLaughlin, D. (2007) *Strategic Market Management*, pp. 225–45. Chichester: John Wiley & Sons.

Grow Wild (2016) About us: the faces behind the food. Available at: www.growwild.co.uk/about

McKinsey (2014) The road to 2020 and beyond: what's driving the global automotive industry? Available at: www.mckinsey.com/client_service/automotive_and_assembly

Maxwell, J. A. and Mitapalli, K. (2008) Explanatory research. In L. M. Given (ed.), *The SAGE Encyclopedia of Qualitative Research Methods.* Thousand Oaks, CA: Sage Publications.

Sheikh, S. and Beise-Zee, R. (2011) Corporate social responsibility or cause-related marketing? The role of cause specificity of CSR. *Journal of Consumer Marketing*, 28 (1), pp. 27–39.

Skoda (2014) The history of Skoda: over 100 years of getting people from A to B. [Online] Available at: www.skoda.co.uk/skoda-history

Skoda Auto (2014) Skoda Auto homepage. [Online] Available at: www.skoda-auto.com

Skoda Auto UAE (2014) Skoda UAE homepage. [Online] Available at: www.skoda-auto.ae

SurveyMonkey (n.d.) SurveyMonkey audience for academics. [Online] Available at: http://help.surveymonkey.com/articles/en_US/kb/How-do-Academics-use-SurveyMonkey-Audience

Sustainable Brands (2014) The widening attitude/behavior gap: the curse of an improving economy? *Behavioral Change, Sustainable Brand Issue in Focus*, 30 July. [Online] Available at: www.sustainablebrands.com/news_and_views/behavior_change/sustainable_brands/widening_attitudebehavior_gap_curse_improving_econ

Torjusen, H., Lieblein, G., Wandel, M. and Francis, C. A. (2001) Food system orientation and quality perception among consumers and producers of organic food in Hedmark County, Norway. *Food Quality and Preference*, 12, pp. 207–16.

Find journal articles and multiple choice questions online at: **https://study.sagepub.com/benzo** to support what you've learnt so far.

CHAPTER 13

Questionnaire Design and Data Preparation for Analysis

LEARNING OBJECTIVES

The key learning objectives of this chapter are:

1. To discuss questionnaire design
2. To explore aspects of questionnaire development, measurement instruments and techniques
3. To identify dos and don'ts in building questionnaires
4. To learn how to prepare the data collected for preliminary analysis

KEY CONCEPTS

By the end of this chapter, the reader should be familiar with the following concepts:

1. Questionnaire design considerations
2. Questionnaire development process
3. Measurement instruments and techniques
4. Selecting measurement scales
5. Pitfalls and guidelines in questionnaire structures
6. Data preparation and organisation
7. Data cleaning and coding for analysis

Marwa G. Mohsen

Introduction

After exploring quantitative research design, approaches and methods, this chapter takes the discussion of using survey research for data collection into more detail. Marketing research using surveys is very common and yields reliable and valid results in as far as the development of the survey is valid and reliable. In market research, survey data inform decision makers in relation to advertising strategies, branding, new product development, customer satisfaction, and so on. As the tool of administering surveys, a questionnaire involves a number of considerations in planning and development; its structure, organisation, wording and administration influence not only the quality of the data generated, but also the number of completed responses retrieved.

A food retailer seeking an understanding of consumer perceptions of the quality of its groceries can conduct a survey with customers visiting its stores using a short questionnaire; the survey can be undertaken on the shop floor by trained researchers who accompany customers as they shop to complete the survey in person, or it can be e-mailed to customers via a loyalty club membership. Questionnaire design and development is not straightforward as the right questions need to be asked in the right way of targeted respondents, and the questionnaire should aim to reach the right respondents to ensure its validity. The key purpose of developing a survey questionnaire is to obtain raw information from participants – i.e. data – which is then organised, 'cleaned' and analysed, with the aim of making sense of the data and providing information that can aid decision makers.

A questionnaire can be very efficient in its design and structure, but it can be ineffective in answering the research question if its measurement scales are mismatched with the research variables it intends to measure; in this case, the usefulness of the data collected in meeting the research aims can be questionable. For instance, a survey of consumer satisfaction with banking services that asks questions related to customer needs for new service offerings may fail to assess customer evaluation of current service provision; hence, the data collected may provide beneficial findings in respect of new banking product launches but miss the mark in providing the information originally sought in conducting the study, i.e. customer satisfaction with the existing service!

The structure of the questions in terms of sequence, logic and flow is a key ingredient of an efficacious questionnaire. Moreover, the choice of question types is an important consideration that has to be linked closely with the research objectives and hypotheses. The analysis strategy and techniques should be planned hand-in-hand with question formulation at an early stage rather than as a post-data collection endeavour. It is worth noting that there is no 'perfect' or ideal questionnaire, but there are a number of quality considerations to make in terms of design to make it optimal. Following survey completion, the data collected go through a number of preparatory steps before in-depth analysis can take place; this partially involves summarising the data using descriptive statistics, as will be discussed in detail in the second part of this chapter.

Snapshot: Setting the Scene – IKEA: Changing a Business Model in Response to Customer Feedback

With big stores and a café renowned for Swedish meatballs, IKEA has become a successful brand in many countries around Europe and the Middle East. However, 18 remote stores in the UK are insufficient to serve high customer demand for convenience and accessibility. Having to travel long hours to spend a day at IKEA is worth it for some, but it can't be a trip frequently taken and customers may tire of having to find the time for it. The open areas and large amounts of space needed for the IKEA business showroom model mean the stores are not in town centres but rather in way-out locations.

To find out how customers perceive IKEA store locations and satisfaction with the shopping channels on offer, a survey was launched to find out whether customers perceive IKEA as conveniently accessible, how often they would be likely to buy from it if there were more stores in town centres, and whether shopping online through 'order and collect' options would increase their likelihood of shopping at IKEA and raise the frequency of purchase. The survey findings reflected consumer frustrations regarding the current distant locations and the need for closer IKEA stores. IKEA hence decided to open smaller stores in more accessible locations, some of which might be in high street sites. They would then include less furniture on display, with more click-to-collect facilities.

What are important considerations in designing the IKEA location satisfaction questionnaire?

1. First, it has to account for the purpose of carrying it out: the study's aim and objectives. So, it should ask the right questions. Moreover, key decisions should be made about the specific sample of respondents who are likely to complete it and how it will be administered.
2. Questions posed should be easy to understand and respond to with a smooth flow. Also, the structure and length should be appropriate to its method of administration; for instance, a respondent intercepted outside an IKEA store or in town will not usually have lots of time to offer a researcher if they agree to take part in the survey, as opposed to a respondent receiving the questionnaire in the post. The questionnaire needs to be structured in a way that eases subsequent data entry.

Nowadays, technology via online survey software such as Qualtrics and Survey Monkey allows for survey administration online via user-friendly and guided tools for design, administration and data analysis. Hence, researchers and companies no longer need professional research agencies to carry out online surveys on their behalf.

Questionnaire Design

The development of questionnaires as the execution tool of surveys is principally driven by the research objectives and conceptual rationale. The focal purpose of any questionnaire is to collect data to address the relationships or differences between/among variables posed in the objectives and to find answers that assist in the systematic examination of proposed hypotheses. Thus, the research data needed are translated into a specific set of questions posed to target respondents in a way they can understand and ably respond to.

It is of essence, when developing each of the questions, to stay on track and for the purpose of the question and the research objective(s) it attempts to address to be kept in mind and threaded through the different parts of the questionnaire. Good practice for researchers is to start a *code book* at an early stage of designing the questionnaire to ensure each item is clearly linked to the specific research objective(s)/question(s) that it is aiming to speak for. The code book of the study archives

A **code book** is a reference book where the questionnaire content and variables are assembled and recorded, and the data coding instructions and data codes associated with the data file are documented. It can also provide a record of the virtual lines running between the questions on the questionnaire and the related variables/relationships being measured

all questions, their sequence, the research variables, the tested relationships and the question routes that different respondents may follow (see Skip Logic under the Measurement Instruments and Techniques section). Thus, it helps keep a record of the detailed parts of the questionnaire, including the coded names of the variables used, which will be used later in the analysis. In summary, the code book serves as a crucial internal document for the researcher to keep the data assembly phase directed, organised and documented.

Primary tips for questionnaire design

A key tip in the design stage is keeping the questionnaire focused and as simple and short as optimally needed; including questions that are not relevant to the research objectives or hypotheses will only elongate the time taken to complete it and respondents may get bored and drop out. For instance, if only age and gender are the classification variables being examined in the study, there is no need to ask respondents questions about social class and profession under the personal questions section just because 'most surveys do'. On the other hand, excluding questions that are core to the study means that the research will have incomplete findings, and the missed data cannot be retrieved afterwards. So, if social status or presence of children in the household is a significant variable in the study, questions about them should be included in the questionnaire.

Questionnaire Organisation

A questionnaire is customarily organised into sections. At the forefront, a short introduction paragraph is provided to give respondents an idea of what the survey is about, its purpose and who the beneficiary (ies) of the data collected is/are. The ethical issue of data confidentiality is usually stated in this summary to address any such concerns for respondents from early on. It is good practice at this point to note to respondents that the data collected is anonymous and will only be used for the stated research purposes. An estimated duration for the completion of the questionnaire – in minutes, based on trialling it prior to full administration – offers a sense of its length and the time one would commit in consenting to taking part (e.g. 'This questionnaire takes 10 minutes to complete').

A good questionnaire adopts the funnel approach (Smith, n.d.) in organising the questions, such that they start from the general and then swiftly move to the specific, with a proper organisation of the topics of query. It then concludes with the more 'threatening' demographic questions of age, gender, social class, income level, level of education, and so on, after rapport has been established with the respondents. Hence, it is best to keep these personal questions to the last section of the questionnaire. A note at that point to respondents that these background questions are only posed to better understand the aggregate data and will not be used to identify individual respondents can help alleviate any concerns and encourage honest answers. A good tip is to start with the easier questions first and move on to the harder later. Respondents need to move easily through the questions in a logical flow that does not make them pause and feel uncomfortable as they complete the questionnaire; otherwise, there is a risk of quitting or providing incomplete/arbitrary responses.

Level of Structure

In terms of level of structure, surveys can be *structured* or *semi-structured*. Surveys are *structured* when the questionnaire is composed of questions that are pre-arranged in a systematic order which all respondents follow, with mostly *closed-ended questions*; this refers to questions that either have a single numerical answer that respondents provide (e.g. 'How many times a month do you buy organic foods?') or questions that are followed by fixed and pre-determined response alternatives (see examples in the next Research in Practice box). The instructions that accompany each question guide the respondent to select from the pre-set answer options; the options are drawn from existing literature and/or a preliminary exploratory study that precedes the quantitative study.

Closed-ended questions are fixed-option questions where the possible responses to a question are pre-determined and set for respondents to select one or more based on the question instructions

Open-ended questions are questions where the respondents are allowed to provide their own responses by writing their answers in the blank space provided

On the other hand, a survey may be *semi-structured* when it is composed of a mixed set of both closed-ended and open-ended questions; *open-ended questions* are those where respondents are provided with a blank space and are requested to formulate their own short answers and write them down. They can be a question on their own or part of a closed-ended question where the last option is: 'If other, please specify', which allows respondents to put forth their response if it is not in the pre-determined list of alternatives. In this case, the question enables diverse responses that respondents may come up with from 'outside the box'. Also, an open-ended question may follow up on a closed-ended question, where respondents are asked to provide more details in their own words; for instance, 'If your answer to the previous question is YES, please explain why/how so'.

Open-Ended Versus Closed-Ended Questions

The use of a mix of closed-ended and open-ended questions in semi-structured form varies in proportion across questionnaires. Some questionnaires are mostly based on closed-ended questions which are structured with literature-grounded response alternatives; only a few open-ended questions may be included to support them. In other questionnaires, there might be more use of open-ended questions that stand on their own to probe certain areas and bring out undetermined themes. Given that we are here considering quantitative research designs that follow a positivist philosophical approach relying on objective numerical data, the use of open-ended questions is best kept to a minimum and should only be used in support of the closed-ended questions. Too many open-ended questions turn the survey into an interview, which in turn can confuse the research design and methodology. Thus, reducing open-ended questions keeps the analysis process simple and keeps the research design as originally planned.

Research in Practice

In a semi-structured, large-scale survey investigating the speed of consumer adoption of organic food as a healthier eating option, a sample of the target population was asked to take part in survey research. The survey took place in the UK where the questionnaire was sent to target respondents in the post; they were asked to complete it at their own convenience and to send back the completed forms in the pre-paid envelopes provided.

(Continued)

(Continued)

- Examples of closed-ended questions in the questionnaire:

Q1. How important is each of the following benefits to you in consuming organic food? *Please circle ONE point for each benefit along the scale provided*:

	Very Important						Not at all Important
Enjoying the taste	1	2	3	4	5	6	7
Benefiting from safer food	1	2	3	4	5	6	7
Bettering the future health of me/my family	1	2	3	4	5	6	7
Supporting environmental welfare	1	2	3	4	5	6	7
Gaining a better long-term nutritional value	1	2	3	4	5	6	7
Supporting animal welfare	1	2	3	4	5	6	7

Q2. Which organic food(s) have you *previously* tried? *Please tick ALL those that apply*:

☐ Vegetables ☐ Fruits ☐ Tea or Coffee ☐ Milk

☐ Juices ☐ Eggs ☐ Meat

☐ None

- Examples of open-ended questions in the questionnaire – the last option in Q3 and Q4 below:

Q3. Having tried organic food, I decided to... *Please tick one or more statements that apply to you*:

☐ adopt organic foods fully into my routine grocery shopping.

☐ buy certain organic foods a lot more frequently.

☐ buy certain organic foods only very occasionally.

☐ try other organic foods that I have not tried before.

☐ never buy organic foods again.

☐ Other (please specify) ______________________

Q4. Why did you make this specific decision? *Please provide your answer here*:

____

____

Types of Research Variables

Formulating research questions based on a critical literature review that focuses the investigation on specific variables is a substantial step in addressing these questions within a given study; this consistently flows from the aim and objectives, and then the hypotheses. In subsequently building a survey, it becomes imperative to use the correct questions that gauge what you specifically set out to measure. This way, the questionnaire minimises the *response error*; a response error refers to the inaccuracy that arises when respondents provide incorrect responses (e.g. when the wording of the questions are vague or there are unclear terms/jargon used with no definition provided) or when the responses are inaccurately recorded. Before discussing how to measure variables, it is important to first explore the basic types of research variables.

Dependent and independent variables

For every hypothesis developed, whether it is one of correlation, difference or causation, there are two key variables under study: a variable that is proposed as doing the effect and a variable that is hypothesised as being possibly affected by it. The variable that is manipulated to determine whether varying it will make an effect on some other variable(s) is the *independent* variable, whereas the variable on which the effect is being observed is the *dependent* variable.

In research aiming at determining the influence of the use of technology-based learning on student satisfaction with a business management course, the dependent variable is student satisfaction whilst the technology-based learning factor is the independent, or the *predictor*, variable. In this case, as the researcher, you can undertake an experiment where you may teach a class session using the traditional lecture teaching practices, without the use of technology-based learning tools, and then teach another session using technology-based learning methods. Collecting data from the students after both sessions and comparing the resulting levels of student satisfaction can determine whether a correlation exists between the two variables, and, if so, can identify its strength and maybe also the power of technology-based learning in predicting student satisfaction. Hence, varying the independent variable can help determine the possible effect on the dependent variable so that the tested hypothesis is supported or dismissed.

Control, extraneous and confounding variables

Linked to the above example, you need to determine the predictive power of the technology-based learning as the independent variable for the same level of students. If the technology-based learning class is given to postgraduate students whilst the traditional lecture is given to undergraduate students, the student level and stage of learning development may influence the results. Thus, you must keep the variable 'student UG/PG level' controlled as it is an extraneous variable that is not being examined in the study at this point. It becomes a *control* variable in this case, where the researcher keeps it constant by administering both approaches to teaching and learning at just one level – undergraduates only or postgraduates only. The study can be duplicated for the other level, but both comparative class approaches have to be done for each group. A control variable is also known as a *covariate* in data analysis.

If the two sessions taught with the two varying approaches for the undergraduate students cover different topics, then this might muddle the resulting student satisfaction data; it is a given that the subject matter itself is perceived differently by students and engages them in differing ways. A 'different topic' may hence interfere with the relationship examined through its possible effect on student satisfaction; such a factor is referred to as an *extraneous variable*; the latter can explain the results of the study without invoking the hypothesis (Stern, 1979). Such variables need to be identified and controlled for, as appropriate, in the design of the intervention or taken into consideration in interpreting the results.

Hence, in the above example, controlling for the topic taught and the time of day of the session is important to ensure extraneous variables are not affecting the findings. *Confounding* variables are a type of extraneous variable which are 'lurking' in the background of the study; if not known or acknowledged, they can threaten the study as they may influence the dependent variable and lead to alternative interpretations of the results. For example, if the layout of the teaching room affects student satisfaction and it remains a confounding factor which is not accounted for or controlled, it could potentially distort the results and interpretation of the findings.

Important Considerations in Questionnaire Development

In developing a questionnaire for a survey study, a good researcher pays close attention to *the Why, the How and the Who*: *why* is this study undertaken? (operationally: the research objectives); *how* will the questionnaire be administered? (in person, by phone, by post or online/ by e-mail); and *who* are the intended respondents? (the sample of the population of interest).

In relation to the *why*, as emphasised before, the research objectives should be closely tied into the questionnaire. The variables to be investigated must be specific and clear in a way that the questions gauge their occurrence, intensity and significance systematically. If the study is examining consumer preferences for shopping in store versus online and one of the objectives is to find out how often consumers shop via both methods, an initial question should ask whether the respondents shop through both channels, rather than assuming this is the case. Subsequent questions can then branch out to measure frequency, attitudes and preferences based on the initial response.

As for the *how*, the administration technique may dictate the wording and the types of questions included in the questionnaire. If the survey will be administered by post, it can be relatively lengthier as respondents can answer it at their own convenience, though the questions have to be crystal clear in their meaning so the participants can independently comprehend them. If the survey will be administered by phone, it necessitates more closed-ended than open-ended questions to enable fast recording of data to be completed in as little time as possible, as respondents are usually impatient to get off the phone. If the survey will be administered online, some open-ended questions can be included as typing can be easier than manual writing.

However, for the latter this assumption may be erroneous depending on the *who*; if respondents are not digitally active or come from an older generation where typing is not their forte, then assuming that open-ended questions will be completed easily is presumptuous and inaccurate. Thus, considering the sample frame and the profile of the intended respondents will influence the means by which the 'why' and the 'how' are coherently implemented to appropriately serve the 'who' towards increasing response rate, thus minimising incomplete questionnaires and reducing response error.

Ethics: Survey Administration

Ethical practices and checks constitute critical considerations from the point a seed of research is planted until its completion. Part of the design process of a survey questionnaire is taking into account the respondents and the way the questions are posed, such that they are right for them. Not only is this important to ensure quality and reliable responses, but also in order to ethically approach them using the right terminology without being emotionally demanding or stretching them mentally.

An important ethical consideration in the questionnaire administration process involves determining whether the researcher administers the questions face-to-face and can hence put participants at ease, or whether the process is self-administered and hence all the questions should be self-explanatory and evident in meaning. In any case, ensuring the suitability of questions used is part of the ethical approval process prior to data collection. Offering an indication to participants of how long it will take them to complete the questionnaire should be accurate and not underestimated; participants should be treated as intelligent and should not be tricked.

Using international surveys across countries involves ethical considerations in studying the codes of practice, cultural expectations and taboos in every country, and ensuring that measurement scales are reliable and valid in whichever language the questionnaire is implemented and managed.

Measurement Instruments and Techniques

Survey measurement instruments are questions and question items that gauge research variables and encapsulate response alternatives and ways for capturing and recording data in completing a questionnaire

Deciding how to transform the information required in a study into questions that respondents can complete is a critical part of designing the questionnaire. Survey measurement instruments involve the statements, items or questions, the response alternatives and how the answers are recorded. Guidance should be given as to what is expected every time the respondent is asked to provide a response (e.g. choose one of the following options; choose ALL applicable answers; circle the appropriate point on the scale; put X next to the answer that best describes your view on… etc.) and on how to record that response for accuracy and consistency.

Different measurement techniques can be used depending on the purpose of the response for a particular question, the type of data required and how the analysis of the data obtained will subsequently be carried out. For example, questions that require Yes/No responses are suitable in simple cases when a straightforward, zero-extent reply is needed. Such questions may not provide an opportunity for rich and rigorous analysis tools, but they can be openers for subsequent questions. When a question asks respondents whether they like products produced by the Apple brand with a Yes/No option, this can lead on to a following question that rates their level of liking Apple products if the answer to the first question is 'YES'. If, however, the respondent answers 'NO', the researcher can use a Skip Logic approach to branch the questions out so the respondent is directed to another question that asks: 'If NO, what are the reasons you do not like Apple products?'

The use of question branching and Skip Logic emanates from having a number of routes along which respondents can progress through the questionnaire. Different groups will take different paths depending on choosing one option versus another on a specific question. Conditional rules are then set such that, if response alternative 1 is selected, the respondent moves to the next question, whereas if response alternative 2 is picked, the respondent is guided to jump ahead to another section or a forward question. The routing for every group of respondents has to be determined and sketched out by the researcher before the questionnaire is designed and assembled, so that it is clear which questions are unconditional (i.e. all respondents will move ordinarily to the following question) and which are conditional; where branching takes places, a Skip Logic instruction must be clearly set in place to guide respondents.

Reflective Activity: Survey Example – Question Branching and Using Skip Logic

With the aim of identifying the reasons for consumer complaints about the IKEA store locations and the best solutions to improve customer satisfaction, the survey could include the following questions:

Q1. Referring to your last visit to an IKEA store, did you visit it on a weekend, i.e. a Saturday or Sunday? Please choose ONE of the following options:

1. Yes.
2. No.

If you selected option '1', please go to Q2. If you selected option '2', please go to Q4.

Q2. Are weekends the typical time of the week when you are most likely to visit IKEA? Please choose one of the following options:

1. Yes.
2. No, sometimes I visit IKEA during the week and sometimes on weekends.

If you selected option '1', please go to Q3. If you selected option '2', please go to Q4.

Q3. I typically visit IKEA on weekends because... (Please choose ALL applicable options):

1. I am only free to go shopping generally on weekends.
2. IKEA is too far away to visit after work on my work days.
3. An IKEA outing is a social occasion so it is always planned on a weekend for me.
4. Other reason(s):... [Please provide your reason(s)]

Q4. To what extent do you agree or disagree with the following statement? Please choose along the scale provided.

I find it convenient to visit IKEA on weekdays:

Strongly Agree						Strongly Disagree
1	2	3	4	5	6	7

Activity: As a researcher on the team conducting this research for IKEA, please work in groups of 2-3 to explain the conditional rule linked to the Skip Logic above. Then, work together to progress the design of Q5, Q6 and Q7 using another Skip Logic routing. Explain the rationale for the conditional rules you set.

Selecting Measurement Scales

The decision of which measurement scale to use for collecting data on a variable depends on how much data are sought and in what form. If you need only to find out whether a consumer has officially made a complaint about their Internet service provision over the last 12 months, then the question may be posed as:

Have you raised a formal complaint over the last 12 months about the Internet service you have been receiving? Please choose one of the following options:

1. *Yes.*
2. *No.*

This is a called a ***dichotomous* question**, where there are only two alternative responses offered. This is also a *nominal measurement scale* as it includes categories with no order involved. A Yes or No answer may be all that the researcher is looking for at that point, and the 1 or 2 next to the answer signifies no order – it is merely an answer code (which should be recorded in the code book).

Categorical questions are those which are closed-ended and provide a number of discrete, pre-set response alternatives; these alternatives can be Nominal or Ordinal. *Nominal* scale questions involve a categorisation of data that names or labels variables rather than ordering or measuring them; hence, the number assigned to each unit has no quantitative significance. So, a question may ask respondents:

Which retail grocery stores do you visit in a month?

1. Sainsbury's 2. Tesco 3. Morrison 4. Aldi 5. Lidl

Participants can be instructed to choose *one* option or to choose *all* that apply, depending on the researcher's plan, but in any case the number next to each alternative is assigned only for coding purposes. When it comes to statistical analysis, the numbers carry no numerical consequence and these are the simplest questions to use. However, they do not offer very rich data and cannot be analysed using powerful parametric statistical techniques, such as correlation or regression analysis. Nominal data can be analysed using non-parametric statistics, for example cross-tabulations such as Chi-square. Non-parametric techniques are less sensitive in detecting differences and relationships among groups than parametric statistical techniques (more details on this in Chapter 14).

Alternatively, categorical variables which are measured using an *ordinal scale* carry an order significance to them and hence the numerical sequence matters, yet the difference between each interval and the next is not known or equal. For example:

What would you say your level of education is?

1. Secondary school 2. College level 3. UG university level 4. PG university level

This exemplar question specifies a number of order-based alternatives. In this case, the alternatives flow in an increasing sequential order of level of education so 2 is higher than 1, but no one can necessarily say that the difference between 1 and 2 is equal to that between 2 and 3, or that such a difference is even known or can be quantified. Ordinal questions provide richer data than nominal questions but, as categorical data, are still limited in the statistical techniques with which the data can be analysed. Examples of statistical techniques that can explore categorical data as independent variable(s) are independent t-tests and ANOVA (see Chapter 14 for more details).

On the other hand, variables can be measured non-categorically through *interval* or *ratio* scale variables. *Interval scales* are ordinal, but with the additional feature that the difference between each interval is consistently equal. These questions provide rich data where many inferential statistical tools can be employed in their analysis (more details in Chapter 14). Examples include:

> How satisfied are you with your Internet service provision? (Please choose along the scale provided):
>
> Strongly Agree Strongly Disagree
>
> 1 2 3 4 5 6 7

The intervals from 1 to 7 (i.e. 1–2, 2–3, 3–4, etc.) are equidistant, can be measured and are consistent along such a scale. This type of scale is known as a *Likert scale* (which can be on a 5-point, 7-point or 9-point scale, depending on the research needs and country norms). The use of odd-numbered scales is better than the use of even-numbered scales as it allows respondents to have a mid-point response alternative or a neutral stance as suits them. The Celsius temperature scale is another example of an interval scale. Interval scales have no Absolute Zero (or True Zero, i.e. there is no 0 point along this scale where the variable has no level), so they cannot measure ratios.

Ratio scale questions are optimal in terms of allowing the possible use of an array of different inferential statistics in the analysis. This is because they encapsulate all the properties of the above scales; they offer an order, they provide exact discrete value between units, but they can also have an Absolute Zero. Examples include measuring weight, height, age (where the question offers a space for respondents to write the exact number), number of years of using a product, and so on, rather than offering respondents a range of alternative categories to choose from; to emphasise, a small space is given for a specific number to be written by the respondents themselves. Scale variables, whether interval or ratio, provide the highest level of data in terms of richness and the multitude of statistical techniques that can be used to analyse them. Parametric techniques including correlation, regression and factor analyses are appropriate for use with scale variables.

Semantic differential questions are also rating questions where the variable in question is rated along bipolar scale(s) that represent opposite adjectives representing the meaning sought. Dotted lines are provided between the poles along which respondents are asked to mark a point of choice. For example:

> Self-service technology to me is: (Please mark an 'X' along the lines provided):
>
> Not needed .... Needed
>
> Not for me .... For me
>
> Difficult .... Easy

In semantic differential questions, respondents are free to point to where they rate the variable in the absence of numbers. In the analysis, the researcher still calculates a numerical value for respondents' answers, and means can be calculated and used for further analysis. If the positive and negative adjectives at both ends of the scales used are mixed (e.g. putting the positive at the first end and the negative at the other end for some of the items) to avoid flat-lining – where respondents monotonously pick the same answer to speed through the questions – then the scoring of the scales should be adjusted in one overall direction at the point of analysis before a combined response can be scored.

Dos and don'ts in constructing a questionnaire

1. Keep the questions simple and concise, with no jargon or acronyms that respondents are unfamiliar with – remember that surveys are objective even in face-to-face administration, so no clarification can be offered beyond what is on the questionnaire. Accordingly, all questions and response alternatives should be clear and easy to answer. Once respondents start exerting effort to make sense of the questions or the optional answers, there is a high risk of wear-out and inept responses developing.
2. Keep it short and focused – a lengthy questionnaire may be turned down by respondents, may lead to drop-outs and may result in redundant responses due to boredom or incompletion. As a rough guide, one two-sided A4 page should suffice.
3. Make sure you provide clear instructions for each question – also, explain to respondents why a question is asked if it requires sensitive information or does not make sense within the context and stated purpose of the survey.
4. Be clear which variables you are measuring (validity is making sure you are measuring what you set out to measure) and which measurement scales are best to use. Otherwise, you may obtain useless data that do not aid your study's aim.
5. Search for existing measurement scales that have been previously developed/adopted by other researchers who have investigated these variables – existing scales are tried and tested for validity and reliability and are better to adapt to the specific study and to be used instead of creating totally new scales. If you need rich data, use scale rather than nominal measurements.
6. Ensure the questions are linked to the research objectives and only seek to collect enough data to address the research aim and objectives, no more and no less.

Figure 13.1 Avoid using jargon/unfamiliar words in questionnaires

7. Avoid negative or biasing questions that take respondents in a specific direction. Do not let your personal views or judgements feature in the questions on a questionnaire as this can easily bias the respondents' expressed answers.
8. Refrain from using ambiguous terms that are not defined specifically within the questionnaire document – for example, 'rarely', 'frequently', 'usually', 'often', 'sometimes' or 'in the last week' can mean different things to different people. Respondents should all be able to understand a term in one consistent manner. There is no problem with providing specific definitions to converge understanding in one clear frame.
9. Avoid overlapping interval options and double-barrelled questions, including the use of and/or – an example of an *overlapping interval* is asking respondents to choose their age from a range of options such as: A. 18–25, B. 25–35, C. 35–45. These intervals are overlapping because if a respondent is 35 years old, he/she would not know whether to tick option B or C, and they may be likely to leave it empty, in addition to the analysis problems this can incur.

   Double-barrelled questions ask two things at the same time, which confuses the respondents if their response to one thing is different to the other as to which option they choose; for example:

   I do not shop online *or* use click-and-collect shopping methods (Please choose one of the following options):

   1. *Yes*
   2. *No*

   If the respondent does not shop online but uses click-and-collect for shopping, should they choose Yes or No?

   Similarly:

   I like shopping in store *and* I like shopping online (Please choose one of the following options):

   1. *Yes*
   2. *No*

   The use of 'and' in the second example, just like the use of 'or' in the first, is perplexing as the respondent may agree with the first part of the statement but disagree with the second.

10. Use consistent coding values for your questionnaire options and responses and record them in your code book; this makes it easier to compare responses and to conduct analysis – for instance, assign the highest value to the positive outcomes and the lowest value to the negative outcomes, such as 5 = Strongly agree and 1 = Strongly disagree, or 5 = High and 1 = Low. Keeping the direction of coding values consistent throughout the questions also aids respondents in recording their responses and guards against confusing them when different scales on the various questions have different directions. If some of the items in the measurement scale are negatively worded to boost respondents' attention, these items should be reverse-coded in the analysis to put them back in the direction of the rest of the questions.

Figure 13.2 Questionnaire testing and administration to the right target sample

11. Keep the questionnaire simple; avoid offensive language; use colourful paper to attract attention and keep the respondents amused (pastel colours are a good choice); and make sure you have a 'Thank you' note in the introduction section and again at the end of the questionnaire.

12. Pre-test the questionnaire and pilot test it – in the *pre-test*, you can give the questionnaire to a few research colleagues and/or subject experts to assess its wording, logic, flow and face validity. Face validity, also called surface validity, refers to the extent to which the questionnaire appears to measure what it purports to measure; in other words, if the questions are measuring brand loyalty as a construct, the aim is to validate the relevance of the measurement scale used. Systematically, research experts can inspect the applicability and transparency of the questionnaire to highlight any ambiguity, errors or jargon which target respondents may not comprehend or if the measurement scales used are not pertinent to the constructs/variables being tested. Though it is based on common sense and judgement at face value, because researchers are undertaking it, it is a dependable and commonly used approach. Following the pre-test feedback, amendments can be undertaken and you can then move on to conduct a pilot test on the new questionnaire draft.

    A *pilot test* is a small-scale administration of the questionnaire to a narrow group of respondents – customarily, it can be 10% or less of the planned sample size – who represent the target sample and population of interest. The aim of the pilot test is to trial the questionnaire in order to study its procedures and dynamics, to determine respondent receptivity and comprehension, and to obtain some comments on any typographical mistakes or problems faced in completing it. The pilot test can also help assess the time it takes, on average, to complete it, to determine whether it is reasonable in length and to include the expected completion time in the information provided at the top of the questionnaire in its large-scale administration.

Research in Practice: Research Mistakes that are NO-NOs – JCPenney: Why did the Ship Sink?

One of the key elements of success in business is conveying a clear positioning and market focus to customers so that brand image is sharp rather than diluted. Wanting a share of too many pies may result in losing that sharpness, and this is the ailment that caught up with JCPenney when it attempted to recover from declining sales that started in 2009. As a retailer with 1,000 department stores across the country, its stores served middle-income families with clothing for men, women and children as well as homewares. Its discounted pricing strategy appealed to families looking to manage their costs of living by seeking out deals and discounts. But this identity could not withstand other discount competitors such as T.K.Maxx and Target. There was no clear differentiation that offered JCPenney a competitive edge. Hence, sales declined from $18 billion to $17 billion between 2009 and 2011 (Lal, 2013).

To deal with this, Ron Johnson – previously successful at leading Apple's retail efforts in 2000–2011 – became JCPenney's CEO in June 2011. Yet, rather than conduct marketing research to better understand actual consumer attitudes and perceptions, he thought he understood the target consumer and acted on ungrounded assumptions; to distinguish JCPenney stores and give them an edge, he introduced the *Apple-successful* concept of 'store-within-a-store', where he opened small boutiques inside each of the JCPenney outlets, selling a variety of products and services. He also moved away from discount pricing which was based on sales and coupons and adopted a 'fair and square' pricing approach or, in other words, an everyday low-pricing strategy. The new approach did not go down well with target customers who abandoned the stores, causing less traffic and sliding sales; in 2012, sales declined by 25%, leading to a net loss of $985 million. Changes to JCPenney did not coincide with what target customers really wanted from shopping there and with their perceptions of the brand, resulting in a negative shift in their attitudes and shopping intentions (BrandIndex, 2013).

Conducting consumer research before and after any changes to a business's strategic or operational plans is critical to its survival. Engaging with what the customer thinks is the key to saving sinking ships in an ever-changing marketplace. Thus, JCPenney's customer needs and perceptions should have been gauged and captured, with the right questions asked of the right target group at the right time.

Data Preparation and Organisation

Once the completed questionnaires are retrieved, the process of preparing the raw data for analysis starts as a pre-analysis phase. This involves reviewing all questionnaires for validity and completeness, determining the quality of those completed to check if they include redundant responses/flat-lining (e.g. a respondent selects only 4s all along for all questions measured on a 7-point Likert scale), sorting out ambiguities (e.g. questions where some responses are circled and others ticked; questions where only one option is required and there is more than one option selected), as well as reviewing questionnaires with missing pages and/or those where Skip Logic was confused or filter-question guidance was ignored.

Editing and getting organised

Based on the issues identified, completed questionnaires should then be counted and organised. If the survey was conducted online, data entry time is saved, but it is still important to check the data and separate the completed questionnaires which are usable from those that have issues, such as those mentioned above. Illegible, incomplete or unsatisfactory questionnaires must be set aside and a decision made as to whether they can be saved, or whether more data are needed through extending the survey administration period to collect more completed questionnaires. The latter can be an attractive option if time allows, but administering the survey at a different time or using a different administration technique can affect the results. Thus, if the plan is to have one unified data set, caution is needed in deciding on the feasibility of the researcher going back to data collection again.

Alternatively, as a researcher, you may consider the potential of saving some of the seemingly unusable questionnaires; if the number of complete/usable questionnaires retrieved hits the pre-planned sample size, then unusable questionnaires can be fully discarded. If however, more questionnaires are needed to achieve the required sample size, then incomplete questionnaires need to be scrutinised to find out if they can be edited without affecting any of the responses. Editing here refers to assigning missing values to responses on the questionnaire which are carelessly recorded (e.g. flat-lining) or missing, or excluding the data from these questions for these specific questionnaires. Editing, however, is conditional and has to be approached with caution so that the data are not altered by the researcher. It works if the number of questionnaires with missing, illegible or unsatisfactory responses is limited; if these questionnaires have a small number of missing responses; and if the affected questions are not related to the key variables and relationships being investigated. If these conditions are not satisfied, the affected questionnaires have to be excluded from data analysis to maintain an objective and reliable data set.

After organising all eligible and usable questionnaires, you can give each a number; numbering is a very important step early on in the data preparation process as it makes it easier to input the data and be able to trace any data entry errors incurred back to its specific case (respondent number). Subsequently, coding should be undertaken in line with the code book. The coding process and the code book are further explained in the next section.

Coding and the code book

As explained in Chapter 12, a code book is best started at the design stage of the questionnaire. It contains coding guidelines and information about each question and response alternative. Its purpose is to record all questions and all possible answers using a coding system of numbers, draw all potential routes respondents can take if Skip Logic is used, setting the conditional rules clearly, as well as highlighting the filter questions. A coding system of numbers is important given that quantitative data analysis will be conducted after data collection and it can only use numerical data, not letters. In the code book, links can be drawn to join each question to the research objectives and hypotheses so that the relevance is illustrated for ease of the subsequent data analysis process and to ensure no extra unneeded questions are added and no important questions are missed in the questionnaire. Usually, the code book is structured into a column identifier, question name, question description and coding instructions. However, this is only a suggestion and researchers can organise the code book in a way that makes sense for them and aids the analysis process.

Coding involves providing numbers to each response alternative to aid the subsequent quantitative analysis. So, if the Gender question provided two answer options of *A. Male* and *B. Female*, coding can transform *A to 1* and *B to 2* (A = 1; B = 2). Alternatively, the researcher can choose to code A as 0 and B as 1 (A = 0; B = 1). Both coding systems are the same in having no effect on the analysis process or results as long as a consistent system of coding is followed for all the questions. If the first system is selected, in coding the response alternatives question for Age, where the options are A. 18–24, B. 25–34, C. 35–44 and D. 45–54, the coding becomes: A = 1; B = 2; C = 3; D = 4. Even if pre-coding takes place early on in the building of the questionnaire (so the response alternatives were set in number format rather than letter format), the coding of each question's optional answers is still required at this point in data preparation to ensure all coding instructions follow one consistent system. Otherwise, analysis can be confused and yield incorrect findings, or results can be interpreted inaccurately. The code book helps to keep everything on record so the researcher can consult it at various times rather than relying only on memory.

Data entry and cleaning: is it ready?

Once all completed questionnaires are numbered and organised, they are ready for entry into a computer software program for analysis. Long ago, statistical analysis was undertaken manually by statisticians and was a time-consuming practice. Nowadays, statistical packages for data management and analysis, such as IBM SPSS Statistics (which is the most commonly used software for researchers in the social sciences) and STATA, can ease the process as long as the researcher has a clear understanding of the appropriate statistical techniques to employ in every analysis. If the survey was administered online, the step of manual data entry is not needed; yet it is still essential to undertake the preparatory steps of checking the data for validity and completeness, editing them as needed, and excluding unusable questionnaires. Most online survey tools have the option of directly transferring the data to SPSS to start analysis after the data collection phase is complete. It is important to note that deciding on the suitable statistical tools to use does not start after data are collected and inputted but rather at the phase of questionnaire design, including choosing the formatting for the different questions. (This was discussed earlier under Measurement Instruments and Techniques and will be further elaborated on in Chapter 14.)

The quantitative data entered into the software should then be checked for accuracy. For example, if the possible range of response options for a question is 1 to 4, a response of 5 does not make sense. Spotting such observation point mistakes is crucial at this point, especially for manually entered data sets. The error may result from the visual confusion that leads to recording a wrong number or confusion between the coding of questions. The researcher thus needs to check the question and response options in the code book, the relevant coding and range set in the instructions, then go back to the specific completed questionnaire where the error is. This step highlights the significance of numbering the questionnaires as it will only be easy to refer back to the correct questionnaire if it has a recorded case number. Otherwise, and particularly in a large data set of hundreds or thousands of questionnaires, tracing back an observation point to its original questionnaire to check the respondent's actual choice can be a challenge, or practically impossible.

An **outlier** is an observation point within a data set that stands outside the pattern of distribution of other observations as too distant from them. It may be the result of detected variability in the data or due to an error during data inputting

In order to systematically ensure no erroneous numbers can threaten the accuracy of the data analysis and lead to unwanted *outliers*, the researcher should examine the descriptive statistics for each question. This preliminary data navigation approach involves checking the mean score for the question's response across the data set and the range, as well as looking at the minimum and maximum values; the latter should respectively represent the lower and higher poles of the possible response alternatives according to the coding system used.

Open-ended questions: qualitative data from the questionnaire

A researcher will, though, be faced with both qualitative and quantitative data from the questionnaire if some open-ended questions were used and an 'Other (please specify)' response alternative was given. Qualitative data are based on words and have to be handled differently given that they cannot be coded in the same way as quantitative data obtained from categorical and scale questions and, hence, will not be numerically analysed. Time should be taken at this point to go through all the qualitative responses to find some patterns and themes that emerge. If a theme is repeated by a large number of respondents, then it can be given a numerical code, thus considering it a new emergent response alternative and recording this process in the code book. If, however, the data are variable and offer new insights that cannot be categorised into new codes at this time, then they have to be taken out and analysed qualitatively using qualitative analysis techniques (see Chapter 10), such as content analysis or thematic analysis. Given the need for this step, researchers usually opt for only a few qualitative questions in a structured survey so that the time required for analysis is not too great. The qualitative findings in this instance can be brought back into the discussion of the data analysis results following completion of the quantitative analysis to help interpret the overall findings and shed more light on hypothesis-testing outcomes.

Reflective Activity: Data Preparation or Jumping to Analysis?

Fred embarked on a research study on behalf of a local charity with the aim of determining the feasibility of developing a commercial arm that may help it raise money for sustainability. Given that a small budget was available for the study, the charity required a focused survey of opinions of the target group who could benefit from the commercial projects potentially on offer. Time was also restricted as Fred had only two months to hand in the report of findings in order to start the project on time.

Fred designed the questionnaire for face-to-face administration, aiming at a sample size of 100. There were 16 questions in all, 7 of which were open-ended. The pilot study showed that it would take 15 minutes for a respondent to complete the questionnaire, but Fred continued with the questionnaire in its same length and form. Data collection was scheduled to take two weeks but instead took four to achieve the set sample size. Fred felt that he was running out of time, so he rushed the data entry as quickly as he could. A full day into it, he realised he did not give a number to each of the questionnaires and had to go through the whole stack again, hoping the case numbers corresponded to the number assigned to the hard copies.

With time getting tighter, Fred thought it best to get into the statistical analysis head on in order to bring findings into the report in time for the charity's deadline. Data cleaning seemed secondary at this point for him as it meant more time before the 'real' analysis. Given that he only had 100 filled out questionnaires, he

(Continued)

(Continued)

could not afford to exclude any unusable ones so he included them all, though there were incomplete cases which were missing responses on key variables. Proceeding with hypothesis testing straight on, the study findings seemed puzzling and inconsistent with the charity's expectations. Fred was unable to recommend to the charity whether or not to proceed with its commercial project towards achieving a sustainable income.

Activity: Having read the above research scenario, what do you think are some of the problems that could have contributed to the final outcome? Discuss the issues that Fred faced and the decisions he made, highlighting how they could have affected his research. Where could he have gone wrong, and why?

Advanced: Measurement Scales and International Perspectives

Continuous scales are one of the best measurement scales to use in obtaining rich data in surveys; interval scales using Likert scales are commonly used in designing questionnaires, given that the continuous data generated allow for analysis using a wide array of statistical analysis techniques. They hence enable a robust approach in determining the significance and direction of the relationships and differences under investigation. Likert scales, however, vary in the number of intervals used; 5-point and 7-point Likert scales are widely used, but, in research carried out in some countries, this may be extended to 9-point or 10-point. The use of an odd rather than an even number of intervals, nevertheless, allows respondents the mid-point neutral response where they can express neither agreement nor disagreement. For some, this can initiate straight easy answers all in the mid-point, but researchers would consider such questionnaires a sign of lack of interest and may exclude them so as not to poorly influence the distribution of data and the combined data analysis results.

Even for researchers globally using the 5-point Likert scale, the format can differ among countries and research cultures, and may yield different results. For instance, the two poles of 1 and 5 may be entitled: Strongly Disagree and Strongly Agree, respectively, but with 2, 3 and 4 left with no description. Alternatively, another format is to give a label to each point on the scale, such as:

Very Poor	Poor	Average	Good	Excellent
1	2	3	4	5

In other formats, the numbers may be depicted with no description, and respondents are expected to make sense of what each means. There may be advantages and disadvantages to each approach, but what matters is testing whatever format is used for reliability and internal consistency before it is used. In this way, the researcher can guard against non-sampling errors linked with the measurement tools used. Therefore, researchers conducting international studies need to be aware of how formatting differences may be needed to suit the country or research culture, but may also play a role in the different research findings achieved. Just like administering the questionnaire in different languages and translating/back translating for reliability, question formatting requires attention and scrutiny.

An important consideration also in deciding on measurement scales and question formatting is to write questionnaires in a way that engages respondents to achieve quality rather than quantity only. The more engaged the respondents are, the more likely they are to provide spontaneous and high quality responses and the less likely they will drop out prior to survey completion. A new innovation in survey design towards that end is the use of gamification which involves making the questions game-based and exciting, using fun imagery and bringing the questions emotionally and personally close to participants. Any new trend has both pros and cons, nonetheless, so these have to be assessed by the researcher as part of survey planning and design.

Chapter Summary

This chapter is the third in a series of four chapters under Part IV, covering quantitative research in marketing. After discussing quantitative research designs and methods in Chapter 12, this chapter took the discussion of survey methods forward into a more detailed understanding of questionnaire development and design. It offered examples and tips on question formats, measurement scales and considerations in the effective planning and design of questionnaire forms.

The chapter also discussed the importance of linking the questions to the research objectives, with the hypotheses clearly active in the background. The use of measurement scales and ensuring clarity about the suitable analysis methods in the planning of question formats highlight key elements of effective questionnaire design. The discussion emphasised that there is no perfect questionnaire, but there are tried-and-tested means of improving its structure, contemplating its wording and length, and considering ethical standards throughout the whole process. Data preparation following data collection was also discussed in the run-up to subsequent full-scale analysis.

In the next chapter (Chapter 14), preliminary analysis to summarise the data using univariate statistics will be explored through the use of descriptive statistics. Inferential analysis will then be discussed through reflecting on various statistical methods that may be employed in hypothesis testing (such as SPSS).

Case Study: Twinings – A Brand Re-Positioned in the Consumer Mind

Established in 1706, Twinings enjoys over 300 years of providing quality tea blends. With history and expertise on its side, the English brand name has always been associated with a special quality of tea. This promotional strategy over the years has positioned Twinings at an elevated place for tea drinkers, but, on the other hand, has meant that many consumers only drink it occasionally, opting for the other 'daily' brands as their everyday tea. To gain a larger market share and convert occasional drinkers into daily/regular Twinings consumers, the brand set out to amend its positioning and persuade customers that they are 'worthy' of drinking Twinings every day.

A better understanding of its unique selling point for its loyal consumers could thus provide insights into how best to communicate its brand to tea drinkers. Twinings carried out research focusing on its main target segment: core tea-drinking female consumers who comprised loyal Twinings customers. A survey of their brand opinions and consumption motivations highlighted an emotional connection beyond a cup of daily tea. Women expressed how they played a number of roles in their everyday lives, to the point of being unclear about their real identity; in the midst of being a wife, a mother, a sister, a daughter, an employee and a friend, women's lives are so busy that the lines blur between where these roles end and where they exist as themselves. Twinings tea was expressed as enabling these women to feel like their real selves again as the restorative nature of its tea offerings emotionally empowered them to better handle their busy lives.

Findings led to a new promotional campaign using an emotional appeal and creatively executed with the theme of 'Get you back to you'; it used animation and drama to symbolise a strenuous journey well understood by women in their everyday lives, whereby Twinings offered these women quality moments of restorative power to return to themselves. The campaign was well received and its effectiveness with target consumers earned the company a rise of 14.1% in its market share through a surge in sales in 2012.

(Continued)

(Continued)

To determine whether this expresses a sustainable change in consumer perceptions of Twinings and its market positioning, Twinings needs to conduct new research. Surveying current consumer usage patterns and changed attitudes to the brand can help identify the market segments taking up Twinings tea as their daily hot beverage based on the new concept established through its successful promotional campaign; it can also examine how loyal Twinings consumers reacted to the campaign and whether it resonated with them and/or changed their consumption patterns.

Case study questions:

1. As the researcher commissioned by Twinings to carry out the research, how would you express the aim and objectives of the new study?
2. In designing the survey questionnaire, where would you place the section containing personal questions about the study participants? Why?
3. How would you determine which measurement scales to use in relation to the research variables? If you want to measure *usage patterns*, is it better to use existing scales from the marketing literature or develop a new scale?
4. You decide to conduct an online survey using *Qualtrics*. This online questionnaire software is giving you a number of question format options using nominal, ordinal or interval scales. How would you determine which scale to use for a given question? For example, which scale would you use for a question about the extent of *advert likeability*, and which scale for a question on the *frequency of purchase* of Twinings English Breakfast tea? Formulate two exemplar questions accordingly.
5. If you administer the questionnaire by post, what steps would you take after data collection is complete and questionnaires are retrieved?

Now put the following steps in the right order:

A. Start data analysis for hypothesis testing

B. Check the data for accuracy of recording and for outliers

C. Assign a number to each of the questionnaires retrieved

D. Conduct descriptive data analysis to summarise the data

E. Enter the data on SPSS

F. Check which questionnaires are useable and which ones to exclude

G. Clean the data, dealing with missing responses and incomplete questionnaires

End of Chapter Questions

These questions should help you reflect on your understanding of this chapter:

1. What are the important considerations in questionnaire design?
2. How important is it that the research aim, objectives and hypotheses are closely linked to the questionnaire design? Why?

3. What are different types of questions to include in a questionnaire?
4. What are the common errors that researchers fall into in questionnaire design?
5. What is a code book and why should it be used in survey research?
6. What are the key steps in data preparation and organisation?
7. What are the different measurement instruments and techniques that can be used in designing survey questions?

Checklist

After studying Chapter 13, you should now be familiar with these key concepts:

1. Questionnaire development as relevant to the research aim, objectives and hypotheses
2. Questionnaire design considerations, dos and don'ts
3. Measurement instruments, techniques and question types
4. Data preparation and data cleaning for analysis

Further Reading (in sequence from beginners to advanced)

Brace, I. (2008) *Questionnaire Design: How to Plan, Structure and Write Survey Material for Effective Market Research*. London: Kogan Page.

Kolb, B. (2008) *Marketing Research: A Practical Approach*. London: Sage Publications (Chapter 12).

Hague, P., Hague, N. and Morgan, C. (2013) *Market Research in Practice: How to get Greater Insight from Your Market* (2nd edition). London: Kogan Page.

Schuman, H. and Presser, S. (1996) *Questions and Answers in Attitude Surveys: Experiments on Question Form, Wording, and Context*. London: Sage Publications.

Tourangeau, R., Rips, L. J. and Rasinski, K. (2000) *The Psychology of Survey Response*. Cambridge: Cambridge University Press.

Bibliography

BrandIndex (April 24, 2013). 'Long-Term Look At Brand Perception Shows J.C. Penney Losing Ground Vs. Kohl's', *Forbes*. [Online] Available at: https://www.forbes.com/sites/brandindex/2013/04/24/long-term-look-at-brand-perception-shows-j-c-penney-losing-ground-vs-kohls/#7e56d6d26213

Fisher, C. (2007) *Researching and Writing a Dissertation: A Guidebook for Business Students*. London: Pearson Education.

Lal, R. (2013) What went wrong at JCPenney's? August. [Online] Available at: www.hbs.edu/news/articles/Pages/rajiv-lal-on-jcpenney.aspx

Market Research Society (MRS) (n.d.) Introduction to gamification: how to change our industry and respondents' experience for the better. [Online] Available at: www.mrs.org.uk/event/course/313/id/7775 [accessed June 2016].

Marketing Society (2012) 2012: Twinings – brand revitalisation – case study. [Online] Available at: www.marketingsociety.com/the-library/2012-twinings-brand-revitalisation-case-study [accessed 18 September 2016].

Smith, S. M. (n.d.) 7 tips for writing surveys. *Qualtrics*. Available at: https://success.qualtrics.com/download-7-tips-for-writing-surveys.html

Stern, P. C. (1979) *Evaluating Social Science Research*. New York: Oxford University Press.

Find journal articles and multiple choice questions online at: **https://study.sagepub.com/benzo** to support what you've learnt so far.

CHAPTER 14

Data Analysis Using Descriptive and Inferential Statistics

LEARNING OBJECTIVES

The key learning objectives of this chapter are:

1. To understand the difference between descriptive and inferential statistics
2. To discuss quantitative data analysis approaches and techniques
3. To learn how to choose the right statistical technique in an analysis situation
4. To explore how to interpret the results in relation to the formulated hypotheses

KEY CONCEPTS

By the end of this chapter, the reader should be familiar with the following concepts:

1. Preliminary analysis using descriptive statistics
2. Data handling prior to commencing analysis
3. Analysis using inferential statistics
4. Parametric statistical techniques
5. Non-parametric statistical techniques
6. Choosing the suitable statistical test for data analysis
7. Interpreting analysis findings for hypothesis testing

Marwa G. Mohsen

Introduction

Data preparation was introduced in Chapter 13 through laying the grounds for making sense of the data obtained from quantitative data collection, such as through survey research. The purpose of data analysis is to organise the questionnaire data into a structure that enables the researcher to answer the research question and address the study's SMART objectives; using suitable analysis techniques, the data can then be summarised and unpacked to determine the extent to which the hypotheses are supported.

Findings should be communicated such that they offer value to the study's users; hence, the structure of the findings should follow the requirements of the users. For example, if CHANEL commissions a piece of research in Egypt to find out the level of awareness of target consumers in relation to its N°5 fragrance, the research brief (i.e. the document which CHANEL's management presents to the marketing research team to clarify the purpose of the study, its requirements and expectations) may establish that the research report needs to be more visual than verbal, where findings are depicted through summary tables, graphical displays and charts. In other instances, the researcher(s) may be required to present a discussion based on the research results as an executive summary that spells out the findings, with few numbers/graphs and tables involved. For a research student, both approaches may be needed to bring out the richness of the data and its analysis steps, and to make sense of the results in relation to the extant literature (the existing studies in the same domain). In any case, both descriptive and inferential statistics might be required for a comprehensive and rigorous analysis.

Descriptive statistics explore data related to the target population through evaluating frequencies, percentages, central tendencies, spread, variance, and so on, which can then be visually reported through graphs, charts (e.g. pie charts, bar graphs, histograms) and tables. Data summaries are valuable in drawing an initial picture of the sample through making quick comparisons within and between data sets; however, they are insufficient in depicting the fuller picture of the relationships or differences under study, or in generalising to others through hypothesis testing. Based on the representative sample drawn, inferential statistics can then be employed to make generalisations (taking into consideration the sampling errors discussed in Chapter 11) through an estimation of parameters and hypothesis testing. For example, inferential statistical analysis can be used to make predictions beyond the immediate data about awareness and take-up among the wider Egyptian female target population. Thus, by using descriptive and inferential statistics together, analysis can provide valuable results for decision makers to rely on.

This chapter will look at the use of both descriptive and inferential statistics in quantitative data analysis. Univariate and bivariate data analysis will be explored, as well as multivariate analyses through parametric and non-parametric techniques. The aim is to demonstrate their combined use towards addressing the research objectives, as well as the conditions underlying their suitability in varying analysis situations. The chapter concludes by offering advice about the interpretation of data analysis for hypothesis testing to establish support, or lack thereof, and thus the extent of the contribution to knowledge.

Snapshot: Setting the Scene – CHANEL: Strategic Plans to Increase its Presence in the Middle East

As a global luxury fashion brand with continuing aspirations for uniqueness and differentiation, CHANEL seeks a share of the luxury market pie. Thus, targeting the affluent Middle Eastern consumer creates a lucrative potential for the French Haute Couture house. Market intelligence becomes increasingly imperative in studying emerging markets such as Dubai, in order to determine the strategies and tactics needed to increase CHANEL's presence there. In 2015, CHANEL took to Dubai for the launch of its Cruise 2015 collection to mark the brand's first showing in the Middle East (Jones, 2014). To uncover consumer attitudes and behaviour in response to this direct business strategy, a researcher carried out a study a few months after the show on a sample of luxury fashion consumers. Utilising a survey tool, the aim of the study was at the heart of the questionnaire design.

For example, to determine whether consumers of CHANEL's beauty and fragrance lines were swayed by the fashion show to also purchase CHANEL's Haute Couture products, respondents were asked:

> Did you purchase any CHANEL Haute Couture products (clothing or handbags) following the 2015 Dubai collection show? (Please choose only ONE option from the following):
>
> 1. Yes   2. No

The nominal data obtained can only be analysed using limited statistical tools, including *non-parametric* statistical methods, due to its categorical nature. To complement this question and increase the richness of the data obtained towards further analysis, interval scale data were obtained from other questions as follows:

> Please choose along the following scale as best describes your opinion:
> There are products in the CHANEL 2015 collection show that could be part of my wardrobe.
>
> Strongly Disagree 1 2 3 4 5 6 7 Strongly Agree

As a Likert-scale rating question, the data obtained can be analysed using a broad range of statistical test options, including many *parametric* statistical tests. It is an example of how data collection can be expanded so that analysis can help the company in making deductions and predictions about the effectiveness of its approach in achieving its strategic goals. It is imperative that the statistical techniques to be used are envisaged at the questionnaire planning and design stage, in order to ensure that data are collected in a form appropriate for the analysis tools that will later be employed.

Using Univariate Statistics to Summarise the Data

As a researcher, there is an exhilarating joy felt at the point when data, the fruition of fieldwork effort, is ready for analysis. At this point, you face the task of making sense of the collected data. The key advice here is to do so without losing sight of the original aim of the research and its objectives.

A researcher may be tempted to prematurely jump into conducting big statistical tests to uncover insights into the phenomenon under study and test the research hypotheses.

Figure 14.1 Data should be explored after collection prior to any hypothesis testing

However, it is vital to start by exploring the characteristics of the data set and its variables; this step involves unravelling the properties of the measured variables and the characteristics of the respondents based on classification questions asked on the survey (e.g. age, gender, income level, presence of children, education).

Consider, for example, that you need to determine: *How many males versus females completed the survey? Are the majority of the respondents employed in full-time jobs?* These examples assume that gender and employment status are variables that are important in this study and were captured in the personal data section at the end of the questionnaire. An important reminder here is that gender is not a required variable in every study, but most studies will want to establish an understanding of the respondent's profile and, hence, gender proportions within the full data set; this might influence data interpretation or reflect the fact that the findings apply more to one group than the other in some studies (if a higher percentage of females than males, for instance, completed the survey). This could have been purposive based on the pre-planned target sample profile, or it could be incidental if gender was not part of the sampling characteristics.

An example of a summary table that highlights the characteristics of a data sample, comprising age, gender, education level and income level, is exhibited in Table 14.1; the table is an extract from a piece of research on influences of situational and personal factors on food portion decisions.

Other examples of summarising the data set's characteristics are establishing the *average age* of the participants, the *mean* of the level of education and/or social class/income level, and so on. This thus sets the stage for exploring data patterns using descriptive statistics, such as measures of frequency, central tendency and dispersion, not only for the classification questions but also for the key research variables investigated. Given that each of the variables in a study, as recorded in the code book, is analysed on its own to describe its individual characteristics, this type of analysis is called *univariate analysis*; it refers to the analysis of a single variable at a time, prior to the next phase of testing for significant relationships or differences between or among variables. This will be discussed in more detail later in the chapter.

Table 14.1 Food portion size decisions: demographic characteristics of the data set

Research Sample Profile (N = 261)						
Age:	18–26: 11.5%	27–34: 13.4%	45–54: 24.5%	55–60: 16.1%	61+: 8%	
Gender:	Male: 43%	Female: 57%				
Education level:	Secondary school: 13.4%	College: 26.4%	University undergrad: 20.7%	University postgrad: 30.7%		
Annual income level:	Unemployed–£3000: 10%	£3000–10,000: 6.1%	£11,000–25,000: 16.9%	£26,000–40,000: 16.1%	£41,000–60,000: 17.6%	61,000+: 20.3%

Frequency analysis

In the IKEA study discussed in the mini case at the start of Chapter 13, consider that respondents were asked how often they would be likely to visit the IKEA store if a smaller branch was located in their town centre. The categorical question gives them five response alternatives: (1) weekly; (2) fortnightly; (3) monthly; (4) every two months; and (5) only when an IKEA item is needed. If in a sample size of 500 only 440 were usable questionnaires, the researcher could find out how frequently each of the categories was selected by the usable sample through running a frequency test with SPSS, using the menu sequence: *Analyse > Descriptive Statistics > Frequencies*. Table 14.2 indicates the possible results.

Table 14.2 Expected frequency of visits to IKEA if located in town centre

Expected frequency of visit	Number	Percentage
Weekly	75	17%
Fortnightly	100	22.7%
Monthly	**150**	**34.1%**
Every two months	50	11.4%
Only when an IKEA item is needed	45	10.2%
No response	20	4.5%
Total	440	100%

Based on these results, there are 20 non-responses which imply that only 420 responses were valid and complete for this specific question. The highest frequency is detected in the 'monthly' response. This gives a general pattern for this variable, although the 4.5% non-response is not ideal.

For categorical variables, which encompass both nominal and ordinal measures, the frequency analysis provides an overall idea of where most of the similarity lies in the recorded observations. It also indicates the number of missing values in the responses for each question. A percentage can also be obtained using SPSS, which determines the frequency of each category calculated in relation to the valid number of overall responses, excluding those who did not provide a response; this is called 'valid percentage'. A *valid percentage* for the question on the expected frequency of visits to IKEA calculates the percentage of occurrence in each category relative to a total of 420 rather than 440 responses. In some studies, researchers prefer to rely on the valid percentage statistic as it is a more realistic indicator of frequency ratio.

Descriptive statistics

For continuous variables (i.e. scale and ratio measures), preliminary data exploration describes the distribution of responses for the sample representing the population for each measured variable. Using descriptive summaries and graphs offers many benefits in preparing the data for further analysis, including: (1) checking for data entry errors that can then be corrected in the data file (e.g. if a variable is out of range, where minimum value = 1 and maximum value = 7, but the inputted value is 8); (2) describing the characteristics of the sample reported in any research report (e.g. mean and range of age groups, average level of education/income level); and (3) checking that there is no violation of the assumptions underlying each statistical technique employed for the analysis (more on this later under the inferential statistical methods), such as the shape of the data distribution curve, the sample size and/or the sampling technique employed.

Normal distribution is a key statistical data distribution histogram that shows a symmetric normal curve with data equally distributed around the mean. Variables which are normally distributed have an equal mean and median, with 50% of the data falling to the right and 50% of the data falling to the left of centre

Using descriptive statistics assists in presenting a ground picture for the study's variables before hypothesis testing is undertaken. One of the important considerations at this stage of preliminary analysis is to look for patterns in the data and to check if any specific variable looks extremely erratic. For example, if a variable is not *normally distributed* but is excessively skewed with many outliers, it is important to find out whether there are any errors in data entry or this is how the actual data are represented. *Normal distribution*, or the 'bell-shaped curve', is a principal statistical distribution pattern where data are depicted on a graphical histogram symmetrically in what is also termed the 'normal curve'. With a single central peak showing equal distribution of the data falling on both sides of the mean (see Figure 14.2), in a normal distribution both the mean and the median are equal.

If data for a variable does not seem right, then there might in fact be a human error in relation to confused coding, data entry mistakes or sampling errors. Hence, getting a sense of the descriptives of the variables early on can help draw attention to potential issues that should be rectified before diving into full-scale analysis. However, there are instances where there are no errors in data collection, but the actual data for a variable indicate *skewness* or *kurtosis* in their graphical distribution. In a skewed data set (skewness), one tail may be longer than the other to the left or the right, leading to asymmetric distribution. Kurtosis affects the peaked-ness of the data distribution, and it takes place when it is too peaked or too flat. Normally, distributed data have zero skewness and zero kurtosis, but in most data sets there will be some level of skewness and/or kurtosis; the key thing is to check that it is within acceptable limits, with statistics books offering a number of recommendations

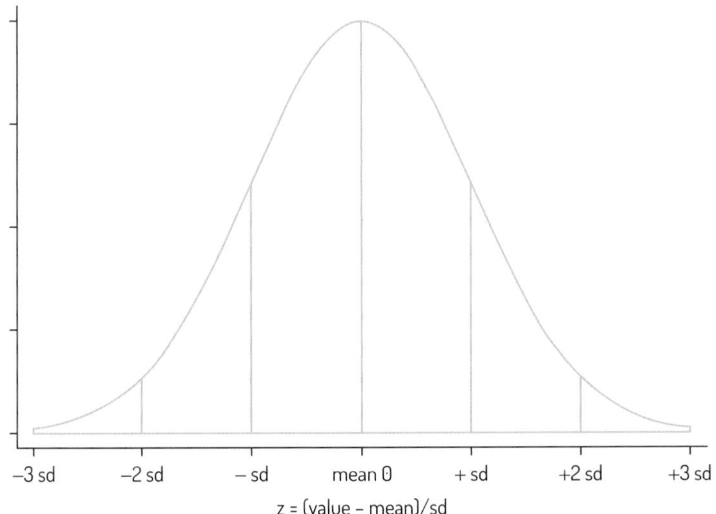

Figure 14.2 Normal distribution 'bell-shaped curve'

Source: www2.connectseward.org/shs/dal/review07/symmetric%20graph.jpg

on this. For instance, Tabachnick and Fidell (2013) posit the acceptable range to be in the region of −1.5 and +1.5, whereas George and Mallery (2010) hold that the values for asymmetry and kurtosis can be considered acceptable in the range of −2 and +2.

Descriptive statistics encompass methods of determining how often a response alternative was selected (frequency and percentages), checking the mean, median and the mode to identify the central location and tendencies for the measured variables, and examining how dispersed around the centre are the data using measures of dispersion, such as the standard deviation, variance and the range.

Central tendency

Referred to in common everyday language as the *average*, central tendency coins a middle point within a distribution of data points. The average helps us to get an idea about the mid-point of things; for instance, in establishing a grade profile of a taught module's assessment, the tutor checks the average grade point achieved to determine where the majority of the class is concentrated. To measure central tendency, there are three possible methods: the mode, the mean and the median.

Mode: The mode is the simplest tool given that it only determines the most recurring response. It is usually used in univariate analysis of categorical variables where data are nominal or ordinal, and where a calculated average does not make sense given that the coded numbers are used only for classification, but have no other meaning. To understand the gender profile of a sample, for instance, it makes sense to employ the mode method in understanding the sample distribution and general central tendency. If 1 = male and 2 = female, with a frequency of males being 300 and females being 140, the mode for Gender = 1. The mode hence specifies the most frequent or repeated response for this specific variable.

Median: Where the mid-point is sought, the median can be used specifically with ordinal data where there is a ranking order involved and the difference between the one alternative and the next has a meaning. So, based on Table 14.1, the median for this variable would involve organising the frequencies in ascending or descending order, and finding the mid-point, after excluding the 'no responses' so as not to alienate the median result. As such, the median would be 75, indicating a 'Weekly' visit as the half-way point of the responses.

Mean: This represents the average point that gives us a calculated perspective of the central tendency of the data for a continuous variable. The mean is calculated by adding up all the responses and then dividing them by the number of respondents who participated in the survey. In the IKEA study, where respondents are asked about how satisfied they are with the location of the nearest IKEA store along a Likert scale of 1 to 7, adding up all the scores recorded for this question in the data set and dividing it by the number of study participants can provide a calculated mean of the level of satisfaction. If 1 = strongly dissatisfied and 7 = strongly satisfied and the mean is 2.2, it indicates that the responses are more concentrated at the lower end, roughly implying high levels of dissatisfaction among respondents.

Measures of dispersion

The other side of determining central tendencies of response for measured variables is checking how the responses vary around the calculated mean score within a data set. It can also provide a benchmark for making comparisons among the response variability for groups in the data set; examining the dispersion of responses around the mean for level of satisfaction with the IKEA location for males versus females can indicate the extent of variability for both groups of respondents. This can be undertaken through calculating the range, variance or standard deviation.

Range: The simplest way to detect variability is to check the range of responses from the minimum value to the maximum value; dispersion is determined by calculating the range as: 'maximum value – minimum value'. If the study participants were asked to indicate how much they spent on average on their last visit to IKEA, the range would involve deducting the lowest amount given from the highest spend. Comparing this across age groups can give a sense of variability in expenditure within each group to determine if age makes a significant difference in spending patterns.

Variance: This method of checking for response variability involves a more sophisticated calculation than the range. It involves checking the difference between each response on the variable and the calculated mean score, squaring it and then summing up the answers. The sum is then divided by the number of responses minus 1 [= Sum (response – mean)^2/ N–1, provided that N = overall number of responses]. These calculations are undertaken by the computer software (SPSS, for example), which simplifies your analysis and takes care of the accuracy of the outcomes generated. A higher variance indicates a greater dispersion of responses around the mean.

Standard deviation: Another statistical method for calculating data dispersion around the mean is the standard deviation. It comprises a step ahead after calculating the variance and constitutes the square root of the variance; given that the variance being squared does not give a clear meaning that can be interpreted, square rooting it provides the standard deviation at the same numerical level as the responses, so it makes more sense. A higher standard deviation for a group of respondents, for instance for males in the sample when asked about their willingness to go to remote IKEA stores versus females, indicates that there is more variation within the responses of one group over another, here males over females.

Research in Practice: Visual Depiction of Descriptive Summaries (Bar Charts, Pie Charts and Histograms)

Preliminary analysis that summarises research data and describes its key characteristics can also be used to portray a frequency of responses for each of the key study variables.

In a survey completed by 125 respondents on the adoption of government e-services in the United Arab Emirates (UAE), the following question was asked:

> What would you say is the main reason for not using government e-services? Please choose ONE from the following options by circling the appropriate number:
>
> 1 Lack of awareness about the e-service government service option
>
> 2 Lack of knowledge on how to use it
>
> 3 High Internet and computer costs
>
> 4 Distrusting online transactions, especially electronic payments
>
> 5 Government e-services still need more enhancements
>
> 6 Preference for manual and face-to-face services

Descriptive analysis of the data collected is depicted in the following bar chart (Figure 14.3), which indicates that preferring manual/face-to-face services is the key reason for not taking up the government e-service alternative, followed by its need for improvement, and then lack of awareness.

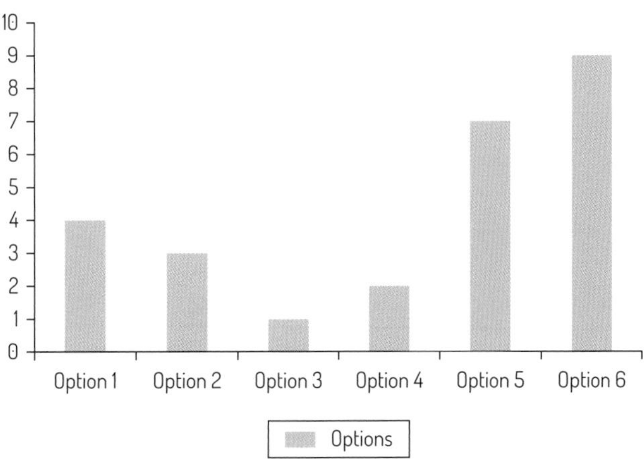

Figure 14.3 Reasons for not using government e-services in the UAE

(Continued)

(Continued)

Data were also sought on level of agreement on the movement by the UAE government to e-services through the question:

> Do you agree with the conversion of the UAE government services from conventional (manual) to electronic? Please choose along the following scale:

Strongly Agree	Agree	Neither Agree nor Disagree	Disagree	Strongly Disagree
1	2	3	4	5

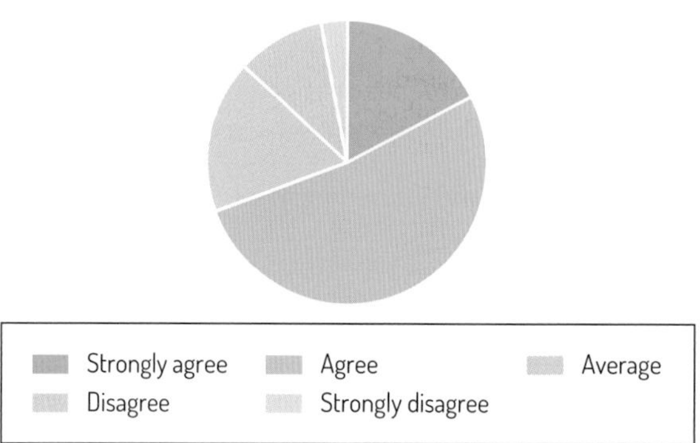

Figure 14.4 Level of agreement with conversion to e-services in the UAE

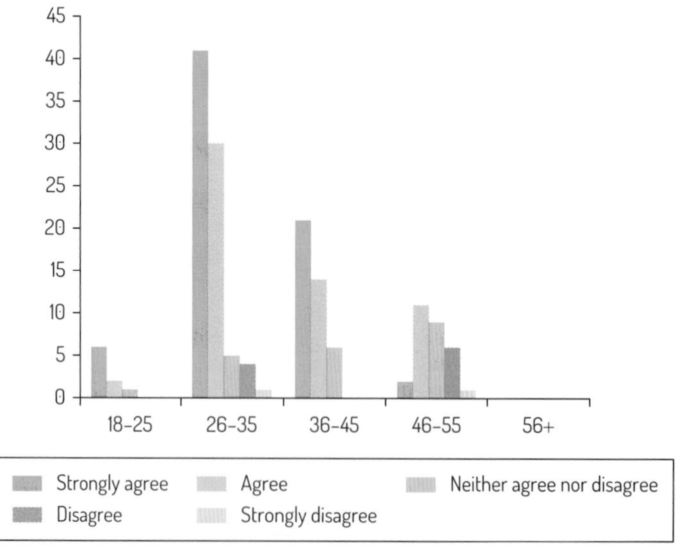

Figure 14.5 End user agreement about e-government based on ages in sample

Descriptive analysis of the data collected can be depicted in the pie chart in Figure 14.4, which indicates that there is a majority agreement with conversion to e-services (70%), with a low percentage of disagreement (13%) and around 17% neutral opinion.

Pie charts visually reflect different response categories on a variable as slices of the total. However, to diagrammatically compare response categories against each other for the variable (males versus females or older versus younger respondents), histograms are a good visual tool.

So, in comparing age groups within the sample on the extent of agreement with transitioning to e-government services, responses were reflected in the histogram in Figure 14.5. By comparing the heights of the columns, a clearer idea of the data distribution for age versus extent of agreement with move to e-services can be better visualised using a histogram.

Descriptive statistics and handling missing data

Data validation is imperative before effort is put into in-depth analysis to bring out patterns and insights of value for decision makers. Following data entry on an Excel spreadsheet or into data analysis software, it is important that the researcher scans the columns and rows to spot clear errors in data entry or careless responses. It is surprising how many 'blunders' a manual check by the analyst can yield. Counts of responses and mean scores can also be tallied to ensure consistency and help in going back to the original data source for amendments. With the support of technology, errors can be reduced through automated data entry optical scanning, using optical character recognition and image technologies, to read paper survey responses and transport them digitally into a data file, with high levels of accuracy (Dillman, 2011).

Commands on SPSS can also guide the analyst to find the specific case (the questionnaire number) for a variable where the blunder is, in order to correct it using descriptive statistics. On SPSS, follow the menu sequence: *Analyse > Descriptive Statistics > Explore*. Maximum and minimum values guide the process in spotting irregular out-of-place values. Non-responses which arise when some questions are left unanswered on the questionnaire can be tracked, and decisions for dealing with them should then be articulated.

Solutions can be determined by the level of importance of the question, whether it is a question on its own or part of a bigger scale of measurement items used to measure one variable, and by the extent of incomplete questionnaires found; if only a small number are found with incomplete responses, the researcher may decide to exclude them fully from the analysis. The disadvantage of this option is that responses for completed questions will be lost, which could have yielded important data. This option works well if these questionnaires have a large number of unanswered questions, so they are useless anyway given so many blanks. In other instances, the analyst may decide to exclude the questionnaire only for the specific variable affected; this entails that the sample size will be different in the analysis undertaken for different questions, so sample size has to be repeatedly stated. The other alternative, which can bring in a new analysis perspective, is to give all missing values on any particular variable a unique number code (e.g. 99 or any number which is not used throughout the data file), and then analyse them in case a pattern arises from the missing responses; this pattern may itself tell a story that assists the interpretation of the analysis (for instance, making sense of why respondents are shying away from answering a particular question).

Reflective Activity: Amazon's Subway Advert for *Man in the High Castle* – Controversy in the USA

As a successful online retailer that has written its place in business history, Amazon continues to seek means of increasing its successful operations worldwide. Yet, some actions carried out in the name of marketing its products can be remiss. An example is the November 2015 advert promoting its most recent TV series *The Man in the High Castle*, which wallpapered the Subway cars between Manhattan Grand Central Terminal and Times Square Terminal in New York City. Described as being insensitive and offensive by many commuters and encouraging a trend for using insignia inspired by Nazi Germany and imperial Japan, Amazon had to pull the advert.

An important question that usually follows such public uproars is around the effects they have on the consumer. Would certain groups now see Amazon in a poor light, leading to negative attitudes towards the online giant and to slower sales? Or, is this just a mistake that was rectified in time by Amazon, who may hence be viewed as customer-centric with a rapid response to public opinion?

Activity: A survey was undertaken among a sample of New Yorkers with the aim of establishing the impact after Amazon pulled the advert. As a researcher, assume you are provided with data from 300 respondents, including data on age, gender, social class, ethnic background, religion, attitude towards Amazon, and perceptions of its social responsibility.

What are the first steps you would take to validate and explore the data to provide a preliminary understanding of the sample's data distribution towards the next analysis phase?

Source: www.theguardian.com/us-news/2015/nov/25/nazi-inspired-ads-for-the-man-in-the-high-castle-pulled-from-new-york-subway

Inferential Statistics

The process of deriving conclusions based on evidence and probability measures denotes inferences or inferring things. Making or drawing inferences is a very important notion in research; observations, experiments, surveys and various modes of data collection are employed to arrive at systematic knowledge that can be put forward as the outcome of probability testing, reasoning and logical thinking. Inferential statistics are mathematical techniques which are used to make judgements (i.e. deduce/infer) about the properties of the population of interest based on data collected from a representative sample. The key idea is that observed differences between the groups or relationships observed between variables in the sample are assessed on the probability that they exist/occur systematically, rather than merely due to chance in the population under study. Systematically here refers to consistent repeatability, reliability and accuracy using the scientific process, and not based on unsupported assumptions.

Consider a survey study conducted among females in the USA which finds that females eat a smaller food portion when in the company of female friends as opposed to when eating with family. Could this difference be generalisable as actual for this populace, or is it occurring only coincidentally? How significant the portion intake difference is as a situational antecedent can be determined through the use of inferential statistics.

As discussed in Chapter 13, data types can be categorical such as nominal and ordinal data variables, or they may be quantity-based such as discrete (counting/ratio) or continuous (measuring/interval) variables. Different data types command the use of different analysis techniques; statistical methods for analysing categorical data are not the same as for continuous data, as also indicated for descriptive statistics. Continuous data are considered more insightful as they allow for the use of a wider variety of statistical analysis methods, yet both types of data are valuable and necessary in any study as relevant to its objectives. It is worth noting that continuous data can be grouped into categories (e.g. numerical data obtained on the number of calories consumed every day by respondents, grouped into: low calorie intake, standard calorie intake and high calorie intake) and hence transformed into categories if this aids the purpose of analysis. However, the detailed richness of the numbers is lost in this process, so it should only be undertaken if it has a clear rationale and only if it eases data handling and sense making.

Tips for choosing the right statistical method for analysis

Univariate analysis through one-way frequencies and descriptive statistics offers a good understanding of variables, but in isolation, i.e. individually; however, to better understand how variables measured in a study are related, bivariate and multivariate analysis is needed. Bivariate statistical methods (such as correlation analysis and cross-tabulations) analyse two variables at a time, whereas multivariate statistical techniques analyse any number of variables and can offer different types of inferences (beyond examining relationships and between group differences, they also assist in making predictions, such as in the use of regression analysis).

Yet, with a wide array of statistical tools, a researcher may be confused as to which one is best to use for which analysis situation. There are a number of criteria that can be used to assess which statistic is best for examining a phenomenon and testing a hypothesis based on the data collected. The following are some tips that offer some guiding criteria.

1. Purpose of the analysis

In order to study cross-relationships, i.e. relationships between two or more of the measured variables, it is important to understand first the aim of the analysis. For example, if the researcher in the CHANEL mini case sought to investigate the link between age and attitude towards CHANEL luxury products, it is important to clearly spell out the purpose of the cross-analysis of these two variables; in this instance, the purpose would be to find out whether there are significant differences in attitude among various consumer age groups. The null hypothesis would be that there are no significant differences among younger and older consumers in their attitude towards CHANEL products. If the analysis indicates a systematic relationship in the data sample, then the null hypothesis would be rejected.

Thus, the purpose here is to assess the *differences between/among groups*. Examples of statistical tools that can be used to analyse differences are: Chi-square, independent sample t-tests, paired t-tests, analysis of variance (ANOVA), multivariate ANOVA (MANOVA) and analysis of covariance (ANCOVA).

If the purpose is to assess the relationships between variables, i.e. whether a variable (or more) relates to or influences another variable (or more), examples of common statistical analysis tools that can be used are: Pearson product-moment correlation, Chi-square, Spearman's rank-order correlation, partial correlation and multiple regression.

Decoding which tool is best to use requires more criteria to narrow it down, as explored next.

2. Number of variables to be analysed

If two variables are to be examined at a time, then bivariate analysis tools should be used; bivariate statistics include: correlation analysis, independent sample t-tests, ANOVA and cross-tabulations. If more than two variables are involved in the analysis, then multivariate analysis is to be used; multivariate statistics include: ANCOVA, MANOVA and regression analysis. The specific statistic to choose among these depends then on the type of variables involved.

3. Type of variables (continuous or categorical, and, if the latter, how many categories)

The way variables were measured in the survey determines the type of variables involved in the analysis. Categorical variables (nominal or ordinal) entail the use of different statistical tools versus continuous variables (scale or ratio). In the case of CHANEL, assume age was measured categorically based on the respondents choosing among a number of age brackets (18–25, 26–35, 36–45, 46–55, 56–65). This means that Age, which is the independent variable (IV), is a categorical variable, namely ordinal due to the rising order of the alternatives, and comprising five categories. Attitude towards CHANEL products, the dependent variable (DV), is measured along a 7-point Likert scale, with *Nothing Special* at one end of the scale and *Outstanding* at the opposite pole; hence, this is a continuous variable.

4. Parametric assumptions underlying the data distribution

Beyond the above three tips, a very important point to consider is: can the data (for the variables to be analysed) provide a *parameter* for the given population?

A *parameter* is a quantity that is constant for a specific population and provides quantitative measures of that population – such as central tendency or variability expressed in a mean of or variance in the distribution of data. This can be obtained from continuous data but not from categorical data, or, more specifically, not from data with discrete categories where the coded numbers have no meaning for the analysis and cannot be used to obtain a mean, standard deviation or variance. Thus, if parameters can be obtained, *parametric statistical techniques* can be employed in the data analysis. These techniques hence entail that the data meets certain assumptions before these tools can be applied, the most common assumption being the shape of the data distribution (that data should be normally distributed when drawn on a histogram); examples of such techniques include ANOVA, product-moment correlation analysis and regression analysis. If, on the other hand, the specific values of a parameter in a given population cannot be estimated for a measured variable (specifically the DV), the data are not normally distributed or only a small data set was collected, the analyst needs to resort to non-parametric (distribution-free) statistical techniques (Pallant, 2013).

Parametric statistical techniques underscore stringent assumptions regarding the distribution of data for the population under study. A key assumption in using them for analysis is that a specific parameter can be estimated for a given population, such as measures of central tendency and variability (e.g. mean, variance). These statistical techniques are best used to analyse continuous data

Non-parametric statistical techniques do not involve knowing/estimating specific values for a parameter (e.g. a mean score of data distribution for a variable) in the population under study. They permit the analysis of small data samples, categorical data, and can be resorted to when there is a violation of parametric statistical assumptions

Non-parametric statistical techniques are the alternatives to parametric methods; examples include: cross-tabulations

(Chi-square test), Kruskal-Wallis, Spearman's rank-order correlation and logistic regression (used as an alternative to multiple regression if the DV is categorical). Parametric statistics are more rigorous and precise, which makes continuous data the preferred type for researchers. Non-parametric statistics are less sensitive in that they may not detect significant relationships or differences when they actually exist. However, there are many instances when categorical data are needed, so non-parametric statistics offer a good alternative. To make sure the latter offer accurate results in hypothesis testing, the analyst should place more stringent demands on statistical significance when using non-parametric statistics (e.g. check significance at different levels of confidence).

Table 14.3 brings together the above four tips by suggesting the most commonly used statistical techniques that are suited to the analysis purpose, number of variables, type of variables and whether parametric statistical assumptions are met.

Table 14.3 does not include every possible analysis technique under parametric and non-parametric statistics. Its aim is to highlight those methods that are most commonly used and which will be explained further in the following sections, together with their underlying assumptions. Some other statistical analysis techniques which are less commonly used will be briefly highlighted in the Advanced box at the end of this chapter (with suggested readings for more details on them).

Parametric Analysis Methods

Parametric statistical tests are rigorous analysis tools that can provide an analyst with accurate answers in hypothesis testing. They underscore stringent assumptions regarding the distribution of data for the specific population under study. One of the key assumptions is that a specific parameter can be estimated, such as measures of central tendency and variability (e.g. mean, variance). Parametric statistics tests are best used to analyse variables when the DV is measured on a continuous scale (see Table 14.3), i.e. interval level: scale and ratio data. The following section discusses some of the most commonly used parametric statistical techniques.

When using any of these tools for data analysis, there are assumptions to be checked to ensure they are not violated. These mainly involve: a continuous rather than categorical DV variable; all the cases constituting independent observations (no interaction between study subjects); homogeneous variance (equal variances of the groups, i.e. the same variability of scores for each group as checked within the tests); the sample being obtained through random sampling; and normal distribution in the population from which the sample was obtained as shown on a histogram. The last two assumptions are rarely easy to achieve, but the robustness of parametric statistical tests makes them 'tolerant' of such violations. Going into these assumptions in depth is beyond the scope of this book, but it is important that analysts check that there is little or no violation of the assumptions underlying each analysis test in undertaking it.

Analysis of Difference-Based Hypotheses

T-tests (independent, paired)

One of the main statistical tools that can be used to compare groups for significant differences is t-tests. These tests are used when the researcher is looking into comparing: (1) two independent

Table 14.3 Choice of statistical methods based on guiding criteria (not inclusive of all analysis techniques, but showing those most commonly used)

Type of Variable (IV and DV)	Purpose of Analysis	Number of Variables	Recommended Statistical Technique	Parametric/Non-parametric
IV: Categorical DV: Categorical	Comparing **differences** between categorical groups	I IV: 2 or more levels I DV: 2 or more levels	Chi-square	Non-parametric
IV: Categorical DV: Continuous	Comparing **differences** between only 2 categorical groups	I IV: 2 levels I DV (assumptions met)	Independent Sample t-test	Parametric
IV: Categorical DV: Continuous	Comparing **differences** between only 2 categorical groups	I IV: 2 levels I DV (assumptions NOT met)	Mann-Whitney U Test	Non-parametric
IV: Categorical DV: Continuous	Comparing **differences** among 3 or more groups	I IV: 3 or more levels I DV (assumptions met)	One-way between groups Analysis of variance (ANOVA)	Parametric
IV: Categorical DV: Continuous	Comparing **differences** among 3 or more groups	I IV: 3 or more levels I DV (assumptions NOT met)	Kruskal-Wallis test	Non-parametric
IV: Categorical DV: Continuous	Comparing **differences** between groups	2 IVs: 2 or more levels each I DV (assumptions met)	Two-way between groups ANOVA	Parametric
IV: Categorical DV: Continuous	Comparing **differences** among groups	3 or more IVs: 3 or more levels each 2 or more DVs (assumptions met)	Multivariate analysis of variance (MANOVA)	Parametric
IV: Categorical DV: Categorical	Examining **relationships** between 2 variables	I IV: 2 or more levels I DV: 2 or more levels	Chi-square	Non-parametric

Type of Variable (IV and DV)	Purpose of Analysis	Number of Variables	Recommended Statistical Technique	Parametric/Non-parametric
IV: Continuous DV: Continuous	Examining **relationships** between 2 variables	1 IV 1 DV (assumptions met)	Pearson product-moment correlation coefficient	Parametric
IV: Continuous DV: Continuous control variable: continuous	Examining **relationships** between 2 variables	1 IV 1 DV (assumptions met) 1 Covariate	Partial correlation	Parametric
IV: Continuous DV: Continuous	Examining **relationships** between 2 variables	1 IV 1 DV (assumptions NOT met for either IV or DV)	Spearman's rank-order correlation (rho)	Non-parametric
IV: Usually continuous DV: Continuous	Explaining how much of the variance can be explained by a set of IVs and determining the best predictors of the DV	A number of IVs 1 DV (assumptions met)	Multiple regression	Parametric
IV: Continuous, categorical or a mix DV: Categorical	Explaining how much of the variance can be explained by a set of IVs and determining the best predictors of the DV	2 or more IVs 1 DV: Discrete categories (2 or more)	Logistic regression	Non-parametric

groups at one point in time; or (2) two sets of data from the same respondents but collected at Time1 and Time2, for their mean score on some continuous variable.

The first type is the *independent t-test*, which compares data about two distinct groups of different (independent) respondents. Consider a study wishing to compare those who smoke and those who do not, on their view on anti-smoking shock advertising campaigns. The IV is a categorical and dichotomous variable comprising 'Yes' and 'No' as its nominal data (*Do you Smoke? Yes/No*). The DV is a continuous variable, where perceptions of anti-smoking shock advertising are measured via a 7-point Likert scale, along negative and positive poles. Analysis would involve using the SPSS menu sequence: *Analyze > Compare Means > Independent Sample T-tests*. The results would help establish whether there is a significant difference in perceptions between the two groups based on comparing their mean scores on the DV.

The second type is the *paired t-test*, which compares two data sets collected at two points in time from the same group of respondents; it may be aimed at finding out the change in response over time following an event or intervention. For example, imagine that Apple wishes to find out consumer opinions of its latest iPad two months and six months after purchase to gauge the usage influences of the product. Data would thus be collected from the same group of respondents, comprising iPad customers, on two occasions and analysed as two data sets. The IV is a categorical variable of two levels (two sets of data) compared on their mean scores for the DV – opinions on the iPad – measured on an interval scale (with *negative* and *positive* as the opposing poles). Analysis would involve using the SPSS menu sequence: *Analyze > Compare Means > Paired Sample T-tests*. The results would help establish whether there is a significant difference between the two related data sets in comparing their mean scores.

ANOVA (one-way ANOVA, ANCOVA, MANOVA)

If the categorical IV has more than two levels, for instance age with a number of different age brackets provided as choice options, and there is only one IV or 'factor', then *one-way between-groups analysis of variance (ANOVA)* can be the chosen parametric statistics test. Like t-tests, the DV should be a continuous variable, where the variability between the groups is compared with the variability within each of the groups. In this way, if there is a significance variance detected, it is systematically due to the IV and not due to chance, thus rejecting H_o. Based on the analysis, an '*F*' statistical value is obtained, representing the variance between the groups divided by the variance within the groups. The higher the *F* value, the more there is an indication of variability between groups as opposed to within groups. Through SPSS analysis functions, post-hoc tests can be generated when using ANOVA to find out where the differences are between the groups. Analysis would involve using the SPSS menu sequence: *Analyze > Compare Means > ANOVA*, checking for violation of the underlying assumptions (e.g. applying homogeneity of the variance test) and looking for post-hoc indicators of which group is significantly different to which other group.

If the analysis involves two rather than one IV, *two-way between-group ANOVA* can be used. For example, if subjects at different levels of income and education are compared on the extent of organic food adoption, then there are two IVs and two-way ANOVA is called for. *One-way analysis of covariance (ANCOVA)* takes the analysis one step further if the analyst is looking to compare between-group variance on a continuous DV, whilst controlling for another continuous variable, referred to as a 'covariate'. This is done if the latter is a confounding variable(s) suspected for influencing the DV, so it is controlled for in the analysis so the power or sensitivity of the *F* statistic can be achieved if there are significant between-group differences.

ANCOVA also has more uses, including comparing two groups after an intervention using pre-test/post-test designs, where you are comparing the results for each of the groups pre and post. In this case, ANCOVA can be used to control for the pre-existing differences between the groups by using the pre-test scores as the covariate. *Multivariate analysis of variance* (MANOVA) is another related test where, in this case, there are two or more continuous DVs, which are related, and on which differences between groups need to be checked for level of significance. MANOVA can be used where there is one or more IVs.

Analysis of Relationship-Based Hypotheses

Correlation analysis (Pearson product-moment correlation, partial correlation)

To investigate relationships, bivariate correlation analysis can be used when the analysis involves two continuous variables. Unlike previous comparisons of groups, where it was important to specify the IV and the DV, in using correlation analysis it does not matter which is the IV and which is the DV; the analyst is aiming to find out whether variable A is significantly associated with variable B, and to uncover the strength and direction (positive or negative) of this association using *Pearson's product-moment correlation coefficient (r)*. This relationship is assumed to be linear, and using a scatterplot can visually confirm this. The Pearson correlation test can also be used if one of the variables is dichotomous (e.g. gender).

An important flag of caution here is not to confuse correlation with causality. Correlation analysis does not examine whether variable A caused B or vice versa, but rather tests whether A is systematically linked with B, whereby if A increases B increases/decreases. The SPSS menu sequence for using the Pearson product-moment correlation analysis is: *Analyze > Correlate > Bivariate*, putting the two variables in for testing, and choosing Pearson under the *Correlation Coefficients* section to determine the strength of the association based on the value of coefficient '*r*'.

Pearson correlation coefficient r values can be anything in the range of –1 to 1. The +ve or –ve sign only indicates the direction of the relationship. Positive values indicate that as variable A increases, variable B increases and vice versa, whereas negative values indicate that as variable A increases, variable B decreases and vice versa, so the latter is an inverse relationship. The numerical value of r indicates the strength of the relationship; the closer r is to 1 or –1, the more powerful the association is between the variables; the closer it is to 0, the weaker the association or effect size. Statistics books provide guidance on r value ranges that are considered small, medium or large effect sizes (statistics reference books are suggested in the Further Reading section at the end of this chapter).

Consider a study of student engagement with technology in the classroom, where the researcher aims to establish the relationship between the extent of using Technology Enhanced Learning (TEL) tools and student engagement. If variable A, the extent of using TEL tools in classroom sessions, and variable B, student engagement levels, are measured using interval scales, correlation analysis can be used to check for a significant association between them and whether this is strong/weak, positive/negative. If the correlation coefficient $r = 0.3$, this means that the H_0 that variable A and B are not associated is rejected in favour of the H_1 that A is significantly and positively associated with B, with a medium effect size (Cohen, 1988).

If a confounding variable, C, might allegedly be influencing the two variables being analysed, you can control for it by using *partial correlation analysis*. In this case, the influence of variable C is separated out and, if indeed it is 'contaminating' the relationship between A and B, the results may indicate a smaller *r* coefficient and hence a smaller association or effect size. The SPSS menu sequence for using partial correlation analysis is: *Analyze > Correlate > Partial*.

For example, if *Unilever* wishes to find out whether the success of its *Sure* compressed deodorant range is related to its perception as a sustainable innovation, controlling for the effect of promotional activities undertaken during the period investigated entails using partial correlation analysis; this would help in determining the real significance and strength of a detected relationship.

Explaining Variance and Determining Best Predictors

Multiple regression analysis

An extension of the investigation of relationships between two variables into a more in-depth exploration of the relationships between a continuous DV and a number of variables entails the use of *multiple regression analysis*. This statistical test enables an understanding of a set of IVs for their ability to explain variance in the DV. The results can be interpreted to find out the power of the IVs together in predicting the DV (i.e. what percentage of the variation in the DV can be explained by this set of *predictors*) as well as the individual relative contribution of each of the IVs examined in relation to the DV (i.e. which of the IVs is relatively better at explaining variance in the DV, or contributing to the model). The IVs are ideally measured on continuous scales, where more variables can be added or removed from the model to determine the effect on the outcome; the analysis also permits determining changes in the predicting power of one variable while controlling for another.

Multiple regression analysis tests can be classified into three types, depending on how the IVs are entered into the equation to assess their predictive powers on the DV relative to others. In *standard multiple regression* analysis, the IVs are entered simultaneously, whereas in *hierarchical multiple regression*, the researcher decides on the order of entry based on the theoretical framework and the study's theoretical conceptualisation. Stepwise multiple regression allows SPSS to decide which IVs to enter into the model and the order of entry based on set statistical criteria. The SPSS menu sequence for using Pearson product-moment correlation analysis is: *Analyze > Regression > Automatic Linear Modelling/Linear*, selecting more details based on the sought test.

Regression analysis has stringent assumptions that must be checked before running the tests to ensure they are not violated in order to achieve a good regression model and generalisable results. Examples include a certain sample size (various statistics books recommend equations to ensure the number of respondents is suited to the number of IVs analysed), linearity, normality of distribution, absence of outliers (extreme values on IVs) and a lack of multicollinearity (i.e. IVs should not be highly correlated), among others. If any of the key

Figure 14.6 Using parametric and non-parametric statistical tests

assumptions are violated or the DV is categorical, *logistic regression* can be used instead as an alternative non-parametric statistical technique; it can also assess the predictive power of a set of IVs and establish their relative individual contribution to the model. For more details about types of regression analysis tests, statistical analysis books can be consulted as suggested in the 'Advanced' section.

Reflective Activity: Robinson's Squash'D Innovation

Innovation has become the name of the day for companies who want to keep aboard the success train and find new market opportunities. In 2014, under its Robinsons brand, Britvic launched *Squash'D*, relying on usage occasion market segmentation. Realising a market gap for customers who want to flavour their water on the go, the product achieved success with £11 million in sales in 2014 through *Squash'D*.

To determine the continued success of this launch, a researcher could study perceptions of the product among target customers a year later to determine if it was just a fad. A number of variables could be examined, including which gender purchases *Squash'D* more frequently, the relationship between purchase frequency and value perception, and factors that determine consumer satisfaction with this innovative product.

(Continued)

(Continued)

Activities:

1. To compare differences between males and females on purchase frequency, measured on a continuous scale of Very infrequent to Very frequent, which statistical test is best to use and why?
2. To determine the relationship between purchase frequency and perceptions of the value of the product, where both are measured on continuous scales, which statistical test is best to use and why?
3. To establish whether frequency of purchase, value perception and perceived healthiness can determine customer satisfaction (also measured as a scale variable), which statistical test is best to use? What other indications may this test provide for the researcher in this case?

Non-Parametric Analysis Techniques

Non-parametric statistical techniques do not involve knowing/estimating specific values for a parameter (e.g. a mean score of data distribution for a variable) in the population under study. They hence do not entail that strict assumptions be applied to the data to be analysed; the only basic assumptions involved are having independent cases or observations, and ideally that data sampling is random. They permit the analysis of categorical data, i.e. nominal and ordinal variables, specifically when the DV is a categorical variable. If the sample size is small (e.g. < 30 cases), or assumptions are violated in relation to the use of the parametric statistics test, then alternative non-parametric measures can be used instead to compare groups on differences and examine relationships.

One of the most commonly used non-parametric statistical tests is the cross-tabulation. These include cross-tabulation tables through the use of the Chi-square test. Additionally, each of the parametric statistical tests discussed earlier has a corresponding alternative non-parametric statistical technique, such as the Mann-Whitney U test, Kruskal-Wallis test and Spearman's rank-order correlation analysis, among others. Some of these techniques will be briefly discussed next.

Chi-square test for independence

One of the main statistical tests commonly used to investigate relationships between categorical variables is cross-tabulation using *Chi-square test for independence*. This test involves examining the relationship between two categorical variables, where each of them can be composed of two or more levels/categories (e.g. 2×2, 2×3, 4×3, 5×6 tables). When analysis involves two categorical variables each with two levels, a 2×2 table is generated which reflects the various combination of variables and the significance of the relationship (p-value) can be determined. The strength of the relationship, if significant, is reported using the Pearson Chi-square value when analysing variables with any number of categories, or through determining the Phi-coefficient (Φ) as recommended by some statistics books in the case of 2×2 tables. The SPSS menu sequence for using the Chi-square test is: *Analyze > Descriptive Statistics > Crosstabs*, followed by a choice of the variables and Chi-square as the test type required (checking also other statistics as relevant, such as *Phi-coefficient*).

One of the main assumptions in using Chi-square tests is that the frequency in each cell is 5 or more, and this assumption is checked in running the test on SPSS and reported below the results table (i.e. *'0 cells have expected count less than 5'*). If any of the cells has a count of less than 5 (or 10 as recommended in some books for 2 × 2 tables in particular), then the *Fisher's Exact Probability test* can be used instead; the latter is always reported as part of the SPSS Chi-square test output table.

Research in Practice: Analysing Categorical Data on Self-Service Technology Use in Banks – An Example

If a researcher seeks to determine whether service customers at a bank opt for the self-service machines or for the manned cashiers based on gender, these could be the two questions on his/her questionnaire:

1. Are you more likely to use the self-service machine at the bank if available when drawing cash rather than the staffed cashier desk?
   - Yes
   - No
2. Gender:
   - Male
   - Female

The characteristics can be applied as follows:

a. *Purpose of the analysis:* to determine whether there is a systematic and significant difference (i.e. if it exists, it is not due to chance) between males and females on their likelihood to choose self-service technology (SST) over manned cashiers in a banking service scape.
b. *Number of variables involved* = 2; one IV: Gender, and one DV: likelihood to choose SST over service staff.
c. *Type of variables:* The IV is a categorical variable comprising two categories (Male and Female), and the DV is a categorical variable also comprising two categories (Yes and No), so both of them are dichotomous variables and constitute nominal data.
d. *Parametric or Non-parametric:* Given that the variables are both categorical, cross tabulations can be used to analyse this relationship, which coins crossing one variable against the other in a 2x2 table. Chi-square tests can be undertaken, which comprise a non-parametric statistical tool as parameters about the population under study are not known/cannot be estimated.

The data collected will provide the numbers of males and females in relation to the likelihood to opt for the use of SST in banking services. Chi-square Independence tests can be used for this purpose as an effective procedure for determining whether there is a significant association between two categorical variables for the sample drawn from the population under study, using the SPSS menu sequence: *Analyze > Descriptive Statistics > Crosstabs.* In the window that opens, the analyst then needs to move one variable to Row(s) (usually

(Continued)

(Continued)

the DV, e.g. likelihood of opting for SST) and one variable to (Columns) [usually the IV, e.g. Gender], and choose Chi-square under the statistics tab, then continue to the analysis.

To make inferences about the wider population of interest, Chi-square tests can indicate the significance of the differences between genders (whether $p< .05$ for the commonly used 95% confidence interval) and the effect size. Effect size is the size or magnitude of the difference in the investigated cross-relationship where, over and above significance, it specifies the strength of the difference numerically.

The two output tables, Table 14.4 and Table 14.5, provide a number of insights.

Given that the two variables have two categories each (2x2), 4 combinations are obtained, portrayed in 4 key 'cells'. These cells indicate the frequency of incidence for each gender versus the Yes and No answers in relation to the DV, as indicated in Table 14.4. However, these numbers could be due to chance for the sample collected. To determine the strength of the association between the variables and the difference between genders for the DV, Table 14.5 offers measures of significance and effect size.

Table 14.4 Gender vs likelihood of choosing SST in bank services over manned cashiers

Count	Male	Female	Total
Yes, opt for SST	52	26	78
No, do not opt for SST	18	54	72
Total	70	80	150

Table 14.5 Chi-square test example

	Chi-Square Tests		
	Value	df	Asymp.Sig.(2-sided)
Pearson Chi-Square	131.206[a]	9	.000
Likelihood Ratio	115.888	9	.000
Linear-by-Linear Association	35.269	1	.000
N of Valid Cases	150		

a. 0 cells (0.0%) have expected count less than 5. The minimum expected count is 5.00

Source: www.spss-tutorials.com/spss-chi-square-independence-test

Two key figures are important to be checked in this table for simplicity. First, the *p*-value illustrated by the 'Asymp. Sig. (2 sided)', is =.000, and hence shows a significant relationship as $p < .05$. A significant relationship refutes H_0 that the two variables are independent through indicating that the observed frequencies (from the sample data) differ from the expected frequencies (what would have been expected if the relationship is merely due to chance).

Second, 'Pearson Chi-square' coefficient provides a value that reflects effect size. This statistic mainly expresses the total difference between the total observed frequencies (in the 4 cells) and their respective expected frequencies. To make sense of the value obtained (131.206) in the example in Table 14.5, the guide is that the larger this value is, the bigger the effect size. In other words, larger values indicate a larger magnitude in the difference between the obtained data (observed) and H_0 (expected). So, in this illustrated example, the alternative hypothesis that there is a significant relationship between the IV and the DV is well supported.

Mann-Whitney U test and Kruskal-Wallis H test

Comparing independent groups within a categorical variable on a continuous variable has been discussed under parametric statistical techniques through using independent t-tests. However, if the assumptions underlying the latter are violated (for example normality of distribution of the DV), or if the sample size is small, an alternative non-parametric test statistic can be used instead, namely the *Mann-Whitney U test*. For instance, a study analysing the difference between males and females on superfoods adoption behaviour, measures the behaviour using a continuous scale; however, illustrating the scores on a histogram does not indicate a normal distribution, but a relatively skewed curve. In this case, Mann-Whitney U test is best used to determine the significance of the between-group differences.

The way this test operates is similar to the independent t-test except for comparing median scores for the two groups rather than their mean scores. To overcome a skewed data distribution on the continuous variable, the test converts the continuous variable into ranks across the groups and compares ranks for the two groups to check for significant differences. The SPSS menu sequence is: *Analyze > Non-parametric Tests >Independent Tests*, then move the continuous DV into the *Test Variable List* box and the categorical variable into the *Grouping Variable* box, choosing *Mann-Whitney U test* from the *Test Type* section.

Similarly, a non-parametric test statistic that can be used as an alternative to ANOVA is the *Kruskal-Wallis H test*. Like the Mann-Whitney U test, it checks for significant differences among groups which represent categories on a categorical IV on a continuous DV. However, the Kruskal-Wallis test is used when the IV has three or more categories, such as three or more levels of education or income. Following the above SPSS menu sequence, the analyst in this case chooses the Kruskal-Wallis H as the test type.

Spearman's rank-order correlation (rho)

In checking for a significant relationship between two continuous variables, correlation analysis is the ideal statistical technique. This was discussed earlier under parametric statistical tests using the Pearson product-moment correlation test, which can also be used if one of the variables is a dichotomous nominal variable. An alternative non-parametric test statistic that examines significant relationships, if one of the variables is measured using ranked or ordinal data, is *Spearman's rank-order correlation (rho)*. The SPSS menu sequence is: *Analyze > Correlate > Bivariate*, placing the two variables in for testing, and choosing *Spearman* under the *Correlation Coefficients* section to determine the strength of the association based on the value of coefficient '*rho*'.

Ethics: Points to Consider

1. Checking the assumptions of any statistical test before employing it ensures its suitability for the data under analysis and the yielding of accurate and reliable results.
2. Researchers should not shy away from presenting findings if the research hypotheses are not supported (H_0 are accepted). Interpreting the results as they are and digging out the rationale, which is embedded in the overall findings and existing research, constitute valuable study contributions.
3. If statistical analysis is considered at an early stage of designing the data collection tool, the right questions will be asked and appropriate data will be obtained, thus avoiding too much data transformation during analysis, which can alter the essence of the original data.

Hypothesis Testing and Data Analysis Interpretations

Research in the social sciences involves both theoretical studies and more practical investigations, where findings in one support research in the other. Using statistical techniques to analyse quantitative data aims at addressing objectives, testing formulated hypotheses and thus answering the main research question. The interpretation of the various statistical test findings provides evidence as to whether each null hypothesis should be accepted or rejected based on the statistical significance obtained; if the null hypothesis is rejected, the tests provide the effect size that indicates the magnitude of the differences between groups or the strength of the relationship between variables stated in the alternative (hence supported) hypothesis.

Notably, the effect size (obtained from the various coefficients that indicate the magnitude of the differences or strength of associations, such as Chi-square coefficient, correlation coefficient, coefficient of determination) should be carefully interpreted by taking into account a number of factors, including the sample size and findings in prior relevant studies in the specific research domain. This illuminates the difference between the statistical significance obtained from the data in isolation, and the practical significance, which is the real value of the results in relation to practical consequence, relative meaning for the sample size under consideration, and its contribution to extant knowledge.

For example, it is usually the case that with large samples it is likely that even small differences or relationships may come out as statistically significant. It is thus your job as a researcher to put it in perspective by interpreting the results based on all available information to reflect the real theoretical or practical significance of the findings.

Advanced: Other Statistical Analysis Techniques and Considerations

- Parametric and non-parametric statistical analysis techniques include a wide range of methods that allow for all sorts of data analysis and hypothesis testing. Some of the most commonly used techniques have been discussed in this chapter, but there are also others available to the analyst for use, for other analysis purposes and situations. It is imperative that any researcher reads up on the statistical methods that are suited to the data and the statistic types that can help interpret the results in specialised quantitative analysis books in the early stages of designing the research methodology and the data collection method (e.g. experiment or survey). This will enable a design and implementation that are consistent with the data type needed and with the specific tools that will be used later on to examine that data for the purpose of hypothesis testing and interpretation of results.

- A key point of consideration in choosing measurement scales is to resort to existing scales, when available, as these have been tried and tested for validity and reliability (i.e. they test what they set out to test and they are free from random error). Such measurement scales (e.g. *Perceived Newness* by Dahl, Chattopadhyay and Gorn, 1999; *Consumer Innovativeness* by Manning, Bearden and Madden, 1995) can be adopted and adapted in newer studies rather than creating totally new scales. The stability of the measures and internal consistency reliability should be checked on SPSS to ensure the scale is reliable for use. For example, it is recommended that internal consistency of the scale's items, indicated by coefficient alpha values, be kept at or above 0.7 (see Nunnally, 1978).
- Some of the other statistical methods that are less commonly employed by younger researchers include factor analysis, logistic regression, cluster analysis, discriminant analysis, and structural equation modelling (SEM). SPSS can be used for most of these analysis methods, yet it is not suited to SEM which requires the analysis of parallel equations and involves more advanced data analysis (such as path modelling and confirmatory factor analysis); these require other data analysis software such as SmartPLS, LISREL or AMOS, among others. For more on statistical analysis methods, including those discussed in this chapter and more advanced techniques, consult the Further Reading list provided at the end of the chapter.

Chapter Summary

Concluding Part IV, Chapter 14 provides a practical treatment of how data collected quantitatively is taken from preparation stage to hypothesis testing to arrive at systematic insights into the phenomenon under study. It began with guidance on how data are summarised after collection and 'cleaning' to describe the sample's profile numerically and visually through tables and graphs. This step lays the foundation for relating back the results to the characteristics of the sample under analysis, and its representation of a given population. Descriptive statistics facilitate this process and can subsequently be followed by the use of inferential statistics to further unravel differences within groups and relationships between variables in relation to the research objectives and hypotheses. One of the key obstacles facing marketing investigators, especially junior researchers, is which statistical test is best to use for a given analysis situation and why. The appropriateness of the selected tests and their effectiveness in providing valid and accurate results are at the heart of a number of criteria that need to be considered and checked, as explained in this chapter. Following a systematic process of analysis assists hypothesis-testing procedures and ensures the research stays on track and provides the answers it originally sought. Interpreting results in relation to support or rejection of the research hypotheses entails considering all available information, not just the statistically significant results, and linking back with existing knowledge to arrive at real theoretical and practical significance.

Case Study: The 'Foodie' Movement and its Intricate Antecedents

The rise of the *foodie* movement around the globe has attracted some research attention in the sociology literature, some critique in food industry trend followers, but little research attention in marketing research. Blurring the lines between mainstream and speciality foods, many questions arise in relation to the rise of the *foodie*; for instance, who is 'the foodie' and what does the term encapsulate? Is it a phenomenon that differs across cultures? Is it about a sophisticated culinary experience, is it related to a deeper sense of self-expression and perceived identity, or is it about a collective food inspiration? In advancing associations around food as a physiological need and its more intricate perception as an emotional encounter, *foodies* emerge possibly as a heterogeneous consumer group that requires further in-depth exploration.

Defined simply as referring to someone who has a refined interest in the latest food fads or a highly sensuous enjoyment of food, the varying and imperfect extant definitions in different sources put the *foodie* phenomenon at an emerging, raw research stage. Intrigued by the *foodie* movement and spotting a gap that, if bridged, has both theoretical and practical implications, a study was commissioned by a global consumer commerce knowledge centre to find some answers. The objective is to describe what it means to be a foodie through probing food attitudes and motivations as antecedents of considering oneself a *foodie*, or labelling others as 'foodies'.

Using a survey research design, a questionnaire was developed to test a set of hypotheses among a sample of self-professed foodies, with a sampling frame derived from existing studies. The questions followed the hypothesis in investigating key variables measured using appropriate measurement scales. The generated demographic data related to gender, age, social class and level of education was categorical, whereas attitudes, motivations and 'foodie' behaviours were measured using continuous scales to provide a mix of rich data for analysis purposes. Following data collection and preparation, analysis was undertaken using both descriptive and inferential statistical methods.

Case study questions:

1. Suggest how descriptive statistics can be used for data analysis, and at which stage(s) of the analysis process.
2. To compare age groups on their different motivations towards *foodie trends*, where the latter is a variable measured along an interval scale, which statistical analysis method do you recommend? Why?
3. Would your answer to Q2 differ if data on motivations towards *foodie trends*, a continuous variable, are not normally distributed based on their histogram? If yes, which statistical analysis method would you use instead? Why?
4. Assuming a correlation analysis indicates a significant association between a high consumption of healthy foods and foodie self-labelling:
    - In determining the strength of the association, which statistical value designates the effect size?
    - Which other information is it important to consider when interpreting the actual theoretical and practical significance of the analysis results?

End of Chapter Questions

These questions should help you reflect on your understanding of this chapter:

1. What are the first, preliminary steps of data analysis that follow from data preparation?
2. How do you use univariate statistics to summarise the data?
3. What are the differences between descriptive statistics and inferential statistics?
4. What are the criteria for selecting a suitable data analysis statistical technique in a specific analysis situation?
5. When are non-parametric statistical techniques an alternative for parametric statistical methods?
6. What are other considerations when interpreting significance results in hypothesis testing?

Checklist

After studying Chapter 14, you should now be familiar with these key concepts:

1. Preparatory steps for data analysis
2. Using univariate descriptive statistics
3. Differentiating descriptive and inferential analysis methods and purposes
4. Criteria for deciding which statistical tools to employ for analysis
5. Parametric and non-parametric statistical techniques
6. Interpretation of findings for hypothesis testing

Further Reading (in sequence from beginners to advanced)

Pallant, J. (2013) *SPSS Survival Manual*. London: McGraw-Hill Education.

Leech, N. L., Barrett, K. C. and Morgan, G. A. (2004) *SPSS for Intermediary Statistics: Use and Interpretation*. Mahwah, NJ: Lawrence Erlbaum.

Cohen, J. (1988) *Statistical Power Analysis for the Behavioral Sciences*. Hillsdale, NJ: Lawrence Erlbaum.

Hair, J. F., Tatham, R. L., Anderson, R. E. and Black, W. C. (1998) *Multivariate Data Analysis* (5th edition). New York: Prentice Hall.

Blaikie, N. (2003) *Analyzing Quantitative Data: From Description to Explanation*. Thousand Oaks, CA: Sage Publications.

Sheskin, D. J. (2003) *Handbook of Parametric and Nonparametric Statistical Procedures*. London: CRC Press.

Bibliography

Cohen, L. S. (1988) *Statistical Power Analysis for the Behavioral Sciences*. Hillsdale, NJ: Lawrence Erlbaum.

Dahl, D. W., Chattopadhyay, A. and Gorn, G. J. (1999) The use of visual mental imagery in new product design. *Journal of Marketing Research*, 36 (1), pp. 18–28.

Dillman, D. A. (2011) *Mail and Internet Surveys: The Tailored Design Method*. New York: John Wiley & Sons.

Fisher, C. (2010) *Researching and Writing a Dissertation: An Essential Guide for Business Students* (3rd edition). Harlow: Pearson Education; New York: FT/Prentice Hall.

George, D. and Mallery, M. (2010) *SPSS for Windows Step by Step: A Simple Guide and Reference*, 17.0 update (10th edition). Boston, MA: Pearson.

Jones, S. (2014) CHANEL shows dedication to Middle East with first runway appearance, 13 February. [Online] Available at: www.luxurydaily.com/chanel-shows-dedication-to-middle-east-with-first-runway-appearance

Manning, K. C., Bearden, W. O. and Madden, T. J. (1995) Consumer innovativeness and the adoption process. *Journal of Consumer Psychology*, 4 (4), pp. 329–45.

Nunnally, J. O. (1978) *Psychometric Theory*. New York: McGraw-Hill.

Pallant, J. (2013) *SPSS Survival Manual*. London: McGraw-Hill Education.

Roderick, L. (2015) What L'Oréal, Britvic and Unilever can teach brands about innovation. *Marketing Week*, 11 December. [Online] Available at: www.marketingweek.com/2015/12/11/what-loreal-britvic-and-unilever-can-teach-brands-about-innovation

Tabachnick, B. G. and Fidell, L. S. (2013) *Using Multivariate Statistics* (4th edition). New York: HarperCollins.

Find journal articles and multiple choice questions online at: **https://study.sagepub.com/benzo** to support what you've learnt so far.

Analysis of data, whether qualitative or quantitative, is not the end of a research cycle. A good researcher needs to make sense of the analysis results and present the findings in a way that answers the research question and talks the language of the target research audience. A research report should provide a discussion of research findings that relates to the focal research objectives and assumptions/hypotheses, bringing out key insights and connecting back to relevant existing studies. There are a number of common considerations in writing an efficient and valuable research report, whether it is an undergraduate project report, a post-graduate dissertation or a management report for decision makers in organisations; these include early planning, using appropriate language, focus and clarity, offering a critical perspective and keeping the expectations of the reader at the forefront of its structure and length.

Chapter 15 presents an overview of how to move on from the research analysis stage to discussing the study's findings towards advancing valuable conclusions and implications. It will also explore the overall process of research writing and its various challenges, offering tips to make it more accessible and efficient.

PART V

Reporting Marketing Research

CHAPTER 15

Discussing Findings, Drawing Recommendations and Conclusions: Writing the Research Report

LEARNING OBJECTIVES

The key learning objectives of this chapter are:

1. To understand how to translate analysis results into an insightful discussion
2. To determine what validity and reliability mean in producing credible research
3. To develop research implications, recommendations and contributions
4. To reflect on research limitations and future directives
5. To write an effective and well-targeted research report and prepare an oral presentation

KEY CONCEPTS

By the end of this chapter, the reader should be familiar with the following concepts:

1. Dos and don'ts in discussing research findings
2. Establishing research value
3. Validity and reliability in high-quality research
4. Research conclusions and contributions
5. Research limitations and future studies
6. Presenting the research in a written report
7. Developing oral research presentations

Marwa G. Mohsen

Introduction

Imagine that you are sitting to read the latest research report on organic food and its health benefits and controversies: you go through lots of graphs and summary statistics. Then the report moves on to the value of organic food, which seems generic and fragmented from the visual data presented earlier. You start to look back at the data and wonder: so what?! What does the data analysis really tell us and what have we learnt about organic food based on this study?

What you are actually missing here is a critical discussion of the findings in a way that puts the results in perspective and provides new insights that can be compared to the existing knowledge. In undertaking a marketing research study, many students lose steam at the point when they finish data analysis, feeling like they are now at the end of the road. Yet, the reality is that data analysis is a starting point for bringing out actual knowledge and presenting information that, ideally, makes sense and opens up horizons, which add value to the research beneficiaries.

In a research report, the discussion chapter or section follows on from the raw findings to intelligibly reflect on how the data supports assumptions or hypotheses, or refutes them. It bridges the analysis with the research conclusions, implications and contributions. Based on the discussion, the researcher can highlight the value of the research, situate it within the extant literature and bring out the study's limitations (no study is flawless! Every study has some exceptions and limitations). Subsequently, new research directives that move the study of that area of research forward can be suggested to provide a motivation and proposal for ensuing further research as the cycle of life continues.

However, it is not always easy to polish up this part of the research and elicit the value of the study's findings, and many students and researchers falter at this point. Such a situation is explicitly clear in a research report that loses both momentum and reader engagement after data analysis is recounted. Thus, the written research report illuminates the scene in the way it is verbalised, structured and presented. A good, well-planned and properly targeted report will offer new value, taking the reader on a journey that flows smoothly with no thuds or abrupt halts, and uses a language appropriate to whoever receives it. A poorly written and loosely focused report superficially states the steps taken in the research study in a summary form, is fragmented and unable to reach its final destination or an engaged, appreciative reader. Moreover, presenting the work verbally provides for an interactive means of reporting the work to its audience and achieving prompt feedback; when done properly, oral presentations can make the work shine and draw out ideas from the audience on its strengths as well as ideas for its further development.

Chapter 15 provides an overview of the steps that follow on from research analysis, drawing on tips for how to ensure they connect back to the research aim and objectives, and the context of the study. The chapter also looks at how to present a research overview with symmetry and efficiency towards bringing out valuable research outcomes. It looks at a writing process that can produce a research report that is well organised, offers intelligent arguments and is clear, logical and creative. Pitfalls are explored and tips are offered throughout the chapter to help avoid the former and make use of the latter in concluding research studies, producing research reports and verbally presenting the work for dissemination.

Snapshot: Setting the Scene with Nestlé's Failure in Africa

Lots of research is conducted in good faith but flops because of its failure to provide actionable and targeted recommendations, or because the way it is reported does not help the target reader/research beneficiary. An example of this is Nestlé's marketing practices in Africa that have led to a boycott campaign against its baby milk products.

Nestlé has been the subject of ethical concerns regarding its marketing strategies and practices due to its efforts in promoting baby milk as a 'natural start' that 'protects' babies in countries where access to pure water to feed babies on formula is not possible. Its actions have been attacked as promoting poverty, putting babies who need milk formula at risk through the failure of its labels to warn mothers that the powdered formula is not sterile and may contain harmful bacteria, especially if used with non-sterile water. Given that breastfeeding can be a lifesaver, particularly in conditions of poverty, compared to formula feeding for babies, Nestlé's actions can be viewed as socially irresponsible.

Marketing research conducted in Africa must have preceded any move of Nestlé to Africa, making it a seemingly lucrative move. Yet, the target market is not just any mother who can move from breastfeeding to formula as a breast milk substitute. Mixed with unclean water, the powdered formula can result in disease for vulnerable infants, thus placing infants in less economically developed countries at risk and breaking international safety and marketing standards. Getting mothers to believe in baby formula as a good option, when it is less healthy and more expensive, has led to a Nestlé scandal.

The recommendation of any marketing research project to move to these African regions required a proper interpretation of research findings as to who best to target: possibly more affluent mothers who have the means to obtain/generate clean water, who are educated to a level where they can understand the risks of using powdered formula and the right portions to use to avoid malnutrition. *Hence, it is not only important to conduct efficient market research that provides an idea on the way forward, but also to provide an interpretation of the findings in context, and the implications that assist decision makers should take into account many external factors and provide specific recommendations that help rather than hinder the reader/research beneficiary in applying the research results.*

Source: Nestlé Boycott: Nestlé Free Zone – www.babymilkaction.org/nestlefree

Discussing Research Findings: Dos and Don'ts

One of the most important sections that makes up a large part of a research report in importance and length is the results section, where the analysis of data is presented. Depending on whether the study is qualitative or quantitative (or is designed on mixed methods which includes both), the structuring of the results section/chapter may vary. The key point is to serve the research purpose and address its aim and objectives; you need to maintain consistency with the research approach that informed the design and the methodology (see Chapter 4). This entails using appropriate language for the task through, for instance, avoiding quantifying qualitative research. You can separate out the results from their discussion by providing, for example, visual tables and graphs (in a quantitative study), then move on to discuss them in a separate discussion section. Alternatively, you can bring out the key themes, for example, based on a thematic analysis (in a qualitative study) and link them directly to each of the research objectives, consistently answering the research question

Figure 15.1 Moving from data analysis to a discussion of findings

as you go along. In quantitative studies where hypotheses are developed for testing, some researchers opt to structure the data analysis results around the hypotheses, where each hypothesis is posed as the results related to it and the discussion of what these results mean, follow in an organised manner.

All of these approaches work and none of them should have any issues as long as the rationale behind the structuring choice is clear and there is a logical and smooth flow. However, problems occur when, for instance, research students think that finding out that Variable A is correlated with Variable B, thus supporting the hypothesis that A and B are significantly related, is enough to present. The real question, though, is: *so what?* In the bigger scheme of things, in looking at the context of the study and what it set out to uncover empirically (i.e. through systematic data collection and analysis), it is imperative that the results are explicated and implications revealed. If, for example, an exploratory study of consumer perceptions of electric cars in Egypt highlights a lack of trust in the efficiency of this emerging technology, the discussion should highlight factors linked with this trust issue and its antecedents within the consumer sample studied. Two different researchers may be presented with the same data analysis results and discuss them differently, uncovering alternative insights linked to the research question, each using a different lens. Hence, the research discussion is important in drawing out the findings and making sense of them towards accentuating the research contribution.

In discussing research findings, Table 15.1 offers some dos and don'ts as tips for consideration.

Table 15.1 Dos and don'ts in discussing research findings

DO...	DON'T...
• ... be clear and concise, using the right variable names and terms that are relevant to the research aim and objectives	• ... assume that the analysis results speak for themselves and that it is enough to throw in a few graphs and tables with no explanation or discourse about what they mean for the study
• ... use authentic research materials and accurate claims in your discussion. Only rely on robust findings in drawing logical arguments that are both valid and reliable	• ... produce a summary of the research results that is very descriptive and adds nothing at all in terms of a critical scrutiny of what it means relative to outstanding assumptions/ hypotheses that it supports or refutes
• ... be careful in interpreting the results, avoiding errors in reporting the meaning of percentages/percentage points (e.g. in quantitative studies) and avoiding inaccuracies in the logic driven by respondents' quotes and what they signify (e.g. in qualitative studies)	• ... have a jumbled comments section that lacks synergy with the results and has no proper organisation in relation to the research objectives and reasoning
• ... think about how you will structure your analysis and discussion section(s) before you set out to present them in writing in the report using a clear rationale	• ... deviate from the main focus of the study and get derailed by some trivial results that came out of the analysis; stay focused on the main objectives and hypotheses. If additional findings emerge, put them in a separate section after the main findings, or discuss them as supplementary outcomes
• ... keep your research objectives (and hypotheses) in mind throughout so you stay true to the main focus of the study in your critical thinking arguments and in presenting your work	• ... jump to big conclusions (yet), as the discussion part is about the results in relation to the research focus and context. The wider inferences and consequences of the study can be presented (prudently) in the following section on research contributions and implications
• ... look at other research papers and the research work of other students to get an idea about optional ways of thinking about and presenting the research analysis results relative to their discussion	• ... lose steam in reporting what you did throughout the research process you undertook; viewing the writing up of what you learnt along the research journey as an exciting endeavour helps you communicate it properly to its planned audience
• ... draft your work and feel free to go back and restructure it again and again if it becomes clear that the way you chose to present it does not serve the expectations of its reader(s) or is vague and/or confusing. You may have an immaculate study in essence, but communicating it poorly may undermine your efforts and reduce its value	• ... forget to bring in existing literature and compare it to your research findings to enrich the insights your data is bringing in, situating your research within extant knowledge, highlighting similarities, add-ons and contradictions

Validity and Reliability in Research

Valid and reliable research is an ever-sought requirement in any credible study, where validity and reliability reflect its quality and relate to the stages of research design and execution. In simple terms, valid means true and accurate, and reliable means consistent and dependable over time.

Valid means true and accurate. Valid research refers to the degree to which it accurately measures what it intends to measure

Reliable means consistent and dependable. Reliable research refers to the degree to which the study's measurements are reliable and dependable if repeated

Valid research is essentially reliable, but reliable research is not necessarily valid

Validity in research refers to the degree to which a study measures what it sets out to measure; this involves using terms and concepts true to the focus of the study, using valid measurements that gauge the specific variables they intend to measure, relying on robust and logical analysis results, and presenting findings that make truthful claims specifically related to their original focus and leading to valid conclusions. *Reliability* refers to the extent to which the study's measurements and findings are consistent and dependable, such that repeating them under the same conditions would yield the same results, interpretations and conclusions over time. Reliability precedes validity, so valid research has to be reliable but reliable research is not essentially valid.

There are different types of validity and reliability, some of which are explored next, and these may also differ based on the nature of the research being qualitative or quantitative based. Validity in qualitative research is mainly related to data interpretation and the themes that arise/conclusions that are drawn based on data transcription. Making sense of qualitative research materials using an interpretivist philosophy entails human reflections that can be questioned for validity of how the data (which involves not just words, but also verbal expressions and other bodily cues) are 'read' and construed. Reliability in the case of qualitative research is about checking and affirming the data collected with the study's subjects to make sure that what was understood by the researcher is what they meant. Also, having more than one researcher independently analyse the data and produce their own interpretations of the analysis results can help test for and ensure consistent and dependable research findings.

In the case of quantitative research, *internal validity* is relevant for experimental research where cause and effect are being investigated; it is about the extent to which the researcher can establish a causal relationship between the independent variable and the dependent variable under study without being confounded by other possible causal factors. *Construct/measurement validity* is relevant in survey research or, more generally, descriptive research using quantitative data collection methodologies; it involves establishing that the measurement scales used are measuring the construct (concept or set of variables) that they set out to measure. This can be assessed using statistical test techniques that test for construct validity (see Hair et al., 1998; Pallant, 2013).

External validity relates to the generalisability of the research and the extent to which the results can be inferred from the sample to the wider population and also applied to other research settings. It is more relevant in quantitative studies where large samples are investigated; however, external validity cannot be tested statistically, yet it may be checked by ensuring the sample size is large enough and the sampling frame and sample selection are efficiently drawing a representative sample so that results may be applied to the wider population under study. In the case of qualitative research, external validity may be referred to as transferability, i.e. whether the elucidations that come out of the data and its analysis may be transferred to a wider context of the population of interest or to other settings (e.g. other customers, industries or organisations). But, given that qualitative studies do not aim to generalise, their small sample-based research need only be rich in the depth of exploration and detailed in its explanation of the topic, such that the research audience can make sense of the potential scope of the findings (Lincoln and Guba, 1985).

Another common type of validity that should also be established is *content validity*; this covers the extent to which there is a match between the content area of the research in terms of its objectives and specifications, on one side, and the test items (various parts of the measurement scale) used in the study, on the other. It is also now and again referred to as *face validity*, and it is usually established at the pre-test stage of a research study where the data collection tool is inspected by experts in the field of research to validate that the measures are pertinent to the intended content. Reliability in quantitative-based studies is about measures being free from error and hence being dependable; these involve the internal consistency of measurement scales (how all the items that make up a test scale measure the same variable, and checking the correlation between them) and the stability of the measurement procedures (the test procedure is conducted and then repeated again on another day to check for its stability). These can be determined using various statistical testing methods.

Establishing Research Value

The basic criterion for determining the value of a research project is how the findings and their interpretation relate to the original research question and the study's objectives. Ask yourself the question: what have I learnt in undertaking this research and how does this reflect on future actions to be taken by the brand, business, industry, individuals or organisation benefiting from the study?

The research value is an insight that should have been theoretically established early on in the research process, where the research gap was proposed and the study's contributions were tentatively advanced. After data analysis and the interpretation of findings, the actual research value is unveiled based on the empirical results, whereby assumptions made or hypotheses developed early in the process are systematically validated. The study's conclusions thus bring out a summary of your creative understanding of the dynamics of the subject or the phenomenon under study in view of the research project's key question and aim.

Research in Practice: How to Produce Research Results that the Marketer Actually Needs

There are many examples in the history of marketing research where research seems to be a crucial answer to saving a business from turmoil by providing key information that the marketing executive lacks. Nonetheless, a research report may look great with all its glamorous-looking figures and its interesting discussion of findings, yet fail to tell the marketer what they need to know most.

(Continued)

(Continued)

For example, when Nestlé identified a market for its baby milk in the African continent, it was logical that the benefits of the product it was offering apply to any developing baby. Universally, mothers seek alternative means of baby nutrition driven by a variety of factors. So, marketing research would have identified that poorer countries in that region would benefit from the nutritional value provided by Nestlé's powdered baby milk formula. The question is: did the research conducted provide insights into who the customer is NOT as opposed to who the customer may be? Did it offer answers to barriers for purchase and adoption of the product category in general due to more basic economic and sanitary conditions that override social and nutritional factors of consideration?

If research offers contributions that are 'off the mark', this might be the result of a breakdown in communication between the researcher and the research beneficiary – what do they already know and where exactly are the knowledge gaps they want filled? But even in academic research conducted by undergraduates or postgraduates, that off-target situation can be the result of a superficial attempt at defining the research gap or coming up with a hurried research question based on little background context and a flawed literature review.

A flipped research design

One of the recommended approaches to ensure the research yields appropriate value by the time it is concluded is to visualise the research process steps in reverse and design it starting at the end, then work backwards. What is the last step in conducting any research? It is broadly an implementation of the outcome – an outcome that makes sense and offers new perspectives to decision makers. Keeping an envisioned original contribution to knowledge in mind, the research report should thus be built in a way that aids the execution of the outcome, both in how the report looks and in its content; the study's implications and recommendations are based on an interpretation of the research results following data collection and analysis. Hence, the analysis should be designed such that it answers the questions raised by the research objectives (is it what, why, how, to what extent or who?). This assists in determining the type of data to be collected to enable the finding of answers to these specific questions. Importantly then, does the existing literature already hold this data, so that secondary research is sufficient to address the study's purpose, and, if not, what are the gaps that primary data can close? As data are being collected, the blanks they are intended to fill need to be continuously checked (particularly in conducting qualitative research where data are collected in parallel to analysis) to ensure the study stays on track for its intended outcome.

Such an outcome needs to significantly link all the way up the process to the research objectives and even further back to the research aim and key question(s). If the research contribution and outcome do not explicitly offer potentially significant value to one or more stakeholder(s), or come across as vague or unclear as to how they consistently address the specific reasons for conducting the study, then you need to go back and alter something in the research plan.

Research Conclusions, Implications and Contributions

The final stage of writing a research report involves pulling it together through a conclusion based on the findings and discussion. A conclusion is not a summary of what the study reached, but it is rather an indication of what the researcher arrived at in pulling together the interpretation of the findings and synthesising the various parts of the study; the result is a symmetric argument built on reason and evidence presented as the study's conclusion (see Chapter 5 for more details on symmetry in research).

Writing a high-quality conclusion involves staying away from two extremes: at one end, you need to avoid offering a mere summary of the steps of the research and everything that has already been said along these steps; at the other end, a good researcher should not suddenly present in the conclusion section new findings that have not been discussed throughout and that are at the core of the study.

Hence, a good conclusion section/chapter should have a structure that brings back what the research set out to do, highlights the significance of the topic of the study and makes logical links between the various parts of the arguments, starting from the hypotheses (in quantitative research, or otherwise the assumptions in qualitative research) to how the findings supported or contradicted them. Along these lines, the conclusion ties the various elements of the research consistently together and shows how the empirical results systematically addressed – or did not manage to address – the research aim and objectives, leading on to the research implications and recommendations.

Research implications can be theoretical or practical, or both. The relevance of the research findings to existing theory needs to be explained by reflecting on how new knowledge obtained from the study complements existing theory, validates it or challenges it. The study may be building on existing theory and coming up with a new theoretical model or framework; the way it ties in with extant models should be elaborated on. Theoretical implications are thus of benefit to marketing theorists and researchers.

The practical implications depend on who the research beneficiary is. If you are producing a research project that focuses on a particular company or brand, the beneficiary is marketing decision makers for that company or brand; hence, the implications should provide actionable recommendations as to how they can make informed decisions based on the research outcomes. If the study is industry-focused (for instance, for food sector marketers), or offering answers for public policy makers (for example, in relation to societal weight management and obesity control), then the implications should highlight the relevance of the study for strategists and policy makers in terms of how its outcomes add to the debate and guide future strategies or policies.

If, alternatively, the research is a social marketing study that also aims to inform consumers about their own behaviours or about certain market forces that influence their decisions (for instance, in relation to promoting ethical and sustainable consumption), then research implications for this group should be explained and means of disseminating the research outcomes to the right consumer groups should also be proposed. Presenting theoretical and practical implications in separate sections is a good approach, so that each is distinct and clear for its target reader or beneficiary.

The implications are critical to advancing the research contributions, which show where the value creation of the research really is. The implications bring to life how the originally identified research gap, which motivated the study and initiated the research question, could be closed via the newly obtained knowledge: what has this knowledge contributed that the research beneficiaries did not know before and how can they make use of it? Yet again, it also identifies the new gaps the study left behind in terms of its boundaries and how to take this forward in future research.

Research Limitations

When you endorse a research project with interest and enthusiasm, the intention is to design it properly so that the process works towards achieving valuable contributions. Yet, there is no such thing as perfection in research; humans conduct research, studying in most cases other humans, or data generated about other humans. In the process of planning, design and implementation, even the most experienced researchers will be faced with obstacles and restrictions. As much as a researcher would aim to overcome these in design and execution, even the data collected and results may involve unintended limitations or inaccuracies beyond the researcher's capacity to overcome them. The first of these may relate to whether or not the study addressed all the research objectives. If the study did not manage to pursue one or more of the originally set objectives, acknowledging this is a positive thing. It sets the boundaries for what was done and reflects on what could not be done, justifying it from your point of view as the researcher.

For example, in the initial phases of planning, access may be a limitation if the study's target sample is in another country, is inaccessible in person or by e-mail, or unwilling to engage with the researcher. An online survey may, for instance, yield responses from a large male sample, with fewer female participants than intended included in the sample. This sample bias has to be acknowledged and its effects investigated in the attained results. In another instance, it might be that a focus group with a mixed sample of genders and ages becomes a challenge due to the inability to find a common time for it to take place for the subjects willing to take part. In this instance, more than one focus group may be conducted with the sample in each not ideally comprising the optimum intended mix of subjects. If there was a limitation and only one focus group was possible, it is important to present this limitation to the reader and explain the foundation for it.

The fact is: no one expects a perfect research study, free of limitations. On the contrary, if limitations are not explicitly recognised and stated, then the research may be seen as weak and lacking depth in showing its coverage boundaries. If the results are attempting to cover every single dimension, then the study may be sceptically viewed as over-ambitious and unrealistic. In other words, if you do not highlight exceptions to your work, there is a high likelihood that the reader will see these limitations as gaps and hence criticise your work and findings, hence the importance of thinking about the limitations facing the study from the planning phase into design and implementation, and putting it all together in a key section in the report. During the analysis and interpretation of the results, other limitations will also emerge in relation to questions that the study could not answer or further questions instigated by its findings.

Sources of limitation are usually related to a study's focus (i.e. the boundaries of what it covers and what it does not cover in relation to the industry, variables and sample characteristics), access to resources in data collection (it might be that only a small sample is accessible or a certain respondent group but not another), or the sampling technique used (e.g. using a non-probability sampling technique such as convenience sampling, with results hence not being fully representative or generalisable). Limitations can also emerge when hypotheses are not supported and further data collection can help to clarify the contributing factors or causes. In some qualitative studies, researcher bias can be a limitation to be reflected on in explaining the possible subjectivities in data analysis or the interpretation of its meaning. As a researcher, you should anticipate the potential research limitations and make every effort to address those that can be handled along the way, explaining the challenges involved and how they were overcome. Fluid limitations that remain unresolved can be viewed constructively as opening up new paths for future research through proposing how the next study can resolve any such limitations.

Figure 15.2 The importance of presenting research limitations

Future Research: The Way Forward

It is often the case that if you want to start new research, you seek new ideas about gaps in existing knowledge through looking at the limitations section of any study. Limitations highlight boundaries and reveal where research in an area has come to and where the next steps could be. The future research section in any research study is crucial as it explains the different dimensions that may inform the next study so that a better understanding of the topic and relevant concepts can be achieved. Future directives build on the present state to determine new applications and potential differences that need to be investigated further; possible extensions that can be made to conceptual frameworks established by the present study; and new perspectives that may emerge in new studies to overcome the current research limitations.

The importance of being critically reflective in presenting the future research section is that it allows for the advent of new arenas of thought that you or other researchers may develop. It can shape the next phase of a study in any particular area by putting the building blocks in place, ready to be picked up, probed and scrutinised by the next researcher. A weak future research section signifies a weak limitations section, which in turn represents a fragile current study lacking rigour, depth and a distinct contribution. Remember how you developed your research question by spotting a gap in the literature which guided your research focus? It came out of scanning the literature and studying what others have researched in your area of interest, but it was also prompted, importantly, by the limitations and future research directives implicated in the existing studies.

A future research direction could be applying the conceptual framework in another context (e.g. on a different consumer group, for a different company, industry, country or culture, or in a different data collection environment) to examine to what extent it is supported and aids generalisation, or it could involve addressing new factors or accounting for other potentially confounding variables that may be influencing the research results. Collecting more data or making comparisons across samples can also be a forward-looking objective in the next study.

Reflective Activity: Examples of How to Report on Limitations

Young researchers find it difficult to critique their own work and admit the exceptions inherent in it. As human beings, admitting that we are not perfect and that there are weaknesses to what we do is always uneasy, but experience makes it easier to do so. The way you phrase research limitations is crucial to explaining them as challenges, some of which could be partially addressed and some of which can only be dealt with in future studies. Limitations are not meant to discredit your research efforts, but rather to frame what was achieved and how it informs both present and future studies.

Qualifiers and quantifiers can help in reporting research limitations. They also linguistically assist in being prudent with presenting arguments and findings.

Examples of qualifiers include the following:

- In most cases, respondents perceived using self-service technology in retail stores as positive and efficient. Yet, there were instances where open-ended comments by some respondents pointed to a reduced efficiency when technology fails them.
- Generally, participants had a favourable attitude to customer-to-customer interactions at the library, but there were exceptions in situations where an employee was not present to deal with a negative incident. This emerging theme needs to be further investigated in future research.
- On average, the sample comprised more respondents with above-average income levels. This might have affected the results and biased them towards this particular group. The next study could complement this research by widening the sample profile to access respondents at more varied levels of income to examine whether similar results arise.

Examples of quantifiers include the following:

- Around half of the respondents reported positive intentions to adopt organic food-buying behaviour.
- Participants highlighted frustration with the government e-service system on two occasions during the focus group. There was not enough time to probe this further, but it opens up a path for delving deeper into the psychological barriers to e-government service adoption.

- The partially supported hypothesis indicates that charities using a fear appeal in marketing communication may reach certain consumer groups but not others. A more specific profiling of consumers who are most likely to be receptive to fear appeal adverts needs further investigation, which was beyond the scope of the present study.

Activity: Reflect on the above examples. Can you highlight the keywords that point to exceptions and limitations? How can you bridge this into the further research section of a research report?

Source: Academic writing: authority and credibility, Monash University, at www.monash.edu.au/lls/llonline/writing/general/academic/2.2.xml

Presenting the Research in Writing: The Research Report

Any research project is a journey, most of it is planned and some of it unravels along the way. Reporting on research is about presenting this journey, not just by describing it, but also through offering clear and evidence-based arguments that explain its design, process and outcomes.

It is important to be excited about the writing and to approach it with enthusiasm; you also need to be organised and follow a structure that enables a logical demonstration of the work carried out, from setting the research question and justifying it to recommending future research and the way ahead.

In writing the research report, Table 15.2 offers some dos and don'ts as tips for consideration.

Table 15.2 Dos and don'ts in writing the research report

DO...	DON'T...
• ... write down the research objectives clearly in the first stage of the research and refine them so they guide the next steps	• ... leave the writing to the end when all the actionable research work is done. Starting early and using drafts will keep a pace and produce a spine to develop on
• ... pull the reader in at the introduction section by being transparent and precise in explaining what the research is about, what it is not about, why it is significant and what valuable contribution it aims to make	• ... ignore the advice of your supervisor or mentor in relation to what they expect to see and the structure of the work
• ... draft a literature review early on after the key research variables are established. This will set the grounding for your work by building on existing studies and clarify the research gap driving the study	• ... lose sight of the reader or beneficiary of the research in planning the structure and content of the report to ensure it is of good value to its audience

(Continued)

Table 15.2 (Continued)

DO...	DON'T...
• ... map out the structure of the report from its outset based on a clear understanding of the expectations of the institution to which your work will be submitted, and having also reviewed previous successful exemplars if you can get access to them	• ... use 'I' or 'We' as it makes the work informal and personal. Expressing yourself as the researcher and explaining the work in objective and formal language reflects high quality and impartial research
• ... check your work for accuracy, be it in terms of the numbers and percentages in quantitative studies or the coding and categories emerging in qualitative studies	• ... start off your introduction chapter with a weak and diluted overview that gives little away about the focal topic and its significance
• ... edit your work for any typos, inconsistent writing styles or erratic section numbering	• ... write in a descriptive style that lacks argument, logic or critical analysis. No one expects a superficial summary presented as a research report
• ... be concise and accurate in your writing language, in the use of titles and subtitles as well as table/figure numbers to smoothly guide the reader through your report	• ... ignore the ethical issues that underpin the work and emerge during its implementation. Ethical considerations should be acknowledged, addressed and reported on in an ethics section within your report

Research Outline Structure: An Example

Every educational institution has guidelines on how to structure an undergraduate research project and postgraduate dissertation; these should be reviewed as templates to follow before the start of any study. Keeping the expected chapters or sections in mind can help to align the subsequent process steps and the write-up within the reader's anticipated frame, which reduces the risk of digressing from the accepted norm. There are basic sections though that any research report has to present, and most structures more or less orbit around these headings and their content.

A general structure forming the outline of a research report involves:

Title page – Mainly comprises the research title, your name, the institution's name and the course or module name (what you are submitting the research project or dissertation in fulfilment of).

Table of contents – Offers an outline of your chapters, section and sub-section titles, and the associated page numbers. It helps guide the reader through the structure of your work.

Acknowledgments – This is optional; you may use it to thank those who supervised, mentored or offered assistance or access in carrying out the research. If you are doing the research using company data or in response to a certain company's research brief, you may need to check whether you can specify them by name based on the agreement. You can also use this page to thank your research participants and respondents for their help in fieldwork and data provision.

Abstract (or in some cases an executive summary may be required instead, where the research is more practical and its beneficiary is a client organisation) – An abstract or executive summary provides a succinct summary of the whole research project. It is usually best written at the end of the project as it provides a brief overview of the research in a snapshot. A good abstract is short, usually 250–300 words (but it depends on the guidance provided by your institution). It should be informative and answer the key questions of what the research is about, its objectives, how the research question was pursued and the objectives addressed, what the results are in a nutshell and what value it contributes and for whom. Sometimes, abstracts are structured around short headings that reflect the research report's key sections, such as: Purpose, Design & Methodology, Findings, Limitations, Implications and Originality.

Introduction – This is a crucial chapter that pulls together a briefing on what the report is about, the research aim, objectives, research gap and significance. It also outlines what comes next in terms of the methodology, and introduces how each of the following chapters inform the reader about the research process. Writing the research question, aim, objectives, potential value and contributions at the outset sets the cornerstone for both the researcher and subsequently the reader. Yet, there are benefits to keeping the completion of this chapter to the end, after all the research work is undertaken and the rest of the chapters are in place; the rationale is that it is introducing what comes next so needs to reflect that. But because you are still developing what comes next, the introduction may change – sometimes considerably – after the rest of the research steps are in place. Feeding back into the introduction chapter throughout the research and writing process is recommended.

Context/Literature Review – This chapter covers both a review of the academic literature and of the industry-based literature. Academic literature covers the key concepts and variables underpinning the research and its objectives; a scan of existing studies highlights what has been done and the gap that exists which motivates the research aim. An industry-based literature review explores the practical environmental context of the focal sector or industry which is the focus of the research, including contextualising the brand – if one is being focused on in the research – and existing competitors, market conditions, the economic, political, social, technological, legal and/or environmental situation that may be of influence. The concluding section of a literature review chapter should pull together the key variables and relationships which will be examined based on the identified gap.

Methodology – This chapter reflects on the research design, whether it is deductive or inductive, and whether it employs a quantitative, qualitative or mixed-methods approach in data collection, offering justification for the choices made in relation to the research objectives. It also highlights the consequential methods used in the fieldwork, explaining the population of interest, the sample frame and the sampling technique employed as well as the sample size. This chapter should also explore the means of accessing participants for the study and how data will be analysed, with a rationale for the choice of suitable analysis methods.

Analysis and Results – Presenting the analysis steps and the emerging findings are different for a qualitative- versus a quantitative-based research study. For instance, analysis associated with hypothesis testing in a quantitative research design takes a different style of reporting to the thematic or content analysis in a qualitative research design. A decision regarding how analysis is organised in relation to the discussion of findings is based on the research approach and the requirements of the reader or research beneficiary. It is advisable to look at previous successful research project submissions at your institution to get a clear sense of how the analysis and results may be structured.

Discussion of Findings – This can be undertaken in a separate section or within the previous chapter/section. Again, you need to make a decision on what works best for the research project in the particular case, for instance where hypothesis testing is undertaken through analysing numerical data or when themes are emerging and developing into theoretical classifications.

Conclusions and Implications – As covered in the present chapter, this is where the research is wrapped up, from its grounding to its outcomes, and its contributions are explained to form implications for marketing researchers and decision makers. As a critical part of the report, conclusions and implications usually form key sections of the final chapter.

Limitations and Future Research – A section reflecting on the exceptions and limitations of the study, and a follow-up section suggesting further study prospects are usually at the concluding end of a research report.

References – These are, crucially, all the academic and industry or practical sources that you used to support your arguments and evidence from the literature you drew on and compared your results with. It must succinctly follow the referencing style required by the institution where the research will be submitted. The same referencing style should have been neatly followed in the in-text citations of the same sources. In some research studies, students may also include a *bibliography*, which goes beyond the sources directly used in the study to include any indirect reading resources that informed the research project.

Appendix/Appendices – An appendix is an optional addendum to the report that is used where there is further supporting information that you want to include to assist in the understanding and assessment of your research work. It can include interview transcripts, code books and coding evidence, online snippets used in netnography studies, a focus group or interview guide, a survey template or a sample of completed questionnaires, analysis tables and graphs generated by the statistical analysis program employed – these may not have been included in the main text but support and provide evidence for the research outcomes.

Ethics: Points to Consider

1. It is important to present in the research report any ethical considerations that were anticipated or that have arisen in the study. Ethical issues may have come up at a variety of points along the way and can be discussed within the individual chapters. Alternatively, a section on ethics can be presented in the final chapter of the report.
2. Writing the research report itself involves ethical reflections; for example, data verification entails making sure the research is reliable and valid, acknowledging any biases that transpired and that the findings are a true representation of the analysis results.

3. Presenting the various elements and steps of the research process ethically also means referencing the work of others with accuracy and consistency, and ensuring that the reader is clear about what constitutes the existing literature and what the original contributions are that form the outcomes of the study.

Presenting the Research Verbally

An important element of presenting a study through a report is that it covers all the details that enable the reader to interact with the research process and outcomes. Yet, any researcher should be ready to put the work done into a shorter, more visually friendly version in the form of a poster or presentation. In doing so, the study's key parts should still be covered in a simple, rationed manner that does not lose the essence of the written report or dilute the storyline. In many instances, presenting the research orally with the aid of some text and visuals (e.g. using PowerPoint or developing a poster) can provide a more lively depiction of its key elements, its significance and the logic followed, allowing the work to shine. Verbal and visual presentations of research work also aid in the dissemination of its outcomes and value, and allow its strengths to be revealed and the gathering of ideas to aid its progress.

The guiding tip for constructing a presentation of the research work is determining who the audience is, in order to meet audience members' expectations and identify the language style that is suitable for them. If you will be presenting your work to your fellow researchers or your supervisor, this is different from presenting the study to a client company or to a wider range of audiences at an event (e.g. a seminar or conference). For the former, a more academic structure is recommended, using the main headings that form the report's sections. Details of literature sources and supportive evidence should be reported, and theories backing up the research variables and key concepts should be explained. In the latter case, where the research is presented to a less academic audience, for example a business or at a conference, it is important that the presentation is more engaging, less theoretical and avoids jargon, as well as bringing out the research value and contributions to life; visuals can give more spirit to the presentation, capturing the interest of the audience and aiding understanding and recall.

Presenting the research orally with the aid of simple text and visuals requires different skills to those utilised in the written report. In the written report, you can go from the general to the specific, you can elaborate on all parts of the work, and the reader has the chance to go back and forth through the work to clarify it once they have it in their hands. In an oral presentation, the start has to be specific and engaging so as not to lose the attention and interest of the audience. You should have a clear vision of what needs to be presented and develop it into a story, using short sentences to guide the oral elaboration, with the support of visual displays (such as images, tables, graphs), as relevant. Some key questions to ask in deciding what to present are: What message do I want to leave the audience with? What areas should be briefly covered and then further elaborated on if questions arise and the audience seeks more information? How can I show support for these arguments?

Remember that oral presentations are usually set at a maximum of 15–20 minutes, which may include a 5-minute Question and Answer (Q&A) subsequent discussion that should be planned for, so there is limited time available for presenting. Rehearsing to make sure you do not finish too early or exceed the maximum time allowed saves you from being cut short before finishing your presentation. There are many instances of researchers running overtime and being required to stop, which did not allow them to offer up the key research implications and contributions, which are essential to the value of the work. Leaving the audience in limbo means you have not been fair to yourself and all the effort you put into the work, and you come across as unprepared or as orally reporting on a weak research project.

It is important to note that orally presenting research work does not allow for all the details to be spelled out, but this is usually expected by the audience and it also leaves room for further questions that ignite the follow-up discussion. A researcher should be prepared to interact with this subsequent discussion, demonstrate openness to any counter-arguments and critique that may emerge, exhibit an awareness of the elements of the work that may initiate questions as well as endorse any suggestions offered by the audience. Being defensive when it comes to responding to critical questions raised by the audience in relation to elements of the research does not support the learning process and leaves the audience sceptical about the work done and about the researcher's developmental abilities. Accordingly, you should approach the oral presentation with a good appreciation of the strengths and weaknesses of your study, an informed understanding of its value and the opportunities it extends for its beneficiaries, and also good ideas about how the work can be enhanced and advanced by overcoming its limitations and expanding its boundaries.

Advanced: More Tips in Research Reporting

1. Any research study is informed by an ethical approval process that has to be undertaken early on and prior to any data collection. Every institution has its research ethics policies and processes that ensure that every researcher follows the code of ethics of the field of study and of the institution to protect their welfare and the welfare of all parties involved in the study (e.g. those conducting the fieldwork, research participants, client companies that may be involved, and any other stakeholders in the research process).
2. In some research reports (such as in postgraduate dissertations), a *Conceptual Development* chapter can be provided between the Literature Review chapter and the Methodology chapter; this is an advanced and expanded version of the summary a researcher would normally provide at the end of the Literature Review chapter. Conceptual development involves outlining in detail the specific constructs, variables and relationships that make up the study. Developing such a framework is the outcome of a critical contextual review that narrows the gap and specifies what is being examined in the research. The conceptual framework for the research can be expressed textually through drawing hypotheses and laying out their underpinning arguments, and it can also be depicted visually through a diagram or model that portrays what is being investigated; it can thus model the relationships being investigated as an adaptation of an existing model.

Chapter Summary

As the concluding part of the book aimed to bring together all the research steps to fruition, this chapter delved into the next steps in a research project following on from data analysis and offered a discussion of how to write a full research report. It highlighted key tips for a good discussion of the research findings, extending some dos and don'ts that can guide the development of this research step. The chapter also explored the concepts of validity and reliability, as well as the importance of assessing both concepts in producing credible quantitative and qualitative studies. Furthermore, it offered a discussion of the next steps in the research cycle, which involve moving forward to highlight the research value as expressed in developing the implications of the study's outcomes and its contribution to theory and practice.

A reflective exercise on this process entails drawing out the research limitations, how some of these limitations may have been addressed during the research study, and how the researcher proposes they may be handled in future studies; at this stage, the researcher is in a position to recommend future research paths that can build on the study. Reporting on the research process from start to end is a crucial part of carrying out effective research. The chapter offered guidelines on how to write a well-targeted and proficient research report, in addition to extending tips on how to present the research orally to various audiences.

Case Study: 'Always' Re-Writing the Rules to Inspire Girls Everywhere

Long-established brand names, like *M&S* and *Always*, sometimes run the risk of becoming associated with older generations just because younger consumers perceive them as having been there 'forever' and being the choice of their parents. Procter & Gamble's *Always* needed to put the right efforts in place to maintain its brand leadership position in the feminine hygiene products market. The brand realised that, being a long-standing name, it may have failed to communicate the core brand purpose to younger consumers – that beyond its functional superiority and quality offering, it is committed to social causes around leveraging the confidence of young women and supporting girls' puberty education into adulthood. While rival brands focus on the use of social media to connect with young consumers, *Always* found that it maintained its focus on promoting its brand performance only.

To gauge brand awareness and perceptions among the younger generation, *Always* carried out research among girls and younger women. Findings highlighted that this target group knew little about what *Always* stood for as a brand and cared little about knowing, beyond the fact that it is a familiar name, trusted over the years and purchased by their mothers. Thus, the research indicated low unaided brand awareness; in addition, young female consumers did not perceive *Always* as supporting their transition from puberty to womanhood. Although acting as an agent of social change is at the heart of its ethos, *Always* marketing communications efforts at that point were clearly ineffective in flagging up its educational endeavours in raising the confidence of young women and becoming part of their lives.

To become relevant to girls and young women and show that the brand share their values, *Always* joined the changing category conversation created by competitors' growing social voices; the *#LikeAGirl* campaign was launched by Leo Burnett Toronto in 2014 to increase top-of-mind awareness of the brand and to reconnect emotionally with consumers by promoting its understanding of the social issues girls face. The online video generated more than 85 million views worldwide and became the #1 viral video in the world in the second week of launch. The campaign proved a success in its attempt to change perceptions of the phrase 'Like a Girl' – it moved it away from a derogatory notion that exudes weakness to getting people to think about its real essence as well as empowering girls and young women with a new resonance to the meaning of confidence.

Assume that *Always* would like to conduct post-campaign research and seeks your research skills in gauging the impact of its change in communication on creating an emotional connection with its target consumers. After conducting some in-depth interviews and launching a survey among the target customers and analysing the data collected, you are expected to produce a full report and present the findings to *Always*.

(Continued)

(Continued)

Case study questions:

1. What are the main elements of the research that should form the key sections of the report?
2. Why is it important to assess the validity and reliability of the study for both its qualitative and quantitative parts?
3. Do you expect the study to have limitations? Why is it important to discuss these limitations in the research report?
4. *Always* has asked you to prepare a 15-minute presentation of the research findings. What are the key points to consider that would guide you in providing an effective and well-targeted presentation?

End of Chapter Questions

These questions should help you reflect on your understanding of this chapter:

1. How can a research discussion effectively interpret data analysis in light of the research objectives?
2. What is the importance of checking for validity and reliability in ensuring the credibility of a study?
3. How do you develop the conclusion chapter of a research report in a way that brings into the spotlight the study's value, implications and contributions?
4. Why is it imperative to reflect on the research limitations and suggest future research directives at the conclusion of any research report?
5. How do you report on the stages of the research from start to end through two well-structured and properly targeted outputs: a written research report and an oral presentation?

Checklist

After studying Chapter 15, you should now be familiar with these key concepts:

1. Research discussion following data analysis
2. Validity and reliability in research
3. Writing the research conclusion, implications and contributions
4. Reflecting on the limitations and bringing out future research directives
5. Research reporting: written and verbal

Further Reading (in sequence from beginners to advanced)

Kraus, J. (2013) How to write high-impact marketing research reports. [Online] Available at: http://researchindustryvoices.com/2013/07/15/how-to-write-high-impact-marketing-research-reports/#sthash.5RrT4fsa.dpuf

Andreasen, A. R. (1985) 'Backward' market research. *Harvard Business Review* (May). [Online] Available at: https://hbr.org/1985/05/backward-market-research

Thody, A. (2006) *Writing and Presenting Research*. London: Sage Publications.

Golafshani, N. (2003) Understanding reliability and validity in qualitative research. *The Qualitative Report*, 8 (4), pp. 597–606.

Carmines, E. G. and Zeller, R. A. (1979) *Reliability and Validity Assessment*. London: Sage Publications.

Bibliography

Andreasen, A. R. (1985) 'Backward' market research. *Harvard Business Review* (May). [Online] Available at: https://hbr.org/1985/05/backward-market-research

Denzin, N. K. and Lincoln, Y. S. (2005) *The Sage Handbook of Qualitative Research*. London: Sage Publications.

Hair, J. F., Tatham, R. L., Anderson, R. E. and Black, W. C. (1998) *Multivariate Data Analysis* (5th edition). New York: Prentice Hall.

Lincoln, Y. S. and Guba, E. G. (1985) *Naturalistic Inquiry* (Vol. 75). London: Sage Publications.

Monash University (n.d.) Acknowledging exceptions and limitations. [Online] Available at: www.monash.edu.au/lls/llonline/writing/general/academic/2.2.xml

Pallant, J. (2013) *SPSS Survival Manual*. London: McGraw-Hill Education.

Peter, J. P. (1979) Reliability: a review of psychometric basics and recent marketing practices. *Journal of Marketing Research*, 16 (1), pp. 6–17.

WARC (2015) Always: #LikeAGirl. European Association of Communications Agencies (EACA) Care Awards. [Online] Available at: www.warc.com/Pages/Taxonomy/Results.aspx?DVals=4294946908&Sort=ContentDate%7c1&Filter=All

Find journal articles and multiple choice questions online at: **https://study.sagepub.com/benzo** to support what you've learnt so far.

Index